Modern Annotated First Nations Legislation

2006 Edition

Paul Salembier
Al Broughton
Jeffery Hutchinson

LexisNexis®
Butterworths

Modern Annotated First Nations Legislation, 2006 Edition
© LexisNexis Canada Inc. 2005
November 2005

Members of the LexisNexis Group worldwide

Canada	LexisNexis Canada Inc, 123 Commerce Valley Dr. E., MARKHAM, Ontario
Argentina	Abeledo Perrot, Jurisprudencia Argentina and Depalma, BUENOS AIRES
Australia	Butterworths, a Division of Reed International Books Australia Pty Ltd, CHATSWOOD, New South Wales
Austria	ARD Betriebsdienst and Verlag Orac, VIENNA
Chile	Publitecsa and Conosur Ltda, SANTIAGO DE CHILE
Czech Republic	Orac sro, PRAGUE
France	Éditions du Juris-Classeur SA, PARIS
Hong Kong	Butterworths Asia (Hong Kong), HONG KONG
Hungary	Hvg Orac, BUDAPEST
India	Butterworths India, NEW DELHI
Ireland	Butterworths (Ireland) Ltd, DUBLIN
Italy	Giuffré, MILAN
Malaysia	Malayan Law Journal Sdn Bhd, KUALA LUMPUR
New Zealand	Butterworths of New Zealand, WELLINGTON
Poland	Wydawnictwa Prawnicze PWN, WARSAW
Singapore	Butterworths Asia, SINGAPORE
South Africa	Butterworth Publishers (Pty) Ltd, DURBAN
Switzerland	Stämpfli Verlag AG, BERNE
United Kingdom	Butterworths Tolley, a Division of Reed Elsevier (UK), LONDON, WC2A
USA	LexisNexis, DAYTON, Ohio

Library and Archives Canada Cataloguing in Publication
Salembier, Paul
    Modern annotated First Nations legislation / Paul Salembier,
Al Broughton, Jeffery Hutchinson. — 2006 ed.

Includes bibliographical references and index.
ISBN 0-433-45042-8

    1. Native peoples—Legal status, laws, etc.—Canada.
I. Broughton, Al II. Hutchinson, Jeffery III. Title.

KE7704 2005   342.7108'72'0263   C2005-906560-5
KF8203 2005

Printed and bound in Canada.

ABOUT THE AUTHORS

Paul Salembier, B.Sc., LL.B., LL.M., is a General Counsel with the federal Department of Justice, in which capacity he provides advice on legislative and regulatory initiatives affecting First Nations. Mr. Salembier has more than two decades of experience in aboriginal law, and has drafted many regulations and statutes relating to first nations. He has also taught regulatory law and statutory interpretation at the University of Ottawa's Faculty of Law. He authored *Regulatory Law and Practice in Canada*, published by LexisNexis in 2004, and has written articles in aboriginal law, regulatory law and statutory interpretation.

Al Broughton, B.A., LL.B., is a General Counsel with the federal Department of Justice, at Indian and Northern Affairs Canada Legal Services. He has been involved in the interpretation and application of legislation affecting First Nations and reserve lands over the course of more than 20 years of public service.

Jeffery Hutchinson, LL.B., is a General Counsel with the federal Department of Justice, at Indian and Northern Affairs Canada Legal Services. He has worked in the area of aboriginal law for 10 years, including litigation at all levels of court. Mr. Hutchinson has worked on all aspects of the Specific Claims process and was extensively involved in the development of the *Specific Claims Resolution Act*.

GENERAL TABLE OF CONTENTS

DETAILED TABLE OF CONTENTS

PART 2

FIRST NATIONS TAX COMMISSION

Interpretation

Purposes

Functions and Powers

Standards and Procedures

Regulations

PART 3

FIRST NATIONS FINANCIAL MANAGEMENT BOARD

Interpretation

Establishment and Organization of Board

PART 4

FIRST NATIONS FINANCE AUTHORITY

Interpretation

PART 5
FIRST NATIONS STATISTICAL INSTITUTE
Interpretation

PART 6

FINANCIAL MANAGEMENT AND CONTROL

PART 7

PROVISIONS OF GENERAL APPLICATION

General

PART 8
TRANSITIONAL PROVISIONS, CONSEQUENTIAL AMENDMENTS, COORDINATING AMENDMENTS AND COMING INTO FORCE

Transitional Provisions

Consequential Amendments

Coordinating Amendments

COMING INTO FORCE

DEBT RESERVE FUND REPLENISHMENT REGULATIONS (PROPOSED)

DEFINITIONS

GENERAL

COMING INTO FORCE

FIRST NATIONS ASSESSMENT APPEAL REGULATIONS (PROPOSED)

INTERPRETATION

PRESCRIBED PROCEDURES

REQUESTS FOR RECONSIDERATION

APPEAL PROCEDURES

HEARING

DOCUMENTS

DECISIONS

REVIEW OF LOCAL REVENUE LAWS

COMPLIANCE REVIEWS

Referral to panel

Documents

Settlement

Hearings

General

FIRST NATIONS TAXATION ENFORCEMENT REGULATIONS (PROPOSED)

LOCAL REVENUE MANAGEMENT IMPLEMENTATION REGULATIONS (PROPOSED)

SHORT-TERM POOLED INVESTMENT FUND REGULATIONS (PROPOSED)

FIRST NATIONS LAND MANAGEMENT ACT

HER MAJESTY

GENERAL

ESTABLISHMENT OF LAND MANAGEMENT REGIME

Land Code and Individual Agreement

Verification

Community Approval and Certification

Coming into Force of Land Code

Rules on Breakdown of Marriage

LAND MANAGEMENT REGIME

First Nation Powers

First Nation Laws

First Nation Land Register

Limitations on Alienation of First Nation Land

FRAMEWORK AGREEMENT ON FIRST NATION LAND MANAGEMENT

PART VI - FUNDING

PART VII - EXPROPRIATION OF FIRST NATION LAND BY CANADA

PART VIII - LANDS ADVISORY BOARD

PART IX - DISPUTE RESOLUTION

PART X - RATIFICATION AND ENACTMENTS BY THE PARTIES

PART XI - OTHER MATTERS

SPECIFIC CLAIMS RESOLUTION ACT

SHORT TITLE

INTERPRETATION

PURPOSE

PART 1

CANADIAN CENTRE FOR THE INDEPENDENT RESOLUTION OF FIRST NATIONS SPECIFIC CLAIMS

Establishment, Composition and Functions

Chief Executive Officer

Personnel Management

General Provisions

PART 2
COMMISSION
Composition and Role
Composition

PART 3
TRIBUNAL
Composition and Role
Composition

PART 4
GENERAL

PART 5
TRANSITIONAL PROVISION, CONSEQUENTIAL AMENDMENTS, COORDINATING AMENDMENT AND COMING INTO FORCE

Transitional Provision

Consequential Amendments

Coordinating Amendment

Coming into Force

INTRODUCTION TO MODERN FIRST NATIONS LEGISLATION

The statutes annotated in this book are the first statutes of general application that have been enacted by the federal government, in consultation with First Nations, to replace the regime that has been in place under the *Indian Act* for more than a century. While this modern First Nations legislation gives First Nations far greater powers than those exercisable under the *Indian Act*, it is also far more complex. This book brings these statutes and their associated regulations together for the first time, offers detailed explanations of how they work, and outlines the case law likely to guide the courts in their interpretation.

Two of the statutes — the *First Nations Fiscal and Statistical Management Act* and the *Specific Claims Resolution Act* — are so new that, although they have been enacted by Parliament, they have not yet been brought into force. The third, the *First Nations Land Management Act*, was enacted in 1999, and is gathering momentum as more and more First Nations opt to manage their lands under it.

A number of regulations relating to the *First Nations Fiscal and Statistical Management Act* are also included. These regulations have not yet been made, but have been released by the government for consultation purposes.[1] The regulations eventually enacted by the Governor in Council are expected to be similar to these consultation regulations in most respects, and they have been included in order to provide a complete picture of the effect of the *First Nations Fiscal and Statistical Management Act*.

Because all of these statutes and regulations are of recent vintage, the courts have had relatively few occasions to consider and comment upon their provisions. However, where these provisions are analogous to other legislative provisions — such as provisions of the *Indian Act* — that have received judicial scrutiny, case law relating to the analogous provisions has been included as an indication of how the courts are likely to treat the newer provisions.

This book is intended to speak to a wide audience, and while it contains detailed case citations and other information useful to lawyers, it is also written with the average person in mind. In this vein, the following explanations may be of assistance to those less practiced in reading federal statutes and related case law.

It may be noted that when the expression "First Nation" is used in the commentary, the expression is capitalized, which reflects the manner in which that expression is traditionally rendered in a non-legislative context. The same expression is generally not capitalized in the original statutes and regulations, however.[2]

In the statutes in this book you will frequently see references to the "Governor in Council". The Governor in Council is the legislative expression

---

[1]   Available at First Nations Fiscal Initiative website at <http://www.fnfi.ca>.

[2]   This reflects current federal legislative practice.

used to denote a combination of two offices — the federal Cabinet and the Governor General of Canada. In Canada, the formal head of state is the Governor General, who in legislative matters must act under the direction of ministers drawn from the party then in power.[3] This group of ministers is the Cabinet. An action taken by the Governor in Council, then, is one taken by the Governor General on the advice of the Cabinet. Because the Governor General's role is purely formal, however, actions taken by the Governor in Council are in fact the actions of the Cabinet.

Throughout the legislation and commentary in this book you will find numerous references to legislative provisions denoted as "sections", "subsections", etc. To assist in comprehending this terminology, a brief explanation is set out below.

NOMENCLATURE FOR LEGISLATIVE PROVISIONS

Statutes and regulations are made up of numbered sentences, referred to generally as "provisions". A number of different labels are used to describe these provisions, such as "section", "subsection" and "paragraph". These reflect the naming conventions for federal statutes. A section is notionally the building block of a statute or regulation, and consists of a complete legislative sentence. An example of a section would be:

> 5. No person shall operate a vehicle with a gross weight of more than 5 tons unless the vehicle is equipped with a fire extinguisher.

A section may contain several subsections. Subsections are similar to sections in that they also set out a complete legislative sentence, but are intended to express an idea that is related to, but subservient to, the idea expressed in the section that contains it.[4] In federal legislation, a subsection is distinguishable from a section by the fact that the number preceding it is in parentheses. In the following example, both s. 5(1) and s. 5(2) are subsections. Together they form a section 5:

> 5. (1) No person shall operate a vehicle with a gross weight of more than 5 tons unless the vehicle is equipped with a fire extinguisher.
>
> (2) Subsection (1) does not apply to forklifts.

Paragraphs are portions of the legislative sentence within a section or subsection, but do not constitute complete sentences themselves. They are preceded by a lower-case letter between parentheses. In the following example, the portions introduced by (a), (b) and (c) are paragraphs:

> 5. (1) No person shall operate a vehicle with a gross weight of more than 5 tons unless the vehicle is equipped with
>
> (a) a fire extinguisher;

---

[3]   P.W. Hogg, *Constitutional Law of Canada* 2nd ed., (Toronto: Carswell, 1985) at p. 191.
[4]   The relationship between ideas expressed in subsections and the idea expressed in a section as a whole is often difficult to ascertain, however, and subsections at times appear to be quite independent of one another.

> *(b) safety flares;*
>
> *(c) a first aid kit approved by*
>
> > *(i)   Health Canada, or*
> >
> > *(ii) the Canadian Standards Association.*

Paragraph (c) in the above example has nested within it two subparagraphs, preceded by lower-case roman numerals between parentheses. These in turn may contain clauses, sub-clauses, and so on.

In the commentary or footnotes you will see that all types of legislative provisions are abbreviated simply by "s." The abbreviation for section 52 is therefore s. 52; for subsection 52(1), it is s. 52(1); and for paragraph 52(1)(a), it is s. 52(1)(a). A listing of two or more provisions is prefaced by the plural "ss." (e.g., ss. 52 and 53). Such abbreviations are not used in the text of statutes or regulations, however, or used at the start of a sentence.

As a final note, many will find the statutes and regulations in this book to be very detailed, very complicated, and very difficult to understand. This should not come as a surprise. Running a government is a very complicated affair, and good government requires mastery of a number of areas of expertise and sophistication. The legislation in this book reflect that complexity, and rightly so. The fact that a law is complex does not mean that it should be incomprehensible, and this book aims to demystify its subject legislation and render it understandable to those who must apply it.

As areas of First Nation governance multiply, the statutes and regulations in this book will no doubt be followed by others, which in turn are likely to be more, rather than less, specialized. Moreover, as questions of application and interpretation of these statutes come before the courts, the volume of case law on modern First Nations legislation will continue to expand. Future editions of this work will track these changes, and endeavour to present the evolution of modern First Nations legislation in a comprehensive and clearly understandable manner.

FIRST NATIONS FISCAL AND STATISTICAL MANAGEMENT ACT

Introductory Commentary

The *First Nations Fiscal and Statistical Management Act*[5] ("the FNFSMA")[6] received royal assent and became law on March 23, 2005. Although it has been enacted by Parliament, at the date of this writing it was not yet in force. It is expected to come into force — and hence to take effect — sometime in the next few months.[7]

The Act has been referred to as being "First Nation-led".[8] As the last recital in the preamble indicates, a group of First Nation leaders, led by former Chief C.T. (Manny) Jules of the Kamloops Band, worked with government officials through the National Table on Fiscal Relations[9] to develop the Act.

The Act is optional legislation. Indian bands that are subject to the *Indian Act* and certain other aboriginal groups[10] can choose to come under the Act,[11] at which point the provisions of the *Indian Act* relating to real property taxation will cease to apply to them.[12]

The stated purpose of the FNFSMA is "to provide First Nations with the practical tools available to other governments for modern fiscal management".[13] It seeks to achieve this objective on the one hand by strengthening First Nations' real property taxation powers and providing greater representation for taxpayers, and on the other by establishing four First Nations institutions to provide service to First Nation governments in areas related to taxation and statistics.[14] The four institutions are:

---

[5]   S.C. 2005, c. 9.

[6]   In commentary relating to regulations made under the *First Nations Fiscal and Statistical Management Act,* the *First Nations Fiscal and Statistical Management Act* is normally referred to simply as "the Act". The abbreviation FNFSMA is used there, however, where it is necessary to distinguish that Act from other statutes being referred to.

[7]   This will be done by an Order in Council made under s. 155 of the Act. The order could bring all of the statute into force at the same time, or different parts at different times.

[8]   Comments by Hon. Stephen Owen (Secretary of State, Indian Affairs and Northern Development), *Hansard*, Vol. 138, No. 49, January 30, 2003 (10:15); Comments made by Hon. Robert Nault, Minister of Indian Affairs and Northern Development, Minutes of Standing Committee on Aboriginal Affairs, Northern Development and Natural Resources, June 9, 2003 (15:30).

[9]   Indian and Northern Affairs Canada *Backgrounder: First Nations Fiscal And Statistical Institutions Initiative*. Available at <http://www.ainc-inac.gc.ca/nr/prs/s-d2002/02218bk_e. html>.

[10]   See Commentary on ss. 141 and 153 of the Act.

[11]   For a discussion of the opt-in mechanism, see Commentary for s. 2(3) of the Act.

[12]   By virtue of s. 15 of the Act.

[13]   Press Release by Department of Indian Affairs and Northern Development, November 2, 2004. Available at <http://www.ainc-inac.gc.ca/nr/prs/s-d2004/2-02521_e.html>.

[14]   Indian and Northern Affairs Canada *Backgrounder: First Nations Fiscal And Statistical Institutions Initiative*. Available at http://www.ainc-inac.gc.ca/nr/prs/s-d2002/02218bk_e.html.

- the First Nations Tax Commission;
- the First Nations Financial Management Board;
- the First Nations Finance Authority; and
- the First Nations Statistical Institute.

The role and functions of each institution are described below.

Legislative History

The Act was first introduced into Parliament in December 2002 as Bill C-19, but died on the order paper[15] when the Parliamentary session ended in November 2003. It was re-introduced in March 2004 as Bill C-23, but once again died when Parliament was dissolved in May 2004. Prior to its dissolution, the House of Commons made significant amendments to the Bill, changing it from an Act of general application to one that was optional in nature.

The Bill was re-introduced in November 2004 as Bill C-20. Bill C-20 incorporated all of the earlier changes that had been made by the House of Commons, including those making it optional legislation. A few minor changes were made to the Bill during the House of Commons committee process.[16] No changes were made in the Senate, and the Bill received royal assent on March 23, 2005.

Changes to First Nations Taxing Powers

Section 5 of the FNFSMA significantly expands the taxing powers of First Nations over those presently provided for under s. 83 of the *Indian Act*. The FNFSMA provides First Nations with specific powers to:

- conduct inspections and requisition information for tax assessments;
- tax business activities;
- impose development cost charges;
- create liens on interests in reserve lands for non-payment of taxes;
- impose interest and penalties on overdue taxes; and
- seize and assign interests or rights in reserve lands or personal property for non-payment of taxes.

The Act also expands the rights of taxpayers. Section 6 of the FNFSMA requires that notice of proposed taxation laws be given to members of the First Nation and other persons who hold interests in the reserve lands affected by the

---

[15]   A bill under consideration by the House of Commons or Senate is considered to have "died on the order paper" if it has not yet received Royal Assent before the end of the Parliamentary session: Fact Sheet, House of Commons - Prorogation General, available at the Parliament of Canada website: <http://www.parl.gc.ca/Search/qfullhit-E.htw?CiWebHitsFile= /information/about/process/house/Procedural_Fact_Sheets/fs_prorogation-e.htm&Ci-Restriction=died+on+the+order+paper&CiBold=True&CiItalic=True&CiBeginHilite=%3Cfo nt+color%3Dred%3E&CiEndHilite=%3C%2Ffont%3E&CiHiliteType=Full&CiUserParam3= %2Fsearch%2Fadvanced%2Easp%3FLanguage%3DE%26Parl%3D38%26Ses%3D1>.
[16]   By the House of Commons Standing Committee on Aboriginal Affairs.

6

taxation law. The Act also provides for rights of appeal of tax assessments,[17] and an opportunity to request a review in respect of any alleged failure to comply with the Act or to apply taxation laws fairly and properly.[18]

Under s. 83 of the *Indian Act*, tax by-laws made by the council of a band must be approved by the Minister of Indian Affairs. Under the FNFSMA, taxation laws made by First Nation councils must still be approved, but are instead approved by the First Nations Tax Commission, which is established under the Act. The Act also requires that all taxation laws approved by the Commission be published by it in the *First Nations Gazette*.

When a First Nation opts into the FNFSMA, any tax by-laws made by it under s. 83 of the *Indian Act* are carried over into the FNFSMA, to the extent that they are consistent with the FNFSMA and the regulations and standards made under it.[19] From that point onward they are treated as if they were taxation laws made under the FNFSMA.

The Institutions — First Nations Tax Commission

The FNFSMA establishes the First Nations Tax Commission,[20] and gives it powers to enter into contracts, hold property and conduct litigation, among other things. All but one of its 10 Commissioners are appointed by the Governor in Council. The remaining Commissioner is to be appointed by a body named in the *First Nations Tax Commissioner Appointment Regulations*.[21] Under s. 20(2) of the Act, three of the Commissioners who are appointed by the Governor in Council must be taxpayers on reserve lands.

The Commission takes over the role formerly played by the Indian Taxation Advisory Board (ITAB). The ITAB was formed after the 1988 amendments to the *Indian Act* introduced the taxing powers found in s. 83 of the *Indian Act*; its purpose is to provide advice to the Minister of Indian Affairs and Northern Development regarding the approval of tax by-laws submitted by First Nations under that section. Unlike ITAB, however, the First Nations Tax Commission's role is not merely advisory: instead, it will exercise powers of approval under the FNFSMA equivalent to those exercised by the Minister under the *Indian Act*. Under s. 143 of the FNFSMA, the staff of the ITAB and its operating rules are carried over into the First Nations Tax Commission. It is expected that the FNFSMA will also continue to fulfill the role played by ITAB in respect of future tax by-laws submitted by First Nations who remain under the *Indian Act*.[22]

The role of the First Nations Tax Commission is set out in s. 29 of the FNFSMA. This includes

---

[17] s. 5(4).

[18] s. 33.

[19] s. 145.

[20] s. 17.

[21] Made under s. 20(3) of the Act. At the time of writing, none of the regulations made under the FNFSMA are yet in force.

[22] First Nations Tax Commission website: <http://www.fntc.ca/faq.phtml> under "Where does the Minister of Indian Affairs fit into this?".

- review of First Nation taxation laws to ensure that they comply with the Act, any standards established by the Commission,[23] and any regulations made by the Governor in Council under the Act,[24] and the approval of laws that do;

- establishing standards for the form and content of First Nation taxation laws;[25]

- establishing procedures for the submission and approval of taxation laws, and for the manner in which taxpayers' interests can be represented in the Commission's decisions;[26]

- arbitrating disputes between First Nation councils and members of First Nations or taxpayers who allege that a First Nation has not complied with the Act or regulations, or has applied a taxation law unfairly or improperly;[27]

- certifying that a First Nation has "unutilized borrowing capacity" for the purpose of applying for loans from the First Nations Finance Authority;[28]

- providing training to First Nation tax administrators and others on the operation of First Nation tax systems;[29] and

- publishing the *First Nations Gazette*.[30]

The First Nations Tax Commission can also initiate its own independent review in any circumstances in which it is of the opinion that a First Nation has not complied with the Act or regulations, or has applied a taxation law unfairly or improperly. On completion of a review under s. 33, the Commission can order a First Nation to remedy the situation that gave rise to the complaint, and can call on the First Nations Financial Management Board to intervene where the First Nation does not comply.

The Institutions — First Nations Finance Authority

The purpose of the First Nations Finance Authority is to provide First Nations with access to capital at interest rates lower than those available on the open market, by pooling the borrowing power of its member First Nations.[31] Although established under the FNFSMA, the Authority continues the

---

[23] Under s. 35.

[24] Primarily the proposed *First Nations Tax Commission Review Procedures Regulations*, *First Nations Taxation Enforcement Regulations*, and *First Nations Assessment Appeal Regulations*.

[25] s. 35(1)(a).

[26] s. 35(2).

[27] s. 33.

[28] s. 32(1)(b).

[29] See <http://www.fntc.ca/about.phtml>.

[30] s. 34(2).

[31] See <http://www.fnfa.ca/about/index.htm>.

operations of the private corporation First Nations Finance Authority Inc.,[32] which is referred to in the preamble to the Act.

Although established by statute, the Authority is independent of the federal government.[33] Unlike the First Nations Tax Commission, its directors are not appointed by the Governor in Council, but are instead elected by the First Nations who are its members.[34] First Nations become investing members of the Authority when they deposit funds with the Authority to invest on their behalf. First Nations become borrowing members of the Authority by making an application to the Authority,[35] supported by the certification of First Nations Financial Management Board that the First Nation's financial management system complies with the Board's standards.[36]

The Authority will borrow on behalf of First Nations primarily by issuing bond securities on the capital markets.[37] These bonds will be secured by the property tax revenues of its borrowing members. The Act provides for a sinking fund[38] and debt reserve fund[39] for each bond issued, as well as a credit enhancement fund,[40] to ensure repayment of the principal for the bonds issued.

Additional security to bondholders is provided by s. 84(5) of the Act, under which the Authority can call upon the tax revenues of any borrowing member to cover a shortfall in funds in relation to any bond issue, whether that borrowing member is participating in the particular bond issue or not. By this mechanism, every bond issue is backed by the revenues of all borrowing members. Borrowing members cannot avoid these obligations — by ceasing to be a borrowing member — without the consent of all other borrowing members.[41]

If a borrowing member fails to make a payment to the First Nations Finance Authority, the Authority can require the First Nations Financial Management Board to impose a co-management arrangement on the borrowing member or assume third-party management of its taxation revenues.[42] If a borrowing member fails to fulfill a non-financial obligation to the Authority, the Authority can request the First Nations Financial Management Board to investigate and report on the reasons for the failure.[43]

---

[32]   See also s. 144 of the Act, under which directors of the First Nations Finance Authority Inc. continue as directors of the Authority under the Act, until new ones are appointed.

[33]   s. 60.

[34]   s. 61.

[35]   s. 76.

[36]   s. 50.

[37]   s. 75(1)(b).

[38]   s. 82.

[39]   s. 84.

[40]   s. 85.

[41]   Unless they opt out of the Act entirely, which they can do (under s. 2(3)(b) of the Act) only if they do not have outstanding financial obligations to the First Nations Finance Authority.

[42]   s. 86(4). These procedures are discussed further below.

[43]   ss. 86(2) and (3).

The Institutions — First Nations Financial Management Board

The purposes of the First Nations Financial Management Board include:

- assisting First Nations to develop their financial management capacity,[44] through training and advisory services related to financial management;[45]

- developing general credit rating criteria[46] and financial management standards[47] for First Nations;

- conducting assessments of the financial practices and financial health of First Nations, particularly in relation to the issuance of bonds;[48] and

- providing co-management and third-party management services.[49]

The First Nations Financial Management Board is managed by a board of directors, appointed primarily by the Governor in Council.[50] Despite this, the Board does not act as an agent of the federal Crown in the performance of its functions.[51]

The First Nations Financial Management Board supports the First Nations Finance Authority by conducting reviews of the financial management system and financial performance of First Nations seeking to become borrowing members of the Authority, and providing certificates of compliance[52] to those who meet standards established by the Board.[53]

The First Nations Financial Management Board also supports the First Nations Finance Authority and First Nations Tax Commission by conducting interventions on their behalf. The First Nations Finance Authority can request intervention by the Board where a borrowing member has failed to make a payment to the Authority.[54] The First Nations Tax Commission can request the Board's intervention where a First Nation has failed to comply with an order of the Commission issued after a hearing under s. 33 of the Act. The First Nations Financial Management Board can also intervene of its own accord if it is of the opinion that there is a serious risk that a First Nation will default on an obligation to the First Nations Finance Authority.[55] Intervention by the First

---

[44] s. 49(a).
[45] First Nations Financial Management Board website, <http://www.fnfmb.com/en/about/index.htm>.
[46] s. 49(d).
[47] Established under s. 55(1).
[48] s. 49(f); First Nations Financial Management Board website, <http://www.fnfmb.com/en/about/index.htm>.
[49] s. 49(h).
[50] ss. 40 and 41(1). Under s. 41(2), up to three of the Board's directors are appointed by the Aboriginal Financial Officers Association of Canada, or another body prescribed by regulation.
[51] s. 39.
[52] s. 50(3).
[53] Under s. 55(1) of the Act.
[54] s. 86(4).
[55] ss. 52(1)(a) and 53(1)(b).

Nations Financial Management Board can take the form of co-management or third-party management.

Under a co-management arrangement, s. 52 of the Act permits the Board to:

- recommend changes to a First Nation's laws, expenditures or budgets;
- recommend improvements to a First Nation's financial management system or the way in which it delivers programs or services;
- require that cheques be co-signed by the Board's manager; or
- exercise any other powers that the First Nation has decided to delegate to the Board in such circumstances.[56]

Where the Board assumes third-party management of a First Nation's property taxation revenues,[57] s. 53 of the Act permits the Board to:

- act in place of the First Nation's council to make or amend property taxation laws;
- manage the First Nation's local revenue account and provide for the delivery of programs and services that are paid for from that account;
- assign rights or interests in reserve land seized for the non-payment of taxes;[58] and
- exercise any other powers that the First Nation has decided to delegate to the Board in such circumstances.[59]

In circumstances where the First Nations Financial Management Board has been called on to assume third-party management to remedy a failure to make a payment to the First Nations Finance Authority, the Board may need to exercise the First Nation's council's law-making powers to raise tax rates, in order to generate additional revenue sufficient to satisfy the First Nation's obligations to the Authority. As ss. 53(2)(c) and (d) of the Act imply, this could involve adjusting the level of programs and services provided out of tax revenues, and collecting outstanding unpaid taxes.

The Institutions — First Nations Statistical Institute

The purposes of the First Nations Statistical Institute include:

- providing and analysing statistical information on the fiscal, economic and social conditions of members of First Nations and other aboriginal groups, as well as others who reside on reserve lands;
- promoting the quality and coherence of those statistics and producing other such statistics in accordance with generally accepted standards and practices;

---

[56]   Under s. 5(1)(g).
[57]   Held in a local revenue account, which must be established by the First Nation under s. 13(1).
[58]   Under s. 5(7).
[59]   Under s. 5(1)(g).

- working with Statistics Canada and other federal departments to ensure that the national statistical system meets the needs of First Nations; and

- building statistical capacity within First Nation governments.[60]

The core activities of the First Nations Statistical Institute include:

- developing a knowledge of, and providing access to, relevant statistical data on First Nations already existing within the Canadian statistical system;

- delivering statistical training and promoting the use of statistical data;

- identifying requirements, potential users and priorities for statistical data; and

- delivering and publishing statistical reports, tabulations and data analysis.[61]

The First Nations Statistical Institute is the only institution established by the FNFSMA that is not strictly financial, although it is intended that it will

- work with the other institutions to identify and market investment opportunities to potential investors;

- work with First Nation tax administrators and the First Nations Tax Commission to improve financial data from local revenue accounts; and

- compile statistical profiles on borrowing members and other participating First Nations.[62]

Unlike the other institutions, which deal only with First Nations who have opted into the FNFSMA, the First Nations Statistical Institute deals with all First Nations in Canada, as well as self-governing aboriginal groups who were formerly, but are no longer, subject to the *Indian Act*. In this sense, Part 5 of the FNFSMA, which governs the Institute, is the only portion of the Act that is not truly optional.

Again, unlike the other institutions, the First Nations Statistical Institute is a Crown corporation.[63] As such, it is subject to the requirements of Part X[64] of the *Financial Administration Act*. The Institute is not, however, an agent of the Crown.[65]

The Institute is governed by a board of directors, who are appointed by the Governor in Council. The Chief Statistician of Canada is also an *ex officio* member[66] of the board of directors.

The activities and powers of the First Nations Statistical Institute in relation to First Nations' statistics are analogous to those of Statistics Canada under the

---

[60] s. 104.

[61] First Nations Statistical Institute presentation dated March 25, 2005, available at <http://www.firststats.ca/home.asp>.

[62] *Ibid.*

[63] s. 92.

[64] ss. 83 to 154.

[65] s. 93.

[66] A person who is a member by virtue of the office he or she holds.

Statistics Act.[67] The FNFSMA similarly requires employees to swear an oath to treat statistical information confidentially,[68] and makes unauthorized disclosure of such information a criminal offence.[69]

Under s. 107 of the Act, the First Nations Statistical Institute can require prescribed federal departments and agencies[70] to share documents or records relating to First Nations, or members of First Nations or other aboriginal groups, that are maintained by that department or agency. Documents that the department or agency is permitted to withhold, or required by law to withhold, are excepted. The Institute is required to enter into an agreement with the department or agency regarding the manner in which the documents and records will be used.

Other Aspects of the FNFSMA

Under s. 141 of the Act, the Governor in Council can make regulations to permit an aboriginal group that is not a band under the *Indian Act* to come under the FNFSMA. These regulations can modify or restrict the application of any provision of the Act, or of any of the regulations made under the Act, in order to enable the aboriginal group to opt into the Act. Section 153 of the Act amends the *Westbank First Nation Self-Government Act*, adding similar regulation-making powers to allow the Westbank First Nation to opt into the Act in the same manner.

The FNFSMA makes only minor consequential amendments to ss. 87 and 88 the *Indian Act.* The amendment to s. 87 permits First Nations to tax reserve lands, which would otherwise be exempt from taxation under that section. The amendment to s. 88 ensures that provincial laws of general application that are inconsistent with the FNFSMA do not apply to Indians living on reserve lands.

The Schedule to the FNFSMA, which was empty when the Act became law, will be completed by way of orders made by the Governor in Council under s. 2(3) of the Act. These orders will add to the Schedule the names of First Nations who have opted to come under the FNFSMA.

---

[67]   R.S.C. 1985, c. S-19.
[68]   s. 103.
[69]   ss. 111 and 112.
[70]   To be prescribed by the proposed *Statistical Data Disclosure Regulations*, made under s. 133 of the Act.

FIRST NATIONS FISCAL AND STATISTICAL MANAGEMENT ACT

S.C. 2005, c. 9

Assented to March 23, 2005

(Not in Force)

An Act to provide for real property taxation powers of first nations, to create a First Nations Tax Commission, First Nations Financial Management Board, First Nations Finance Authority and First Nations Statistical Institute and to make consequential amendments to other Acts

Preamble

Commentary

This preamble, like most, sets out statements of fact related to the context in which the Act was enacted and statements of intention as to what it is intended to achieve. The preamble forms part of the statute and can be used to assist in determining its purpose.[71]

Whereas the Government of Canada has adopted a policy recognizing the inherent right of self-government as an aboriginal right and providing for the negotiation of self-government;

Commentary

The policy referred to in this paragraph of the preamble is the federal government's policy on Implementation of the Inherent Right and the Negotiation of Aboriginal Self-Government, established in 1995. A copy of it can be found on the website of Indian and Northern Affairs Canada.[72]

Whereas this Act is not intended to define the nature and scope of any right of self-government or to prejudge the outcome of any self-government negotiation;

Whereas the creation of national aboriginal institutions will assist first nations that choose to exercise real property taxation jurisdiction on reserve lands;

Whereas economic development through the application of real property tax revenues and other local revenues to support borrowing on capital markets for the development of public infrastructure is available to other governments in Canada;

---

[71] R. Sullivan, *Sullivan and Driedger on the Construction of Statutes*, 4th ed., (Toronto: Butterworths, 2002) at p. 296; P.A. Côté, *The Interpretation of Legislation in Canada*, 3rd ed., (Carswell, Toronto, 2000) at p. 59.
[72] <http://www.ainc-inac.gc.ca/pr/pub/sg/plcy_e.html>.

Whereas real property taxation regimes on reserves should recognize both the interests of on-reserve taxpayers and the rights of members of first nations communities;

Whereas accurate, timely and credible statistics are a key element of sound financial planning, management and reporting available to other governments in Canada;

Whereas first nations led an initiative that resulted in 1988 in an amendment to the *Indian Act* so that their jurisdiction over real property taxation on reserve could be exercised and the Indian Taxation Advisory Board was created to assist in the exercise of that jurisdiction;

Commentary

The initiative referred to in this paragraph led to the passage of Bill C-115 in 1988, which amended the *Indian Act* to introduce First Nation taxation powers for the first time. These powers are set out in s. 83 of the *Indian Act*. The Indian Taxation Advisory Board is a non-statutory body, funded by the Department of Indian Affairs and Northern Development, which has provided advice to the Minister of Indian Affairs and Northern Development regarding the approval of tax by-laws submitted by First Nations under that section.

Whereas, in 1995, the First Nations Finance Authority Inc. was incorporated for the purposes of issuing debentures using real property tax revenues and providing investment opportunities;

Commentary

The First Nations Finance Authority Inc. is a private corporation whose functions are to be taken over by the statutory body known as the First Nations Finance Authority, established under Part 4 of the Act.[73] Under s. 144 of the Act, the directors of the First Nations Finance Authority Inc. continue as directors of the Authority under the Act, until new ones are appointed by the Governor in Council.

Whereas, by 1999, first nations and the Government of Canada recognized the benefits of establishing statutory institutions as part of a comprehensive fiscal and statistical management system;

And whereas first nations have led an initiative culminating in the introduction of this Act;

Commentary

A series of advisory panels, led by First Nation members, were established to develop the concepts that led to the Act. The development of the Act is therefore frequently referred to as being "First Nations-led".

---

[73]   See s. 58.

NOW, THEREFORE, Her Majesty, by and with the advice and consent of the Senate and House of Commons of Canada, enacts as follows:

SHORT TITLE

1. SHORT TITLE — This Act may be cited as the *First Nations Fiscal and Statistical Management Act*.

INTERPRETATION

2. (1) DEFINITIONS — The following definitions apply in this Act.

Commentary

The definitions below are set out alphabetically, and apply to all Parts of the Act.[74] Note that the definitions in the French version of s. 2(1) are also set out alphabetically and, unlike other sections of the Act, are not therefore equivalent to the English definitions printed across from them on the page in a bilingual print format. To assist in locating the equivalent French definition of a particular term, the French equivalent is listed in italics in the marginal note to the definition (e.g., *membre emprunteur* in the first definition below).

"borrowing member"
« membre emprunteur »

"borrowing member" means a first nation that has been accepted as a borrowing member under subsection 76(2) and has not ceased to be a borrowing member under section 77.

Commentary

As the definition indicates, "borrowing members" are First Nations who have applied to the First Nations Finance Authority to become a borrowing member for the purpose of obtaining a loan from the Authority. The other class of members of the First Nations Finance Authority, described in s. 59, is composed of its investing members.[75]

"council"
« conseil de la première nation »

"council" has the same meaning as "council of the band" in subsection 2(1) of the *Indian Act*.

---

[74] By contrast, the definitions set out in ss. 16, 37, 57 and 90 of the Act apply only to the Part of the Act in which they are located.
[75] Defined in s. 57 of the Act.

Commentary

The definition of "council of the band" in s. 2(1) of the *Indian Act* reads as follows:

"council of the band" means

    (a) in the case of a band to which section 74 applies, the council established pursuant to that section,

    (b) in the case of a band to which section 74 does not apply, the council chosen according to the custom of the band, or, where there is no council, the chief of the band chosen according to the custom of the band;

Section 74 of the *Indian Act*, referred to in the definition of "council of the band", permits the Minister of Indian Affairs and Northern Development to declare that the council of a band is to be selected by elections held in accordance with the *Indian Act*.

"First nation"
« première nation »
"First nation" means

    (a) in any provision of Part 5, a band; and

    (b) in any other provision, a band named in the schedule.

Commentary

The effect of paragraph (b) of the definition is that a reference to a First Nation in Part 1 (dealing with taxation powers of First Nations) and Parts 2 to 4 (dealing with the fiscal institutions) is a reference only to the *Indian Act* bands that have opted into the Act, and which are thereupon listed in the Schedule to the Act. Under paragraph (a) of the definition, references to First Nations in Part 5, which deals with the First Nations Statistical Institute, include all *Indian Act* bands, whether they have opted into the Act or not.

"First Nations Finance Authority"
« Administration financière des premières nations »

"First Nations Finance Authority" means the corporation established under section 58.

Commentary

Part 4 of the Act (ss. 57 to 89) deals with the operations of the First Nations Finance Authority.

"First Nations Financial Management Board"
« Conseil de gestion financière des premières nations »

"First Nations Financial Management Board" means the board established under subsection 38(1).

Commentary

Part 3 of the Act (ss. 37 to 56) deals with the operations of the First Nations Financial Management Board.

"First Nations Gazette"
« Gazette des premières nations »
"*First Nations Gazette*" means the publication published under section 34.

Commentary

The *First Nations Gazette* is co-published by the Indian Taxation Advisory Board and the Native Law Centre of Canada at the University of Saskatchewan. Subscriptions for the 2005 year cost $72. Further information can be obtained, and subscriptions ordered, at the *First Nations Gazette* website.[76]

"First Nations Statistical Institute"
« Institut de la statistique des premières nations »
"First Nations Statistical Institute" means the institute established under section 91.

Commentary

Part 5 of the Act (ss. 90 to 113) deals with the operations of the First Nations Statistical Institute.

"First Nations Tax Commission"
« Commission de la fiscalité des premières nations »
"First Nations Tax Commission" means the commission established under subsection 17(1).

Commentary

Part 2 of the Act (ss. 16 to 36) deals with the operations of the First Nations Tax Commission.

"local revenue law"
« texte législatif sur les recettes locales »
"local revenue law" means a law made under subsection 5(1).

Commentary

Local revenue laws include laws relating to taxation of rights and interests in reserve lands (s. 5(1)(a)), authorization of expenditures of revenues derived from

---

[76]   <http://www.usask.ca/nativelaw/publications/desc/fng.html>.

that taxation (s. 5(1)(b)), procedures by which taxpayers' interests may be represented (s. 5(1)(c)), the borrowing of money from the First Nations Finance Authority (s. 5(1)(d)), and the methods by which payment of taxes can be enforced (s. 5(1)(e)).

"local revenues"
« recettes locales »

"local revenues" means moneys raised under a local revenue law.

"Minister"
« ministre »

"Minister" means the Minister of Indian Affairs and Northern Development.

"property taxation law"
« texte législatif relatif à l'imposition foncière »

"property taxation law" means a law made under paragraph 5(1)(a).

Commentary

Note that a property taxation law is different from a local revenue law, in that a property taxation law relates only to the taxation of rights and interests in reserve lands under s. 5(1)(a), and does not include the types of laws made under ss. 5(1)(b) to (g), which are encompassed under the broader definition of "local revenue law". Property taxation laws can, however, encompass areas such as property valuation assessments (s. 5(1)(a)(i)), the taxation of business activities (s. 5(1)(a)(iv)), and the imposition of development cost charges (s. 5(1)(a)(v)).

"third-party management"
Version anglaise seulement

"third-party management" means the management of a first nation's local revenues under section 53.

Commentary

Third-party management refers to the assumption of management of a First Nation's property taxation system, and the revenues derived therefrom, by the First Nations Financial Management Board. The mechanism by which this occurs is set out in s. 53 of the Act. This definition occurs only in the English version of the Act.

(2) *INDIAN ACT* DEFINITIONS — Unless the context otherwise requires, words and expressions used in this Act and not otherwise defined have the same meaning as in the *Indian Act*.

Commentary

Examples of terms used in this Act that take their meaning from the *Indian Act* include "band" and "reserve".

(3) AMENDMENTS TO SCHEDULE — At the request of the council of a band, the Governor in Council may, by order, amend the schedule in order to

    (a)   add or change the name of the band; or

    (b)   delete the name of the band, as long as there are no amounts owing by the band to the First Nations Finance Authority that remain unpaid.

Commentary

This subsection embodies the mechanism by which a First Nation that is a band under the *Indian Act* can opt into the FNFSMA.[77] Once a band's name is added to the Schedule, Parts 1 to 4 of the Act — the sections relating to taxation and the fiscal institutions — apply to it. Note that both opting into the Act under paragraph (a) and opting out of the Act under paragraph (b) require only a request by the band council (normally provided by way of a band council resolution). A band can, however, only opt out of the Act under paragraph (b) if it has no financial obligations to the First Nations Finance Authority — such as outstanding loans or charges imposed under s. 84(5) — that remain unpaid.

Although not mentioned explicitly, because orders under this subsection are by convention forwarded to the Governor in Council on the recommendation of the Minister of Indian Affairs and Northern Development, band council resolutions under the section would normally be forwarded to that Minister's office for transmittal to the Governor in Council.

A First Nation that changes its name can request that the Schedule be amended to reflect the name change by forwarding a band council resolution to the Minister under paragraph (b) to request that the Governor in Council make the necessary amendment. Orders made by the Governor in Council under this subsection will be published in the *Canada Gazette* Part II.

ABORIGINAL RIGHTS

3. ABORIGINAL AND TREATY RIGHTS — For greater certainty, nothing in this Act shall be construed so as to abrogate or derogate from any existing aboriginal or treaty rights of the aboriginal peoples of Canada under section 35 of the *Constitution Act, 1982*.

---

[77]   Aboriginal groups that were once, but are no longer bands under the *Indian Act*, can opt into the Act by requesting the making of a regulation by the Governor in Council under s. 141 of the Act.

Commentary

Provisions such as s. 3 are normally referred to as non-derogation clauses. Section 35 of the *Constitution Act, 1982* reads as follows:

>   35. (1) The existing aboriginal and treaty rights of the aboriginal peoples of Canada are hereby recognized and affirmed.

>   (2) In this Act, "aboriginal peoples of Canada" includes the Indian, Inuit and Métis peoples of Canada.

Case Law

Saskatchewan First Nations and Indian Bands v. Canada (Attorney General), [2002] F.C.J. No. 1517, 223 F.T.R. 64.

The applicants argued that wording identical to s. 3[78] both acknowledged a possible impact of that Act on treaty rights and foreclosed the Crown from justifying the alleged infringement of those rights. Because of the statement in the section that Parliament did not intend to interfere with treaty rights, it was argued that the Crown was estopped from arguing that public safety or public policy justified their infringement.[79]

Delgamuukw v. British Columbia, [1997] S.C.J. No. 108, [1997] 3 S.C.R. 1010.

The Supreme Court of Canada considered similar wording in s. 6(2) of the *Indian Oil and Gas Act*, which stated:

>   (2) Nothing in this Act shall be deemed to abrogate the rights of Indian people or preclude them from negotiating for oil and gas benefits in those areas in which land claims have not been settled.

It concluded that the wording in that subsection reinforced the conclusion that:

>   The statute presumes that the aboriginal interest in reserve land includes mineral rights, a point which this Court unanimously accepted with respect to the *Indian Act* in *Blueberry River Indian Band v. Canada (Department of Indian Affairs and Northern Development)*, [1995] 4 S.C.R. 344. On the basis of *Guerin*,[80] aboriginal title also encompass[es] mineral rights, and lands held pursuant to aboriginal title should be capable of exploitation in the same way, which is certainly not a traditional use for those lands.[81]

---

[78] Found in s. 2(3) of the *Firearms Act*, S.C. 1995, c. 39.
[79] [2002] F.C. J. No. 1517, 223 F.T.R. 64 at 71.
[80] *Guerin v. Canada*, [1984] 2 S.C.R. 335.
[81] [1997] S.C.J. No. 108, [1997] 3 S.C.R. 1010 at 1086-87.

PART 1

FIRST NATIONS FISCAL POWERS

4. FINANCIAL ADMINISTRATION LAWS — The council of a first nation may not make a law under paragraph 5(1)(d) until the council has made a law respecting the financial administration of the first nation under paragraph 9(1)(a) and that law has been approved by the First Nations Financial Management Board.

Commentary

Under paragraph 5(1)(d) of the Act, the council of a First Nation can make a general law regarding the borrowing of money from the First Nations Finance Authority, or a law to authorize entering into a particular loan agreement with the Authority. Section 4 requires that, before making a law to borrow funds from the Authority, the council must first have in place a financial administration law made under paragraph 9(1)(a), and that this law must have been approved by the First Nations Financial Management Board.[82]

Standards for the form and content of financial administration laws are established by the First Nations Financial Management Board under s. 55(1)(a) of the Act. Once established, standards of the Board will be published in the *First Nations Gazette*.[83]

5. LOCAL REVENUE LAWS — (1) Subject to subsections (2) to (6), sections 4 and 6 and any regulations made under paragraph 36(1)(d), the council of a first nation may make laws

Commentary

The powers conferred on First Nation councils under s. 5 of the Act replace (or, more accurately, displace) the taxation powers conferred on Indian band councils under ss. 83(1)(a) and (d) to (g) and s. 84 of the *Indian Act*. Those *Indian Act* provisions read as follows:

> 83. (1) Without prejudice to the powers conferred by section 81, the council of a band may, subject to the approval of the Minister, make by-laws for any or all of the following purposes, namely,

---

[82]   Although s. 9(2) automatically requires that any financial administration law that is made by a borrowing member, at the time a First Nation council first contemplates borrowing from the First Nations Finance Authority it will not yet be a borrowing member.
[83]   This is required under s. 55(4) of the Act.

(a)   subject to subsections (2) and (3), taxation for local purposes of land, or interests in land, in the reserve, including rights to occupy, possess or use land in the reserve;

...

(d)   the payment of remuneration, in such amount as may be approved by the Minister, to chiefs and councillors, out of any moneys raised pursuant to paragraph (a);

(e)   the enforcement of payment of amounts that are payable pursuant to this section, including arrears and interest;

(e.1)   the imposition and recovery of interest on amounts that are payable pursuant to this section, where those amounts are not paid before they are due, and the calculation of that interest

(f)   the raising of money from band members to support band projects; and

(g)   with respect to any matter arising out of or ancillary to the exercise of powers under this section.

...

84. Where a tax that is imposed on an Indian by or under the authority of a by-law made under section 83 is not paid in accordance with the by-law, the Minister may pay the amount owing together with an amount equal to one-half of one per cent thereof out of moneys payable out of the funds of the band to the Indian.

By virtue of s. 15 of the FNFSMA, these *Indian Act* provisions no longer apply to First Nations who opt into the FNFSMA.

The opening words of s. 5(1) set out the powers of First Nation councils in respect of real property taxation. The provision starts out by stipulating that these powers are subject to

- s. 4 – the requirement for an approved financial administration law before making a law under s. 5(1)(d);

- ss. 5(2) and (3) – the requirement for approval of First Nations Tax Commission before a law can come into force;

- ss. 5(4) to (6) – content requirements for particular types of laws;

- s. 6 – notice requirements; and

- regulations made under s. 36(1)(d) – potential restrictions on First Nation law-making powers.

Note that, while ss. 81 and 83 of the *Indian Act* refer to the making of "by-laws", s. 5 of the FNFSMA provides for the making of "laws".

(a) **respecting taxation for local purposes of reserve lands, interests in reserve lands or rights to occupy, possess or use reserve lands, including**

  (i) **the assessment of the value of those lands, interests and rights, the requisition of any information necessary to conduct the assessment and the inspection, in accordance with procedures prescribed by regulation, for assessment purposes of any reserve lands that are subject to taxation for local purposes,**

  (ii) **a mechanism to establish tax rates and apply them to the assessed value of those lands, interests and rights,**

  (iii) **taxation for the provision of services in respect of reserve lands,**

  (iv) **the taxation of business activities on reserve lands, and**

  (v) **the imposition of development cost charges;**

Commentary

Paragraph 5(1)(a) of the Act sets out the property taxation powers of First Nation councils. Under a law made under that paragraph, First Nation councils can tax:

- reserve lands;
- interests in reserve lands; or
- rights to occupy, possess or use reserve lands.

The reference to a power to tax reserve lands *per se*, when considered in conjunction with the distinct powers to tax interests in reserve lands and rights to occupy, possess or use reserve lands, would likely be interpreted to refer to lands in a reserve in respect of which no lease, permit, licence or allotment had been otherwise granted under the *Indian Act* or its regulations. In practice, this might include the power to tax buildings located on First Nation lands in respect of which no right or interest has been granted under the *Indian Act*.[84] The courts have confirmed the right of a First Nation to tax such lands under s. 83 of the *Indian Act*, in *Beattie v. Squamish Indian Band*,[85] discussed below, and it is likely that its reasoning would extend equally to taxation powers under the FNFSMA.

The power to tax interests in reserve lands would include any interests granted pursuant to a surrender under s. 37 to 39 of the *Indian Act* or acquired by assignment under s. 54 of that Act, as well as leases granted under ss. 58(1)(b) or (c) or s. 58(3) of that Act, and leases granted under the *Indian Mining Regulations*.[86]

---

[84] Any such holdings by a non-band member would contravene the prohibitions in ss. 28(1) and 37 of the *Indian Act*.

[85] [2005] F.C.J. No. 391 (T.D.).

[86] C.R.C., c. 956.

The power to tax rights to occupy, possess or use reserve lands would likely encompass rights conferred to use lands under s. 18(2) of the *Indian Act*, allotments of possession obtained by band members[87] under ss. 20, 24, 49 or 50(4) of that Act, permits issued under s. 28(2) of that Act, timber licences conferred under the *Indian Timber Regulations*[88] or *Indian Timber Harvesting Regulations*,[89] and permits issued under the *Indian Mining Regulations*.[90]

It is not entirely clear whether lands subject to a taking under s. 35 of the *Indian Act* would be subject to taxation. The decisions in *Canadian Pacific Ltd. v. Matsqui Indian Band*,[91] *Osoyoos Indian Band v. Oliver (Town)*[92] and *BC Tel v. Seabird Island Indian Band*,[93] discussed below, do not provide definitive guidance on this point.

Subparagraph 5(1)(a)(i) provides for First Nation law-making powers in respect of the assessment of value of properties subject to taxation. A First Nation law can provide for inspections for the purpose of assessing property values, which must be conducted in accordance with the procedures set out in the proposed *First Nations Assessment Inspection Regulations*.[94]

Subparagraph 5(1)(a)(iii) clarifies that one of the purposes for which properties on reserve can be taxed is to defray the cost of providing services to those lands.

Subparagraph 5(1)(a)(iv) provides for the taxation of business activities on reserve lands. Although the opening words of s. 5(1)(a) speak of the taxation of lands or interests and rights in lands, this subparagraph confers a power to tax an activity, as opposed to the land itself. This would appear, in theory, to empower taxation of the operator of a business, irrespective of whether that operator is also the holder of a right or interest in the lands on which the business is conducted.

The development cost charges referred to in s. 5(1)(a)(v) are charges levied by municipalities to finance the capital costs of infrastructure such as roads, water, sewers and parkland. The idea behind these charges is to have developers pay for the cost of the new infrastructure necessitated by their developments, thereby lessening the tax burden on existing homeowners. Such charges are usually levied on a per-dwelling or per-lot basis.[95]

---

[87]   Limited to band members who have Indian status.
[88]   C.R.C., c. 961.
[89]   SOR/2002-109.
[90]   C.R.C., c. 956.
[91]   [1999] F.C.J. No. 1057, 176 D.L.R. (4th) 35 (C.A.).
[92]   [2001] S.C.J. No. 82, [2001] 3 S.C.R. 746, 206 D.L.R. (4th) 385.
[93]   [2002] F.C.J. No. 1032, [2003] 1 F.C. 475 (C.A.).
[94]   Discussed further below, in the commentary devoted to those regulations.
[95]   Subsection 933(1) of the British Columbia *Local Government Act*, R.S.B.C. 1996, c. 323, gives authority to British Columbia municipalities to levy such charges for similar purposes.

Case Law

Given the similarities between s. 83(1) of the *Indian Act* and s. 5(1)(a) of the FNFSMA, it is likely that the following jurisprudence applicable to the former would also apply to the latter.

Westbank First Nation v British Columbia Hydro and Power Authority, [1999] S.C.J. No. 38, 176 D.L.R. (4th) 276.

The Supreme Court of Canada confirmed that a First Nation could not use its taxation powers under s. 83 of the *Indian Act* to tax the interests in reserve lands held by the respondent, which was an agent of the Province of British Columbia. The respondent had been granted rights-of-way for electrical transmission and distribution lines under s. 28(2) of the *Indian Act*. Because s. 125 of the *Constitution Act, 1867* prohibits one level of government from taxing another, however, the assessment and taxation by-laws of the Westbank First Nation, made in the exercise of federal authority, were held to be inapplicable to B.C. Hydro.

St. Mary's Indian Band v. Cranbrook (City), [1997] S.C.J. No. 19, [1997] 2 S.C.R. 657.

The Supreme Court of Canada determined that lands that had been surrendered for sale for the construction of an airport were no longer reserve lands, despite the proviso in the surrender that the lands would revert to the band if they ceased to be used for public purposes. The court found that the context of the surrender made it clear that the band intended to part with the lands on an absolute basis, which was confirmed by the fact that the Crown paid full market value for the lands. As the lands had been surrendered for sale, they were outside the band's property taxation jurisdiction.

Canadian Pacific Ltd. v. Matsqui Indian Band, [1999] F.C.J. No. 1057, 176 D.L.R. (4th) 35 (C.A.).

The Federal Court of Appeal determined that lands conveyed to the Canadian Pacific Railway under s. 35 of the *Indian Act* were not subject to taxation under s. 83 of that Act. Of the two judgments constituting the majority decision, one determined that the lands in question did not form part of the reserve, and were not therefore taxable, while the other determined that the lands were reserve lands, but that the band's taxation by-laws were invalid because they discriminated as between band members and non-band members. The court's ruling was further complicated by the fact that the dissenting judgment concluded that the lands in question were within the reserve, and that the structure of the *Indian Act* authorized the discrimination in the by-laws by necessary implication.

Osoyoos Indian Band v. Oliver (Town), [2001] S.C.J. No. 82, [2001] 3 S.C.R. 746, 206 D.L.R. (4th) 385.

The Supreme Court of Canada held that the expropriation of reserve land for a canal did not result in the transfer of the entire Indian interest in the land, and that a sufficient interest remained with the band to preserve the band's taxation jurisdiction under s. 83 of the *Indian Act*. Because its fiduciary obligations obliged the Crown to transfer only the minimum interest necessary to maintain and operate the canal, the transfer to the town under s. 35 of the *Indian Act* was determined to be limited to a statutory easement. The lands therefore remained part of the reserve, and were subject to taxation under s. 83 of the *Indian Act*.

BC Tel v. Seabird Island Indian Band, [2002] F.C.J. No. 1032, [2003] 1 F.C. 475 (C.A.).

The Federal Court of Appeal considered whether the appellant band had the power to assess and tax property used for a fibre optic cable system that was situated on lands that had been taken for a highway right-of-way under s. 35 of the *Indian Act*. Applying the test in *Osoyoos*, the court determined that the federal Crown had not transferred the entire interest of the band in the subject lands to the respondents, and that the band therefore retained an interest sufficient to consider the land to be reserve land for the purposes of s. 83 of the *Indian Act*.

Beattie v. Squamish Indian Band, [2005] F.C.J. No. 391 (T.D.).

The Federal Court confirmed that a First Nation can validly assess taxes under s. 83 of the *Indian Act* on any person who uses or occupies reserve lands, regardless of whether a legal right or interest has been granted to that person under the *Indian Act*. The court determined that the "manufactured home" in which the appellant resided, which was located in a mobile home park on the reserve, was a fixture, and could therefore be taxed as part of the land to which it was attached. The court further held that the fact that the appellant was not a member of the First Nation, and had no legal interest in the land, did not mean that she had no right to occupy, use or possess the land within the meaning of s. 83 of the *Indian Act*, since her possessory right was exercisable against anyone who did not have better title to the property. The First Nation could therefore tax this right.

Chapman v. Canada, [2001] B.C.J. No. 775, 89 B.C.L.R. (3rd) 124 (S.C.), aff'd [2003] B.C.J. No. 2742, 21 B.C.L.R. (4th) 272 (C.A.).

The plaintiffs alleged that their rights under s. 15(1) of the *Canadian Charter of Rights and Freedoms* had been breached because the Crown had given the band the right to assess property taxes under s. 83 of the *Indian Act* and the plaintiffs had been subjected to taxation without representation.[96] Because the court was considering a procedural application to strike the plaintiff's claim, it did not

---

[96] [2001] B.C.J. No. 775, 89 B.C.L.R. (3d) 124 (S.C.), aff'd [2003] B.C.J. No. 2742, 21 B.C.L.R. (4th) 272 (C.A.) at 148-49.

consider the claim on its merits but, for the purposes of the application, concluded "I can only say that, on the arguments before me, the plaintiffs' chance of success on these Charter arguments would appear tenuous to say the least but I would not be prepared to say that it is plain and obvious that they have no chance to succeed."[97]

(b)   authorizing the expenditure of local revenues;

Commentary

Under s. 13(2) of the Act, local revenues generated by taxation laws can be expended only under the authority of a budget law made under s. 5(1)(b). Subsection 13(3) also provides that such a budget law cannot authorize expenditures that exceed the local revenues estimated for the year, over and above any deficit carried over from prior years.

Paragraph 10(b) also requires that a new budget law be enacted by the First Nation council each year, on the date to be established under the proposed *First Nations Rates and Expenditure Laws Timing Regulations.*[98]

(c)   respecting procedures by which the interests of taxpayers may be represented to the council;

Commentary

As noted in the commentary following the opening words of s. 5(1), the First Nation's law-making powers under this paragraph are subject to the requirements of s. 6 relating to the notice to be given to taxpayers of proposed First Nation laws.

(d)   respecting the borrowing of money from the First Nations Finance Authority, including any authorization to enter into a particular borrowing agreement with that Authority;

Commentary

Under s. 5(1)(d), the council of a First Nation can make either

- a general law regarding the borrowing of money from the First Nations Finance Authority; or

- a law to authorize entering into a particular loan agreement with the Authority.

---

[97]   *Ibid.* at 149.

[98]   The proposed regulations currently establish this date as the date established by the province in which the reserve is located, for the setting of the tax rates applicable to provincial lands adjacent to the reserve.

A general law might authorize the First Nation council to apply to the First Nations Finance Authority under s. 76(1) to become a borrowing member, and undertake the conditions precedent to doing so such as obtaining a certificate from the First Nations Financial Management Board under s. 50(3) and satisfying the First Nations Tax Commission that the First Nation has "unutilized borrowing capacity", as required by s. 32(1)(b). Such a law might also set out the purposes for which funds that might be borrowed from the First Nations Finance Authority can be used.

Once the First Nation has satisfied these conditions precedent and has been accepted by the First Nations Finance Authority as a borrowing member, a subsequent law could be made under s. 5(1)(d) to authorize the First Nation's council to enter into a loan agreement to borrow a specified amount from the First Nations Finance Authority.

(e) **subject to any conditions, and in accordance with any procedures, prescribed by regulation, respecting the enforcement of laws made under paragraph (a) in respect of outstanding taxes or charges, including**

  (i) **the creation of liens on reserve lands and interests in reserve lands,**

  (ii) **the imposition and recovery of interest and penalties on an amount payable pursuant to a law made under that paragraph, where the amount is not paid when it is due, and the rate of interest or the amount of the penalty, as the case may be,**

  (iii) **subject to subsection (7), the seizure, forfeiture and assignment of interests or rights in reserve lands,**

  (iv) **the seizure and sale of personal property located on reserve lands, other than property located in a dwelling, and**

  (v) **the discontinuance of services;**

Commentary

The powers conferred on First Nation councils in respect of the enforcement of property taxation laws are essentially powers for the collection of outstanding taxes. These powers are much more detailed than those conferred under ss. 83(1)(e) and (e.1) of the *Indian Act*, which are limited to the making of by-laws for

> (e) the enforcement of payment of amounts that are payable pursuant to this section, including arrears and interest;
>
> (e.1) the imposition and recovery of interest on amounts that are payable pursuant to this section, where those amounts are not paid before they are due, and the calculation of that interest;

In particular, ss. 5(1)(e)(iii) and (iv) of the FNFSMA give First Nation councils the right to seize, forfeit and assign rights or interests in reserve land or personal property located on reserve lands. These are significant remedies for the non-payment of taxes, and constitute a significant advance over the law-making powers conferred under s. 83 of the *Indian Act*. The power to make laws regarding the seizure of lands under s. 5(1)(e)(iii) is subject to s. 5(7) of the Act, which stipulates that the power can only be exercised if taxes have been outstanding for more than two years.

Like all of the enforcement powers exercisable under s. 5(1)(e), the power to make laws relating to the seizure, forfeiture and assignment of reserve lands or personal property is subject to any conditions and procedures that are prescribed by regulation. The regulations proposed to govern First Nation taxation law enforcement powers are the proposed *First Nations Taxation Enforcement Regulations*, which are discussed in more detail in the commentary devoted to those regulations.

(f)   delegating to any person or body any of the council's powers to make laws under any of paragraphs (a) to (e); and

Commentary

As the text of paragraph (f) indicates, a First Nation council can, by a law made under that paragraph, delegate its law-making powers to another body, such as a tribal council.

(g)   delegating to the First Nations Financial Management Board any other of the council's powers that are required to give effect to a co-management arrangement entered into under section 52 or to give effect to third-party management of the first nation's local revenues.

Commentary

This paragraph operates in conjunction with ss. 52(2)(f) and 53(2)(e) of the Act, which authorize the First Nations Financial Management Board to exercise any powers delegated to it under a law of a First Nation while it is engaged in co-management or third-party management of the First Nation's property tax revenues (defined in s. 2(1) of the Act as "local revenues").

Any delegation of powers by the First Nation council under this paragraph would complement the powers that the First Nation must give to the First Nations Financial Management Board under s. 5(5) of the Act, which allow the Board to act as agent of the First Nation to fulfil the powers and obligations of the council under property taxation laws, the FNFSMA and regulations.

While, like all of the powers conferred under s. 5(1), a First Nation has the discretion whether to exercise the powers conferred under s. 5(1)(g), it is not inconceivable that enacting a law under s. 5(1)(g) would be a condition precedent to acceptance of a First Nation as a borrowing member by the First Nations Finance Authority under s. 76 of the Act.

(2) APPROVAL REQUIRED — A law made under subsection (1) does not have any force or effect until it is approved by the First Nations Tax Commission.

(3) COMING INTO FORCE — A law made under subsection (1) comes into force on the later of

(a)   the day of coming into force set out in the law, and

(b)   the day after it is approved by the First Nations Tax Commission.

Commentary

In combination, ss. 5(2) and (3) of the Act require that the First Nations Tax Commission must approve property taxation laws and other local revenue laws of a First Nation before they can take effect. In this regard, the Commission takes over the role played by the Minister of Indian Affairs and Northern Development in approving property tax by-laws under s. 83 of the *Indian Act*.

Since it is not possible for First Nation members and other citizens to know exactly when an approval by the First Nations Tax Commission has been given, s. (3) provides that a local revenue law comes into force (begins to have legal effect) on the day after it is approved by the Commission. If the law itself specifies that it does not come into force until a later date, then that later date will govern. In either case, by virtue of s. 6(1) of the *Interpretation Act*,[99] the law will come into force at the beginning of the day in question.

(4) APPEALS — A law made under paragraph (1)(a) shall include

(a)   an appeal procedure in respect of assessments, incorporating such procedures as are prescribes by regulation; and

(b)   fixed rates of renumeration and fixed terms of office for any persons designated to decide the appeals.

Commentary

Appeal procedures for property taxation laws will be set out in the proposed *First Nations Assessment Appeal Regulations.*[100]

Case Law

Given the similarities between s. 83(3) of the *Indian Act* and s. 5(4) of the FNFSMA, it is likely that the following jurisprudence would also apply to the latter provision.

---

[99]   R.S.C. 1985, c. I-21.
[100]   Discussed further below, in the commentary devoted to those regulations.

Canadian Pacific Ltd. v Matsqui Indian Band, [1995] S.C.J. No. 1, [1995], 1 S.C.R. 3.

The Supreme Court of Canada addressed the requirement for fixed rates of remuneration and fixed terms of office for members of tribunals established by First Nations, reflected in the requirements of s. 5(4)(b) above:

> Thus, to conform to the requirements of institutional independence, the appellant bands' by-laws will have to guarantee remuneration and stipulate periods of tenure for tribunal members[101]

Huyck v. Musqueam Indian Band, [2000] F.C.J. No. 582, 189 F.T.R. 1, aff'd [2001] F.C.J. No. 754, 272 N.R. 188 (C.A.), appeal to S.C.C. dismissed [2001] S.C.C.A. No. 373.

The Federal Court observed that a reasonable apprehension of bias could arise by virtue of the fact that the band appointed the members of the tax assessment appeal board. It cited the reasoning of Chief Justice Lamer in *Canadian Pacific Ltd. v Matsqui Indian Band*:

> For the Chief Justice, the fact that the Band selects the tribunal members suggests a degree of dependence which in turn, gives rise to a reasonable apprehension of bias. In effect, the Chief Justice affirms that "a party should not be required to present its case before a tribunal whose members have been appointed by an opposing party".[102]

In that case, however, although the assessment review board members were appointed by the band, because the board subsequently appointed outside panels to conduct the appeals, the court held that a reasonable apprehension of bias did not arise.

Canadian Pacific Ltd. v Matsqui Indian Band, [1995] S.C.J. No. 1, [1995] 1 S.C.R. 3.

The Supreme Court of Canada also held that the requirement in s. 83(3) of the *Indian Act* that a taxation by-law must provide an appeal procedure in respect of taxation assessments permitted a band enacting a taxation by-law under s. 83(1) of the *Indian Act* to create a right of appeal to the Federal Court – Trial Division.

Beattie v. Squamish Indian Band[103] confirms that the ruling in *Canadian Pacific Ltd. v Matsqui Indian Band*[104] continues to permit the appeal of a taxation by-law

---

[101]   [1995] S.C.J. No. 1, [1995] 1 S.C.R. 3 at p. 59.

[102]   *Canadian Pacific Ltd. v Matsqui Indian Band*, [1995] S.C.J. No. 1 at 26, [1995], 1 S.C.R. 3 at 57.

[103]   [2005] F.C.J. No. 391.

[104]   [1995] S.C.J. No. 1, [1995] 1 S.C.R. 3.

to the Federal Court, notwithstanding the changes brought to the *Federal Court Act* by the *Courts Administration Service Act.*[105]

(5) THIRD-PARTY MANAGEMENT — A property taxation law shall provide that, if the First Nations Financial Management Board gives notice to the first nation that third-party management of the first nation's local revenues is required, the Board may act as agent of the first nation to fulfil any of the powers and obligations of the council under the property taxation law, this Act and any regulations made under this Act.

Commentary

Unlike the delegation of law-making powers set out in s. 5(1)(g) of the Act, the requirement to give the First Nations Financial Management Board the power to act as agent for the First Nation in situations of third-party management under s. 5(5) is not optional. This subsection therefore requires that every property taxation law made under s. 5(1)(a) of the Act must contain the required delegation to the Board, applicable in situations where the Board gives notice of third-party management under s. 53 of the Act.[106]

(6) SPECIAL LEVY — A property taxation law of a borrowing member shall provide that the borrowing member must make a law under paragraph (1)(a) in order to recover amounts payable under paragraph 84(5)(b).

Commentary

Paragraph 84(5)(b) of the Act gives the First Nations Finance Authority the power to require borrowing members to pay to replenish the Authority's debt reserve fund, in circumstances where defaults in payments by other borrowing members have reduced the balance in that fund to less than 50%. Under s. 5(6), a property taxation law of a borrowing member must require it to make another property taxation law (or to amend the existing one) in order to recover sufficient additional tax revenue to satisfy the charges under s. 84(5)(b).

Oddly enough, although the First Nations Finance Authority can also require a First Nation to raise additional revenue through a charge imposed under s. 84(5)(a), there is no corresponding requirement to provide for that contingency in the First Nation's property taxation laws.

(7) ASSIGNMENT OF RIGHT OR INTEREST — Notwithstanding the *Indian Act* or any instrument conferring a right or interest in reserve lands,

---

[105]   S.C. 2002, c. 8. That Act also changed the name of the *Federal Court Act* to the *Federal Courts Act.*
[106]   The manner of giving such a notice is prescribed in the proposed *Local Revenue Management Implementation Regulations*, made under s. 56(a) of the Act.

if there are outstanding taxes payable pursuant to a law made under paragraph (1)(a) for more than two years, the first nation may assign the right or interest in accordance with the conditions and procedures prescribed by regulation.

Commentary

This subsection confers a significant additional power on First Nation councils under the FNFSMA, as compared to those conferred under s. 83 of the *Indian Act*. The protective regime of the *Indian Act* prohibits the transfer of a lease, permit or other right to use or occupy reserve lands without the approval of the Minister of Indian Affairs and Northern Development:

> 28. (1) Subject to subsection (2), any deed, lease, contract, instrument, document or agreement of any kind, whether written or oral, by which a band or a member of a band purports to permit a person other than a member of that band to occupy or use a reserve or to reside or otherwise exercise any rights on a reserve is void.
>
> ...
>
> 37. (1) Lands in a reserve shall not be sold nor title to them conveyed until they have been absolutely surrendered to Her Majesty pursuant to subsection 38(1) by the band for whose use and benefit in common the reserve was set apart.
>
> (2) Except where this Act otherwise provides,[107] lands in a reserve shall not be leased nor an interest in them granted until they have been surrendered to Her Majesty pursuant to subsection 38(2) by the band for whose use and benefit in common the reserve was set apart.

Subsections 38(1) and (2) set out the mechanisms for surrenders and designations. Because of these statutory protections for the reserve land base, band councils operating under s. 83 were unable themselves to seize and transfer interests in reserve land in order to pay outstanding taxes.

Under this provision of the FNFSMA, however, a First Nation council can seize and, in effect, sell an interest in reserve land to recover unpaid taxes. The power to do so is governed by conditions and procedures prescribed by regulation, which in this case would be the proposed *First Nations Taxation Enforcement Regulations*. As proposed, these regulations would set out required notice periods and auction procedures. They would also limit the assignment of a right or interest to persons or entities who would otherwise have been entitled

---

[107] Examples of instances where the *Indian Act* provides for dispositions without a surrender are ss. 18(2) (use of lands for the general welfare of the band), 28(2) (permit to occupy, use, reside on or otherwise exercise rights on a reserve), 35 (expropriation), 58(1) (agricultural leases), 58(3) (leases of allotted lands on behalf of individual Indians) and 58(4) (disposition of wild grass, fallen timber, sand and gravel and non-metallic minerals).

under the *Indian Act* to hold the interest or right in question.[108] This preserves the *Indian Act*'s limitations on alienation of reserve lands in assignments under the FNFSMA.

(8) JUDICIAL NOTICE — In any proceedings, judicial notice may be taken of a local revenue law.

Commentary

Judicial notice refers to the ability of a court, in conducting a trial or framing a decision, to take cognizance of the truth of certain facts — in this case the content of a local revenue law — without the production of evidence to prove them.[109]

Note that although this provision does not require the courts to take judicial notice of laws made under s. 5(1), it permits them to do so.

(9) *STATUTORY INSTRUMENTS ACT* — The *Statutory Instruments Act* does not apply in respect of local revenue laws or laws made under section 9.

Commentary

Because First Nation property taxation laws would likely be characterized as regulations under the *Statutory Instruments Act*, in the absence of this provision those laws would be subject to the examination, registration and publication requirements of that Act.[110] Tax by-laws made under s. 83 of the *Indian Act* are exempted from registration under the *Statutory Instruments Act* (and therefore also from examination and publication) by virtue of s. 7(1) of the *Statutory Instruments Regulations*.[111]

6. (1) NOTICE OF PROPOSED LAWS — The council of a first nation shall, at least 60 days before making a law under any of paragraphs 5(1)(a) to (c), including a law repealing such a law or an amendment to such a law other than one referred to in paragraph 10(a) or (b),

    (a)   **publish a notice of the proposed law in a local newspaper;**

    (b)   **post the notice in apublic place on the reserve lands of the first nation; and**

    (c)   **send the notice, by mail or electronic means, to the First Nations Tax Commission, to members of the first nation, to others who**

---

[108]   Proposed *First Nations Taxation Enforcement Regulations*, s. 18.

[109]   *Black's Law Dictionary*, 7th ed. (St. Paul, Minn.: West Publishing, 1999).

[110]   For a discussion of why this would be so, see P. Salembier, *Regulatory Law and Practice in Canada* (Toronto: Butterworths, 2004), at pp. 39-48.

[111]   C.R.C., c. 1509.

have interests in those lands or rights to occupy, possess or use those lands and to every government, organization and individual who, in the opinion of the council, may be affected by the proposed law.

Commentary

The notice requirements in this subsection apply to the following types of First Nation laws, as well as to amendments or repeals of them:

- property taxation laws (s. 5(1)(a));
- local revenue budget laws (s. 5(1)(b)); and
- laws respecting how taxpayers' interests are to be represented to the First Nation council (s. 5(1)(c)).

They do not apply to annual rate and expenditure laws, made under ss. 10(a) and (b).

(2) EXEMPTION — The First Nations Tax Commission may exempt a first nation from the requirements of subsection (1) in respect of an amendment of a law if the Commission considers that the amendment is not significant.

Commentary

The FNFSMA nowhere defines which types of amendment would be considered "significant", and which would not. The exemption powers of the Commission under this subsection would therefore likely be exercised on the basis of a request by the First Nation council, based on a draft of the proposed amendment. Standard criteria for such exemptions might also be established by the Commission under s. 35(2) of the Act.

(3) CONTENT OF NOTICE — A notice referred to in subsection (1) shall

(a) describe the proposed law;

(b) state where a copy of the proposed law may be obtained;

(c) invite representations regarding the proposed law to be made, in writing, to the council within 60 days after the date stated in th notice; and

(d) if the council is to review the proposed law at a public meeting, state the time and place of the meeting.

(4) COUNCIL TO CONSIDER REPRESENTATIONS — Before making a law under any of paragraphs 5(1)(a) to (c), the council of a first nation shall consider any representations that were made in accordance with paragraph (3)(c) or at a meeting referred to in paragraph (3)(d).

Commentary

The requirements of this subsection apply to:

- property taxation laws (s. 5(1)(a));
- local revenue budget laws (s. 5(1)(b)); and
- laws respecting how taxpayers' interests are to be represented to the First Nation council (s. 5(1)(c)).

The representations that must be considered are those that were made in writing to the council within 60 days after the date stated in the notice (s. 6(3)(c)), and those made at a public meeting held by the council to review the proposed law (s. 6(3)(d)).

7. FURTHER REPRESENTATIONS — When the council of a first nation sends a property taxation law or a law made under paragraph 5(1)(c) to the First Nations Tax Commission for its approval, the council shall

(a) provide a copy of the law to any persons who made representations under paragraph 6(3)(c); and

(b) invite those persons to make written representations to the Commission within 30 days after the day on which they receive the copy of the law.

Commentary

This section applies to property taxation laws (made under s. 5(1)(a)) and laws respecting how taxpayers' interests are to be represented to the First Nation council (made under s. 5(1)(c)). Persons to whom copies of the law must be sent are those who provided comments in writing to the council within 60 days after the date stated in the notice sent pursuant to s. 6(3).

8. (1) INFORMATION ACCOMPANYING PROPERTY TAXATION LAW — A property taxation law — including an amendment of a property taxation law — shall, when submitted to the First Nations Tax Commission for approval, be accompanied by

(a) a description of the lands, interests or rights subject to the law;

(b) a description of the assessment practices to be applied to each class of land, interest or right;

(c) information regarding services to be provided from local revenues, existing service agreements and any service agreement negotiations under way at the time the law was made;

(d) a description of the notices that were given, any consultation undertaken by the council before making the law and copies of any written representations received by the council; and

(e) evidence that the law was duly made by the council.

(2) EXEMPTION — The First Nations Tax Commission may exempt a first nation from the requirements of subsection (1) in respect of an amendment of a property taxation law if the Commission considers that the amendment is not significant.

Commentary

The FNFSMA nowhere defines which types of amendment would be considered "significant", and which would not. The exemption powers of the Commission under this subsection would therefore likely be exercised on the basis of a request from the First Nation council, at the time the proposed amendment is submitted for approval. Standard criteria for such exemptions might also be established by the Commission under s. 35(2) of the Act.

(3) ACCOMPANYING INFORMATION — A law made under paragraph 5(1)(c), when submitted to the First Nations Tax Commission for approval, shall be accompanied by

(a)   a description of the notices that were given, any concultation undertaken by the council before making the law and copies of any written representations received by the council; and

(b)   evidence that the law was duly made by the council.

Commentary

Laws made under s. 5(1)(c) are laws respecting how taxpayers' interests are to be represented to the First Nation council.

(4) EVIDENCE LAW DULY MADE —A law made under paragraph 5(1)(b), (d) or (e) that is submitted to the First Nations Tax Commission for approval shall be accompanied by evidence that it was duly made by the council.

(5) ADDITIONAL INFORMATION ON REQUEST — At the request of the First Nations Tax Commission, a first nation shall provide any documents that the Commission requires in order to

(a) review a local revenue law;

(b) determine that the law was made in accordance with this Act, the regulations or any standards made under subsection 35(1); or

(c) perform any of its other functions under this Act.

Commentary

Although the test for what documents must be provided is expressed objectively as those *required* by the Commission for the enunciated purposes, in practice, in situations such as this the courts usually give some deference to the opinion of the body in question as to what documents it believes are necessary.[112]

9. (1) FINANCIAL ADMINISTRATION LAWS — Subject to subsections (2) and (3), the council of a first nation may make laws

    (a)   respecting the financial administration of the first nation; and

    (b)   delegating to any person or body its powers to make laws under paragraph (a).

Commentary

This subsection provides a general law-making power to First Nations to make laws respecting financial administration. The qualifications expressed in the opening words relate to requirements for borrowing members (under s. 9(2)) and the various times at which such laws come into force (under s. 9(3)). Financial administration laws that were made under s. 83 of the *Indian Act* by a First Nation that opts into the FNFSMA are deemed by s. 145(1) of that Act to have been made under s. 9(1) of the FNFSMA.

(2) APPROVAL REQUIRED — A law made under subsection (1) by a borrowing member, including any amendment of such a law, does not have any force or effect until it is approved by the First Nations Financial Management Board.

Commentary

In order to become a borrowing member, s. 4 of the Act requires that a First Nation council must first have in place a financial administration law approved by the Board. The effect of this subsection is hence to require that any further amendments to a borrowing member's financial administration law must be approved by the First Nations Financial Management Board before the amendments can come into force.

(3) COMING INTO FORCE — A law made under subsection (1) comes into force on the latest of

    (a)   the day on which it is made,

    (b)   the day of coming into force set out in the law, and

    (c)   in the case of a law or amendment made by a borrowing member, the day after it is approved by the First Nations Financial Management Board.

---

[112]   *Bell Canada v. Canada (Canadian Radio-Television and Telecommunications Commission)*, [1989] S.C.J. No. 68, [1989] 1 S.C.R. 1722 at 1746; *Pezim v. British Columbia (Superintendent of Brokers)* [1994] S.C.J./A.C.S. No. 58, 114 D.L.R. (4th) 385 at 404.

Commentary

The default rule in this subsection is that a financial administration law will come into force on the day on which it is made or, if the law itself specifies that it does not come into force until a later day, then on that later day. The rule, however, is different for financial administration laws made by borrowing members.

For financial administration laws made by borrowing members, this subsection operates in a manner similar to s. 5(3). Since it is not possible for First Nation members and other citizens to know exactly when an approval by the First Nations Financial Management Board has been given, s. 5(3)(c) provides that a financial administration law comes into force (begins to have legal effect) on the day after it is approved by the Board. If the law itself specifies that it does not come into force until a later day, then that later day will govern.

In either case, by virtue of s. 6(1) of the *Interpretation Act*,[113] the law will come into force at the beginning of the day in question.

(4) EVIDENCE LAW DULY MADE — A law made under subsection (1) that is submitted to the First Nations Financial Management Board for approval shall be accompanied by evidence that it was duly made by the council.

(5) ADDITIONAL INFORMATION ON REQUEST — At the request of the First Nations Financial Management Board, a first nation shall provide any documents that the Board requires in order to

(a) review a financial administration law submitted to the Board;

(b) determine that the law was made in accordance with this Act, the regulations or any standards made under subsection 55(1); or

(c) perform any of its other functions under this Act.

Commentary

Although the test for what documents must be provided is expressed objectively as those *required* by the Board for the enunciated purposes, in practice, in situations such as this the courts usually give some deference to the opinion of the body in question as to what documents it believes are necessary.[114]

10. ANNUAL RATE AND EXPENDITURE LAWS — A council of a first nation that makes a property taxation law shall, at least once each year at a time prescribed by regulation, make

---

113   R.S.C. 1985, c. I-21.
114   *Bell Canada v. Canada (Canadian Radio-Television and Telecommunications Commission)*, [1989] S.C.J. No. 68, [1989] 1 S.C.R. 1722 at 1746; *Pezim v. British Columbia (Superintendent of Brokers)* [1994] S.C.J./A.C.S. No. 58, 114 D.L.R. (4th) 385 at 404.

(a) **a law under paragraph 5(1)(a) setting the rate of tax to be applied to the assessed value of each class of lands, interests or rights; and**

(b) **a law under paragraph 5(1)(b) establishing a budget for the expenditure of revenues raised under the property taxation law.**

Commentary

This section requires that every First Nation with a property taxation law (a law made under s. 5(1)(a)) in place must also make an annual tax rate law under s. 5(1)(a) and an annual budget law under s. 5(1)(b). The date by which such laws must be made is to be prescribed by the proposed *First Nations Rates and Expenditure Laws Timing Regulations.*[115]

11. (1) NO REPEAL BY BORROWING MEMBERS — A borrowing member shall not repeal a property taxation law.

Commentary

Because the revenues from property taxation laws of borrowing members are routinely pledged as security for its loan from the First Nations Finance Authority, such laws cannot be repealed while the loan remains outstanding.

(2) PRIORITY TO AUTHORITY — A law made under paragraph 5(1)(b) by a borrowing member shall not authorize the expenditure of local revenues unless the borrowing member's budget provides for the payment of all amounts payable to the First Nations Finance Authority during the budget period.

Commentary

This subsection requires that a First Nation that is a borrowing member must give priority to repayment of financial obligations to the First Nations Finance Authority over other expenditures in its annual budget law.

(3) FINANCIAL COMMITMENT — The borrowing member shall, in every year, reserve such local revenues as are required to ensure that all amounts authorized to be paid to the First Nations Finance Authority in the year are actually paid in that year.

---

[115] The proposed regulations currently establish this date as the date established by the province in which the reserve is located, for the setting of the tax rates applicable to provincial lands adjacent to the reserve.

Commentary

This subsection would appear to require the First Nation to create a reserve fund for payments that are to be made to the First Nations Finance Authority.

12. LEGAL CAPACITY OF FIRST NATIONS — For greater certainty, for the purposes of Part 4, a borrowing member has the capacity to contract and to sue and be sued.

Commentary

Because of uncertainty as to the legal status of First Nations (see discussion below), and because First Nations must be able to enter into binding loan contracts with the First Nations Finance Authority under Part 4 of the Act, this provision provides that, for those purposes at least, a First Nation has the power to contract and to litigate on its own behalf.

Case Law

PSAC v. Francis, [1982] 2 S.C.R. 72.

The Supreme Court of Canada held that, while the *Indian Act* did not establish a band or band council as a corporate body, it did grant the band council certain powers which, if exercised, rendered the band council subject to the same liabilities as the law imposes on natural persons exercising those powers. The band council's status as an entity with legal capacity to act as an employer therefore arose by necessary implication.

Mintuck v. Valley River Band No. 63A (1977), 75 D.L.R. (3d) 589 (Man. C.A.).

In this earlier decision, the Manitoba Court of Appeal held that a band can be sued in tort for the actions of its council, and that it was appropriate to name the chief and council as representatives of the band for that purpose. It also ruled that a judgement obtained in such an action could be executed against the assets of the band.

Horseman v. Horse Lake First Nation, [2005] A.J. No. 24, 248 D.L.R. (4th) 505, (C.A.).

In this recent decision that follows the line of thinking in *Mintuck v. Valley River Band No. 63A*,[116] the Alberta Court of Appeal confirmed that a band is a public body and that if it acts either maliciously or in abuse of its powers it will be liable for the tort of breach of public authority.

---

[116]   (1977), 75 D.L.R. (3d) 589 (Man. C.A.).

R. v. Cochrane, [1977] M.J. No. 301, [1977] 3 W.W.R. 660 (Co. Ct.).

The court held that while a band may be a suable entity, it is neither a natural person nor a corporation.

Cache Creek Motors Ltd. v. Porter, [1979] B.C.J. No. 1602, 14 B.C.L.R. 13 (Co. Ct.).

The court confirmed that a band can be sued in its own right without the involvement of the Minister of Indian Affairs and Northern Development.

Joe v. Findlay, [1987] B.C.J. No. 20, 12 B.C.L.R. (2d) 166 (S.C.).

It was held that a band council's authority to bring and defend legal proceedings on behalf of the band, although not expressly provided for in the *Indian Act*, must be inferred as a necessary adjunct to give effect to the band council's powers under s. 81 of the Act. The court also confirmed that it was not necessary for the council to seek the consent of the band to do so.

King v. Gull Bay Indian Band, [1983] O.J. No. 2152, 38 C.P.C. 1 (Dist. Ct.).

The court found that Indian bands are not unincorporated associations, but are instead legal entities that are therefore capable of being sued. This ruling was followed in *Bannon v. Pervais*,[117] *Springhill Lumber Ltd. v. Lake St. Martin Indian Band*[118] and *Clow Darling Ltd. v. Big Trout Lake Band.*[119]

Kucey v. Peter Ballantyne Indian Band, [1987] S.J. No. 193, [1987] 3 W.W.R. 438 (C.A.).

The court followed the Supreme Court of Canada decision in *PSAC v. Francis*,[120] and held that because Indian band councils are given significant rights to contract and incur legal obligations in the course of fulfilling their statutory mandate, they may sue or be sued in their own name: that they have an existence in law that goes beyond that of their individual members.

Wewayakum Indian Band v. Canada, [1991] F.C.J. No. 213, [1991] 3 F.C. 420 (T.D.).

The court concluded that Indian bands have a special status enabling them to institute, prosecute and defend a court action. It observed that a band has the same power to sue as a corporation, and would consequently be subject to any resulting obligations.[121]

---

[117]   [1989] O.J. No. 426, 68 O.R. (2d) 276 (Dist. Ct.).
[118]   [1985] M.J. No. 425, [1986] 2 C.N.L.R. 179 (Q.B.).
[119]   70 O.R. (2d) 56 (Dist.Ct.).
[120]   [1982] 2 S.C.R. 72.
[121]   [1991] F.C.J. No. 213, [1991] 3 F.C. 420 (T.D.) at 429.

William v. Lake Babine Indian Band, [1999] B.C.J. No. 842, [2000] 1 C.N.L.R. 233 (S.C.).

The British Columbia Supreme Court, in determining how an Indian band could be served with a legal process, commented on the reasoning in *Wewayakum Indian Band v. Canada*. It noted that although an Indian band may have similar obligations and rights to a corporation, that does not mean that it functions as, or assumes the legal status of, a corporation. It concluded instead that a band is more analogous to an unincorporated entity than to a corporation.

Otineka Dev Corp. Ltd v. Canada, [1994] T.C.J./A.C.I. No. 23, [1994] 2 C.N.L.R. 83 (F.C.).

The Tax Court of Canada determined that, for the purposes of the tax exemptions granted by s. 149(1)(d) of the *Income Tax Act*, a band is a municipality.

Montana Band v. Canada, [1997] F.C.J. No. 1486, [1998] 2 F.C. 3 (T.D.).

The Federal Court held that a band's capacity to sue or be sued arises by implication from its statutory powers, but has uncertain boundaries. It confirmed that a band or band council does not have the legal powers of a natural person in the same way a corporation does. It also confirmed that the naming of a band as a party to a legal action, followed by certain named band members (usually the elected councillors) acting on their own behalf as well as on behalf of all other members of the band, was sufficient to resolve any uncertainties about legal status that might exist.[122]

Nelson House Indian Band v. Frost, [1999] M.J. No. 63, 169 D.L.R. (4th) 606 (C.A.).

The court held that an Indian band empowered to control and manage revenue moneys under s. 69 of the *Indian Act* has the capacity to sue for the recovery of revenue moneys that had allegedly been misappropriated.

13. (1) LOCAL REVENUE ACCOUNT — Local revenues of a first nation shall be placed in a local revenue account, separate from other moneys of the first nation.

(2) RESTRICTION ON EXPENDITURES — Local revenues may be expended only under the authority of a law made under paragraph 5(1)(b).

Commentary

Paragraph 5(1)(b) authorizes the making of laws authorizing the expenditure of local revenues.

---

[122]   [1997] F.C.J. No. 1486, [1998] 2 F.C. 3 (T.D.) at 18.

(3) BALANCED BUDGET — Expenditures provided for in a law made under paragraph 5(1)(b) shall not exceed the local revenues estimated for the year in which those expenditures are to be made, less any deficit accumulated from prior years.

Commentary

While this subsection requires a balanced budget, it would appear that an overestimate of the amount of tax revenues to be generated could nonetheless result in a deficit for any particular year.

14. (1) AUDIT — The local revenue account shall be audited at least once each calendar year and reported on separately from other accounts.

(2) ACCESS TO REPORT — The audit report of the local revenue account shall be made available to

(a)   the members of the first nation;

(b)   any other persons who have an interest in, or the right to occupy, possess or use, the first nation's reserve lands;

(c)   the First nations Tax Commission, the First Nations Financial Management Board and the First Nations Finance Authority; and

(d)   the Minister.

Commentary

Note that while this subsection requires that audit reports be *made available* to the parties listed in paragraphs (a) to (d), it does not require that the report actually be sent to those parties.

15. NON-APPLICATION OF CERTAIN PROVISIONS — Paragraphs 83(1)(a) and (d) to (g) and section 84 of the *Indian Act* and any regulations made under paragraph 73(1)(m) of that Act do not apply to a first nation.

Commentary

Once a First Nation has opted into the FNFSMA, the listed provisions of the *Indian Act* cease to apply to that First Nation. The provisions of the *Indian Act* in question are:

> 83. (1) Without prejudice to the powers conferred by section 81, the council of a band may, subject to the approval of the Minister, make by-laws for any or all of the following purposes, namely,
>
> > (a)   subject to subsections (2) and (3), taxation for local purposes of land, or interests in land, in the reserve, including rights to occupy, possess or use land in the reserve;

...

(d)   the payment of remuneration, in such amount as may be approved by the Minister, to chiefs and councillors, out of any moneys raised pursuant to paragraph (a);

(e)   the enforcement of payment of amounts that are payable pursuant to this section, including arrears and interest;

(e.1)   the imposition and recovery of interest on amounts that are payable pursuant to this section, where those amounts are not paid before they are due, and the calculation of that interest;

(f)   the raising of money from band members to support band projects; and

(g)   with respect to any matter arising out of or ancillary to the exercise of powers under this section.

84. Where a tax that is imposed on an Indian by or under the authority of a by-law made under section 83 is not paid in accordance with the by-law, the Minister may pay the amount owing together with an amount equal to one-half of one per cent thereof out of moneys payable out of the funds of the band to the Indian.

Paragraph 73(1)(m) of the *Indian Act* provides for the making of regulations by the Governor in Council:

...

(m)   for empowering and authorizing the council of a band to borrow money for band projects or housing purposes and providing for the making of loans out of moneys so borrowed to members of the band for housing purposes.

The *Indian Band Council Borrowing Regulations* have been made under this paragraph. They contain a single substantive provision that mirrors its enabling power:

2. The council of a band may borrow money for band projects or housing purposes and may make loans out of moneys so borrowed to members of the band for housing purposes, on such terms and conditions as may be determined by the council.

PART 2

FIRST NATIONS TAX COMMISSION

Interpretation

16. DEFINITIONS — The following definitions apply in this Part.

Commentary

These definitions apply in ss. 16 to 36 of the Act.

"Commission"
«Commission »
"Commission" means the First Nations Tax Commission.

"taxpayer"
« contribuable »
"taxpayer" means a person paying tax under a property taxation law.

Establishment and Organization of Commission

17. (1) COMMISSION — There is hereby established a commission, to be known as the First Nations Tax Commission, consisting of 10 commissioners, including a Chief Commissioner and Deputy Chief Commissioner.

(2) CAPACITY, RIGHTS, POWERS AND PRIVILEGES — The Commission has the capacity, rights, powers and privileges of a natural person, including the capacity to

(a)   enter into contracts;

(b)   acquire, hold and dispose of property or an interest in property;

(c)   raise, invest or borrow money; and

(d)   sue and be sued.

18. (1) WHEN AGENT OF HER MAJESTY — The Commission is an agent of Her Majesty only for the approval of local revenue laws.

Commentary

Other functions of the Commission, in respect of which the Commission does not act as an agent of the Crown, include:

- the conduct of reviews under s. 33;

- the delivery of training programs to First Nation real property tax administrators;
- providing advice to First Nations on taxation matters;
- entering into cooperative sales or consultation arrangements;
- maintaining a registry of local revenue and financial administration laws;
- determining or representing that a First Nation has unutilized borrowing capacity under s. 32(1)(b);
- the issuance of certifications under s. 32(2)(b); and
- publishing the *First Nations Gazette*.

(2) SAVINGS — For the purpose of subsection (1), the issuance of a certificate referred to in paragraph 32(2)(b) is deemed not to be an approval of a local revenue law.

19. (1) APPOINTMENT OF CHIEF COMMISSIONER — On the recommendation of the Minister, the Governor in Council shall appoint a Chief Commissioner and Deputy Chief Commissioner.

(2) TENURE — The Chief Commissioner and Deputy Chief Commissioner hold office during good behaviour for a term not exceeding five years, subject to removal by the Governor in Council at any time for cause.

Commentary

A person who holds office during good behaviour can be removed in one of two ways:

- by order of the Governor in Council, on the recommendation of the Canadian Judicial Council,[123] made following an inquiry requested by the Minister of Justice under s. 69 of the *Judges Act*;[124] or
- by an order of the Governor in Council, following any other process that provides the person with an opportunity to be heard in accordance with the principles of natural justice.

In the latter instance, allegations of misfeasance would normally be provided to the Governor in Council, which would then provide the appointee with an opportunity to answer them. The Governor in Council would then make its

---

[123]   Established under s. 59(1) of the *Judges Act*, R.S.C. 1985, c. J-1.
[124]   R.S.C. 1985, c. J-1.

decision whether to remove the appointee based on the written material before it.[125]

Case Law

Weatherill v. Canada (Attorney General), [1999] F.C.J. No. 787, [1999] 4 F.C. 107 (T.D.).

The Federal Court upheld the dismissal by the Governor in Council of the Chairman of the former Canada Labour Relations Board, who held office during good behaviour, for incurring unreasonable hospitality and travel expenses. The applicant had been offered an opportunity to make submissions in response to a report on his expenses and in response to the application to the Governor in Council for his removal, but chose not to do so. The court concluded that the requirements of natural justice had been satisfied, and that a further inquiry under s. 69 of the *Judges Act* was not required.

Wedge v. Canada (Attorney General), [1997] F.C.J. No. 872, 4 Admin. L.R. (3d) 153, 133 F.T.R. 277 (T.D.).

The Federal Court upheld the dismissal by the Governor in Council of a member of the Veterans Appeal Board, who held office during good behaviour, for allegedly having participated in election irregularities. The court found that there had been no breach of procedural fairness in the way in which the applicant had been treated. The applicant had been informed of the allegations against him by letter, and had been given copies of an investigation report and copies of the final report to the Governor in Council. The applicant had had the opportunity to respond orally, and his written responses to the investigation report and final report were submitted to the Governor in Council. The court held that the applicant was not entitled to cross-examine witnesses interviewed, or to a full, formal, court-like hearing. The court also concluded that the standard of good behaviour to which an appointee will be held is in the discretion of the Governor in Council, which extends to its judgment as to whether the appointee's conduct could undermine public confidence in the federal institution with which he had been appointed to serve.

Subsection 19(2), together with ss. 20 and 23(1), parallels the requirements for institutional independence set out by the Supreme Court of Canada in *Canadian Pacific Ltd. v Matsqui Indian Band* in relation to tribunals established by bands themselves:

> Thus, to conform to the requirements of institutional independence, the appellant bands' by-laws will have to guarantee remuneration and stipulate periods of tenure for tribunal members.[126]

---

[125]   A similar procedure was followed, and received judicial approval, in *Weatherill v. Canada (Attorney General)*, [1999] F.C.J. No. 787, [1999] 4 F.C. 107 (T.D.).
[126]   [1995] S.C.J. No. 1, [1995] 1 S.C.R. 3 at 59.

20. (1) APPOINTMENT OF COMMISSIONERS — On the recom-mendation of the Minister, the Governor in Council shall appoint four commissioners to hold office during good behaviour for a term not exceeding five years, subject to removal by the Governor in Council at any time for cause.

(2) APPOINTMENT OF COMMISSIONERS — On the recom-mendation of the Minister, the Governor in Council shall appoint three additional commissioners — one of whom shall be a taxpayer using reserve lands for commercial, one for residential and one for utility purposes — to hold office during good behaviour for a term not exceeding five years, subject to removal by the Governor in Council at any time for cause.

Commentary

A person who holds office during good behaviour can be removed in one of two ways:

- by order of the Governor in Council, on the recommendation of the Canadian Judicial Council,[127] made following an inquiry requested by the Minister of Justice under s. 69 of the *Judges Act*;[128] or

- by an order of the Governor in Council, following any other process that provides the person with an opportunity to be heard in accordance with the principles of natural justice.

In the latter instance, allegations of misfeasance would normally be provided to the Governor in Council, which would then provide the appointee with an opportunity to answer them. The Governor in Council would then make its decision whether to remove the appointee based on the written material before it.[129]

Case Law

Weatherill v. Canada (Attorney General), [1999] F.C.J. No. 787, [1999] 4 F.C. 107 (T.D.).

The Federal Court upheld the dismissal by the Governor in Council of the Chairman of the former Canada Labour Relations Board, who held office during good behaviour, for incurring unreasonable hospitality and travel expenses. The applicant had been offered an opportunity to make submissions in response to a report on his expenses and in response to the application to the Governor in Council for his removal, but chose not to do so. The court concluded that the requirements of natural justice had been satisfied, and that a further inquiry under s. 69 of the *Judges Act* was not required.

---

[127] Established under s. 59(1) of the *Judges Act*, R.S.C. 1985, c. J-1.

[128] R.S.C. 1985, c. J-1.

[129] A similar procedure was followed, and received judicial approval, in *Weatherill v. Canada (Attorney General)*, [1999] F.C.J. No. 787, [1999] 4 F.C. 107 (T.D.).

Wedge v. Canada (Attorney General), [1997] F.C.J. No. 872, 4 Admin. L.R. (3d) 153, 133 F.T.R. 277 (T.D.).

The Federal Court upheld the dismissal by the Governor in Council of a member of the Veterans Appeal Board, who held office during good behaviour, for allegedly having participated in election irregularities. The court found that there had been no breach of procedural fairness in the way in which the applicant had been treated. The applicant had been informed of the allegations against him by letter, and had been given copies of an investigation report and copies of the final report to the Governor in Council. The applicant had had the opportunity to respond orally, and his written responses to the investigation report and final report were submitted to the Governor in Council. The court held that the applicant was not entitled to cross-examine witnesses interviewed, or to a full, formal, court-like hearing. The court also concluded that the standard of good behaviour to which an appointee will be held is in the discretion of the Governor in Council, which extends to its judgment as to whether the appointee's conduct could undermine public confidence in the federal institution with which he had been appointed to serve.

Subsection 20, together with ss. 19(2) and 23(1), parallels the requirements for institutional independence set out by the Supreme Court of Canada in *Canadian Pacific Ltd. v Matsqui Indian Band* in relation to tribunals established by bands themselves:

> Thus, to conform to the requirements of institutional independence, the appellant bands' by-laws will have to guarantee remuneration and stipulate periods of tenure for tribunal members.[130]

(3) APPOINTMENT OF ADDITIONAL COMMISSIONER — A body prescribed by regulation shall appoint an additional commissioner to hold office during pleasure for a term not exceeding five years.

Commentary

A body to appoint the additional commissioner is to be prescried by the proposed *First Nations Tax Commissioner Appointment Regulations*. Note that the additional commissioner appointed by this body holds office only "during pleasure", which means that the commissioner can be removed at any time without a judicial enquiry or the need to show cause.

(4) STAGGERED TERMS — In determining the term of appointment of commissioners, the Governor in Council shall endeavour to ensure that the terms of no more than three commissioners expire in any one calendar year.

---

[130]   [1995] S.C.J. No. 1, [1995] 1 S.C.R. 3 at 59.

(5) QUALIFICATIONS — The Commission shall be composed of men and women from across Canada, including members of first nations, who are committed to the development of a system of first nations real property taxation and who have the experience or capacity to enable the Commission to fulfil its mandate.

21. STATUS — The Chief Commissioner shall hold office on a full-time basis, while the other commissioners shall hold office on a part-time basis.

22. REAPPOINTMENT — A commissioner may be reappointed for a second or subsequent term of office.

23. (1) REMUNERATION — Commissioners shall be paid the remuneration determined by the Governor in Council.

Case Law

This subsection, together with ss. 19(2) and 20 above, parallels the requirements for institutional independence set out by the Supreme Court of Canada in *Canadian Pacific Ltd. v Matsqui Indian Band* in relation to tribunals established by bands themselves:

> Thus, to conform to the requirements of institutional independence, the appellant bands' by-laws will have to guarantee remuneration and stipulate periods of tenure for tribunal members[131]

(2) EXPENSES — The Chief Commissioner shall be reimbursed for reasonable travel and other expenses incurred in performing duties while absent from his or her ordinary place of work. Other Commissioners shall be reimbursed for such expenses incurred in performing duties while absent from their ordinary place of residence.

24. CHIEF COMMISSIONER — **FUNCTIONS** — The Chief Commissioner is the chief executive officer of the Commission and has supervision over, and direction of, the work and staff of the Commission.

25. DEPUTY CHIEF COMMISSIONER — **FUNCTIONS** — In the event of the absence or incapacity of the Chief Commissioner, or if the office of Chief Commissioner is vacant, the Deputy Chief Commissioner shall assume the duties and functions of the Chief Commissioner.

---

[131]   *Ibid.*

26. (1) HEAD OFFICE — The head office of the Commission shall be on the reserve lands of the Kamloops Band or at any other location that the Governor in Council determines.

Commentary

At the time of publication, no alternate location for the Commission's head office had been determined by the Governor in Council.

(2) ADDITIONAL OFFICE — The Commission shall maintain an additional office in the National Capital Region described in the schedule to the *National Capital Act*.

Commentary

The National Capital Region is generally the area comprised of Ottawa, Ontario and Gatineau, Quebec.

27. RULES OF PROCEDURE — The Commission may make any rules that it considers necessary for the conduct of, and the fixing of a quorum for, its meetings.

28. (1) STAFF — The Commission may

(a) hire any staff that is necessary to conduct the work of the Commission; and

(b) determine the duties of those persons and the conditions of their employment.

(2) SALARIES AND BENEFITS — Persons hired under subsection (1) shall be paid the salaries and benefits fixed by the Commission.

Commentary

Note that the powers of the Commission under this section are constrained by s. 143(1) of the Act, which provides that persons who are employees of the Indian Taxation Advisory Board at the time that the First Nations Tax Commission is established must be offered employment with the Commission, at the same salary and with equivalent terms and conditions of employment.

Purposes

29. MANDATE — The purposes of the Commission are to

(a) ensure the integrity of the system of first nations real property taxation and promote a common approach to first nations real property taxation nationwide, having regard to variations in provincial real property taxation systems;

(b) ensure that the real property taxation systems of first nations reconcile the interests of taxpayers with the responsibilities of chiefs and councils to govern the affairs of first nations;

(c) prevent, or provide for the timely resolution of, disputes in relation to the application of local revenue laws;

(d) assist first nations in the exercise of their jurisdiction over real property taxation on reserve lands and build capacity in first nations to administer their taxation systems;

(e) develop training programs for first nation real property tax administrators;

(f) assist first nations to achieve sustainable economic development through the generation of stable local revenues;

(g) promote a transparent first nations real property taxation regime that provides certainty to taxpayers;

(h) promote understanding of the real property taxation systems of first nations; and

(i) provide advice to the Minister regarding future development of the framework within which local revenue laws are made.

Commentary

In addition to the purposes set out in the Act, the First Nations Tax Commission describes its purposes as follows:

> The FNTC will represent the collective interests of First Nations and taxpayers and will promote economic development by enhancing the administrative efficiency and fairness of the First Nation property tax system. Its chief aims are to protect First Nation jurisdiction, safeguard taxpayer interests and increase the value of real property tax on-reserve. It will also ensure the effective administration of the tax system while protecting its integrity by reconciling the interests of First Nation tax authorities and taxpayers, thus creating benefits to all.[132]

Functions and Powers

30. POWERS — In furtherance of the purposes set out in section 29, the Commission may enter into cooperative arrangements and shared-cost ventures with national and international organizations to consult on or sell products or services developed for first nations who have made property taxation laws.

---

[132]   First Nations Tax Commission website: "About the Commission" at <http://www.fntc.ca/about.phtml>.

Commentary

Note that s. 117 of the Act permits the First Nations Tax Commission to expend any revenues that it receives through the conduct of operations, such as those referred to in s. 30, during the financial year in which they are received or in the following year.

31. (1) LOCAL REVENUE LAW REVIEW — The Commission shall review every local revenue law.

Commentary

The requirement for a First Nation to forward local revenue laws (laws made under s. 5(1)) to the First Nations Tax Commission for review is implicit in the wording of ss. 5(2) and (3), which provide that local revenue laws do not come into force until after they are approved by the Commission, and s. 8, which refers to the documentation that must accompany a local revenue law when it is submitted to the First Nations Tax Commission for approval.

(2) WRITTEN SUBMISSIONS — Before approving a local revenue law, the Commission shall consider, in accordance with any regulations made under paragraph 36(1)(b), any representations made to it under paragraph 7(b) in respect of the law by members of the first nation or others who have interests in the reserve lands of the first nation or rights to occupy, possess or use those lands.

Commentary

Paragraph 7(b) requires a First Nation that makes a property taxation law[133] or a law respecting procedures by which the interests of taxpayers may be represented to the council[134] must invite any persons who made prior representations[135] about the law to make written representations to the Commission within 30 days after they receive the copy of the law.

The proposed *First Nations Tax Commission Review Procedures Regulations*, which are to be made under s. 36(1)(b) of the Act, do not at the time of publication contain any procedures for the consideration of representations made to it under paragraph 7(b).

(3) LOCAL REVENUE LAW APPROVAL — Subject to section 32, the Commission shall approve a local revenue law that complies with this Act and with any standards and regulations made under this Act.

---

[133]   Under s. 5(1)(a).
[134]   Under s. 5(1)(c).
[135]   Under s. 6(3)(c).

Commentary

Note that the Commission *must* approve a local revenue law that complies with the Act, the regulations and any standards made by the Commission under s. 35(1). Once those criteria have been met, the Commission has no discretion to withhold approval. Note, however, that this subsection does not prevent the Commission from approving a local revenue law that does *not* comply with the Act, regulations and standards.[136]

The exception referred to in s. 32 relates to criteria that must be satisfied before the Commission can approve a law respecting the borrowing of money from the First Nations Finance Authority.

(4) REGISTRY — The Commission shall maintain a registry of every law approved by it under this section and every financial administration law made under section 9.

32. (1) RESTRICTIONS — The Commission shall not approve a law made under paragraph 5(1)(d) for financing capital infrastructure for the provision of local services on reserve lands unless

(a) the first nation has obtained and forwarded to the Commission a certificate of the First Nations Financial Management Board under subsection 50(3); and

(b) the first nation has unutilized borrowing capacity.

Commentary

The certificate referred to in paragraph (a) is a certificate from the First Nations Financial Management Board stating that the Board is of the opinion that the First Nation was in compliance with the standards set by the Board under s. 55(1).

The Act nowhere defines "unutilized borrowing capacity", although under s. 35(1) the Commission can establish standards criteria for the approval under this subsection of s. 5(1)(d) laws.

(2) COPY AND CERTIFICATE — On approving a law made by a first nation under paragraph 5(1)(d) for financing capital infrastructure for the provision of local services on reserve lands, the Commission shall provide the First Nations Finance Authority with

(a) a true copy of the law registered under subsection 31(4); and

---

[136] Aside, possibly, for the approval of laws made under s. 5(1)(d) for financing capital infrastructure for the provision of local services on reserve lands, since s. 32(2) requires the Commission to issue a certificate after approving such a law stating that the law complies with the Act and regulations (but not its standards).

(b)   **a certificate stating that the law meets all the requirements of this Act and the regulations made under this Act.**

Commentary

The requirement to issue the certificate under paragraph (b) would presumably preclude the Commission from approving a law under s. 31(3) that did not meet the requirements of this Act and regulations, although there is no mention of compliance with the standards referred to in s. 31(3).

(3) NOTICE OF JUDICIAL REVIEW — If the Commission becomes aware that judicial review proceedings have been undertaken in respect of a law made by a first nation under paragraph 5(1)(d) for financing capital infrastructure for the provision of local services on reserve lands, the Commission shall without delay inform the First Nations Finance Authority of those proceedings.

Commentary

Note that this section does not expressly require the Commission to take any concrete steps to ascertain whether judicial review proceedings have been commenced in respect of any particular law.

(4) CERTIFICATE IS EVIDENCE — A certificate referred to in paragraph (2)(b) is, in the absence of evidence to the contrary, conclusive evidence in any judicial proceedings of the facts contained in it.

33. (1) REVIEW ON REQUEST — On the request in writing by a member of a first nation, or by a person who holds an interest in reserve lands or has a right to occupy, possess or use the reserve lands, who

(a)   **is of the opinion that the first nation has not complied with this Part or Part 1 or with a regulation made under either Part or section 141 or 142 or that a law has been unfairly or improperly applied,**

(b)   **has requested the council of the first nation to remedy the situation, and**

(c)   **is of the opinion that the council has not remedied the situation,**

the Commission shall conduct a review of the matter in accordance with the regulations.

Commentary

This subsection gives a right to members of First Nations or taxpayers to request that the Commission conduct a review to determine

- whether the First Nation council has complied with Parts 1 and 2 of the Act and the regulations, or
- whether the First Nation has unfairly or improperly applied a property tax law.

Before requesting a review under this subsection, paragraph (b) requires that the person requesting the review must first have attempted to resolve the complaint with the First Nation council.

The procedures for conducting these reviews are set out in ss. 4 to 37 of the proposed *First Nations Tax Commission Review Procedures Regulations.*

Note that a person cannot request a review under this section as to whether a property taxation law complies with the standards established by the Commission under s. 35(1). Since the standards essentially set out the Commission's criteria for approving proposed property taxation laws under s. 31, any review on compliance with these standards would constitute a review by the Commission of its own actions in approving the law in question, and might lack the appearance of impartiality.

(2) INDEPENDENT REVIEW — If the Commission is of the opinion that a first nation has not complied with this Part or Part 1 or with a regulation made under either Part or section 141 or 142 or that a law has been unfairly or improperly applied, it shall conduct a review of the matter in accordance with the regulations.

Commentary

Subsection 33(2) permits the Commission to launch its own review of whether the First Nation council has complied with Parts 1 and 2 of the Act and the regulations, or has unfairly or improperly applied a property tax law.

The procedures for conducting such a review are set out in ss. 38 to 42 of the proposed *First Nations Tax Commission Review Procedures Regulations.*

(3) REMEDY — If, after conducting a review, the Commission considers that a first nation has not complied with this Part or Part 1 or with a regulation made under either Part or section 141 or 142 or that a law has been unfairly or improperly applied, the Commission

(a) shall order the first nation to remedy the situation; and

(b) may, if the first nation does not remedy the situation within the time set out in the order, by notice in writing, require the First Nations Financial Management Board to either — at the Board's discretion — impose a co-management arrangement on the first nation or assume third-party management of the first nation's local revenues to remedy the situation.

Commentary

This subsection sets out the powers the First Nations Tax Commission can exercise where it determines after a review under s. 33(1) or (2) that

- a First Nation has not complied with Part 1 or 2 of the Act or with the regulations, or
- a property taxation law has been unfairly or improperly applied.

Upon making such a determination, the Commission can order the council or tax administrator of the First Nation to take whatever action is needed to remedy the situation. While the Act does not give these orders the same force as a court order, the Commission can call on the First Nations Financial Management Board under s. 33(3)(b) to impose a co-management arrangement or assume third-party management of the First Nation's tax system if the First Nation fails to comply with the Commission's order. Section 51 of the Act obligates the First Nations Financial Management Board to respond to a request from the Commission under this subsection.

Note that the Commission's request to the Board is simply to intervene; it is up to the Board to determine whether to impose a co-management arrangement or assume third-party management.

34. (1) *FIRST NATIONS GAZETTE* — All local revenue laws approved by the Commission and all standards and procedures established by the Commission under section 35 shall be published in the *First Nations Gazette*.

Commentary

The *First Nations Gazette* is co-published by the Indian Taxation Advisory Board and the Native Law Centre of Canada at the University of Saskatchewan. Subscriptions for the 2005 year cost $72. Further information can be obtained, and subscriptions ordered, at the *First Nations Gazette* website.[137]

(2) FREQUENCY OF PUBLICATION — The Commission shall publish the *First Nations Gazette* at least once in each calendar year.

Commentary

The *First Nations Gazette* is currently published semi-annually.[138]

Standards and Procedures

35. (1) STANDARDS — The Commission may establish standards, not inconsistent with the regulations, respecting

---

[137]   <://www.usask.ca/nativelaw/publications/desc/fng.html>.
[138]   *Ibid.*

(a)   the form and content of local revenue laws;

(b)   enforcement procedures to be included in those laws;

(c)   criteria for the approval of laws made under paragraph 5(1)(d); and

(d)   the form in which information required under section 8 is to be provided to the Commission.

Commentary

Subsection 34(1) requires that these standards be published in the *First Nations Gazette.*

(2) PROCEDURES — The Commission may establish procedures respecting

(a)   submission for approval of local revenue laws;

(b)   approval of those laws;

(c)   representation of taxpayers' interests in the decisions of the Commission; and

(d)   resolution of disputes with first nations concerning the taxation of rights and interests on reserve lands.

(3) *STATUTORY INSTRUMENTS ACT* — The *Statutory Instruments Act* does not apply to a standard established under subsection (1) or a procedure established under subsection (2).

Regulations

36. (1) REGULATIONS — The Governor in Council may, on the recommendation of the Minister made having regard to any representations by the Commission, make regulations

(a)   prescribing anything that is to be prescribed under subparagraph 5(1)(a)(i), paragraph 5(1)(e) or (4)(a), subsection 5(7) or section 10;

(b)   establishing the procedures to be followed in reviewing laws submitted under section 7 and conducting reviews under section 33, including procedures

(i)   for requiring the production of documents from a first nation or person requesting a review under subsection 33(1),

(ii) for conducting hearings, and

(iii) authorizing the Commission to apply to a justice of the peace for a subpoena compelling a person to appear before the Commission to give evidence and bring any documents specified in the subpoena, and to pay associated travel expenses;

(c) **prescribing fees to be charged by the Commission for services to first nations and other organizations; and**

(d) **respecting the exercise of the law-making powers of first nations under subsection 5(1).**

Commentary

The following regulations are proposed to be made[139] under paragraph (a):

- *First Nations Assessment Inspection Regulations*;
- *First Nations Rates and Expenditure Laws Timing Regulations*;
- *First Nations Taxation Enforcement Regulations*;
- *First Nations Assessment Appeal Regulations*; and
- *First Nations Tax Commissioner Appointment Regulations*.

The First Nations Tax Commission Review Procedures Regulations are proposed pursuant to paragraph (b).

No regulations are currently proposed under paragraph (c).

Regulations are proposed under paragraph (d) that will mirror the *Property Assessment and Taxation (Railway Right-of-Way) Regulations*[140] made under the *Indian Act*, but at the time of publication had not been made public.

(2) PROVINCIAL DIFFERENCES — Regulations made under paragraph (1)(a) may vary from province to province.

(3) AUTHORITY TO VARY — Regulations made under paragraph (1)(b)may authorize the Commission to

(a) **vary the procedures to accommodate the customs or culture of a first nation in respect of which a hearing is being held;**

(b) **extend or shorten any period provided for in those regulations;**

(c) **dispense with compliance with any procedure provided for in the regulations in the interest of securing a just, expeditious and inexpensive hearing of a complaint; and**

(d) **delegate any of the powers of the Commission under section 31 or 33 to one or more commissioners.Commentary**

The powers conferred under paragraphs (a) and (c) are exercised in s. 36 of the proposed *First Nations Tax Commission Review Procedures Regulations*, which are proposed to be made under s. 36(1)(b). Powers to extend or shorten periods pursuant to paragraph (b) are exercised in s. 35 of those regulations, while the delegations referred to in paragraph (d) are exercised in s. 2 of those regulations.

---

[139] Proposed regulations under the FNFSMA are posted on the INAC website: <http://www.ainc-inac.gc.ca/nr/prs/s-d2002/02218bk_e.html>.
[140] SOR/2001-493.

(4) INCONSISTENCIES — In the event of an inconsistency between a law made under subsection 5(1) and regulations made under subsection (1), the regulations prevail to the extent of the inconsistency.

Commentary

This subsection provides a legislative override to judicial rulings in cases such as *R. v. Blackbird*,[141] *R. v. Jimmy*,[142] *R. v. Baker*,[143] and *R. v. Meechance*,[144] which have held that band by-laws made under s. 81 of the *Indian Act* can in certain circumstances override competing federal regulations.

PART 3

FIRST NATIONS FINANCIAL MANAGEMENT BOARD

Interpretation

37. DEFINITION OF "BOARD" — In this Part, "Board" means the First Nations Financial Management Board.

Commentary

This definition applies in ss. 37 to 56 of the Act.

Establishment and Organization of Board

38. (1) ESTABLISHMENT — There is hereby established a board, to be known as the First Nations Financial Management Board, to be managed by a board of directors consisting of a minimum of nine and a maximum of 15 directors, including a Chairperson and Vice-Chairperson.

(2) CAPACITY, RIGHTS, POWERS AND PRIVILEGES — The Board has the capacity, rights, powers and privileges of a natural person, including the capacity to

(a) enter into contracts;

(b) acquire, hold and dispose of property or an interest in property;

(c) raise, invest or borrow money; and

(d) sue and be sued.

---

[141] [2003] O.J. No. 1102 (S.C.).
[142] [1987] B.C.J. No. 1516, [1987] 5 W.W.R. 755 (C.A.).
[143] [1983] B.C.J. No. 2383, [1983] 4 C.N.L.R. 73 (Co.).
[144] [2000] S.J. No. 203, 193 Sask. R. 109 (Q.B.).

39. NOT AGENT OF HER MAJESTY — The Board is not an agent of Her Majesty.

Commentary

Note that the First Nations Financial Management Board differs from the First Nations Tax Commission in this regard, in that the latter is an agent of Her Majesty for the approval of local revenue laws. Neither the First Nations Finance Authority nor the First Nations Statistical Institute is an agent of the Crown, either.

40. APPOINTMENT OF CHAIRPERSON — On the recommendation of the Minister, the Governor in Council shall appoint a Chairperson to hold office during good behaviour for a term not exceeding five years, subject to removal by the Governor in Council at any time for cause.

Commentary

A person who holds office during good behaviour can be removed in one of two ways:

- by order of the Governor in Council, on the recommendation of the Canadian Judicial Council,[145] made following an inquiry requested by the Minister of Justice under s. 69 of the *Judges Act*;[146] or

- by an order of the Governor in Council, following any other process that provides the person with an opportunity to be heard in accordance with the principles of natural justice.

In the latter instance, allegations of misfeasance would normally be provided to the Governor in Council, which would then provide the appointee with an opportunity to answer them. The Governor in Council would then make its decision whether to remove the appointee based on the written material before it.[147]

Case Law

Weatherill v. Canada (Attorney General), [1999] F.C.J. No. 787, [1999] 4 F.C. 107 (T.D.).

The Federal Court upheld the dismissal by the Governor in Council of the Chairman of the former Canada Labour Relations Board, who held office during good behaviour, for incurring unreasonable hospitality and travel expenses. The applicant had been offered an opportunity to make submissions in response to a report on his expenses and in response to the application to the Governor in Council for his removal, but chose not to do so. The court concluded that the

---

[145] Established under s. 59(1) of the *Judges Act*, R.S.C. 1985, c. J-1.
[146] R.S.C. 1985, c. J-1.
[147] A similar procedure was followed, and received judicial approval, in *Weatherill v. Canada (Attorney General)*, [1999] F.C.J. No. 787, [1999] 4 F.C. 107 (T.D.).

requirements of natural justice had been satisfied, and that a further inquiry under s. 69 of the *Judges Act* was not required.

Wedge v. Canada (Attorney General), [1997] F.C.J. No. 872, 4 Admin. L.R. (3d) 153, 133 F.T.R. 277 (T.D.).

The Federal Court upheld the dismissal by the Governor in Council of a member of the Veterans Appeal Board, who held office during good behaviour, for allegedly having participated in election irregularities. The court found that there had been no breach of procedural fairness in the way in which the applicant had been treated. The applicant had been informed of the allegations against him by letter, and had been given copies of an investigation report and copies of the final report to the Governor in Council. The applicant had had the opportunity to respond orally, and his written responses to the investigation report and final report were submitted to the Governor in Council. The court held that the applicant was not entitled to cross-examine witnesses interviewed, or to a full, formal, court-like hearing. The court also concluded that the standard of good behaviour to which an appointee will be held is in the discretion of the Governor in Council, which extends to its judgment as to whether the appointee's conduct could undermine public confidence in the federal institution with which he had been appointed to serve.

Section 40, together with ss. 19(2), 20 and 23(1), parallels the requirements for institutional independence set out by the Supreme Court of Canada in *Canadian Pacific Ltd. v Matsqui Indian Band* in relation to tribunals established by bands themselves:

> Thus, to conform to the requirements of institutional independence, the appellant bands' by-laws will have to guarantee remuneration and stipulate periods of tenure for tribunal members.[148]

41. (1) APPOINTMENT OF ADDITIONAL DIRECTORS — The Governor in Council, on the recommendation of the Minister, shall appoint a minimum of five, and a maximum of eleven, other directors to hold office during good behaviour for a term not exceeding five years, subject to removal by the Governor in Council at any time for cause.

Commentary

A person who holds office during good behaviour can be removed in one of two ways:

- by order of the Governor in Council, on the recommendation of the Canadian Judicial Council,[149] made following an inquiry requested by the Minister of Justice under s. 69 of the *Judges Act*;[150] or

---

[148]   [1995] S.C.J. No. 1, [1995] 1 S.C.R. 3 at 59.
[149]   Established under s. 59(1) of the *Judges Act*, R.S.C. 1985, c. J-1.
[150]   R.S.C. 1985, c. J-1.

- by an order of the Governor in Council, following any other process that provides the person with an opportunity to be heard in accordance with the principles of natural justice.

In the latter instance, allegations of misfeasance would normally be provided to the Governor in Council, which would then provide the appointee with an opportunity to answer them. The Governor in Council would then make its decision whether to remove the appointee based on the written material before it.[151]

Case Law

Weatherill v. Canada (Attorney General), [1999] F.C.J. No. 787, [1999] 4 F.C. 107 (T.D.).

The Federal Court upheld the dismissal by the Governor in Council of the Chairman of the former Canada Labour Relations Board, who held office during good behaviour, for incurring unreasonable hospitality and travel expenses. The applicant had been offered an opportunity to make submissions in response to a report on his expenses and in response to the application to the Governor in Council for his removal, but chose not to do so. The court concluded that the requirements of natural justice had been satisfied, and that a further inquiry under s. 69 of the *Judges Act* was not required.

Wedge v. Canada (Attorney General), [1997] F.C.J. No. 872, 4 Admin. L.R. (3d) 153, 133 F.T.R. 277 (T.D.).

The Federal Court upheld the dismissal by the Governor in Council of a member of the Veterans Appeal Board, who held office during good behaviour, for allegedly having participated in election irregularities. The court found that there had been no breach of procedural fairness in the way in which the applicant had been treated. The applicant had been informed of the allegations against him by letter, and had been given copies of an investigation report and copies of the final report to the Governor in Council. The applicant had had the opportunity to respond orally, and his written responses to the investigation report and final report were submitted to the Governor in Council. The court held that the applicant was not entitled to cross-examine witnesses interviewed, or to a full, formal, court-like hearing. The court also concluded that the standard of good behaviour to which an appointee will be held is in the discretion of the Governor in Council, which extends to its judgment as to whether the appointee's conduct could undermine public confidence in the federal institution with which he had been appointed to serve.

Subsection 41(1), together with ss. 19(2), 20, 23(1) and 40, parallels the requirements for institutional independence set out by the Supreme Court of Canada in *Canadian Pacific Ltd. v Matsqui Indian Band* in relation to tribunals established by bands themselves:

---

[151]   A similar procedure was followed, and received judicial approval, in *Weatherill v. Canada (Attorney General)*, [1999] F.C.J. No. 787, [1999] 4 F.C. 107(T.D.).

Thus, to conform to the requirements of institutional independence, the appellant bands' by-laws will have to guarantee remuneration and stipulate periods of tenure for tribunal members.[152]

(2) APPOINTMENT BY AFOA — The Aboriginal Financial Officers Association of Canada, or any other body prescribed by regulation, shall appoint up to three additional directors to hold office during pleasure for a term not exceeding five years.

Commentary

At the date of publication, no alternative appointing body had been proposed to be prescribed by regulation. Note that the additional commissioners appointed by the Aboriginal Financial Officers Association of Canada hold office only "during pleasure", which means that they can be removed at any time without a judicial enquiry or the need to show cause.

(3) STAGGERED TERMS — In determining the term of appointment of directors, the Governor in Council shall endeavour to ensure that the terms of no more than three directors expire in any one calendar year.

(4) QUALIFICATIONS — The board of directors shall be composed of men and women from across Canada, including members of first nations, who are committed to the strengthening of first nation financial management and who have the experience or capacity to enable the Board to fulfil its mandate.

42. (1) ELECTION OF VICE-CHAIRPERSON — The board of directors shall elect a Vice-Chairperson from among the directors.

(2) FUNCTIONS — In the event of the absence or incapacity of the Chairperson, or if the office of Chairperson is vacant, the Vice-Chairperson shall assume the duties and functions of the Chairperson.

43. REAPPOINTMENT — Directors may be reappointed for a second or subsequent term of office.

44. STATUS — Directors shall hold office on a part-time basis.

45. (1) REMUNERATION — Directors shall be paid the remuneration determined by the Governor in Council.

---

[152]   [1995] S.C.J. No. 1, [1995] 1 S.C.R. 3 at 59.

(2) EXPENSES — Directors shall be reimbursed for reasonable travel and other expenses incurred in performing duties while absent from their ordinary place of residence.

46. RULES OF PROCEDURE — The board of directors may make any rules that it considers necessary for the conduct of its meetings.

47. HEAD OFFICE — The head office of the Board shall be at a location determined by the Governor in Council.

Commentary

At the date of publication, no location had been proposed for the head office of the Board.

48. (1) STAFF — The board of directors may

(a) hire any staff that is necessary to conduct the work of the Board; and

(b) determine the duties of those persons and the conditions of their employment.

(2) SALARIES AND BENEFITS — Persons hired under subsection (1) shall be paid the salary and benefits fixed by the board of directors.

Purposes

49. MANDATE — The purposes of the Board are to

(a) assist first nations in developing the capacity to meet their financial management requirements;

(b) assist first nations in their dealings with other governments respecting financial management, including matters of accountability and shared fiscal responsibility;

(c) assist first nations in the development, implementation and improvement of financial relationships with financial institutions, business partners and other governments, to enable the economic and social development of first nations;

(d) develop and support the application of general credit rating criteria to first nations;

(e) provide review and audit services respecting first nation financial management;

(f) provide assessment and certification services respecting first nation financial management and financial performance;

(g)   provide financial monitoring services respecting first nation financial management and financial performance;

(h)   provide co-management and third-party management services; and

(i)   provide advice, policy research and review and evaluative services on the development of fiscal arrangements between first nations' governments and other governments.

Commentary

In addition to the purposes set out in the Act, the First Nations Financial Management Board describes its purposes as follows:

> To assist First Nations in building their capacity in all areas related to the development and maintenance of quality financial management systems.

> To conduct assessments of the financial practices and overall financial health of First Nations. Assessments will be objective, technically competent and recognize the requirements of financial institutions, particularly as they relate to debenture issues processes.

> To set guidelines for financial management and reporting.

> To identify and promote best practices in the management of assets, human resources, finance and risk.

> To provide advice and guidance to First Nations on specific issues related to financial management and program and service delivery.

> To support capacity building through financial management training for First Nations and their institutions.

> To develop and implement a communications plan in support of increased awareness by the general and First Nations publics concerning financial management issues.

> To support First Nations in strengthening the links between policy making, planning and budgeting and more effective program and service delivery.

> To support the prevention and resolution of disputes on matters concerning financial management on an "as-requested" basis.

> To develop nationally accepted standards that reflect the unique financial management requirements of First Nations and provide an optional basis for economic development.

> To function as a regulatory body through the development and ongoing maintenance of a system of certification that oversees

the activity and involvement of First Nations within a syndicated borrowing regime.[153]

Functions and Powers

50. (1) REVIEW OF FINANCIAL MANAGEMENT SYSTEM — On the request of the council of a first nation, the Board may review the first nation's financial management system or financial performance for compliance with the standards established under subsection 55(1).

Commentary

The review provided for in this subsection, which leads to the issuance of a certificate under s. 50(3), is required before the First Nations Tax Commission can approve a First Nation's borrowing law (under s. 32(1)(a)) and before the First Nations Finance Authority can accept a First Nation as a borrowing member (under s. 76(2)).

(2) REPORT — On completion of a review under subsection (1), the Board shall provide to the first nation a report setting out

(a) the scope of the review undertaken; and

(b) an opinion as to the extent to which the first nation was in compliance with the standards.

(3) CERTIFICATE — If after completing a review under subsection (1) the Board is of the opinion that the first nation was in compliance with the standards, it shall issue to the first nation a certificate to that effect.

(4) REVOCATION OF CERTIFICATE — The Board may, on giving notice to a council, revoke a certificate issued under subsection (3) if, on the basis of financial or other information available to the Board, it is of the opinion that the basis upon which the certificate was issued has materially changed.

Commentary

Subsection 76(2) provides that revocation of a certificate under this subsection will render a First Nation ineligible to become a borrowing member. See also s. 50(6), which requires a borrowing member that has had its certificate revoked to take such measures as are required to re-establish its certification.

(5) FORM AND CONTENT — The Board may determine the form and content of certificates issued under subsection (3), including any restrictions

---

[153]   From First Nations Financial Management Board website: <http://www.fnfmb.com/en/about/index.htm>.

as to the purposes for which, and the persons by whom, they are intended to be used.

(6) REMEDIAL MEASURES REQUIRED — If a borrowing member's certificate is revoked, the borrowing member shall, without delay, take any measures required to re-establish its certification.

Commentary

Certificates can be revoked under s. 50(4).

(7) OPINION FINAL — An opinion of the Board referred to in this section is final and conclusive and is not subject to appeal.

51. REQUIRED INTERVENTION — On receipt of a notice from the First Nations Tax Commission under paragraph 33(3)(b) or from the First Nations Finance Authority under subsection 86(4), the Board shall either require the first nation to enter into a co-management arrangement in accordance with section 52 or assume third-party management of the first nation's local revenues in accordance with section 53, as the Board sees fit.

Commentary

Under s. 33(3)(b) of the Act, the First Nations Tax Commission can call on the First Nations Financial Management Board to impose a co-management arrangement or assume third-party management of the First Nation's tax system, if the First Nation has failed to comply with an order of the Commission issued under s. 33(3)(a). Such orders are issued if the Commission determines after a review under s. 33(1) or (2) that

- a First Nation has not complied with Part 1 or 2 of the Act or with the regulations, or
- a property taxation law has been unfairly or improperly applied.

Under s. 86(4) of the Act, the First Nations Finance Authority can require the Board to impose a co-management arrangement on a borrowing member or assume third-party management of its revenues if

- the borrowing member has failed to make a payment to the Authority on a bond issue, or has failed to pay a charge imposed by the Authority under s. 84(5) of the Act;[154] or
- on receipt of a report of the Board under s. 84(3) of the Act in relation to a request to the Board to investigate a failure to fulfill an obligation of a non-financial nature under a borrowing agreement with the Authority.

---

[154] The mechanism for imposing these charges is set out in the proposed *Debt Reserve Fund Replenishment Regulations*.

As the closing words of s. 51 indicate, the Board has the discretion to determine whether co-management or third-party management is warranted in any particular case.

52. (1) IMPOSED CO-MANAGEMENT — The Board may, on giving notice to the council of a first nation, require the first nation to enter into a co-management arrangement in respect of the first nation's local revenues, including its local revenue account,

(a) **if, in the opinion of the Board, there is a serious risk that the first nation will default on an obligation to the First Nations Finance Authority; or**

(b) **on receipt of a request or demand to do so under paragraph 33(3)(b) or subsection 86(4).**

Commentary

Under this provision, the First Nations Financial Management Board can impose a co-management arrangement on a First Nation in three circumstances:

1.   if it determines of its own accord that a serious risk exists that the First Nation will default on an obligation (financial or non-financial) to the First Nations Finance Authority;

2.   if it receives a request from the First Nations Tax Commission to enforce an order of the Commission under s. 33(3)(b) of the Act; or

3.   if it receives a request from the First Nations Finance Authority under s. 86(4) of the Act.

The procedures governing the imposition of co-management arrangements are set out in the proposed *Local Revenue Management Implementation Regulations*. Under s. 17(1)(a) of those regulations, the notice required under this subsection must be in writing, and under s. 18(1) of those regulations a copy of it must be provided to the First Nations Finance Authority and First Nations Tax Commission.

(2) POWERS — Under a co-management arrangement, the Board may

(a) **recommend amendments to a law of the first nation made under this Act;**

(b) **recommend changes to the first nation's expenditures or budgets;**

(c) **recommend improvements to the first nation's financial management system;**

(d) **recommend changes to the delivery of programs and services;**

(e) **order that expenditures of local revenues of the first nation be approved by, or paid with cheques co-signed by, a manager appointed by the Board; and**

(f)   exercise any powers delegated to the Board under a law of the first nation or under an agreement between the first nation and the Board or the first nation and the First Nations Finance Authority.

Commentary

Note that the powers of the First Nations Financial Management Board under paragraphs (a) to (d) of this subsection are limited to making recommendations; it does not have the power to require the listed amendments, changes or improvements. In contrast, under paragraph (e) the Board can require that expenditures from the First Nation's local revenue account be approved by its manager, and that cheques drawn on that account be co-signed by the manager as well.

A delegation referred to in paragraph (f) of this subsection could be made under a law made under s. 5(1)(g) of the Act, under which the council of the First Nation can make laws:

> (g) delegating to the First Nations Financial Management Board any other of the council's powers that are required to give effect to a co-management arrangement entered into under section 52 . . .

An example of an agreement with the Board referred to in this paragraph might be an agreement to enter into a co-management arrangement as a condition of termination of third-party management under s. 53(6). An agreement with the First Nations Finance Authority might, for example, be one flowing from the contractual obligations undertaken by the First Nation as a condition to becoming a borrowing member.

(3) TERMINATION BY BOARD — The Board may terminate a co-management arrangement with a first nation on giving notice to its council that the Board is of the opinion that

(a)   there is no longer a serious risk that the first nation will default on an obligation to the First Nations Finance Authority;

(b)   where the first nation was in default of a payment obligation to the First Nations Finance Authority, the first nation has remedied the default;

(c)   a co-management arrangement requested or demanded under paragraph 33(3)(b) or subsection 86(4) is no longer required; or

(d)   third-party management of the first nation's local revenues is required.

Commentary

Under paragraph (d) of this subsection the Board can move out of co-management and into third-party management under s. 53 if it considers it necessary to do so.

Subsection 17(1) of the proposed *Local Revenue Management Implementation Regulations* requires that a notice under this subsection be given in writing.

(4) OPINION FINAL — An opinion given by the Board under this section is final and conclusive and is not subject to appeal.

(5) NOTICE — The Board shall advise the First Nations Finance Authority and the First Nations Tax Commission of the commencement or termination of a co-management arrangement.

Commentary

Subsection 18(1) of the proposed *Local Revenue Management Implementation Regulations* requires that a copy of a notice of termination by the First Nations Financial Management Board must be provided to the First Nations Finance Authority and First Nations Tax Commission.

53. (1) THIRD-PARTY MANAGEMENT — The Board may, on giving notice to the council of a first nation and to the Minister, assume management of the first nation's local revenues, including its local revenue account,

(a) **if, in the opinion of the Board, a co-management arrangement under section 52 has not been effective;**

(b) **if, in the opinion of the Board, there is a serious risk that the first nation will default on an obligation to the First Nations Finance Authority; or**

(c) **on receipt of a request or demand to do so under paragraph 33(3)(b) or subsection 86(4).**

Commentary

Under this provision, the First Nations Financial Management Board can impose a co-management arrangement on a First Nation in any of the following circumstances:

1. if it determines that a co-management arrangement imposed under s. 52 has not remedied the circumstances that led to its imposition;

2. if it determines of its own accord that a serious risk exists that a First Nation will default on an obligation (financial or non-financial) to the First Nations Finance Authority;

3. if it receives a request from the First Nations Tax Commission to enforce an order of the Commission under s. 33(3)(b) of the Act; or

4. if it receives a request from the First Nations Finance Authority under s. 86(4) of the Act.

The procedures governing the imposition of third-party management are set out in the proposed *Local Revenue Management Implementation Regulations*.

Under s. 17(1)(b) of those regulations, the notice required under this subsection must be in writing, and under s. 18(3) of those regulations a copy of it must be provided to the First Nations Finance Authority and First Nations Tax Commission.

(2) POWERS — If the Board assumes third-party management of the local revenues of a first nation, the Board has the exclusive right to

   (a) **subject to subsection (3), act in the place of the council of the first nation to make laws under paragraphs 5(1)(a) to (f);**

   (b) **act in the place of the council of the first nation under laws made under paragraphs 5(1)(a) to (e) and manage the first nation's local revenue account, including any necessary borrowing;**

   (c) **provide for the delivery of programs and services that are paid for out of local revenues;**

   (d) **assign rights or interests under subsection 5(7); and**

   (e) **exercise any powers delegated to the Board under a law of the first nation or an agreement between the first nation and the Board or between the first nation and the First Nations Finance Authority.**

Commentary

This subsection confers very broad powers on the First Nations Financial Management Board in cases where it has assumed third-party management over the property taxation system of a First Nation. Note that the rights conferred are *exclusive* rights, which implies that in such circumstances the First Nation council can no longer exercise the enumerated powers.

Under paragraph (a) of this subsection, the Board can exercise any of the law-making powers of the First Nation council under s. 5(1)(a) to (f) of the Act, including the power to amend or repeal property taxation laws, budget laws or borrowing laws of the First Nation, or to make new laws where none exist. The caveat "subject to subsection (3)" in that paragraph refers to the restriction that the Board cannot make or change a law delegating law-making powers to another person without the consent of the First Nation council.

Paragraph (b) of this subsection permits the Board to assume management of the First Nation's local revenue account, in which revenues from property taxation laws are deposited. Under paragraph (c), the Board can assume responsibility for the provision of municipal services that are funded from property taxation revenues.

Under paragraph (d) of this subsection, the Board has the power, if necessary, to seize and auction off rights and interests in reserve lands held by delinquent taxpayers, under the procedures provided for in the proposed *First Nations Taxation Enforcement Regulations*. It can then exercise the power of the

First Nation under s. 5(7) of the Act to transfer those rights or interest to the successful bidder.[155]

A delegation referred to in paragraph (e) of this subsection could be made under a law made under s. 5(1)(g) of the Act, under which the council of the First Nation can make laws:

> (g) delegating to the First Nations Financial Management Board any other of the council's powers that are required to give effect to a co-management arrangement entered into ... to give effect to third-party management of the First Nation's local revenues.

An example of an agreement with the First Nations Finance Authority might be one flowing from the contractual obligations undertaken by the First Nation as a condition to becoming a borrowing member.

(3) CONSENT OF COUNCIL REQUIRED — The Board shall not make a law under paragraph 5(1)(f) that delegates a power to a person or body to whom a power was not delegated at the time the Board assumed third-party management of the local revenues of a first nation, unless the council of the first nation gives its consent.

Commentary

This subsection limits the Board's powers to make laws in place of the First Nation's council under 53(2)(a).

(4) PROHIBITION — The council of the first nation shall not, during the time that the board assumes third-party management of the first nation's local revenues, repeal any law made under paragraph 5(1)(g).

Commentary

While it is under third-party management, the council of the First Nation continues to have the ability to make laws under s. 5(1)(g) of the Act, under which the council of the First Nation can make laws:

> (g)   delegating to the First Nations Financial Management Board any other of the council's powers that are required to give effect to ... third-party management of the First Nation's local revenues.

This subsection prevents the First Nation council from repealing such a law (and thereby removing powers from the Board) during a period of third-party management.

---

[155]   Subject to the limitation, set out in s. 19(1) of those regulations, that a right or interest cannot be assigned to a person or entity who would not otherwise have been entitled under the *Indian Act* to obtain the right or interest in question.

(5) REVIEW EVERY SIX MONTHS — Where the Board has assumed third-party management of a first nation's local revenues, it shall review the need for third-party management at least once every six months and advise the First Nations Finance Authority, the First Nations Tax Commission and the council of the first nation of the results of its review.

(6) TERMINATION BY BOARD — The Board may terminate third-party management of a first nation's local revenues, on giving notice to the council of the first nation, if

(a) it is of the opinion that there is no longer a serious risk that the first nation will default on an obligation to the First Nations Finance Authority and the Authority consents to the termination in writing;

(b) where the first nation was in default of an obligation to the First Nations Finance Authority, it is of the opinion that the first nation has remedied the default and the Authority consents to the termination in writing; or

(c) it is of the opinion that the situation for which third-party management of the first nation's local revenues was required under paragraph 33(3)(b) or subsection 86(4) has been remedied.

Commentary

Paragraph 17(1)(b) of the proposed *Local Revenue Management Implementation Regulations* requires that a notice under this subsection be given in writing, and s. 18(3) of those regulations requires that a copy of the notice be provided to the First Nations Finance Authority and First Nations Tax Commission.

(7) OPINION FINAL — An opinion given by the Board under this section is final and conclusive and is not subject to appeal.

(8) NOTICE — The Board shall advise the First Nations Finance Authority and First Nations Tax Commission of the assumption or termination of third-party management of a first nation's local revenues.

Commentary

Subsection 18(3) of the proposed *Local Revenue Management Implementation Regulations* requires that a copy of a notice of termination given by the First Nations Financial Management Board to the council of the First Nation must also be provided to the First Nations Finance Authority and First Nations Tax Commission.

54. REQUIRED INFORMATION — At the request of the Board, a first nation that has made a local revenue law shall provide to the Board any information about the first nation's financial management system and financial performance that the Board requires for a decision regarding a co-management arrangement or third-party management of the first nation's local revenues.

Commentary

This section appears to require the employees of a First Nation to provide the First Nations Financial Management Board with any explanations about the First Nation's financial management system and financial performance required to enable the Board to implement a co-management or third-party management situation.

Standards And Procedures

55. (1) STANDARDS — The Board may establish standards, not inconsistent with the regulations, respecting

(a)　**the form and content of laws made under section 9;**

(b)　**approvals of the Board under Part 1;**

(c)　**certification of first nations under section 50; and**

(d) **financial reporting under subsection 14(1).**

Commentary

Subsection 55(4) requires that these standards be published in the *First Nations Gazette.*

(2) PROCEDURES — The Board may establish procedures respecting

(a)　**the submission for approval and approval of laws made under section 9;**

(b)　**the issuance of a certificate under subsection 50(3); and**

(c)　**the implementation or termination of a co-management arrangement or third-party management of a first nation's local revenues.**

(3) *STATUTORY INSTRUMENTS ACT* — The *Statutory Instruments Act* does not apply to a standard established under subsection (1) or a procedure established under subsection (2).

(4) *FIRST NATIONS GAZETTE* — All laws made under section 9 and approved by the Board and all standards established by the Board under subsection (1) shall be published in the *First Nations Gazette*.

Commentary

The *First Nations Gazette* is co-published by the Indian Taxation Advisory Board and the Native Law Centre of Canada at the University of Saskatchewan.

Subscriptions for the 2005 year cost $72. Further information can be obtained, and subscriptions ordered, at the *First Nations Gazette* website.[156]

Regulations

56. REGULATIONS — The Governor in Council may, on the recommendation of the Minister made having regard to any representations by the Board, make regulations
  (a) **respecting the implementation of a co-management arrangement or third-party management of a first nation's local revenues, including the obligations of affected first nations to provide access to financial records; and**
  (b) **fixing fees that the Board may charge for services, including fees to first nations for co-management and third-party management services, and the manner in which the fees may be recovered.**

Commentary

The *Local Revenue Management Implementation Regulations* are proposed[157] under paragraph (a).

At the time of publication, no regulations fixing fees had been proposed under paragraph (b).

Note that s. 117 of the Act permits the First Nations Financial Management Board to expend any revenues that it receives through the conduct of operations, such as those referred to in s. 56(b), during the financial year in which they are received or in the following year.

PART 4

FIRST NATIONS FINANCE AUTHORITY

Interpretation

57. DEFINITIONS — The following definitions apply in this Part.

Commentary

These definitions apply in ss. 57 to 89 of the Act.

---

[156]   <http://www.usask.ca/nativelaw/publications/desc/fng.html>.
[157]   Proposed regulations under the FNFSMA are posted on the INAC website: <http://www .ainc-inac.gc.ca/nr/prs/s-d2002/02218bk_e.html>.

"Authority"
« Administration »
"Authority" means the First Nations Finance Authority.

"investing member"
« membre investisseur »
"investing member" means a first nation that has invested in a short-term investment pool managed by the Authority.

Commentary

Investing members are one of the two classes of members of the First Nations Finance Authority under s. 59 of the Act. The other class consists of borrowing members.[158] The two provisions pertaining particularly to investing members are ss. 59 and 63(3), although other provisions of the Act relating to "members" in general also apply to investing members.

"long-term loan"
« prêt à long terme »
"long-term loan" means a loan the term of which is one year or longer.

"property tax revenues"
« recettes fiscales foncières »
"property tax revenues" means moneys raised under a law made under paragraph 5(1)(a).

Commentary

Laws made under s. 5(1)(a) are property taxation laws.[159]

"representative"
« représentant »
"representative", in respect of a first nation that is a member, means the chief or a councillor of the first nation who is designated as a representative by a resolution of its council.

Commentary

Note that representatives are limited to persons who are chiefs or councillors of First Nations that are either investing or borrowing members. Subsection 63(3) sets out the circumstances under which a person will cease to be a representative, including loss of office as chief or councillor.

---

[158]   Defined in s. 2 of the Act.
[159]   *Ibid.*

"security"
« titre »

"security" means a security of the Authority issued under paragraph 75(1)(b).

"short-term loan"
« prêt à court terme »

"short-term loan" means a loan the term of which is less than one year.

Establishment and Organization of Authority

58. ESTABLISHMENT — There is hereby established a non-profit corporation without share capital, to be known as the First Nations Finance Authority.

59. MEMBERSHIP — The members of the Authority shall be its borrowing members and investing members.

60. (1) NOT AGENT OF HER MAJESTY — The Authority is not an agent of Her Majesty or a Crown corporation within the meaning of the *Financial Administration Act*,[160] and its officers and employees are not part of the public service of Canada.

Commentary

Note that under s. 154(2) of the FNFSMA, the reference in this subsection to the "public service of Canada" was changed to the "federal public administration" as of April 1, 2005, when section 8 of the *Public Service Modernization Act* came into force.[161]

(2) NO GUARANTEES — No person shall give a guarantee on behalf of Her Majesty for the discharge of an obligation or liability of the Authority.

Commentary

Subsections 60(1) and (2) affirm that the Authority operates independently of the federal Crown.

---

[160]   R.S.C. 1985, c. F-11.
[161]   SI/2005-25

61. (1) BOARD OF DIRECTORS — The Authority shall be managed by a board of directors, consisting of from 5 to 11 directors, including a Chairperson and Deputy Chairperson.

(2) NOMINATION OF DIRECTORS — A representative of a borrowing member may nominate

  (a) **a representative of a borrowing member for election as Chairperson or Deputy Chairperson; and**

  (b) **any representative for election as a director other than the Chairperson or Deputy Chairperson.**

Commentary

Note that only the representatives of borrowing members — and not representatives of investing members — may nominate persons for election to the board of directors of the First Nations Finance Authority. Only persons who are representatives of borrowing members are eligible to be nominated for Chairperson or Deputy Chairperson, while representatives of either borrowing members or investing members are eligible to be nominated for other directorships.

(3) ELECTION OF DIRECTORS — Directors shall be elected by representatives of borrowing members.

Commentary

Note that only representatives of borrowing members — and not representatives of investing members — may vote to elect directors.

62. FUNCTION OF DEPUTY CHAIRPERSON — In the event of the absence or incapacity of the Chairperson, or if the office of Chairperson is vacant, the Deputy Chairperson shall assume the duties and functions of the Chairperson.

63. (1) TERM OF OFFICE — Directors shall hold office on a part-time basis for a term of one year.

(2) ADDITIONAL TERMS — A director is eligible to be re-elected for a second or subsequent term of office.

(3) CEASING TO BE DIRECTOR — A person ceases to be a director when

  (a) **the person ceases to hold office as a chief or councillor of a first nation that is a borrowing member or investing member;**

  (b) **the person's designation as a representative of a borrowing member or investing member is revoked by a resolution of the council of that first nation; or**

(c) **the person is removed from office before the expiry of the term of the appointment by a special resolution of the board of directors.**

Commentary

"Special resolution", used in paragraph 63(3)(c), is not defined in the FNFSMA. The expression is defined in s. 2(1) of the *Canada Business Corporations Act* as a resolution passed by a majority of not less than two-thirds of the votes cast by the shareholders who voted in respect of that resolution or signed by all the shareholders entitled to vote on that resolution. It is not used in respect of resolutions of boards of directors.

Note that under s. 109(1) of the *Canada Business Corporations Act*, directors of a corporation may be removed by an ordinary resolution at a special meeting of shareholders.

64. QUORUM — Two thirds of the directors constitute a quorum at any meeting of the board of directors.

65. MAJORITY VOTE — Decisions by the board of directors shall be made by a majority vote of the directors present.

66. (1) *CANADA CORPORATIONS ACT* — The *Canada Corporations Act* does not apply to the Authority.

Commentary

The *Canada Corporations Act*[162] applies to certain not-for-profit and non-share capital corporations, as well as other companies incorporated by the Crown for purposes set out in that Act. Section 158 of the *Canada Corporations Act* provides that certain portions of that Act apply to

> ... any corporation without share capital incorporated by Special Act of the Parliament of Canada for the purpose of carrying on, without pecuniary gain to its members, objects, to which the legislative authority of the Parliament of Canada extends, of a national, patriotic, religious, philanthropic, charitable, scientific, artistic, social, professional or sporting character, or the like objects.

Given the inherent uncertainty as to whether this description would capture the First Nations Finance Authority, s. 66(1) of the FNFSMA confirms that the *Canada Corporations Act* does not apply.

---

[162] R.S.C. 1970, c. C-32.

(2) *CANADA BUSINESS CORPORATIONS ACT* — **The following provisions of the *Canada Business Corporations Act* apply, with any modifications that the circumstances require, to the Authority and its directors, members, officers and employees as if the Authority were a corporation incorporated under that Act, this Part were its articles of incorporation and its members were its shareholders:**

(a) subsection 15(1) (capacity of a natural person);

Commentary

Subsection 15(1) of the *Canada Business Corporations Act*[163] (CBCA) reads as follows:

> 15. (1) A corporation has the capacity and, subject to this Act, the rights, powers and privileges of a natural person.

(b)   section 16 (by-law not required to confer powers on Authority, restriction on powers of Authority, and validity of acts of Authority);

Commentary

Section 16 of the CBCA reads as follows:

> 16. (1) It is not necessary for a by-law to be passed in order to confer any particular power on the corporation or its directors.

> (2) A corporation shall not carry on any business or exercise any power that it is restricted by its articles from carrying on or exercising, nor shall the corporation exercise any of its powers in a manner contrary to its articles.

> (3) No act of a corporation, including any transfer of property to or by a corporation, is invalid by reason only that the act or transfer is contrary to its articles or this Act.

(c)   subsection 21(1) (access to Authority's records by members and creditors);

Commentary

Subsection 21(1) of the CBCA reads as follows:

> 21. (1) Subject to subsection (1.1), shareholders and creditors of a corporation, their personal representatives and the Director may examine the records described in subsection 20(1) during the usual business hours of the corporation, and

---

[163]   R.S.C. 1985, c. C-44.

may take extracts from the records, free of charge, and, if the corporation is a distributing corporation, any other person may do so on payment of a reasonable fee.

The records referred to are:

(a) the articles and the by-laws, and all amendments thereto, and a copy of any unanimous shareholder agreement;

(b) minutes of meetings and resolutions of shareholders;

(c) copies of every notice of directors (which entitles directors to hold office from the issuance of the certificate of incorporation until the first meeting of shareholders) and copies of every notice of change of address of a director; and

(d) a securities register that indicates

- the names and the latest known addresses of security holders;

- the number of securities held by each security holder; and

- the date and particulars of the issuance and transfer of each security.

It is unclear whether the qualification that the rights in s. 21(1) of the CBCA are subject to the requirements of s. 21(1.1) of that Act is carried over into the FNFSMA. The fact that s. 21(1.1) of the CBCA was not incorporated by reference into the FNFSMA suggests that they are not.

(d)   section 23 (corporate seal not needed to validate instrument);

Commentary

Section 23 of the CBCA reads as follows:

23. (1) A corporation may, but need not, adopt a corporate seal, and may change a corporate seal that is adopted.

(2) A document executed on behalf of a corporation is not invalid merely because a corporate seal is not affixed to it.

(e)   subsections 103(1) to (4) (powers of directors to make and amend by-laws, member approval of by-laws and effective date of by-laws);

Commentary

Subsections 103(1) to (4) of the CBCA read as follows:

103. (1) Unless the articles, by-laws or a unanimous shareholder agreement otherwise provide, the directors may,

by resolution, make, amend or repeal any by-laws that regulate the business or affairs of the corporation.

(2) The directors shall submit a by-law, or an amendment or a repeal of a by-law, made under subsection (1) to the shareholders at the next meeting of shareholders, and the shareholders may, by ordinary resolution, confirm, reject or amend the by-law, amendment or repeal.

(3) A by-law, or an amendment or a repeal of a by-law, is effective from the date of the resolution of the directors under subsection (1) until it is confirmed, confirmed as amended or rejected by the shareholders under subsection (2) or until it ceases to be effective under subsection (4) and, where the by-law is confirmed or confirmed as amended, it continues in effect in the form in which it was so confirmed.

(4) If a by-law, an amendment or a repeal is rejected by the shareholders, or if the directors do not submit a by-law, an amendment or a repeal to the shareholders as required under subsection (2), the by-law, amendment or repeal ceases to be effective and no subsequent resolution of the directors to make, amend or repeal a by-law having substantially the same purpose or effect is effective until it is confirmed or confirmed as amended by the shareholders.

(f)   subsection 105(1) (qualifications of directors);

Commentary

Section 105(1) of the CBCA reads as follows:

105. (1) The following persons are disqualified from being a director of a corporation:

(a) anyone who is less than eighteen years of age;

(b) anyone who is of unsound mind and has been so found by a court in Canada or elsewhere;

(c) a person who is not an individual; or

(d) a person who has the status of bankrupt.

Corporations, which are persons at law,[164] are exempted by paragraph (c), which excludes persons who are not individuals.

(g)   subsection 108(2) (resignation of director);

---

[164]   Subsection 35(1) of the *Interpretation Act* defines "person" to include a corporation.

Commentary

Subsection 108(2) of the CBCA reads as follows:

> (2) A resignation of a director becomes effective at the time a written resignation is sent to the corporation, or at the time specified in the resignation, whichever is later.

(h) section 110 (right of director to attend members' meetings and statements by retiring directors);

Commentary

Section 110 of the CBCA reads as follows:

> 110. (1) A director of a corporation is entitled to receive notice of and to attend and be heard at every meeting of shareholders.
>
> (2) A director who
>
> (a) resigns,
>
> (b) receives a notice or otherwise learns of a meeting of shareholders called for the purpose of removing the director from office, or
>
> (c) receives a notice or otherwise learns of a meeting of directors or shareholders at which another person is to be appointed or elected to fill the office of director, whether because of the director's resignation or removal or because the director's term of office has expired or is about to expire,
>
> is entitled to submit to the corporation a written statement giving reasons for resigning or for opposing any proposed action or resolution.
>
> (3) A corporation shall forthwith send a copy of the statement referred to in subsection (2) to every shareholder entitled to receive notice of any meeting referred to in subsection (1) and to the Director unless the statement is included in or attached to a management proxy circular required by section 150.
>
> (4) No corporation or person acting on its behalf incurs any liability by reason only of circulating a director's statement in compliance with subsection (3).

(i) subsection 114(1) (place of directors' meetings);

Commentary

Subsection 114(1) of the CBCA reads as follows:

114. (1) Unless the articles or by-laws otherwise provide, the directors may meet at any place and on such notice as the by-laws require.

(j)   section 116 (validity of acts of directors and officers);

Commentary

Section 116 of the CBCA reads as follows:

116. An act of a director or officer is valid notwithstanding an irregularity in their election or appointment or a defect in their qualification.

(k)   section 117 (validity of directors' resolutions not passed at meeting);

Commentary

Section 117 of the CBCA reads as follows:

117. (1) A resolution in writing, signed by all the directors entitled to vote on that resolution at a meeting of directors or committee of directors, is as valid as if it had been passed at a meeting of directors or committee of directors.

(2) A copy of every resolution referred to in subsection (1) shall be kept with the minutes of the proceedings of the directors or committee of directors.

(3) Unless a ballot is demanded, an entry in the minutes of a meeting to the effect that the chairperson of the meeting declared a resolution to be carried or defeated is, in the absence of evidence to the contrary, proof of the fact without proof of the number or proportion of the votes recorded in favour of or against the resolution.

(l)   subsections 119(1) and (4) (liability of directors);

Commentary

Subsections 119(1) and (4) of the CBCA read as follows:

119. (1) Directors of a corporation are jointly and severally, or solidarily, liable to employees of the corporation for all debts not exceeding six months wages payable to each such employee for services performed for the corporation while they are such directors respectively.

(4) Where execution referred to in paragraph (2)(a) has issued, the amount recoverable from a director is the amount remaining unsatisfied after execution.

The expression "solidarily liable", as used in s. 119(1) of the CBCA, is the civil law equivalent of jointly and severally liable. The "execution referred to in paragraph (2)(a)" mentioned in s. 119(4) is an execution,[165] issued in an action arising out of a debt of the corporation, that has been returned unsatisfied in whole or in part.

(m) section 120 (conflict of interests of directors);

Commentary

Section 120 of the CBCA reads as follows:

120. (1) A director or an officer of a corporation shall disclose to the corporation, in writing or by requesting to have it entered in the minutes of meetings of directors or of meetings of committees of directors, the nature and extent of any interest that he or she has in a material contract or material transaction, whether made or proposed, with the corporation, if the director or officer

(a) is a party to the contract or transaction;

(b) is a director or an officer, or an individual acting in a similar capacity, of a party to the contract or transaction; or

(c) has a material interest in a party to the contract or transaction.

(2) The disclosure required by subsection (1) shall be made, in the case of a director,

(a) at the meeting at which a proposed contract or transaction is first considered;

(b) if the director was not, at the time of the meeting referred to in paragraph (a), interested in a proposed contract or transaction, at the first meeting after he or she becomes so interested;

(c) if the director becomes interested after a contract or transaction is made, at the first meeting after he or she becomes so interested; or

---

[165] An execution is a command to a sheriff to seize and sell the goods of a judgment debtor to satisfy the amount of the judgment: *Black's Law Dictionary*, 7th ed. (St. Paul, Minn.: West Publishing, 1999).

(d) if an individual who is interested in a contract or transaction later becomes a director, at the first meeting after he or she becomes a director.

(3) The disclosure required by subsection (1) shall be made, in the case of an officer who is not a director,

(a) immediately after he or she becomes aware that the contract, transaction, proposed contract or proposed transaction is to be considered or has been considered at a meeting;

(b) if the officer becomes interested after a contract or transaction is made, immediately after he or she becomes so interested; or

(c) if an individual who is interested in a contract later becomes an officer, immediately after he or she becomes an officer.

(4) If a material contract or material transaction, whether entered into or proposed, is one that, in the ordinary course of the corporation's business, would not require approval by the directors or shareholders, a director or officer shall disclose, in writing to the corporation or request to have it entered in the minutes of meetings of directors or of meetings of committees of directors, the nature and extent of his or her interest immediately after he or she becomes aware of the contract or transaction.

(5) A director required to make a disclosure under subsection (1) shall not vote on any resolution to approve the contract or transaction unless the contract or transaction

(a) relates primarily to his or her remuneration as a director, officer, employee or agent of the corporation or an affiliate;

(b) is for indemnity or insurance under section 124; or

(c) is with an affiliate.

(6) For the purposes of this section, a general notice to the directors declaring that a director or an officer is to be regarded as interested, for any of the following reasons, in a contract or transaction made with a party, is a sufficient declaration of interest in relation to the contract or transaction:

(a) the director or officer is a director or officer, or acting in a similar capacity, of a party referred to in paragraph (1)(b) or (c);

(b) the director or officer has a material interest in the party; or

(c) there has been a material change in the nature of the director's or the officer's interest in the party.

(6.1) The shareholders of the corporation may examine the portions of any minutes of meetings of directors or of committees of directors that contain disclosures under this section, and any other documents that contain those disclosures, during the usual business hours of the corporation.

(7) A contract or transaction for which disclosure is required under subsection (1) is not invalid, and the director or officer is not accountable to the corporation or its shareholders for any profit realized from the contract or transaction, because of the director's or officer's interest in the contract or transaction or because the director was present or was counted to determine whether a quorum existed at the meeting of directors or committee of directors that considered the contract or transaction, if

(a) disclosure of the interest was made in accordance with subsections (1) to (6);

(b) the directors approved the contract or transaction; and

(c) the contract or transaction was reasonable and fair to the corporation when it was approved.

(7.1) Even if the conditions of subsection (7) are not met, a director or officer, acting honestly and in good faith, is not accountable to the corporation or to its shareholders for any profit realized from a contract or transaction for which disclosure is required under subsection (1), and the contract or transaction is not invalid by reason only of the interest of the director or officer in the contract or transaction, if

(a) the contract or transaction is approved or confirmed by special resolution at a meeting of the shareholders;

(b) disclosure of the interest was made to the shareholders in a manner sufficient to indicate its nature before the contract or transaction was approved or confirmed; and

(c) the contract or transaction was reasonable and fair to the corporation when it was approved or confirmed.

(8) If a director or an officer of a corporation fails to comply with this section, a court may, on application of the corporation or any of its shareholders, set aside the contract or transaction on any terms that it thinks fit, or require the director or officer to account to the corporation for any profit or gain realized on it, or do both those things.

(n) section 123 (directors' dissents);

Commentary

Section 123 of the CBCA reads as follows:

123. (1) A director who is present at a meeting of directors or committee of directors is deemed to have consented to any resolution passed or action taken at the meeting unless

(a) the director requests a dissent to be entered in the minutes of the meeting, or the dissent has been entered in the minutes;

(b) the director sends a written dissent to the secretary of the meeting before the meeting is adjourned; or

(c) the director sends a dissent by registered mail or delivers it to the registered office of the corporation immediately after the meeting is adjourned.

(2) A director who votes for or consents to a resolution is not entitled to dissent under subsection (1).

(3) A director who was not present at a meeting at which a resolution was passed or action taken is deemed to have consented thereto unless within seven days after becoming aware of the resolution, the director

(a) causes a dissent to be placed with the minutes of the meeting; or

(b) sends a dissent by registered mail or delivers it to the registered office of the corporation.

(4) A director is not liable under section 118 or 119, and has complied with his or her duties under subsection 122(2), if the director exercised the care, diligence and skill that a reasonably prudent person would have exercised in comparable circumstances, including reliance in good faith on

(a) financial statements of the corporation represented to the director by an officer of the corporation or in a written report of the auditor of the corporation fairly to reflect the financial condition of the corporation; or

(b) a report of a person whose profession lends credibility to a statement made by the professional person.

(5) A director has complied with his or her duties under subsection 122(1) if the director relied in good faith on

(a) financial statements of the corporation represented to the director by an officer of the corporation or in a written report of the auditor of the corporation fairly to reflect the financial condition of the corporation; or

(b) a report of a person whose profession lends credibility to a statement made by the professional person.

The liability under s. 118 of the CBCA referred to in s. 123(4) of that Act relates to liability of directors for things such as issuance of shares for consideration other than money, and to authorization of share purchases or redemptions, payment of commissions, dividends or indemnities, or payments to shareholders, that are contrary to the Act. The liability under s. 119 of the

CBCA (set out above in the commentary to s. 66(2)(l)) that is referred to in s. 123(4) of the CBCA relates to the liability of directors to employees for unpaid wages. The duties of directors under ss. 122(1) and (2) of the CBCA, referred to in ss. 123(4) and (5) of that act, relate to duties to act honestly and in good faith, with due diligence, and in accordance with the requirements of the CBCA.

(o) **section 124 (directors' indemnity);**

Commentary

Section 124 of the CBCA reads as follows:

124. (1) A corporation may indemnify a director or officer of the corporation, a former director or officer of the corporation or another individual who acts or acted at the corporation's request as a director or officer, or an individual acting in a similar capacity, of another entity, against all costs, charges and expenses, including an amount paid to settle an action or satisfy a judgment, reasonably incurred by the individual in respect of any civil, criminal, administrative, investigative or other proceeding in which the individual is involved because of that association with the corporation or other entity.

(2) A corporation may advance moneys to a director, officer or other individual for the costs, charges and expenses of a proceeding referred to in subsection (1). The individual shall repay the moneys if the individual does not fulfil the conditions of subsection (3).

(3) A corporation may not indemnify an individual under subsection (1) unless the individual

(a) acted honestly and in good faith with a view to the best interests of the corporation, or, as the case may be, to the best interests of the other entity for which the individual acted as director or officer or in a similar capacity at the corporation's request; and

(b) in the case of a criminal or administrative action or proceeding that is enforced by a monetary penalty, the individual had reasonable grounds for believing that the individual's conduct was lawful.

(4) A corporation may with the approval of a court, indemnify an individual referred to in subsection (1), or advance moneys under subsection (2), in respect of an action by or on behalf of the corporation or other entity to procure a judgment in its favour, to which the individual is made a party because of the individual's association with the corporation or other entity as described in subsection (1) against all costs,

charges and expenses reasonably incurred by the individual in connection with such action, if the individual fulfils the conditions set out in subsection (3).

(5) Despite subsection (1), an individual referred to in that subsection is entitled to indemnity from the corporation in respect of all costs, charges and expenses reasonably incurred by the individual in connection with the defence of any civil, criminal, administrative, investigative or other proceeding to which the individual is subject because of the individual's association with the corporation or other entity as described in subsection (1), if the individual seeking indemnity

(a) was not judged by the court or other competent authority to have committed any fault or omitted to do anything that the individual ought to have done; and

(b) fulfils the conditions set out in subsection (3).

(6) A corporation may purchase and maintain insurance for the benefit of an individual referred to in subsection (1) against any liability incurred by the individual

(a) in the individual's capacity as a director or officer of the corporation; or

(b) in the individual's capacity as a director or officer, or similar capacity, of another entity, if the individual acts or acted in that capacity at the corporation's request.

(7) A corporation, an individual or an entity referred to in subsection (1) may apply to a court for an order approving an indemnity under this section and the court may so order and make any further order that it sees fit.

(8) An applicant under subsection (7) shall give the Director notice of the application and the Director is entitled to appear and be heard in person or by counsel.

(9) On an application under subsection (7) the court may order notice to be given to any interested person and the person is entitled to appear and be heard in person or by counsel.

(p)   section 155 (financial statements);

Commentary

Section 155 of the CBCA reads as follows:

155. (1) Subject to section 156, the directors of a corporation shall place before the shareholders at every annual meeting

(a) comparative financial statements as prescribed relating separately to

      (i) the period that began on the date the corporation came into existence and ended not more than six months before the annual meeting or, if the corporation has completed a financial year, the period that began immediately after the end of the last completed financial year and ended not more than six months before the annual meeting, and

      (ii) the immediately preceding financial year;

    (b) the report of the auditor, if any; and

    (c) any further information respecting the financial position of the corporation and the results of its operations required by the articles, the by-laws or any unanimous shareholder agreement.

(2) Notwithstanding paragraph (1)(a), the financial statements referred to in subparagraph (1)(a)(ii) may be omitted if the reason for the omission is set out in the financial statements, or in a note thereto, to be placed before the shareholders at an annual meeting.

(q)   section 158 (approval of financial statements by directors);

Commentary

Section 158 of the CBCA reads as follows:

158. (1) The directors of a corporation shall approve the financial statements referred to in section 155 and the approval shall be evidenced by the manual signature of one or more directors or a facsimile of the signatures reproduced in the statements.

(2) A corporation shall not issue, publish or circulate copies of the financial statements referred to in section 155 unless the financial statements are

    (a) approved and signed in accordance with subsection (1); and

    (b) accompanied by the report of the auditor of the corporation, if any.

(r)   section 159 (sending financial statements to members before annual meeting);

Commentary

Section 159 of the CBCA reads as follows:

159. (1) A corporation shall, not less than twenty-one days before each annual meeting of shareholders or before the signing of a resolution under paragraph 142(1)(b) in lieu of the annual meeting, send a copy of the documents referred to in section 155 to each shareholder, except to a shareholder who has informed the corporation in writing that he or she does not want a copy of those documents.

(2) A corporation that, without reasonable cause, fails to comply with subsection (1) is guilty of an offence and liable on summary conviction to a fine not exceeding five thousand dollars.

(s)   sections 161 and 162 (qualifications and appointment of auditor);

Commentary

Sections 161 and 162 of the CBCA read as follows:

161. (1) Subject to subsection (5), a person is disqualified from being an auditor of a corporation if the person is not independent of the corporation, any of its affiliates, or the directors or officers of any such corporation or its affiliates.

(2) For the purposes of this section,

(a) independence is a question of fact; and

(b) a person is deemed not to be independent if he or his business partner

    (i) is a business partner, a director, an officer or an employee of the corporation or any of its affiliates, or a business partner of any director, officer or employee of any such corporation or any of its affiliates,

    (ii) beneficially owns or controls, directly or indirectly, a material interest in the securities of the corporation or any of its affiliates, or

    (iii) has been a receiver, receiver-manager, liquidator or trustee in bankruptcy of the corporation or any of its affiliates within two years of his proposed appointment as auditor of the corporation.

(2.1) For the purposes of subsection (2), a person's business partner includes a shareholder of that person.

(3) An auditor who becomes disqualified under this section shall, subject to subsection (5), resign forthwith after becoming aware of the disqualification.

(4) An interested person may apply to a court for an order declaring an auditor to be disqualified under this section and the office of auditor to be vacant.

(5) An interested person may apply to a court for an order exempting an auditor from disqualification under this section and the court may, if it is satisfied that an exemption would not unfairly prejudice the shareholders, make an exemption order on such terms as it thinks fit, which order may have retrospective effect.

162. (1) Subject to section 163, shareholders of a corporation shall, by ordinary resolution, at the first annual meeting of shareholders and at each succeeding annual meeting, appoint an auditor to hold office until the close of the next annual meeting.

(2) An auditor appointed under section 104 is eligible for appointment under subsection (1).

(3) Notwithstanding subsection (1), if an auditor is not appointed at a meeting of shareholders, the incumbent auditor continues in office until a successor is appointed.

(4) The remuneration of an auditor may be fixed by ordinary resolution of the shareholders or, if not so fixed, may be fixed by the directors.

The qualification "Subject to section 163" in the opening words of s. 162(1) of the CBCA exempts shareholders of corporations that are not distributing corporations from the requirement to appoint an auditor, if all shareholders consent. Given that s. 163 of the CBCA is not incorporated by reference into the FNFSMA, it is unclear whether this option is open to the First Nations Finance Authority.

(t)   section 168 (rights and duties of auditor);

Commentary

Section 168 of the CBCA reads as follows:

168. (1) The auditor of a corporation is entitled to receive notice of every meeting of shareholders and, at the expense of the corporation, to attend and be heard on matters relating to the auditor's duties.

(2) If a director or shareholder of a corporation, whether or not the shareholder is entitled to vote at the meeting, gives written notice not less than ten days before a meeting of shareholders to the auditor or a former auditor of the corporation, the auditor or former auditor shall attend the meeting at the expense of the corporation and answer questions relating to their duties as auditor.

(3) A director or shareholder who sends a notice referred to in subsection (2) shall send concurrently a copy of the notice to the corporation.

(4) An auditor or former auditor of a corporation who fails without reasonable cause to comply with subsection (2) is guilty of an offence and liable on summary conviction to a fine not exceeding five thousand dollars or to imprisonment for a term not exceeding six months or to both.

(5) An auditor is entitled to submit to the corporation a written statement giving reasons for resigning or for opposing any proposed action or resolution when the auditor

(a) resigns;

(b) receives a notice or otherwise learns of a meeting of shareholders called for the purpose of removing the auditor from office;

(c) receives a notice or otherwise learns of a meeting of directors or shareholders at which another person is to be appointed to fill the office of auditor, whether because of the resignation or removal of the incumbent auditor or because the auditor's term of office has expired or is about to expire; or

(d) receives a notice or otherwise learns of a meeting of shareholders at which a resolution referred to in section 163 is to be proposed.

(5.1) In the case of a proposed replacement of an auditor, whether through removal or at the end of the auditor's term, the following rules apply with respect to other statements:

(a) the corporation shall make a statement on the reasons for the proposed replacement; and

(b) the proposed replacement auditor may make a statement in which he or she comments on the reasons referred to in paragraph (a).

(6) The corporation shall send a copy of the statements referred to in subsections (5) and (5.1) without delay to every shareholder entitled to receive notice of a meeting referred to in subsection (1) and to the Director, unless the statement is included in or attached to a management proxy circular required by section 150.

(7) No person shall accept appointment or consent to be appointed as auditor of a corporation to replace an auditor who has resigned, been removed or whose term of office has expired or is about to expire until the person has requested and received from that auditor a written statement of the circumstances and the reasons, in that auditor's opinion, for their replacement.

(8) Notwithstanding subsection (7), a person otherwise qualified may accept appointment or consent to be appointed as auditor of a corporation if, within fifteen days after making

the request referred to in that subsection, the person does not receive a reply.

(9) Unless subsection (8) applies, an appointment as auditor of a corporation of a person who has not complied with subsection (7) is void.

(u)   section 169 (examination by auditor);

Commentary

Section 169 of the CBCA reads as follows:

169. (1) An auditor of a corporation shall make the examination that is in their opinion necessary to enable them to report in the prescribed manner on the financial statements required by this Act to be placed before the shareholders, except such financial statements or part thereof that relate to the period referred to in subparagraph 155(1)(a)(ii).

(2) Notwithstanding section 170, an auditor of a corporation may reasonably rely on the report of an auditor of a body corporate or an unincorporated business the accounts of which are included in whole or in part in the financial statements of the corporation.

(3) For the purpose of subsection (2), reasonableness is a question of fact.

(4) Subsection (2) applies whether or not the financial statements of the holding corporation reported on by the auditor are in consolidated form.

The text of s. 155(1)(a)(ii) of the CBCA, referred to in subsection 169(1) of the Act, is set out above in the commentary following paragraph (p) of this subsection. The text of s. 170 of the CBCA, referred to in subsection 169(2) above, is set out below in the commentary following paragraph (v) of this subsection.

(v)   section 170 (auditor's right to information);

Commentary

Section 170 of the CBCA reads as follows:

170. (1) On the demand of an auditor of a corporation, the present or former directors, officers, employees or agents of the corporation shall furnish such

(a) information and explanations, and

(b) access to records, documents, books, accounts and vouchers of the corporation or any of its subsidiaries as are, in the opinion of the auditor, necessary to enable the auditor to make the examination and report required under section 169 and that the directors, officers, employees or agents are reasonably able to furnish.

(2) On the demand of the auditor of a corporation, the directors of the corporation shall

(a) obtain from the present or former directors, officers, employees and agents of any subsidiary of the corporation the information and explanations that the present or former directors, officers, employees and agents are reasonably able to furnish and that are, in the opinion of the auditor, necessary to enable the auditor to make the examination and report required under section 169; and

(b) furnish the auditor with the information and explanations so obtained.

(3) A person who in good faith makes an oral or written communication under subsection (1) or (2) is not liable in any civil proceeding arising from having made the communication.

The text of s. 169 of the CBCA, referred to in paragraph 170(2)(a) of the CBCA, is set out above in the commentary following paragraph (u) of this subsection.

(w) subsections 171(3) to (9) (duty and administration of audit committee and penalty for failure to comply);

Commentary

Subsections 171(3) to (9) of the CBCA read as follows:

(3) An audit committee shall review the financial statements of the corporation before such financial statements are approved under section 158.

(4) The auditor of a corporation is entitled to receive notice of every meeting of the audit committee and, at the expense of the corporation, to attend and be heard thereat; and, if so requested by a member of the audit committee, shall attend every meeting of the committee held during the term of office of the auditor.

(5) The auditor of a corporation or a member of the audit committee may call a meeting of the committee.

(6) A director or an officer of a corporation shall forthwith notify the audit committee and the auditor of any error or mis-statement of which the director or officer becomes aware in a

financial statement that the auditor or a former auditor has reported on.

(7) An auditor or former auditor of a corporation who is notified or becomes aware of an error or mis-statement in a financial statement on which they have reported, if in their opinion the error or mis-statement is material, shall inform each director accordingly.

(8) When under subsection (7) the auditor or former auditor informs the directors of an error or mis-statement in a financial statement, the directors shall

(a) prepare and issue revised financial statements; or

(b) otherwise inform the shareholders and, if the corporation is one that is required to comply with section 160, it shall inform the Director of the error or mis-statement in the same manner as it informs the share-holders.

(9) Every director or officer of a corporation who knowingly fails to comply with subsection (6) or (8) is guilty of an offence and liable on summary conviction to a fine not exceeding five thousand dollars or to imprisonment for a term not exceeding six months or to both.

The text of s. 158 of the CBCA, referred to in s. 171(3) of that Act, is set out above in the commentary following s. 66(2)(q). The corporations, referred to in s. 171(8)(b) above, are distributing corporations whose issued securities are held by more than one person.

(x) section 172 (qualified privilege in defamation for auditor's statements); and

Commentary

Section 172 of the CBCA reads as follows:

172. Any oral or written statement or report made under this Act by the auditor or former auditor of a corporation has qualified privilege.

(y) subsections 257(1) and (2) (certificates of Authority as evidence).

Commentary

Subsections 257(1) and (2) of the CBCA read as follows:

257. (1) A certificate issued on behalf of a corporation stating any fact that is set out in the articles, the by-laws, a unanimous shareholder agreement, the minutes of the meetings of the directors, a committee of directors or the

shareholders, or in a trust indenture or other contract to which the corporation is a party, may be signed by a director, an officer or a transfer agent of the corporation.

(2) When introduced as evidence in any civil, criminal or administrative action or proceeding,

   (a) a fact stated in a certificate referred to in subsection (1),

   (b) a certified extract from a securities register of a corporation, or

   (c) a certified copy of minutes or extract from minutes of a meeting of shareholders, directors or a committee of directors of a corporation,

is, in the absence of evidence to the contrary, proof of the facts so certified without proof of the signature or official character of the person appearing to have signed the certificate.

67. REMUNERATION OF DIRECTORS — Directors shall be paid a fee for attendance at meetings of the board of directors, as fixed by the by-laws of the Authority.

68. (1) DUTY OF CARE — The directors and officers of the Authority in exercising their powers and performing their duties shall

(a)   act honestly and in good faith with a view to the best interests of the Authority; and

(b)   exercise the care, diligence and skill that a reasonably prudent person would exercise in comparable circumstances.

(2) LIMIT OF LIABILITY — Directors and officers are not liable for a failure to comply with subsection (1) if they rely in good faith on

(a)   a written report of the auditor of the Authority or financial statements represented by an officer of the Authority as fairly reflecting the financial condition of the Authority; or

(b)   a report of a lawyer, notary, accountant, engineer, appraiser or other person whose position or profession lends credibility to a statement made by that person.

69. (1) PRESIDENT — The board of directors shall appoint a President to act as the chief executive officer of the Authority.

(2) OTHER STAFF — The President may employ any other officers and employees that are necessary to conduct the work of the Authority.

70. ANNUAL GENERAL MEETING — The Authority shall hold an annual general meeting of representatives for the purpose of

(a)   presenting the annual report and audited financial statements of the Authority;

(b)   electing the board of directors; and

(c)   dealing with any other business of the Authority that may be presented by the board of directors.

71. BY-LAWS — The board of directors may make by-laws

(a)   respecting the calling and conduct of meetings of the board, including the holding of meetings by teleconference;

(b)   fixing the fees to be paid to directors for attendance at meetings of the board and the reimbursement of reasonable travel and living expenses to directors;

(c)   respecting the duties and conduct of the directors, officers and employees of the Authority and the terms and conditions of employment and of the termination of employment of officers and employees of the Authority;

(d)   respecting the signing and sealing of securities and interest coupons issued by the Authority; and

(e)   generally for the conduct and management of the affairs of the Authority.

72. HEAD OFFICE — The head office of the Authority shall be on reserve lands at a location determined by the board of directors.

73. ANNUAL BUDGET — At the beginning of every year, the President shall prepare an annual budget of the Authority and present it to the board of directors for approval.

Purposes

74. MANDATE — The purposes of the Authority are to

(a)   secure for its borrowing members, through the use of property tax revenues,

   (i)   long-term financing of capital infrastructure for the provision of local services on reserve lands,

   (ii) lease financing of capital assets for the provision of local services on reserve lands, or

   (iii) short-term financing to meet cash-flow requirements for operating or capital purposes under a law made under paragraph 5(1)(b), or to refinance a short-term debt incurred for capital purposes;

(b) secure for its borrowing members, through the use of other revenues prescribed by regulation, financing for any purpose prescribed by regulation;

(c) secure the best possible credit terms for its borrowing members;

(d) provide investment services to its members and first nations organizations; and

(e) provide advice regarding the development of long-term financing mechanisms for first nations.

Commentary

In addition to the purposes set out in the Act, the First Nations Finance Authority describes its purposes as follows:

> the primary purpose of the FNFA will be to raise capital by issuing bonds on behalf of its member First Nation governments. The proceeds of the bond issues will be used by First Nations to build community infrastructure such as sewer, roads and water. The investment grade bonds will be backed by the property taxation revenues of the First Nation governments and the collective credit of the borrowing pool.[166]

> The FNFA will improve access to capital by pooling borrowing through greater cooperation among First Nations, creating advantages of size and diversifying risk and revenue streams and by supplying expertise and sophisticated financial opportunities to First Nations. By pooling, the cost of borrowing will be significantly reduced making capital affordable to all First Nations including small First Nations.[167]

At the time of publication, no regulations prescribing other types of revenue had been made under s. 74(b).

Functions And Powers

75. (1) POWERS OF BOARD OF DIRECTORS — For the purposes of this Part, the board of directors may by resolution

(a) borrow money in an amount authorized by the resolution;

(b) issue securities of the Authority;

(c) lend securities to generate income, if the loan is fully secured;

(d) enter into agreements for risk management purposes, including swaps; and

(e) provide for

    (i) payments related to the issuance of securities,

---

[166] From First Nations Finance Authority website: <http://www.fnfa.ca/>.
[167] From First Nations Finance Authority website: <http://www.fnfa.ca/about/index.htm>.

(ii) the registration, transfer, management and redemption of securities,

(iii) the re-issuance, reinstatement or other disposition of lost, stolen, destroyed or damaged securities or interest coupons,

(iv) the examination, cancellation or destruction of securities and of materials used in their production, or

(v) the timing of the issuance of securities.

Commentary

The securities referred to in paragraph (b) are the bonds that the First Nations Finance Authority proposes to issue on behalf of its member First Nation governments.

The swap agreements referred to in paragraph (d) are a form of derivative transaction involving the exchange of cash flows over a period of time, based on a defined market index and a notional value that never actually changes hands.[168]

(2) SECURITY ISSUANCE REQUIREMENTS — A resolution respecting the issuance of securities shall set out

(a)   the rate of interest;

(b)   the time and place of repayment of principal and interest; and

(c)   the currency in which repayment of principal and interest will be made.

(3) SECURITY ISSUANCE RESOLUTIONS — A resolution respecting the issuance of securities may provide that

(a)   the securities are to be redeemable in advance of maturity at a time and price set out in the resolution;

(b)   all or any part of the securities may be paid, refunded or renewed;

(c)   the securities are to be issued in an amount sufficient to realize the amount of any securities called in and paid before maturity, for a term not longer than the remainder of the term of the securities called in and paid; or

(d)   the securities and any interest coupons attached to them are to be in the form set out in the resolution, and are to be exchangeable for other securities of the same issue on any terms and conditions set out in the resolution.

(4) AMOUNT OF ISSUE — The Authority may issue securities the principal amounts of which, after payment of any discount and the costs of

---

[168]   See *Proctor & Gamble Co. v. Bankers Trust Co.* (1996), 925 F. Supp. 1270, for a further discussion of the legal effects of swaps.

issue and sale, will realize the net amount authorized by the board of directors in a resolution made under paragraph (1)(a).

Commentary

The s. 75(1)(a) resolution referred to in s. 75(4) is a resolution to borrow a specified amount of money.

(5) DECLARATION CONCLUSIVE — A declaration in a resolution authorizing the issuance of securities that it is necessary to issue securities in the principal amount authorized in order to realize the net amount authorized is conclusive evidence of that fact.

(6) SALE PRICE — The board of directors may sell securities at their par value or at other than par value.

(7) DELEGATION — The board of directors may delegate its powers under this section to a committee of directors and officers of the Authority, subject to any limitations that the board of directors may impose.

76. (1) APPLICATION TO BECOME BORROWING MEMBER — A first nation may apply to the Authority to become a borrowing member.

Commentary

A formal request to become a borrowing member would likely be made by the council of a First Nation by way of a law made under s. 5(1)(d).

(2) CRITERIA — The Authority shall accept a first nation as a borrowing member only if the First Nations Financial Management Board has issued to the first nation a certificate under subsection 50(3) and has not subsequently revoked it.

Commentary

In order to obtain a certificate under s. 50(3) of the Act, the council of a First Nation must request the First Nations Financial Management Board to review its financial management system and/or financial performance for compliance with the standards established by the Board under s. 55(1) of the Act.

77. CEASING TO BE A BORROWING MEMBER — A first nation may cease to be a borrowing member only with the consent of all other borrowing members.

Commentary

Note that, by virtue of this section, a First Nation does not cease to be a borrowing member when any bond issue in which it participated is retired. Unless the consent of all other borrowing members is obtained, a First Nation that becomes a borrowing member retains that status indefinitely. The only way in which a First Nation can cease to be a borrowing member without such consent is by opting out of the Act entirely under s. 2(3)(b), which it can do only if all of its financial obligations to the First Nations Finance Authority have been met.

This provision is sometimes referred to as the Hotel California clause.

78. (1) PRIORITY — The Authority has a priority over all other creditors of a first nation that is insolvent, for any moneys that are authorized to be paid to the Authority under a law made under paragraph 5(1)(b) or (d).

(2) DEBTS TO THE CROWN — For greater certainty, subsection (1) does not apply to Her Majesty.

Commentary

While under this provision claims by the First Nations Finance Authority would likely take priority over other claims set out in s. 136 of the *Bankruptcy and Insolvency Act*,[169] it is uncertain what priority a claim by the Authority would have in relation to claims for legal costs set out in s. 197(6) of that Act.

Note that the exclusion of claims by Her Majesty from the priority accorded to the Authority under this section is not limited to Her Majesty in right of Canada, and therefore presumably includes the provincial Crown as well.

79. LIMITATIONS — INFRASTRUCTURE LOANS — The Authority shall not make a long-term loan to a borrowing member for the purpose of financing capital infrastructure for the provision of local services on reserve lands unless

(a)   the First Nations Tax Commission has approved a law made by the borrowing member under paragraph 5(1)(d); and

(b)   the loan is to be paid out of the property tax revenues of the borrowing member in priority to other creditors of the borrowing member.

---

[169]   R.S.C. 1985, c. B-3.

Commentary

This section prohibits the Authority from granting a long-term loan to a borrowing member for the purpose of financing capital infrastructure for the provision of local services on reserve lands unless

- the First Nation has made a law under s. 5(1)(d) authorizing the borrowing; and

- it has arranged with any other creditors who have a claim to payment from its property taxation revenues to postpone their priorities to that of the Authority.

Although this section prohibits the Authority from making long-term loans to a borrowing member for the purpose of financing capital infrastructure for the provision of local services on reserve lands, it is not clear whether the Authority could nonetheless make long-term loans to a borrowing member for some other purpose.

80. RESTRICTION ON FINANCING — A borrowing member shall not obtain long-term financing secured by property tax revenues from any person other than the First Nations Finance Authority.

Commentary

Under s. 80 of the Act, a First Nation that is a borrowing member cannot use its property taxation revenues as security for a long-term loan from any person other than the First Nations Finance Authority.

81. LIMITATIONS — SHORT-TERM LOANS — The Authority shall not make a short-term loan to a borrowing member for a purpose described in subparagraph 74(a)(iii) unless the loan is made in anticipation of local revenues of the borrowing member set out in a law made under paragraph 5(1)(b).

Commentary

Subparagraph 74(a)(iii) refers to short-term financing to meet cash-flow requirements for operating or capital purposes, or to refinance a short-term debt incurred for capital purposes. Laws made under s. 5(1)(b) are budget expenditure laws.

82. (1) SINKING FUND — The Authority shall establish a sinking fund, or any other system of repayment prescribed by regulation, to fulfil its repayment obligations to the holders of each security issued by the Authority.

Commentary

At the time of publication, no regulations prescribing an alternate system of repayment had been proposed.

(2) SEPARATE ACCOUNTS — Where a sinking fund is established, a separate sinking fund account shall be kept for each borrowing member participating in a security issued by the Authority.

(3) SINKING FUND INVESTMENTS — Funds in a sinking fund may be invested only in

(a) **securities issued or guaranteed by Canada or a province;**

(b) **securities of a local, municipal or regional government in Canada;**

(c) **investments guaranteed by a bank, trust company or credit union; or**

(d) **deposits in a bank or trust company in Canada or non-equity or membership shares in a credit union.**

83. (1) SURPLUSES — The Authority may declare a surplus in a sinking fund and use the surplus, in order of priority, to

(a) **replenish any amounts paid out of the debt reserve fund; and**

(b) **make a distribution to borrowing members who are participating in that fund.**

Commentary

Such a surplus would arise from investments made under s. 82(3). The debt reserve fund referred to in paragraph (a) is established under s. 84 of the Act.

(2) RECOVERY FROM SINKING FUND — The Authority may recover fees payable by a borrowing member from any surplus to be distributed to that member under paragraph (1)(b).

84. (1) DEBT RESERVE FUND — The Authority shall establish a debt reserve fund to make payments or sinking fund contributions for which insufficient moneys are available from borrowing members.

(2) PROVISIONING OF FUND — Subject to the regulations, the Authority shall withhold 5% of the amount of any long-term loan to a borrowing member for financing capital infrastructure for the provision of local services on reserve lands and deposit that amount in the debt reserve fund.

(3) SEPARATE ACCOUNT — A separate account shall be kept for each security issued and for each borrowing member contributing to the debt reserve fund.

(4) INVESTMENTS — The funds of the debt reserve fund may be invested only in securities, investments or deposits referred to in paragraph 82(3)(a), (c) or (d) that mature or are callable within five years, 25% of which must be callable within 90 days.

(5) LIABILITY FOR SHORTFALL — If payments from the debt reserve fund reduce its balance

(a)   by less than 50% of the total amount contributed by borrowing members, the Authority may, in accordance with the regulations, require all borrowing members to pay amounts sufficient to replenish the debt reserve fund; and

(b)   by 50% or more of the total amount contributed by borrowing members,

    (i)   the Authority shall, in accordance with the regulations, require all borrowing members to pay without delay amounts sufficient to replenish the debt reserve fund, and

    (ii)   the borrowing members shall recover those amounts under their property taxation laws.

Commentary

Note that amounts required to be paid by borrowing members under subparagraph (b)(i) must be paid immediately and must be recovered by use of property taxation laws, while neither of these requirements exists in respect of amounts required to be paid under paragraph (a). Note too that charges must be assessed on *all* borrowing members, not just on those borrowing members who are participating in the bond in respect of which the shortfall occurred.

The mechanisms for recovering such charges from borrowing members are set out in the proposed *Debt Reserve Fund Replenishment Regulations*, which are made under s. 89(c) of the Act.

(6) REPAYMENT — Money contributed by a borrowing member to the debt reserve fund and investment income received on it shall be repaid by the Authority to the borrowing member when all obligations in respect of the security in respect of which the money was contributed have been satisfied.

85. (1) CREDIT ENHANCEMENT FUND — The Authority shall establish a fund for the enhancement of the Authority's credit rating.

Commentary

The credit enhancement fund is proposed to be funded with funds provided by the Government of Canada, up to a maximum of $10 million.[170]

(2) INVESTMENTS — The funds of the credit enhancement fund may be invested only in securities, investments or deposits referred to in paragraph 82(3)(a), (c) or (d) that mature or are callable within five years, 25% of which must be callable within 90 days.

Commentary

The deposits referred to in ss. 82(3)(a), (c) or (d) are:

- securities issued or guaranteed by Canada or a province;
- investments guaranteed by a bank, trust company or credit union; and
- deposits in a bank or trust company in Canada or non-equity or membership shares in a credit union.

(3) INVESTMENT INCOME — Investment income from the credit enhancement fund may be used

(a)   to temporarily offset any shortfalls in the debt reserve fund;

(b)   to defray the Authority's costs of operation; and

(c)   for any other purpose prescribed by regulation.

Commentary

At the time of publication, there were no regulations proposed under s. 85(3)(c).

(4) CAPITAL — The capital of the credit enhancement fund may be used

(a)   to temporarily offset any shortfalls in the debt reserve fund; and

(b)   for any other purpose prescribed by regulation.

Commentary

At the time of publication, there were no regulations proposed under s. 85(4)(b).

---

[170]   From "Investor Information", First Nations Finance Authority website: <http://www.fnfa .ca/forms/investor_information.pdf>.

86. (1) DEFAULT BY FIRST NATION — If a borrowing member fails to make a payment to the Authority, to fulfil any other obligation under a borrowing agreement with the Authority or to pay a charge imposed by the Authority under this Part, the Authority shall

   (a) notify the borrowing member of the failure; and

   (b) send a notice of the failure to the First Nations Financial Management Board and the First Nations Tax Commission, together with evidence of the failure and a copy of any relevant documents and records.

Commentary

A default under this subsection can occur if a First Nation that is a borrowing member

- fails to make a scheduled payment on a loan from the First Nations Finance Authority;

- breaches some other provision of its agreement with the Authority; or

- fails to pay a charge imposed by the Authority under s. 84(5).

Note that although this subsection provides for notification of the First Nations Financial Management Board and First Nations Tax Commission, it does not obligate or empower either of those institutions to take remedial action.

(2) REQUIREMENT FOR REPORT — If a failure referred to in subsection (1) relates to an obligation other than payment, the Authority may require that the First Nations Financial Management Board review and report on the reasons for the failure.

Commentary

Note that the power of the First Nations Finance Authority under this subsection is discretionary; it can choose whether or not to request the review and report in question.

(3) REPORT — On receipt of a notice referred to in paragraph (1)(b) in respect of a failure related to an obligation other than payment, the First Nations Financial Management Board shall advise the Authority in writing of its opinion on the reasons for the failure and recommend any intervention under section 52 or 53 that it considers appropriate.

Commentary

An intervention under s. 52 would be an imposed co-management arrangement. An intervention under s. 53 would be the assumption of third-party management of the First Nation's property tax revenue system.

(4) REQUIRED INTERVENTION — The Authority may, by notice in writing, require the First Nations Financial Management Board to either — at the Board's discretion — impose a co-management arrangement on a borrowing member or assume third-party management of the first nation's local revenues

  (a)   where the borrowing member fails to make a payment to the Authority under a borrowing agreement with the Authority, or to pay a charge imposed by the Authority under this Part; or

  (b)   on receipt of a report of the Board under subsection (3) in respect of the borrowing member.

Commentary

Note that while the First Nations Finance Authority can require the First Nations Financial Management Board to take action, the decision as to whether to impose a co-management arrangement on a borrowing member or to assume third-party management of its property tax revenue system is left up to the Board.

The report referred to in paragraph (b) is a report by the First Nations Financial Management Board on the reasons for the First Nation's failure to comply with a requirement (other than repayment) in its borrowing agreement with the First Nations Finance Authority.

87. (1) SHORT-TERM POOLED INVESTMENT FUNDS — The Authority may establish short-term pooled investment funds.

Commentary

While the Act does not define what constitutes a short-term pooled investment fund, examples of the types of investment funds currently offered by the First Nations Finance Authority Inc. can be examined at the website of the First Nations Finance Authority. The current funds are described as funds that "offer high levels of protection of investor capital, combined with flexibility of subscription and redemption."[171] The pooled investment activities of the Authority are not connected to its capital financing activities.[172] Additional information on the Authority's pooled investment funds is available at <http://www.fnfa.ca/forms/pooled_invest_funds.pdf>.

(2) INVESTMENTS — Funds in a short-term pooled investment fund may be invested only in

---

[171]   First Nations Finance Authority website: <http://www.fnfa.ca/member/pooled_ investments.htm>.

[172]   *Ibid.*

(a) securities issued or guaranteed by Canada, a province or the United States;

(b) fixed-term deposits, notes, certificates or other short-term paper of, or guaranteed by, a bank, trust company or credit union, including swaps in United States currency;

(c) securities issued by the Authority or by a local, municipal or regional government in Canada;

(d) commercial paper issued by a Canadian company that is rated in the highest category by at least two recognized security-rating institutions;

(e) any class of investments permitted under an Act of a province relating to trustees; or

(f) any other investments or class of investments prescribed by regulation.

Commentary

Additional classes of permitted investments are provided for in the proposed *Short-term Pooled Investment Fund Regulations*.

General

88. (1) ANNUAL REPORT — The Chairperson shall, within four months after the end of each fiscal year, submit to the Authority's members and the Minister a report of the operations of the Authority for that fiscal year.

Commentary

"Fiscal year" is not defined in respect of the First Nations Finance Authority. Paragraph 37(1)(b) of the *Interpretation Act*[173] provides that:

37. (1) ... a reference ..

(b) to a "financial year" ... means, *in relation to money provided by Parliament*, or the Consolidated Revenue Fund, or the accounts, taxes or finances of Canada, the period beginning on April 1 in one calendar year and ending on March 31 in the next calendar year; ...

If this definition is considered to apply in relation to "fiscal year" as it is used in s. 88(1) of the FNFSMA, the fiscal year end for the Authority would be March 31. The four-month period referred to in s. 88(1) would therefore end on July 31 of each year.

Under s. 116 of the Act, the financial years for the First Nations Tax Commission and First Nations Financial Management Board end on March 31.

---

[173] R.S.C. 1985, c. I-21.

The financial year for the First Nations Statistical Institute is governed by s. 121(1) of the *Financial Administration Act*,[174] which establishes it as December 31.

(2) CONTENTS — The annual report shall include the financial statements of the Authority and its auditor's opinion on them.

Regulations

89. REGULATIONS — The Governor in Council may, on the recommendation of the Minister after consultation by the Minister with the Authority, make regulations

(a) **prescribing anything that is to be prescribed under subsection 82(1) and paragraphs 85(3)(c) and (4)(b) and 87(2)(f);**

(b) **increasing or decreasing the amount to be withheld from a loan under subsection 84(2);**

(c) **respecting the imposition of charges under subsection 84(5), including the manner of calculating those charges and the share of those charges to be paid by each borrowing member; and**

(d) **extending the application of this Part to any non-profit organization established to provide social welfare, housing, recreational or cultural services to first nations or their members on reserve lands and making any adaptations to the provisions of this Act that are necessary for that purpose.**

Commentary

At the time of publication,

- the *Short-term Pooled Investment Fund Regulations* were proposed to be made[175] under paragraph (a):

- no regulations were proposed to be made under paragraph (b);

- the *Debt Reserve Fund Replenishment Regulations* were proposed to be made under paragraph (c); and

- no regulations were proposed to be made under paragraph (d).

---

[174]   R.S.C. 1985, c. F-11.

[175]   Proposed regulations under the FNFSMA are posted on the INAC website: <http://www.ainc-inac.gc.ca/nr/prs/s-d2002/02218bk_e.html>.

PART 5

FIRST NATIONS STATISTICAL INSTITUTE

Interpretation

90. DEFINITIONS — The following definitions apply in this Part.

Commentary

These definitions apply in ss. 90 to 113 of the Act.

"Institute"
« Institut »

"Institute" means the First Nations Statistical Institute.

"other aboriginal group"
« autre groupe autochtone »

"other aboriginal group" means an aboriginal group that was formerly a band under the *Indian Act* and that is a party to a treaty, land claim agreement or self-government agreement with Canada.

Commentary

In essence, this definition encompasses former *Indian Act* bands that have negotiated self-government or other agreements pursuant to which they are no longer subject to the *Indian Act*.

"respondent"
« intéressé »

"respondent" means a person in respect of whom, or in respect of whose activities, a report or information is sought or provided under this Part.

Establishment and Organization of Institute

91. INSTITUTE — There is hereby established an institute, to be known as the First Nations Statistical Institute, which may carry on business under the name of "First Nations Statistics".

92. CROWN CORPORATION — The Institute is a Crown corporation and is governed by Part X of the *Financial Administration Act*, but to the extent that any provisions of this Part are inconsistent with sections 105 and 121 of that Act, the provisions of this Part prevail.

Commentary

Part X of the *Financial Administration Act*[176] (ss. 83 to 154 of that Act) sets out the rules relating to Crown corporations. While those rules are too lengthy to set out here, they relate to the accountability of Crown corporations to Parliament, restrictions on the transactions they can engage in, the appointment of their directors and officers, and financial management, auditing and reporting requirements.

Section 92 of the FNFSMA provides, however, that the provisions of the FNFSMA override ss. 105 and 121 of the *Financial Administration Act* to the extent that they conflict. Section 105 of the *Financial Administration Act* deals with the appointment of directors, and the rules in ss. 94 to 100 of the FNFSMA would therefore largely replace those in s. 105 of the *Financial Administration Act*. Section 121 of the *Financial Administration Act* establishes the financial year of a Crown corporation as the calendar year:

> 121. (1) The financial year of a parent Crown corporation is the calendar year, unless the Governor in Council otherwise directs.
>
> (2) [Not applicable.]

Since there is no provision for a financial year of the First Nations Statistical Institute in the FNFSMA, s. 121 of the *Financial Administration Act* would appear to continue to apply.

93. NOT AN AGENT OF HER MAJESTY — The Institute is not an agent of Her Majesty.

94. (1) BOARD OF DIRECTORS — The Institute shall be managed by a board of directors, consisting of 10 to 15 directors, including the Chairperson and Vice-Chairperson.

(2) EX OFFICIO DIRECTOR — The Chief Statistician of Canada shall be a member of the board of directors.

95. APPOINTMENT OF CHAIRPERSON — On the recommendation of the Minister, the Governor in Council shall appoint a Chairperson to hold office during pleasure for a term not exceeding five years.

Commentary

Note that, unlike the Commissioners and directors appointed under Parts 2 and 3, the members of the First Nations Statistical Institute's board of directors, like all directors of Crown corporations, hold office at pleasure, rather than on

---

[176]   R.S.C. 1985, c. F-11.

good behaviour. This means that they can be dismissed without the requirement to show misfeasance on their part.

96. APPOINTMENT OF OTHER DIRECTORS — On the recommendation of the Minister, the Governor in Council shall appoint a minimum of eight, and a maximum of 13, additional directors to hold office during pleasure for a term not exceeding five years.

Commentary

Note that, unlike the Commissioners and directors appointed under Parts 2 and 3, the members of the First Nations Statistical Institute's board of directors, like all directors of Crown corporations, hold office at pleasure, rather than on good behaviour. This means that they can be dismissed without the requirement to show misfeasance on their part.

97. (1) STAGGERED TERMS — In determining the term of appointment of directors, the Governor in Council shall endeavour to ensure that the terms of no more than three directors expire in any one calendar year.

(2) QUALIFICATIONS — The board of directors shall be composed of men and women from across Canada, including members of first nations, who are committed to improving first nations statistical information and fulfill its mandate.

98. STATUS — The Chairperson and other directors shall hold office on a part-time basis.

99. (1) ELECTION OF VICE-CHAIRPERSON — The board of directors shall elect a Vice-Chairperson from among the directors.

(2) FUNCTIONS — In the event of the absence or incapacity of the Chairperson, or if the office of Chairperson is vacant, the Vice-Chairperson shall assume the duties and functions of the Chairperson.

100. REAPPOINTMENT — A director may be reappointed for a second or subsequent term of office.

101. HEAD OFFICE — The head office of the Institute shall be at a location determined by the Governor in Council.

102. (1) FIRST NATIONS CHIEF STATISTICIAN — On the recommendation of the Minister, the Governor in Council shall appoint a First Nations Chief Statistician to hold office during pleasure on a full-time basis for a term not exceeding five years.

Commentary

Note that the First Nation's Chief Statistician is not a member of the First Nations Statistical Institute's board of directors.

(2) REMUNERATION — The First Nations Chief Statistician shall be paid the remuneration determined by the Governor in Council.

(3) STAFF — The board of directors shall determine the duties of other officers and employees and the conditions of their employment.

(4) STAFF — The First Nations Chief Statistician may hire any other officers and employees that are necessary to conduct the work of the Institute.

(5) SALARIES AND BENEFITS — Persons hired under subsection (4) shall be paid salaries and benefits fixed by the board of directors.

103. OATH OF OFFICE — The First Nations Chief Statistician, every person employed by the Institute, every person retained under contract by the Institute and every employee and agent of a person retained under contract by the Institute shall, before commencing their duties, swear or solemnly affirm that he or she will comply with section 108 and will not without authority disclose any information acquired in the course of his or her duties that can be related to any identifiable individual, first nation, business or organization.

Commentary

This provision is equivalent to the requirements of s. 6 of the *Statistics Act*.[177]

Purposes

104. MANDATE — The purposes of the Institute are to

(a) **provide statistical information on, and analysis of, the fiscal, economic and social conditions of**

   (i) **Indians and other members of first nations,**

   (ii) **members of other aboriginal groups, and**

   (iii) **other persons who reside on reserve lands or lands of other aboriginal groups;**

(b) **promote the quality, coherence and compatibility of first nations statistics and their production in accordance with generally accepted standards and practices through collaboration with first**

---

[177] R.S.C. 1985, c. S-19.

    nations, federal departments and agencies, provincial departments and agencies and other organizations;

(c)   work with, and provide advice to, federal departments and agencies and provincial departments and agencies on first nations statistics;

(d)   work in cooperation with Statistics Canada to ensure that the national statistical system meets the needs of first nations and Canada; and

(e)   build statistical capacity within first nation governments.

Commentary

Subparagraph 104(a)(i) refers to both Indians and other members of First Nations because, under the *Indian Act*, a First Nation can have as members persons who are not Indians. Note that under s. 104(a)(iii) the First Nations Statistical Institute is tasked with providing statistical information on other non-Indian residents of reserve lands as well, who may reside there by virtue of leases of reserve lands granted under the *Indian Act* or *First Nations Land Management Act*.

Powers

105. (1) GENERAL POWERS — In furtherance of the purposes set out in section 104, the Institute may enter into agreements with aboriginal and other governments and organizations.

(2) PARTICULAR POWERS — The Institute may collect, compile, analyze and abstract data for statistical purposes respecting any of the following matters as they relate to first nations, to reserve lands, to Indians and other members of first nations, to members of other aboriginal groups, and to other persons who reside on reserve lands or lands of other aboriginal groups:

(a)   **population;**

(b)   **agriculture;**

(c)   **health and welfare;**

(d)   **commercial and industrial activities;**

(e)   **law enforcement, the administration of justice and corrections;**

(f)   **finance;**

(g)   **education;**

(h)   **language, culture and traditional activities;**

(i)   **labour and employment;**

(j)   **prices and the cost of living;**

(k)   **transportation and communications;**

(l)   **electric power, gas and water utilities;**

(m) **public administration;**

(n) **community services;**

(o) **the environment;**

(p) **forestry, fishing and trapping; and**

(q) **any other matter prescribed by regulation.**

Commentary

This subsection roughly parallels the powers given to Statistics Canada under s. 22 of the *Statistics Act*.[178] At the time of publication, no regulations had been proposed under paragraph (q).

(3) PUBLICATION — The Institute shall publish and make publicly available statistical information collected, compiled, analysed or abstracted under subsection (2) in a manner that does not permit the information to be related to any identifiable individual, business or organization.

Commentary

This subsection roughly parallels the restrictions on Statistics Canada imposed under s. 17(1)(b) of the *Statistics Act*.[179]

106. (1) SHARING OF INFORMATION — The Institute may enter into an agreement with a first nation or other aboriginal group, federal department or agency, provincial department or agency, municipality, corporation or other organization for the sharing of information collected by or on behalf of either party and for its subsequent tabulation or publication.

Commentary

This subsection roughly parallels the requirements of s. 12(1) of the *Statistics Act*.[180]

(2) AGREEMENT — An agreement under subsection (1) shall provide that

(a) **respondents from whom information is collected are to be informed by notice that the information is being collected on behalf of the Institute and the first nation, other aboriginal group,**

---

[178] *Ibid.*
[179] *Ibid.*
[180] *Ibid.*

department, agency, municipality, corporation or organization, as the case may be; and

(b) if the respondents object by notice in writing to the First Nations Chief Statistician to the sharing of the information by the Institute, the information will not be shared unless the first nation, other aboriginal group, department, agency, municipality, corporation or organization is authorized by law to require respondents to provide that information.

Commentary

This subsection roughly parallels the requirements of s. 12(2) of the *Statistics Act.*[181]

107. (1) FEDERAL DATA — Subject to subsection (2), documents or records relating to first nations, Indians or other members of first nations, or to members of other aboriginal groups, that are maintained by any department, body or corporation set out in any of Schedules I to III to the *Financial Administration Act*[182] that is prescribed by regulation shall be disclosed to the Institute for the purposes of this Part in accordance with an agreement referred to in subsection (3).

Commentary

The requirements of this subsection are analogous to those of s. 13 of the *Statistics Act,*[183] although the access given to the First Nations Statistical Institute under this provision excludes access to municipal offices, corporations, businesses and organizations referred to in the *Statistics Act.*[184]

Access to documents and records under this subsection is limited to federal departments, and agencies or corporations established by the federal government, that are prescribed by regulation. The proposed regulation in which these departments, agencies and corporations are to be prescribed is the *Statistical Data Disclosure Regulations.*

Access to documents and records under this subsection is also limited by the requirements of the following subsection.

(2) EXCEPTION — A department, body or corporation referred to in subsection (1) is not required to disclose any information that it is required to, or may, withhold under any federal law or under any privilege at law.

---

[181] *Ibid.*
[182] R.S.C. 1985, c. F-11.
[183] *Ibid.*
[184] *Ibid.*

Commentary

This provision permits a department, body or corporation referred to in s. 107(1) to decline to disclose any information that

- it is required by statute to keep confidential, such as information referred to in ss. 13(1), 16(3) and 19, 20 and 24(1) of the *Access to Information Act*;[185] or

- it is permitted by statute to refuse to disclose, such as information referred to in ss. 14, 15, 16(1) and (2), 17, 18, 21 to 23 and 26 of the *Access to Information Act*.

Documents that are privileged at law would include documents such as legal opinions for which a privilege exists at common law,[186] as well documents privileged by statute. The latter include reports of accidents made under the *Bridges Act*,[187] returns made by corporations under the *Corporations Returns Act*,[188] reports made by the Privacy Commissioner,[189] and confidences of the Queen's Privy Council.[190]

(3) AGREEMENT REQUIRED — The Institute shall enter into an agreement for the collection and use of information referred to in subsection (1) with the department, body or corporation from whose documents or records it is to be obtained.

Commentary

This subsection requires the First Nations Statistical Institute to enter into an agreement with each department, agency or corporation from which it is entitled to obtain documents or records under s. 107(1), setting out the agreed upon uses to which the information will be put. It is unclear in what respect the agreement is to address collection of the information.

General

108. (1) PROTECTION OF INFORMATION — Except for the purpose of communicating information in accordance with the conditions of an agreement made under section 106, for the conduct of a prosecution under this Act or for the purposes of subsection (2),

---

[185]   R.S.C. 1985, c. A-1.

[186]   See *Lavallee, Rackel & Heintz v. Canada (Attorney General)*, [2002] S.C.J. No. 61, [2002] 3 S.C.R. 209, at 230. See generally J. Sopinka, S.N. Lederman and A.W. Bryant, *The Law of Evidence in Canada* (Toronto: Butterworths, 1992) at pp. 635-36.

[187]   R.S.C. 1985, c. B-8, s. 19

[188]   R.S.C. 1985, c. C-43, s. 18

[189]   *Privacy Act*, R.S.C. 1985, c. P-21, s. 67(2)(b).

[190]   *Canada Evidence Act*, R.S.C. 1985, c. C-5, s. 39.

(a) no person, other than a person employed by, or under contract to, the Institute and sworn or affirmed under section 103, shall be permitted to examine any identifiable individual return made for the purposes of this Part; and

(b) no person who has been sworn or affirmed under section 103 shall knowingly disclose any information obtained by the Institute that can be related to any identifiable individual, first nation, business or organization.

Commentary

This subsection roughly parallels the requirements of s. 17(1) of the *Statistics Act*.[191]

(2) **PERMISSIBLE DISCLOSURE** — The First Nations Chief Statistician may authorize the following information to be disclosed:

(a) information collected by persons, first nations, organizations or departments for their own purposes and communicated to the Institute, subject to the same secrecy requirements applicable to it when it was collected, and in the manner and to the extent agreed on by its collector and the First Nations Chief Statistician;

(b) information relating to a person, first nation, business or organization in respect of which disclosure is consented to in writing by that person, first nation, business or organization;

(c) information available to the public under an Act of Parliament or of the legislature of a province;

(d) information relating to a hospital, institution for individuals with a mental health disability, library, educational institution or other similar non-commercial institution that cannot be related to an individual to whom services were or are provided by that institution; and

(e) a list of businesses, showing

(i) their names and addresses,

(ii) the telephone numbers at which they may be reached in relation to statistical matters,

(iii) the official language in which they prefer to be addressed in relation to statistical matters,

(iv) the products they produce, transport, store, purchase or sell, or the services they provide, in the course of their business, or

(v) the number of persons they employ, as a specified range.

---

[191] R.S.C. 1985, c. S-19.

Commentary

This subsection roughly parallels the requirements of s. 17(2) of the *Statistics Act*.[192]

109. (1) INFORMATION PRIVILEGED — Except for the purpose of conducting a prosecution under this Act, information obtained by the Institute that can be related to any identifiable individual, business, organization or first nation is privileged and shall not be used as evidence in a legal proceeding.

Commentary

This subsection roughly parallels the requirements of s. 18(1) of the *Statistics Act*.[193]

(2) NO COMPULSION TO PRODUCE — No person referred to in section 103 shall be required by an order of a court, tribunal or other body to give testimony in respect of any information referred to in subsection (1).

Commentary

This subsection roughly parallels the requirements of s. 18(2) of the *Statistics Act*.[194]

110. POWERS OF STATISTICS CANADA — Nothing in this Act shall be construed so as to limit the powers and duties of Statistics Canada under the *Statistics Act*.[195]

Offences

111. OFFENCE — Every person who, after making an oath or solemn affirmation under section 103,

(a)   wilfully makes a false declaration, statement or return in the performance of his or her duties,

(b)   in the pretended performance of his or her duties, obtains or seeks to obtain information that the person is not authorized to obtain, or

(c)   contravenes section 108

---

[192]   *Ibid.*
[193]   *Ibid.*
[194]   *Ibid.*
[195]   *Ibid.*

is guilty of an offence and liable on summary conviction to a fine not exceeding $1,000 or to imprisonment for a term not exceeding six months, or to both.

Commentary

This subsection roughly parallels the requirements of s. 30 of the *Statistics Act.*[196]

112. SECRET INFORMATION — Every person who, after making an oath or solemn affirmation under section 103,

    (a) **wilfully discloses, directly or indirectly, information obtained in the course of his or her duties that might affect the market value of a security or commodity, including any information referred to in subsection 108(2), to any person who has not been sworn or affirmed under section 103, or**

    (b) **uses any information described in paragraph (a) for the purpose of speculating in a security or commodity**

is guilty of an offence and liable on summary conviction to a fine not exceeding the aggregate of $5,000 and double the amount of any benefit obtained from speculation referred to in paragraph (b) or to imprisonment for a term not exceeding five years, or to both.

Commentary

This subsection roughly parallels the requirements of s. 34 of the *Statistics Act.*[197]

Regulations

113. REGULATIONS — The Governor in Council may, on the recommendation of the Minister made having regard to any representations by the Institute, make regulations prescribing anything to be prescribed under paragraph 105(2)(q) or subsection 107(1).

Commentary

At the time of publication, no regulations have been proposed under 105(2)(q).

Regulations proposed to be made under s. 107(1) are the *Statistical Data Disclosure Regulations.*

---

[196] *Ibid.*
[197] *Ibid.*

PART 6

FINANCIAL MANAGEMENT AND CONTROL

114. DEFINITIONS — The following definitions apply in this Part.

"board of directors"
" conseil d'administration »

"board of directors" includes

(a) in respect of the First Nations Tax Commission, the commissioners referred to in section 17; and

(b) in respect of the First Nations Financial Management Board, the directors referred to in section 38.

"institution"
" institution »

"institution" means the First Nations Tax Commission or the First Nations Financial Management Board.

Commentary

Note that, because of the definition of "institution", the application of this Part is limited to the First Nations Tax Commission and the First Nations Financial Management Board. Similar rules apply to the First Nations Statistical Institute under Part X of the *Financial Administration Act*[198] (see Commentary following s. 92).

115. (1) EXCLUSION FROM PUBLIC SERVICE — The officers and employees of an institution are not part of the public service of Canada.

Commentary

Note that under s. 154(2) of the Act, the reference in this subsection to the "public service of Canada" was changed to the "federal public administration" as of April 1, 2005 when section 8 of the *Public Service Modernization Act* came into force.[199]

(2) NO GUARANTEES — No person shall give a guarantee on behalf of Her Majesty for the discharge of an obligation or liability of an institution.

---

[198] R.S.C. 1985, c. F-11.
[199] SI/2005-25

116. FINANCIAL YEAR — The financial year of each institution is the period from April 1 to March 31, unless otherwise prescribed by regulation.

Commentary

At the time of publication, no regulations had been proposed to change the financial year under this section.

117. EXPENDITURE OF REVENUES — Subject to any terms and conditions that the Treasury Board may direct, for the purposes of the institution, an institution may expend, during a financial year or the following year, any revenues that it receives in that financial year through the conduct of its operations.

Commentary

This permits the First Nations Tax Commission and First Nations Financial Management Board to spend money that they earn by way of contracts or collect through the imposition of fees. Such funds would otherwise go directly to government revenues [200] and would be unavailable to the institutions.

118. (1) CORPORATE PLANS — Each institution shall, in accordance with any directions given by the Minister, establish a corporate plan and budget for each financial year and submit them to the Minister for approval.

Commentary

This provision sets out requirements similar to those for Crown corporations in s. 122(1) of the *Financial Administration Act*.[201]

(2) SCOPE AND CONTENTS OF CORPORATE PLAN — The corporate plan of each institution shall encompass all of the businesses and activities of the institution and include a statement of

    (a) the objects or purposes of the institution;

    (b) the institution's objectives for the financial year and the strategy it intends to employ to achieve those objectives; and

    (c) the institution's expected performance for the financial year as compared to its objectives for that year as set out in the last corporate plan.

---

[200]   They would fall within the definition of "public monies" in s. 2 of the *Financial Administration Act*, R.S.C. 1985, c. F-11, and would therefore be required to be deposited in the Consolidated Revenue Fund under s. 17(1) of that Act.

[201]   R.S.C. 1985, c. F-11.

Commentary

This provision sets out requirements similar to those for Crown corporations in ss. 122(2) and (3) of the *Financial Administration Act*.[202]

(3) CONTENTS OF BUDGET — The budget of each institution must include a statement of the institution's projected revenues and expenses for the financial year on account of capital and operations.

Commentary

This provision sets out requirements similar to those for Crown corporations in s. 123 of the *Financial Administration Act*.[203]

(4) FORM OF CORPORATE PLAN — The corporate plan of each institution shall be prepared in a form that clearly sets out information according to the major businesses or activities of the institution.

Commentary

This provision sets out requirements similar to those for Crown corporations in s. 122(4) of the *Financial Administration Act*.[204]

(5) RESTRICTION ON BUSINESS OR ACTIVITY — No institution may carry on any business or activity in any financial year in a manner that is not consistent with its corporate plan for that year.

Commentary

This provision parallels the requirements for Crown corporations set out in s. 122(5) of the *Financial Administration Act*.[205]

(6) AMENDMENT — Any amendment by an institution to its corporate plan or budget shall be submitted to the Minister for approval.

Commentary

This provision sets out requirements similar to those for Crown corporations in s. 122(6) of the *Financial Administration Act*.[206]

---

[202]   *Ibid.*
[203]   *Ibid.*
[204]   *Ibid.*
[205]   *Ibid.*
[206]   *Ibid.*

119. (1) BOOKS AND SYSTEMS — Each institution shall

(a) keep books of account and records in relation to them; and

(b) maintain financial and management control and information systems.

(2) BOOKS AND SYSTEMS — The books, records and systems referred to in subsection (1) shall be kept and maintained in such a manner as will provide reasonable assurance that

(a) the institution's assets are safeguarded and controlled;

(b) its transactions are in accordance with this Act;

(c) its financial, human and physical resources are managed economically and efficiently; and

(d) its operations are carried out effectively.

(3) INTERNAL AUDIT — An institution may cause internal audits to be conducted to assess compliance with subsections (1) and (2).

(4) FINANCIAL STATEMENTS — Each institution shall annually prepare financial statements, in accordance with generally accepted accounting principles, as supplemented by any directions given by the Minister under subsection (6).

(5) FORM OF FINANCIAL STATEMENTS — The financial statements of an institution shall be prepared in a form that clearly sets out information according to the major businesses or activities of the institution.

(6) DIRECTIONS — The Minister may give directions respecting the preparation of financial statements, to supplement generally accepted accounting principles.

Commentary

Subsections 119(1) to (6) set out requirements similar to those for Crown corporations under ss. 131(1) to (6) of the *Financial Administration Act*.[207]

120. (1) ANNUAL AUDITOR'S REPORT — Each institution shall cause an annual auditor's report to be prepared in accordance with any directions of the Minister, on

(a) its financial statements; and

(b) any quantitative information required to be audited under subsection (3).

---

[207]   *Ibid.*

Commentary

This provision sets out requirements similar to those for Crown corporations in s. 132(1) of the *Financial Administration Act*.[208]

(2) CONTENTS — A report under subsection (1) shall

(a)   include separate statements as to whether in the auditor's opinion

    (i)   the financial statements are presented fairly, in accordance with generally accepted accounting principles, applied on a basis consistent with that of the preceding year,

    (ii)   the quantitative information is accurate in all material respects and, if applicable, was prepared on a basis consistent with that of the preceding year, and

    (iii) the transactions of the institution that have come to the auditor's notice in the course of his or her examination for the report were carried out in accordance with this Act; and

(b)   call attention to any other matter falling within the scope of the auditor's examination for the report that, in his or her opinion, should be brought to the attention of the institution or the Minister.

Commentary

This provision sets out requirements similar to those for Crown corporations in s. 132(2) of the *Financial Administration Act*.[209]

(3) AUDIT OF QUANTITATIVE INFORMATION — The Minister may require that any quantitative information required to be included in an institution's annual report pursuant to paragraph (2)(a) be audited.

Commentary

This provision sets out requirements similar to those for Crown corporations in s. 132(5) of the *Financial Administration Act*.[210]

(4) PRESENTATION TO MINISTER — Each institution shall submit its audited financial statements to the Minister at least 30 days before the day of its annual meeting.

121. (1) SPECIAL EXAMINATION — Each institution shall, at least once every five years and at any other time required by its board of

---

[208]   *Ibid.*
[209]   *Ibid.*
[210]   *Ibid.*

directors or by the Minister, cause a special examination to be carried out in respect of its operations to determine if the books, records, systems and practices referred to in section 119 were, in the period under examination, maintained in a manner that met the requirements of that section.

(2) PLAN — Before commencing a special examination, an examiner shall survey the systems and practices of the institution to be examined and submit a plan for the examination, including a statement of the criteria to be applied in the examination, to the audit committee of the institution.

(3) RESOLUTION OF DISAGREEMENTS — Any disagreement between the examiner and the audit committee or board of directors of an institution with respect to a plan referred to in subsection (2) shall be resolved by the Minister.

(4) RELIANCE ON INTERNAL AUDIT — An examiner shall, as far as is practicable, rely on any internal audit conducted pursuant to subsection 119(3) in respect of the institution being examined.

Commentary

Subsections 121(1) to (4) set out requirements similar to those for Crown corporations under ss. 138(1) to (5) of the *Financial Administration Act*.[211]

122. (1) REPORT — An examiner shall, on completion of a special examination in respect of an institution, submit a report on his or her findings, and a summary of that report, to the Minister and to the board of directors of the institution.

Commentary

This provision sets out requirements similar to those for Crown corporations in s. 139(1) of the *Financial Administration Act*.[212]

(2) CONTENTS — The report of an examiner shall include

(a) a statement whether in the examiner's opinion, having regard to the criteria referred to in subsection 119(2), there is a reasonable assurance that there are no significant deficiencies in the systems and practices examined; and

(b) a statement of the extent to which the examiner relied on internal audits.

---

[211] *Ibid.*
[212] *Ibid.*

Commentary

This provision sets out requirements similar to those for Crown corporations in s. 139(2) of the *Financial Administration Act*.[213]

(3) POSTING OF REPORT — An institution shall, as soon as possible after receipt of an examiner's report, post a summary of the report on an Internet website maintained by the institution.

123. (1) EXAMINER — Subject to subsection (2), a special examination shall be carried out by the auditor of the institution.

Commentary

This provision sets out requirements similar to those for Crown corporations in s. 142(1) of the *Financial Administration Act*.[214]

(2) OTHER AUDITOR — If, in the opinion of the Minister, a person other than the auditor of an institution should carry out a special examination in respect of the institution, the Minister may, after consulting with the board of directors of the institution, direct that the examination be carried out by another auditor who is qualified for the purpose.

Commentary

This provision sets out requirements similar to those for Crown corporations in s. 142(2) of the *Financial Administration Act*.[215]

124. CONSULTATION WITH AUDITOR GENERAL — The auditor or examiner of an institution may at any time consult the Auditor General of Canada on any matter relating to an audit or special examination.

125. (1) RIGHT TO INFORMATION — At the request of the auditor or examiner of an institution, the present or former commissioners, directors, officers, employees or agents of the institution shall provide any information and explanations, and give access to any records, documents, books, accounts and vouchers of the institution that are under their control, that the auditor or examiner considers necessary to prepare a report required under this Act.

---

[213]   *Ibid.*
[214]   *Ibid.*
[215]   *Ibid.*

(2) OBLIGATION TO INFORM — **If a commissioner or director of an institution does not have information or an explanation requested by an auditor or examiner under subsection (1), the commissioner or director shall obtain the information or explanation and provide it to the auditor or examiner.**

Commentary

Subsections 125(1) and (2) set out requirements similar to those for Crown corporations under ss. 144(1) and (2) of the *Financial Administration Act.*[216]

126. RESTRICTION — **Nothing in this Part or in any directions of the Minister shall be construed as authorizing the auditor or examiner of an institution to express any opinion on the merits of matters of policy, including the merits of**

(a) **the objects or purposes for which the institution was established or the restrictions on the businesses or activities that it may carry on, as set out in this Act; or**

(b) **any business or policy decision of the institution.**

Commentary

This provision sets out requirements similar to those for Crown corporations in s. 145 of the *Financial Administration Act.*[217]

127. QUALIFIED PRIVILEGE — **An oral or written statement or report made under this Part by an auditor or examiner has qualified privilege.**

Commentary

This provision sets out requirements similar to those for Crown corporations in s. 146 of the *Financial Administration Act.*[218]

128. (1) AUDIT COMMITTEE — **Each institution shall establish an audit committee composed of not less than three commissioners or directors who are not officers of the institution and who are competent to perform the duties set out in subsection (2).**

(2) **DUTIES** — **An audit committee shall**

---

[216]   *Ibid.*
[217]   *Ibid.*
[218]   *Ibid.*

(a) review, and advise the board of directors in respect of, the financial statements that are to be included in the annual report of the institution;

(b) oversee any internal audit of the institution;

(c) review, and advise the board of directors in respect of, the annual auditor's report in respect of the institution;

(d) review, and advise the board of directors in respect of, any plan and report of a special examiner; and

(e) perform any other functions that are assigned to it by the board of directors of the institution.

(3) AUDITOR'S OR EXAMINER'S ATTENDANCE — An auditor and any examiner of an institution are entitled to receive notice of every meeting of the audit committee and, at the expense of the institution, to attend and be heard at each meeting.

(4) REQUIRED ATTENDANCE — The auditor or examiner of an institution shall attend any meeting of the institution's audit committee at which he or she is requested to attend by a member of that committee.

(5) CALLING MEETING — The auditor or examiner of an institution or a member of the institution's audit committee may call a meeting of that committee.

Commentary

Subsections 128(1) to (5) set out requirements similar to those for Crown corporations under ss. 148(1), (3), (4) and (5) of the *Financial Administration Act*.[219]

129. DISCLOSURE OF MATERIAL DEVELOPMENTS — The chief executive officer of an institution shall, as soon as reasonably practicable, notify the Minister and any commissioner or director of the institution not already aware of them of any financial or other developments that, in the chief executive officer's opinion, are likely to have a material effect on the performance of the institution, relative to its objectives or requirements for funding.

Commentary

This provision sets out requirements similar to those for Crown corporations in s. 149(2) of the *Financial Administration Act*.[220]

---

[219]   *Ibid.*
[220]   *Ibid.*

130. (1) ANNUAL REPORT — Each institution shall, within four months after the end of each financial year, submit to the Minister an annual report on the operations of the institution in that year.

Commentary

This provision sets out requirements similar to those for Crown corporations in s. 150(1) of the *Financial Administration Act*.[221]

(2) FORM AND CONTENTS — The annual report of an institution shall be prepared in a form that clearly sets out information according to the major businesses or activities of the institution and shall include

(a)   the financial statements of the institution;

(b)   the annual auditor's report;

(c)   a statement on the extent to which the institution has met its objectives for the financial year;

(d)   any quantitative information respecting the performance of the institution that the Minister may require to be included; and

(e)   any other information that is required under this Act or any other Act of Parliament.

Commentary

This provision sets out requirements similar to those for Crown corporations in s. 150(3) of the *Financial Administration Act*.[222]

131. (1) ANNUAL MEETING — The board of directors of an institution shall call an annual meeting not later than 18 months after the institution is established and subsequently not later than 15 months after the preceding annual meeting.

(2) NOTICE OF MEETING — An institution shall, at least 30 days before the annual meeting, publish a notice in a major newspaper setting out the time and location of the meeting and specifying that the institution's annual report may be accessed on an Internet website to be maintained by the institution.

Commentary

The present website for the First Nations Tax Commission is <http://www.fntc.ca/main.phtml>. The present website for the First Nations Financial Management Board is <http://www.fnfmb.com/en/index.htm>.

---

[221]   *Ibid.*

[222]   *Ibid.*

(3) AVAILABILITY TO PUBLIC — At the annual meeting, the board of directors shall ensure that

(a)   there are available a sufficient number of copies of the institution's most recent annual report for those present at the meeting; and

(b)   the chief executive officer and the commissioners or directors of the institution are available to those present at the meeting to answer any questions about the institution's operations.

PART 7

PROVISIONS OF GENERAL APPLICATION

General

132. (1) CONFLICT OF INTEREST — No person who is appointed to, or is employed by, a commission, board, authority or institute established under this Act shall be appointed to, or be employed by, any other commission, board, authority or institute established under this Act.

(2) CONFLICT OF INTEREST — No person referred to in subsection (1) shall accept or hold any office or employment that is inconsistent with that person's duties or take part in any matter involving the commission, board, authority or institute in which that person has an interest.

(3) CONFLICT OF INTEREST — All persons appointed to a commission, board or institute established under this Act shall comply with the *Conflict of Interest and Post-Employment Code for Public Office Holders*, issued by the Office of the Ethics Counsellor, as amended from time to time, as though they were public office holders as defined in that Code.

Commentary

A copy of the *Conflict of Interest and Post-Employment Code for Public Office Holders* can be obtained at the Privy Council Office website at http:// strategis.ic.gc.ca/epic/internet/inoec-bce.nsf/vwapj/coi_2004.pdf/$FILE /coi_2004.pdf.

133. (1) LIABILITY OF HER MAJESTY — No person has a right to receive any compensation, damages, indemnity or other relief from Her Majesty in right of Canada in respect of any claim against the First Nations Tax Commission, First Nations Financial Management Board, First Nations Finance Authority or First Nations Statistical Institute arising from its exercise of, or its failure to exercise, any of the powers or functions of that Commission, Board, Authority or Institute, as the case may be, including any claim against the First Nations Tax Commission as an agent of Her Majesty in right of Canada.

(2) INSURANCE REQUIRED — The First Nations Tax Commission, First Nations Financial Management Board, First Nations Finance Authority and First Nations Statistical Institute shall maintain in good standing at all times the insurance coverage required by any regulations made under paragraph 140(b).

Commentary

At the time of publication, no regulations had been proposed to be made under this subsection.

134. NO APPROPRIATION — No payment to the First Nations Tax Commission, First Nations Financial Management Board, First Nations Finance Authority or First Nations Statistical Institute may be made under an appropriation by Parliament authorized under an Act of Parliament to enable the Commission, Board, Authority or Institute to satisfy any claim referred to in subsection 133(1).

135. NO COMPENSATION — No person has a right to receive any compensation, damages, indemnity or other relief from Her Majesty in right of Canada, or from the First Nations Tax Commission, for any acquired, vested or future right, or for any prospect of such a right, that is affected by a law approved by the First Nations Tax Commission under subsection 31(3), or for any duty or liability imposed on that person as a result of such a law.

136. LIMIT OF LIABILITY — No civil proceedings lie against a commissioner or employee of the First Nations Tax Commission, or any director or employee of the First Nations Financial Management Board or First Nations Statistical Institute, for anything done, or omitted to be done, in the exercise or purported exercise in good faith of any power, or in the performance or purported performance in good faith of any duty, of that person in accordance with this Act.

137. LIMIT OF LIABILITY — No civil proceedings lie against a member of a council or an employee of a first nation for anything done, or omitted to be done, during the course of the exercise or purported exercise in good faith of any power, or the performance or purported performance in good faith of any duty, of that member or employee in accordance with this Act, regulations made under this Act or a law made by the council of a first nation under this Act.

138. (1) CONFLICT WITH OTHER LAWS — In the event of a conflict between a local revenue law and an Act of Parliament or any regulations made under an Act of Parliament or a code made by a first nation under another Act of Parliament, the Act, regulations or code prevails to the extent of the conflict.

Commentary

This provision overrides judicial rulings made in cases such as *R. v. Blackbird*,[223] *R. v. Jimmy*,[224] *R. v. Baker*,[225] and *R. v. Meechance*,[226] which have suggested that in some circumstances band by-laws made under the *Indian Act* have priority over federal regulations.

An example of a code referred to in this subsection would be land codes adopted under s. 6(1) of the *First Nations Land Management Act*.[227]

(2) CONFLICT WITH OTHER FIRST NATION LAWS — In the event of a conflict between a law made by a first nation under this Act and a law, other than a code, made by the first nation under another Act of Parliament, the law made by the first nation under this Act prevails to the extent of the conflict.

139. (1) OFFICIAL LANGUAGES — For greater certainty, the provisions of the *Official Languages Act* applicable to federal institutions apply to the First Nations Tax Commission and First Nations Statistical Institute.

Commentary

The First Nations Tax Commission and First Nations Statistical Institute qualify as federal institutions under paragraphs (g) and (h) of the definition of that term in s. 3(1) of the *Official Languages Act*:[228]

> "federal institution" includes any of the following institutions of the Parliament or government of Canada: ...
>
> > (g) a Crown corporation established by or pursuant to an Act of Parliament, and
> >
> > (h) any other body that is specified by an Act of Parliament to be an agent of Her Majesty in right of Canada or to be subject to the direction of the Governor in Council or a minister of the Crown, ...

---

[223] [2003] O.J. No. 1102 (S.C.).
[224] [1987] B.C.J. No. 1516, [1987] 5 W.W.R. 755 (C.A.).
[225] [1983] B.C.J. No. 2383, [1983] 4 C.N.L.R. 73 (Co. Ct.).
[226] [2000] S.J. No. 203, 193 Sask. R. 109 (Q.B.).
[227] S.C. 1999, c. 24.
[228] R.S., 1985, c. 31 (4th Supp.).

They are therefore required by s. 22 of that Act to provide certain services in both official languages:

> 22. Every federal institution has the duty to ensure that any member of the public can communicate with and obtain available services from its head or central office in either official language, and has the same duty with respect to any of its other offices or facilities
>
> (a) within the National Capital Region; or
>
> (b) in Canada or elsewhere, where there is significant demand for communications with and services from that office or facility in that language.

(2) OFFICIAL LANGUAGES — Where there is a significant demand for services in a particular official language, the First Nations Financial Management Board and First Nations Finance Authority shall offer services in that language.

Commentary

Although the First Nations Financial Management Board and First Nations Finance Authority do not qualify as "federal institutions" for the purposes of the *Official Languages Act*,[229] this subsection sets out a lesser requirement for bilingual services where a demand exists.

Regulations

140. REGULATIONS — The Governor in Council may make regulations

(a) prescribing anything that is to be prescribed under subsection 20(3) or 41(2) or section 116; and

(b) prescribing the insurance coverage required to be maintained by the First Nations Tax Commission, First Nations Financial Management Board, First Nations Finance Authority and First Nations Statistical Institute in respect of liabilities referred to in subsection 133(1).

Commentary

The regulations proposed to be made under s. 20(3) are the *First Nations Tax Commissioner Appointment Regulations*.

At the time of publication, no regulations have been proposed to be made under s. 41(2), 116 or 133(1).

---

[229]   *Ibid.*

141. REGULATIONS — For the purpose of enabling an aboriginal group that is not a band as defined in subsection 2(1) of the *Indian Act* but is a party to a treaty, land claims agreement or self-government agreement with Canada to benefit from the provisions of this Act or obtain the services of any body established under this Act, the Governor in Council may make any regulations that the Governor in Council considers necessary, including regulations

(a) adapting any provision of this Act or of any regulation made under this Act; and

(b) restricting the application of any provision of this Act or of any regulation made under this Act.

Commentary

Because additions to the schedule to the Act under s. 2(3) are limited to bands under the *Indian Act*, this provision is necessary to enable aboriginal groups that are not bands to opt into the Act if they so choose. The definition of "band" in s. 2(1) of the *Indian Act* reads as follows:

"band" means a body of Indians

(a) for whose use and benefit in common, lands, the legal title to which is vested in Her Majesty, have been set apart before, on or after September 4, 1951,

(b) for whose use and benefit in common, moneys are held by Her Majesty, or

(c) declared by the Governor in Council to be a band for the purposes of this Act;

Although some aboriginal groups that have negotiated self-government agreements might technically meet the requirements of at least paragraph (a) and therefore theoretically be considered as a "band" within the meaning of that definition, most such groups are no longer considered to be bands for the purposes of the *Indian Act*. These groups could, however, request that regulations be made under this section to enable them to exercise powers or become borrowing members under the FNFSMA. Because the FNFSMA is geared to First Nations that have been exercising taxation powers under s. 83 of the *Indian Act*, certain accommodations may be necessary in order for the FNFSMA to apply properly to such self-governing aboriginal groups. Regulations made under this section can therefore adapt the provisions of the FNFSMA in whatever manner is necessary in order to achieve this objective.

Regulation-making powers of this sort are often referred to as "Henry VIII clauses".

In order to address uncertainties as to whether this section would apply to the Westbank First Nation, which exercises some governmental powers under the *Westbank First Nation Self-Government Act*[230] and other powers under the

---

[230]   S.C. 2004, c. 17.

Indian Act, amendments to the *Westbank First Nation Self-Government Act* were made by s. 153 of this Act to provide a similar option to the Westbank First Nation.

142. REGULATIONS — The Governor in Council may make regulations

(a) **prescribing anything that is to be prescribed for the purposes of paragraph 74(b); and**

(b) **adapting or restricting any provision of this Act or of any regulation made under this Act for the purposes of paragraph 74(b).**

Commentary

Paragraph 74(b) of the Act relates to the ability of the First Nations Finance Authority to secure financing for its borrowing members through the use of revenues, other than property taxation revenues, that are prescribed by regulation. Such regulations would also prescribe the purpose for which such financing could be used.

At the time of publication, no regulations had been proposed under this section.

PART 8

TRANSITIONAL PROVISIONS, CONSEQUENTIAL AMENDMENTS, COORDINATING AMENDMENTS AND COMING INTO FORCE

Transitional Provisions

143. (1) ITAB EMPLOYEES — Persons who are employed by the Indian Taxation Advisory Board at the time that the First Nations Tax Commission is established shall be offered employment with the Commission, at the same salary and with equivalent terms and conditions of employment.

Commentary

This subsection constrains the powers of the First Nations Tax Commission to fix the salaries and benefits of its employees under s. 28(2) of the Act.

(2) INTERIM RULES OF PROCEDURE — Until new rules are established by the First Nations Tax Commission, the Commission shall conduct itself in accordance with the rules of procedure established by the Indian Taxation Advisory Board.

Commentary

Although s. 34(1) requires the procedures established by the Commission to be published in the *First Nations Gazette*, no mention is made under that section regarding publication of the rules of procedure referred to in this section.

144. CONTINUATION OF DIRECTORS — Persons who are directors of the First Nations Finance Authority Inc., a corporation incorporated under the *Canada Business Corporations Act*, on the day on which section 58 comes into force shall continue as directors of the First Nations Finance Authority until new directors are elected.

Commentary

The First Nations Finance Authority Inc. is a private sector corporation that is a legal entity distinct from the First Nations Finance Authority established under s. 58 of the Act. As mentioned in the 8th preamble, it has been in operation since 1995.

145. (1) CONTINUATION OF EXISTING BY-LAWS — By-laws made by a first nation under paragraph 83(1)(a), or any of paragraphs 83(1)(d) to (g), of the *Indian Act* that are in force on the day on which the name of the first nation is added to the schedule are deemed to be laws made under section 5 or 9, as the case may be, to the extent that they are not inconsistent with section 5 or 9, and remain in force until they are repealed or replaced.

Commentary

This subsection provides that taxation by-laws and financial administration by-laws that were made by a First Nation under s. 83 of the *Indian Act* will be treated as laws made under s. 5 or 9 of the FNFSMA, when a First Nation opts into the FNFSMA. They will be operative, however, only to the extent that they conform to the requirements of ss. 5 and 9 of the Act, and to the requirements of the regulations made under those sections.

(2) AMENDMENT OF EXISTING BY-LAWS — For greater certainty, subsections 5(2) to (7) apply to amendments of by-laws referred to in subsection (1).

Commentary

This subsection essentially confirms that, after *Indian Act* by-laws referred to in s. 145(1) are deemed to be laws made under this Act, the requirements of ss. 5(2) to (7) of the Act will apply to all subsequent amendments to them. This includes the requirement that any subsequent amendments be approved by the First Nations Tax Commission under s. 5(2).

146. REVIEW AND EVALUATION — **Within seven years after the day on which this Act receives royal assent, the Minister, after consultation with the First Nations Tax Commission, First Nations Financial Management Board, First Nations Finance Authority and First Nations Statistical Institute, shall review the provisions and operation of this Act and the operations of those institutions, and submit a report to each House of Parliament on that review, including any changes that the Minister recommends relating to the evolution of the mandate and operation of those institutions.**

Commentary

Note that the requirement under this section is to report *within* seven years, which would technically permit the Minister to conduct a review at an earlier date if he or she so chose.

Consequential Amendments

ACCESS TO INFORMATION ACT

147. Schedule I to the *Access to Information Act* is amended by adding the following in alphabetical order under the heading "Other Government Institutions":

First Nations Financial Management Board
   Conseil de gestion financière des premières nations

First Nations Statistical Institute
   Institut de la statistique des premières nations

First Nations Tax Commission
   Commission de la fiscalité des premières nations

Commentary

The effect of this amendment to the *Access to Information Act*[231] is to include the First Nations Financial Management Board, First Nations Statistical Institute and First Nations Tax Commission within the category of bodies considered to be government institutions under that Act. The purpose of the *Access to Information Act* is to provide a right of access to information in records under the control of government institutions.[232]

148. Schedule II to the Act is amended by adding, in alphabetical order, a reference to

---

[231] R.S.C. 1985, c. A-1.
[232] *Access to Information Act*, s. 2(1).

First Nations Fiscal and Statistical Management Act

Loi sur la gestion financière et statistique des premières nations

and a corresponding reference in respect of that Act to "section 108".

Commentary

The effect of this amendment to the *Access to Information Act*[233] is to provide that information in records referred to in s. 108 of the FNFSMA are exempt from the disclosure requirements under the *Access to Information Act*.

FINANCIAL ADMINISTRATION ACT

149. Part I of Schedule III to the *Financial Administration Act* is amended by adding the following in alphabetical order:

First Nations Statistical Institute

Institut de la statistique des premières nations

Commentary

This amendment adds the First Nations Statistical Institute to Part 1 of the Schedule III to the *Financial Administration Act*,[234] which sets out Crown corporations that are essentially non-profit.[235]

INDIAN ACT

150. The portion of subsection 87(1) of the *Indian Act* before paragraph (a) is replaced by the following:

87. (1) PROPERTY EXEMPT FROM TAXATION — Notwithstanding any other Act of Parliament or any Act of the legislature of a province, but subject to section 83 and section 5 of the *First Nations Fiscal and Statistical Management Act*, the following property is exempt from taxation:

Commentary

Subsection 87(1) of the *Indian Act* exempts reserve lands and the property of Indians on reserve lands from taxation:

> 87. (1) Notwithstanding any other Act of Parliament or any
> Act of the legislature of a province, but subject to section 83,
> the following property is exempt from taxation, namely,

---

[233] R.S.C. 1985, c. A-1.

[234] R.S.C. 1985, c. F-11.

[235] Crown corporations that are expected to earn a return on equity and pay dividends are set out in Part II of Schedule III of that Act: see s. 3(5) of the *Financial Administration Act*.

(a) the interest of an Indian or a band in reserve lands or surrendered lands; and

(b) the personal property of an Indian or a band situated on a reserve.

The effect of the amendment made by s. 150 of the FNFSMA is to except out taxation under the FNFSMA from the s. 87 *Indian Act* exemption. Without this amendment First Nations would not be able to use the FNFSMA to tax interests in reserve lands held by Indians.

151. Section 88 of the Act is replaced by the following:

88. GENERAL PROVINCIAL LAWS APPLICABLE TO INDIANS — Subject to the terms of any treaty and any other Act of Parliament, all laws of general application from time to time in force in any province are applicable to and in respect of Indians in the province, except to the extent that those laws are inconsistent with this Act or the *First Nations Fiscal and Statistical Management Act*, or with any order, rule, regulation or law of a band made under those Acts, and except to the extent that those provincial laws make provision for any matter for which provision is made by or under those Acts.

Commentary

This amendment adds the words "or the *First Nations Fiscal and Statistical Management Act*" to s. 88 of the *Indian Act*, and makes consequential grammatical changes. The effect of this amendment to s. 88 of the *Indian Act* is to provide that provincial laws of general application will not apply to Indians if the provincial laws are inconsistent with the FNFSMA. The exclusion of provincial laws that are inconsistent with the *Indian Act*, which the section already provided for before the amendment, remains in place under the amendment.

PRIVACY ACT

152. The schedule to the *Privacy Act* is amended by adding the following in alphabetical order under the heading "Other Government Institutions":

First Nations Financial Management Board
Conseil de gestion financière des premières nations

First Nations Statistical Institute
Institut de la statistique des premières nations

First Nations Tax Commission
Commission de la fiscalité des premières nations

Commentary

The effect of this amendment to the *Privacy Act*[236] is to include the First Nations Financial Management Board, First Nations Statistical Institute and First Nations Tax Commission within the category of bodies considered to be government institutions under that Act. The purpose of the *Privacy Act* is to protect the privacy of the personal information of individuals held by government institutions.[237]

WESTBANK FIRST NATION SELF-GOVERNMENT ACT

153. The *Westbank First Nation Self-Government Act* **is amended by adding the following after section 8:**

8.1 *FIRST NATIONS FISCAL AND STATISTICAL MANAGEMENT ACT* — **Notwithstanding any provision of this Act or the Agreement, for the purpose of enabling the Westbank First Nation to benefit from the provisions of the** *First Nations Fiscal and Statistical Management Act* **or obtain the services of any body established under that Act, the Governor in Council may make any regulations that the Governor in Council considers necessary, including regulations**

   (a)   adapting any provision of that Act or of any regulation made under that Act; and

   (b)   restricting the application of any provision of that Act or of any regulation made under that Act.

Commentary

In order to address uncertainties as to whether section 141 of the Act would apply to the Westbank First Nation, which exercises some governmental powers under the *Westbank First Nation Self-Government Act*[238] and other powers under the *Indian Act*, amendments to the *Westbank First Nation Self-Government Act* were made by this section to provide an option to the Westbank First Nation to request regulations to come under this Act.

Regulations made under this section can adapt the provisions of the Act in whatever manner is necessary in order to make the Act properly apply to the Westbank First Nation. Regulation-making powers of this sort are often referred to as "Henry VIII clauses".

---

[236]   R.S.C. 1985, c. P-21.
[237]   *Privacy Act*, s. 2.
[238]   S.C. 2004, c. 17.

Coordinating Amendments

154. (1) On the later of the coming into force of section 8 of the *Public Service Modernization Act* **and subsection 60(1) of this Act, subsection 60(1) of the English version of this Act is replaced by the following:**

60. (1) NOT AGENT OF HER MAJESTY — The Authority is not an agent of Her Majesty or a Crown corporation within the meaning of the *Financial Administration Act,*[239] **and its officers and employees are not part of the federal public administration.**

Commentary

Section 8 of the *Public Service Modernization Act* changes the terminology used in statutes from the "public service", which is used in s. 60(1) of the FNFSMA, to the "federal public administration". Because the *Public Service Modernization Act* was not in force when the FNFSMA was introduced in Parliament, the change of wording could not be immediately introduced into the FNFSMA. Subsection 154(1) was therefore added to make the appropriate change automatically when s. 8 of the *Public Service Modernization Act* came into force, which occurred on April 1, 2005.[240]

(2) On the later of the coming into force of section 8 of the *Public Service Modernization Act* **and subsection 115(1) of this Act, subsection 115(1) of the English version of this Act is replaced by the following:**

115. (1) EXCLUSION FROM FEDERAL PUBLIC ADMINIS-TRATION — The officers and employees of an institution are not part of the federal public administration.

Commentary

Section 8 of the *Public Service Modernization Act* changes the terminology used in statutes from the "public service", which is used in s. 115(1) of the FNFSMA, to the "federal public administration". Because the *Public Service Modernization Act* was not in force when the FNFSMA was introduced in Parliament, the change of wording could not be immediately introduced into the FNFSMA. Subsection 154(2) was therefore added to make the appropriate change automatically when s. 8 of the *Public Service Modernization Act* came into force.

---

[239]   R.S.C. 1985, c. F-11.
[240]   SI/2005-25.

COMING INTO FORCE

155. ORDER IN COUNCIL — The provisions of this Act, other than section 154, come into force on a day or days to be fixed by order of the Governor in Council.

Commentary

Under this section, the provisions of the FNFSMA, other than the coordinating provisions set out in ss. 154(1) and (2), take effect only when they are brought into force by an order of the Governor in Council. The dates on which such orders are made can be determined by consulting the Table of Public Statutes, which is published in print form by the Department of Justice on an annual basis. It can be accessed on the website of the Department of Justice.[241]

SCHEDULE

(Subsections 2(1) and (3))

Commentary

By virtue of paragraph (b) of the definition of "First Nation" in s. 2(1), a reference to a First Nation in Part 1 (dealing with taxation powers of First Nations) or any of Parts 2 to 4 (dealing with the fiscal institutions) is a reference only to the *Indian Act* bands that are listed in the Schedule. Part 5, which deals with the First Nations Statistical Institute, applies to all *Indian Act* bands, whether they are listed in the Schedule or not.

The names of First Nations that have opted into the Act are added to the Schedule by Orders made by the Governor in Council under s. 2(3) of the Act. These Orders will be published in the *Canada Gazette* Part II.

---

[241]   <http://laws.justice.gc.ca/en/publaw/>

DEBT RESERVE FUND REPLENISHMENT REGULATIONS

Introductory Commentary

The *Debt Reserve Fund Replenishment Regulations* are one of the set of regulations proposed to be made under the *First Nations Fiscal and Statistical Management Act*.[242] The regulations have not yet been made, but have been released by the government for consultation purposes.[243]

The regulations are to be made under ss. 84(5) and 89(c) of the *First Nations Fiscal and Statistical Management Act*, respecting the imposition of charges to replenish shortfalls in the First Nations Finance Authority's debt reserve fund, including the manner of calculating those charges and the share of those charges to be paid by each borrowing member. The debt reserve fund is a fund established under s. 84(1) of the Act to make payments or sinking fund contributions on bond issues if there are insufficient moneys available from the borrowing members participating in the bond issue. The fund is initially capitalized by holding back 5 per cent of the amount of funds borrowed by First Nations on bond issues.

The regulations:

- provide for advance notice to borrowing members prior to imposing charges; and

- determine how the amount of the charge for each borrowing member is to be determined.

The regulations are expected to come into force on the same date on which the *First Nations Fiscal and Statistical Management Act* comes into force.

---

[242] S.C. 2005, c. 9.
[243] Available at First Nations Fiscal Initiative website at <http://www.fnfi.ca>.

DEBT RESERVE FUND REPLENISHMENT REGULATIONS
(PROPOSED)

Her Excellency the Governor in Council, on the recommendation of the Minister of Indian Affairs and Northern Development, pursuant to subsection 84(5) and paragraph 89(*c*) of the *First Nations Fiscal and Statistical Management Act*, hereby makes the annexed *Debt Reserve Fund Replenishment Regulations*.

Commentary

The introductory Order in Council sets out the enabling authorities for the *Debt Reserve Fund Replenishment Regulations*, which are ss. 84(5) and 89(c) of the *First Nations Fiscal and Statistical Management Act*. Paragraph 89(c) is the general regulation-making power:

> 89. The Governor in Council may, on the recommendation of the Minister after consultation by the Minister with the Authority, make regulations ...

> (c) respecting the imposition of charges under subsection 84(5), including the manner of calculating those charges and the share of those charges to be paid by each borrowing member;

Note that the regulations are to be made on the recommendation of the Minister of Indian Affairs and Northern Development, after consultation by the Minister with the First Nations Finance Authority. The italicized text in paragraph (a) establishes the link to the requirement for regulations setting out a scheme for the imposition of charges to replenish shortfalls in the debt reserve fund in s. 84(5). It reads as follows:

> (5) If payments from the debt reserve fund reduce its balance

> (a) by less than 50% of the total amount contributed by borrowing members, the Authority may, *in accordance with the regulations*, require all borrowing members to pay amounts sufficient to replenish the debt reserve fund; and

> (b) by 50% or more of the total amount contributed by borrowing members,

> (i) the Authority shall, *in accordance with the regulations*, require all borrowing members to pay without delay amounts sufficient to replenish the debt reserve fund, and

> (ii) the borrowing members shall recover those amounts under their property taxation laws.

The italicised wording provides the link between the Act and the *Debt Reserve Fund Replenishment Regulations*.

DEBT RESERVE FUND REPLENISHMENT REGULATIONS

DEFINITIONS

1. DEFINITIONS — The following definitions apply in these Regulations.

"Act"
« Loi »

"Act" means the *First Nations Fiscal and Statistical Management Act*.

"defaulting member"
« membre en défaut »

"defaulting member" means a borrowing member whose failure to make a payment under a loan obligation agreement with the Authority or to pay a charge imposed under subsection 84(5) of the Act has led to a reduction in the debt reserve fund.

Commentary

A "borrowing member" is defined in s. 2(1) of the Act as a First Nation that has been accepted as a borrowing member by the First Nations Finance Authority under s. 76(2) of the Act. The debt reserve fund is a fund established under s. 84(1) of the Act to make payments or sinking fund contributions on bond issues if there are insufficient moneys available from the borrowing members participating in the bond issue. The fund is initially capitalized by holding back 5 per cent of the amount of funds borrowed by First Nations on bond issues.

Subsection 84(5) of the Act permits the Authority to impose charges on all of its borrowing members (whether they are participating in the bond issue or not) to replenish the debt reserve fund if it has fallen by less than 50 per cent. If the fund has fallen by more than 50 per cent, the Authority is required to impose such charges.

GENERAL

2. (1) NOTICE OF PROPOSED CHARGE — The Authority shall send a notice to the council of every borrowing member of the amount of the shortfall in the fund, and of any intention to require borrowing members to replenish the debt reserve fund under paragraph 84(5)(*a*) or (*b*) of the Act, at least 90 days in advance of imposing charges under that paragraph.

(2) CONTENT OF NOTICE — A notice referred to in subsection **(1)** shall identify each defaulting member and, if there are two or more defaulting members, the amount of the shortfall attributable to each.

3. DEFAULTING MEMBER — During the period referred to in section **2**, the Authority shall determine what amount each defaulting member is able to pay as a charge for the purpose of replenishing the debt reserve fund.

Commentary

This provision contemplates that the same circumstances that led a defaulting member to default on its payment obligations to the First Nations Finance Authority may prevent it from paying a full pro-rata share of the shortfall.

4. CALCULATION OF CHARGES — On the expiry of the period referred to in section **2**, the Authority

(*a*) shall send to the council of each defaulting member a notice imposing a charge on that borrowing member equal to the amount negotiated under section **3**; and

(*b*) shall send to the council of every other borrowing member a notice imposing a charge on that borrowing member equal to the amount determined by the formula

$A/(B-C) \times (D-E)$

where

A   is the gross annual property tax revenue of the borrowing member,

B   is the aggregate gross annual property tax revenue of all borrowing members,

C   is the aggregate gross annual property tax revenue by defaulting members,

D   is the amount of the shortfall in the debt reserve fund set out in the notice referred to in section **2**, and

E   is the amount charged to defaulting members under section **3**.

Commentary

The repayment formula is premised on each non-defaulting borrowing member paying a share of the shortfall based on that borrowing member's tax revenues. The first part of the formula $A/(B-C)$ calculates the borrowing member's tax revenues as a proportion of the tax revenues of all borrowing members combined, less the tax revenues of the defaulting members. The borrowing member's proportion of the total tax revenues is then multiplied by the amount of the shortfall (D), less any amounts that the Authority has managed to negotiate from the defaulting members (E).

COMING INTO FORCE

5. COMING INTO FORCE DATE — These Regulations come into force on [the day on which they are registered/specified date].

Commentary

The regulations are expected to come into force on the same date on which tthe *First Nations Fiscal and Statistical Management Act* comes into force.

FIRST NATIONS ASSESSMENT APPEAL REGULATIONS

Introductory Commentary

The *First Nations Assessment Appeal Regulations* are one of the set of regulations proposed to be made under the *First Nations Fiscal and Statistical Management Act*.[244] The regulations have not yet been made, but have been released by the government for consultation purposes.[245]

The regulations are made under ss. 36(1)(a) and (d) of the *First Nations Fiscal and Statistical Management Act*, and set out the procedures required by s. 5(4)(a) of the Act to be included in First Nation property taxation laws.

The regulations establish a minimum limitation period for the appeal of an assessment under a First Nation law. The regulations also require that First Nation property taxation laws include a number of specified procedures:

- for requesting reconsideration of an assessment by the First Nation tax administrator;
- for the composition of an Assessment Review Board;
- prescribing the content of notices of appeal;
- for the exchange of documentation; and
- for the conduct of hearing.

The regulations are expected to come into force on the same date on which the *First Nations Fiscal and Statistical Management Act* comes into force.

---

[244] S.C. 2005, c. 9.
[245] Available at First Nations Fiscal Initiative website at <http://www.fnfi.ca>.

FIRST NATIONS ASSESSMENT APPEAL REGULATIONS
(PROPOSED)

Her Excellency the Governor in Council, on the recommendation of the Minister of Indian Affairs and Northern Development, pursuant to paragraphs 5(4)(*a*) and 36(1)(*a*) and (*d*) of the *First Nations Fiscal and Statistical Management Act*, hereby makes the annexed *First Nations Assessment Appeal Regulations*.

Commentary

The introductory Order in Council sets out the enabling authorities for the *First Nations Assessment Appeal Regulations*, which are ss. 5(4)(*a*) and 36(1)(*a*) and (*d*) of the *First Nations Fiscal and Statistical Management Act*. Paragraphs 36(1)(*a*) and (*d*) are the general regulation-making powers:

> 36. (1) The Governor in Council may, on the recommendation of the Minister made having regard to any representations by the Commission, make regulations
>
> (a) *prescribing anything that is to be prescribed under* subparagraph 5(1)(a)(i), *paragraph* 5(1)(e) *or (4)(a)*, subsection 5(7) or section 10; ...
>
> (d) *respecting the exercise of the law-making powers of first nations under subsection 5(1)*.

Note that the regulations are to be made on the recommendation of the Minister of Indian Affairs and Northern Development, after consultation by the Minister with the First Nations Tax Commission.

The italicized text in paragraph (a) establishes the link to the requirement for regulations set out in s. 5(4)(a) of the Act. Paragraph 5(4)(a) requires property taxation laws to include an appeal procedure:

> (4) A law made under paragraph (1)(a) shall include
>
> (a) an appeal procedure in respect of assessments, *incorporating such procedures as are prescribed by regulation*; and
>
> (b) fixed rates of remuneration and fixed terms of office for any persons designated to decide the appeals.

The italicised wording provides the link between the Act and the *First Nations Assessment Appeal Regulations*.

FIRST NATIONS ASSESSMENT APPEAL REGULATIONS

INTERPRETATION

1. DEFINITIONS — The following definitions apply in these Regulations.

"appellant"
« appelant »
"appellant" means a person who commences an appeal under section 6.

Commentary

Section 6 provides for appeals of property tax assessments.

"Assessment Review Board"
« comité »
"Assessment Review Board" means the committee referred to in section 6.

Commentary

Section 6 requires that such committees be composed of at least 3 members.

"parties"
« parties »
"parties" means the appellant, the first nation and the first nation's tax assessor and tax administrator.

Commentary

The terms "tax assessor" and "tax administrator" are defined below.

"registered"
« enregistré »
"registered", in respect of an interest in reserve lands or a right to occupy, possess or use reserve lands, means registered in the Reserve Land Register, the Surrendered and Designated Lands Register, the First Nations Land Register or a provincial registry or land titles system.

Commentary

The Reserve Land Register is established under s. 21 of the *Indian Act*. The Surrendered and Designated Lands Register is established under s. 55(1) of the

Indian Act. The First Nations Land Register is established under s. 25(1) of the *First Nation Land Management Act.*[246]

"tax administrator"
« *administrateur fiscal* »

"tax administrator" means the person designated by a first nation to administer a property taxation law.

"tax assessor"
« *évaluateur* »

"tax assessor" means the person designated by a first nation to conduct assessments of taxable property.

"taxable property"
« *bien imposable* »

"taxable property" means an interest in reserve lands, or a right to occupy, possess or use reserve lands, that is subject to taxation under a property taxation law.

Commentary

The definition of taxable property follows the wording of s. 5(1)(a) of the Act that describes the types of rights and interests in reserve land that can be taxed.

PRESCRIBED PROCEDURES

2. REQUIRED PROCEDURES — A property taxation law shall incorporate the procedures set out in sections 3 to 16.

Commentary

Paragraph 5(4)(a) of the Act provides that property taxation laws are to include the appeal procedures that are prescribed by regulation. Although the requirements of ss. 3 to 16 of the regulations do not refer to property taxation laws *per se*, by virtue of s. 2 the procedures and requirements set out in those sections are required to be incorporated into every property taxation law.

REQUESTS FOR RECONSIDERATION

3. (1) REQUEST FOR RECONSIDERATION — Within 30 days after receipt of an assessment notice in respect of taxable property, a taxpayer may request a reconsideration of the assessment of the property.

---

[246] S.C. 1999, c. 24.

(2) FORM OF REQUEST — A request for reconsideration of an assessment shall be made in writing and delivered to the tax administrator of the first nation on behalf of whom the assessment was made.

4. REVIEW BY TAX ASSESSOR — Within 30 days after receipt of a request for reconsideration of an assessment, the tax assessor shall review the assessment of the taxable property in question, and provide the taxpayer with the results of his or her reconsideration.

5. (1) OFFER TO MODIFY ASSESSMENT — Where after reconsideration of an assessment a tax assessor concludes that the taxable property should have been assessed at a different value, the assessor shall offer to modify the assessment to reflect that value.

(2) MODIFICATION OF TAX ROLL — Where the taxpayer accepts the offer to modify the assessment, the tax assessor shall modify the tax roll to reflect the revised value.

(3) NO APPEAL — A taxpayer who accepts an offer to modify the assessment shall not appeal the assessment and shall withdraw any Notice of Appeal filed under section 8.

Commentary

Sections 3 to 5 of the regulations put in place an informal procedure by which the taxpayer can obtain a review of a property tax assessment without implementing a formal appeal. Note that although s. 3 speaks of a "request" for a reconsideration, because the tax assessor is required to conduct the reconsideration, the request is more in the nature of a right.

Under s. 5(3), a taxpayer who accepts the reconsidered assessment is bound by that figure and cannot thereafter appeal the assessment in the hopes of lowering it further.

APPEAL PROCEDURES

6. (1) REVIEW BOARD MEMBERSHIP — An assessment may be appealed to an Assessment Review Board composed of not less than three members.

Case Law

The decisions in *Canadian Pacific Ltd. v Matsqui Indian Band*[247] and *Beattie v. Squamish Indian Band*[248] confirmed that taxation by-laws made under s. 83 of the *Indian Act* could provide for appeals of assessments to the Federal Court of Canada. The implicit requirement in this subsection that assessment appeals

---

[247]   [1995] S.C.J. No. 1, [1995] 1 S.C.R. 3.
[248]   [2005] F.C.J. No. 391.

must be brought to an Assessment Review Board may preclude a First Nation from providing for appeals to the Federal Court in property taxation laws made under the FNFSMA.

(2) CONFLICTS OF INTEREST — A person shall not serve as a member of an Assessment Review Board if the person has a personal or financial interest in the property that is the subject of the appeal.

(3) QUALIFICATIONS — At least one member of an Assessment Review Board shall be a member of the law society of the province in which the taxable property is situated and at least one other member shall have experience in assessment appeals in the province in which the taxable property is situated.

Case Law

Given the similarities between s. 83(3) of the *Indian Act* and s. 5(4) of the FNFSMA, under which this regulation is made, it is likely that the jurisprudence relating to s. 83(3) would also apply to the FNFSMA.

Canadian Pacific Ltd. v Matsqui Indian Band, [1995] S.C.J. No. 1, [1995] 1 S.C.R. 3.

The Supreme Court of Canada dismissed allegations of bias on the part of band members sitting on an assessment appeal board, noting that it was appropriate to have band members as board members because they represented community interests. It dismissed allegations that band members might have a pecuniary interest in imposing higher tax assessments, noting that such members might equally prefer lower rates to encourage investment. The court did raise concerns about an absence of financial security and of security of tenure for board members, although it found that insufficient evidence on these points was available to the court to rule against the band on that ground.

Huyck v. Musqueam Indian Band, [2000] F.C.J. No. 582, 189 F.T.R. 1, aff'd [2001] F.C.J. No. 754, 272 N.R. 188(C.A.), appeal to S.C.C. dismissed [2001] S.C.C.A. No. 373.

The Federal Court observed that a reasonable apprehension of bias could arise by virtue of the fact that the band appointed the members of the tax assessment appeal board. It cited the reasoning of Lamer CJ. in *Canadian Pacific Ltd. v Matsqui Indian Band*:

> For the Chief Justice, the fact that the Band selects the tribunal members suggests a degree of dependence which in turn, gives rise to a reasonable apprehension of bias. In effect, the Chief Justice affirms that "a party should not be required to present

its case before a tribunal whose members have been appointed by an opposing party".[249]

In that case, however, although the assessment review board members were appointed by the band, because the board subsequently appointed outside panels to conduct the appeals, the court held that a reasonable apprehension of bias did not arise.

7. MINIMUM LIMITATION PERIOD — If a property taxation law establishes a period beyond which assessments may not be appealed, that period shall not be shorter than 81 days after the date on which notice of the assessment is delivered to the taxpayer.

Commentary

The 81-day period provides at a minimum for 30 days to request a reconsideration, 30 days to receive the results from it, and an additional 3 weeks to launch an appeal.

8. (1) GROUNDS FOR APPEAL — A notice of appeal shall indicate whether the appeal is in respect of

(a)   the assessed value of the property;

(b)   the assessment classification of the property; or

(c)   any alleged error or omission in an assessment notice.

(2) COMMENCEMENT OF APPEAL — The appeal is commenced by delivery to the Assessment Review Board of a Notice of Appeal, at an address set out in the property taxation law.

(3) CONTENT OF NOTICE — A Notice of Appeal shall be accompanied by a copy of the assessment notice and shall include

(a)   the name and mailing address of the appellant and of any representative acting on behalf of the appellant;

(b)   the description of the taxable property set out on the assessment notice.

HEARING

9. (1) SCHEDULING OF HEARING — On receipt of a Notice of Appeal, the Assessment Review Board shall schedule an appeal hearing, giving at least 30 days written notice to all parties.

(2) TIMING — An appeal hearing shall be conducted by the Assessment Review Board within 90 days after receiving the Notice of Appeal unless all parties consent to the delay.

---

[249]   [2000] F.C.J. No. 582, 189 F.T.R. 1 at para. 64.

(3) NOTICE — Where an appeal relates to land in which a person other than the appellant has a registered interest, the Assessment Review Board shall provide that person with written notice of the time, date, and place of the hearing of the appeal.

Commentary

This section provides that notice of an assessment appeal will be given to persons who are co-owners or co-tenants to the person bringing the appeal.

10. HEARING DEFERRED — Where an appellant commences an appeal while a matter with respect to liability for taxes for the same property is before a court of competent jurisdiction, the Assessment Review Board shall defer hearing the appeal until the matter is finally determined by that court.

11. COMBINED HEARING — The Assessment Review Board may conduct a single hearing of two or more appeals related to the same assessment roll.

12. *IN CAMERA* HEARING — At the request of a party, the Assessment Review Board may conduct a hearing *in camera*.

13. ATTENDANCE REQUIRED — The tax assessor and the tax administrator of the first nation shall be present at an appeal hearing.

DOCUMENTS

14. DOCUMENTATION — The Assessment Review Board shall deliver the Notice of Appeal, and any submissions and other documents filed by the appellant to all other parties within seven days after their receipt by the Committee.

15. EVIDENCE OF VALUE — If the hearing relates to a dispute over the assessed value of taxable property,

(a) the tax assessor shall deliver to the Assessment Review Board and parties, not less than 21 days before the hearing, the entire assessment roll and a written explanation of how the assessment was established for the property; and

(b) the appellant shall deliver to the Assessment Review Board and parties, not less than 10 days before the hearing, evidence in support of his or her opinion of the value of the property.

DECISIONS

16. (1) DECISIONS — Within five days after the completion of the hearing of an appeal, the Assessment Review Board shall deliver its written decision on the appeal to all parties.

(2) JUDICIAL REVIEW — The written decision shall be accompanied by a statement that the parties have the right to judicial review of the Assessment Review Board's decision by a court of competent jurisdiction.

Commentary

If Assessment Review Boards are determined to be a "federal board, commission or other tribunal" for the purposes of the *Federal Courts Act*,[250] then applications for judicial review of their decisions could be brought to the Federal Court of Canada.

COMING INTO FORCE

17. COMING INTO FORCE — These Regulations come into force on [the day on which they are registered/ specified date].

Commentary

The regulations are expected to come into force on the same date on which the *First Nations Fiscal and Statistical Management Act* comes into force.

---

[250]   R.S.C. 1985, c. F-7.

FIRST NATIONS ASSESSMENT INSPECTION REGULATIONS

Introductory Commentary

The *First Nations Assessment Inspection Regulations* are one of the set of regulations proposed to be made under the *First Nations Fiscal and Statistical Management Act*.[251] The regulations have not yet been made, but have been released by the government for consultation purposes.[252]

The regulations are to be made under s. 36(1)(a) of the *First Nations Fiscal and Statistical Management Act*, and set out the procedures required under s. 5(1)(a)(i) of the Act to be incorporated in property taxation laws that provide for property assessment inspections.

The regulations establish procedures that must be followed by the First Nation's tax assessors, if they wish to conduct an inspection of taxable property for the purpose of assessing its value. These procedures include:

- notice requirements;
- permitted hours for inspections; and
- procedures for dealing with refusals to allow an inspection.

The regulations essentially put in place a procedure for obtaining an inspection that incorporates common-sense protections and courtesies to the owner or occupant, while at the same time permitting the tax assessor to make a (presumably higher) estimate of value based on other information, if an inspection proves impossible.

The regulations are expected to come into force on the same date on which the *First Nations Fiscal and Statistical Management Act* comes into force.

---

[251] S.C. 2005, c. 9.
[252] Available at First Nations Fiscal Initiative website at <http://www.fnfi.ca>.

FIRST NATIONS ASSESSMENT INSPECTION REGULATIONS
(PROPOSED)

Her Excellency the Governor General in Council, on the recommendation of the Minister of Indian Affairs and Northern Development, pursuant to subparagraph 5(1)(*a*)(i) and paragraph 36(1)(*a*) of the *First Nations Fiscal and Statistical Management Act*, hereby makes the annexed *First Nations Assessment Inspection Regulations*.

Commentary

The introductory Order in Council sets out the enabling authority for the *First Nations Assessment Inspection Regulations*, which are ss. 5(1)(a)(i) and 36(1)(a) of the *First Nations Fiscal and Statistical Management Act*. Paragraphs 36(1)(a) is the general regulation-making power:

> 36. (1) The Governor in Council may, on the recommendation of the Minister made having regard to any representations by the Commission, make regulations
>
> (a) *prescribing anything that is to be prescribed under subparagraph 5(1)(a)(i), paragraph 5(1)(e) or (4)(a), subsection 5(7) or section 10;* ...

Note that the regulations are to be made on the recommendation of the Minister of Indian Affairs and Northern Development, after consultation by the Minister with the First Nations Tax Commission.

The italicized text in paragraph (a) establishes the link to the requirement for regulations set out in s. 5(1)(a)(i). Subparagraph 5(1)(a)(i) authorizes First Nation councils to make property taxation laws incorporating property assessment inspections, conducted in accordance with procedures prescribed by regulation:

> 5. (1) ... the council of a first nation may make laws
>
> (a) respecting taxation for local purposes of reserve lands, interests in reserve lands or rights to occupy, possess or use reserve lands, including
>
> (i) the assessment of the value of those lands, interests and rights, the requisition of any information necessary to conduct the assessment and the inspection, *in accordance with procedures prescribed by regulation*, for assessment purposes of any reserve lands that are subject to taxation for local purposes,

The italicised wording provides the link to the *First Nations Assessment Inspection Regulations*.

FIRST NATIONS ASSESSMENT INSPECTION REGULATIONS

INTERPRETATION

1. DEFINITIONS — The following definitions apply in these Regulations.

"taxable property"
« bien imposable »

"taxable property" means an interest in reserve lands, or a right to occupy, possess or use reserve lands, that is subject to taxation under a property taxation law.

Commentary

The definition of taxable property follows the wording of s. 5(1)(a) of the FNFSMA that describes the types of rights and interests in reserve land that can be taxed.

"tax assessor"
« évaluateur »

"tax assessor" means the person designated by a first nation to conduct assessments of taxable property.

INSPECTIONS

2. PROCEDURES — Inspections of taxable property for assessment purposes that are provided for in a property taxation law shall be carried out in accordance with the procedures prescribed in sections 3 to 6.

Commentary

Subparagraph 5(1)(a)(i) of the FNFSMA provides that property taxation laws providing for assessment inspections must include the procedures that are prescribed by regulation. Although the requirements of ss. 3 to 6 of the regulations do not refer to property taxation laws *per se*, by virtue of s. 2 the procedures set out in those sections are required to be incorporated into a First Nation's property taxation laws.

3. (1) NOTICE — A tax assessor who wishes to conduct an inspection of taxable property for the purpose of assessing its value shall send a notice of assessment inspection by registered mail to the taxpayer at the taxpayer's address indicated on the assessment roll.

(2) CONTENT OF NOTICE — A notice of assessment inspection shall

(a) include a description of the taxable property;

(b) **advise of the time and date on which the inspection will take place and invite the taxpayer to contact the tax assessor at a telephone number set out in the notice to make arrangements for an alternate time and date, if necessary; and**

(c) **advise the taxpayer of the alternate assessment procedure set out in section 6.**

Commentary

Paragraph 3(2)(c) refers to the procedure in section 6, which permits the assessor, if an inspection is impossible or is refused, to assess the property based on whatever information is available to him or her.

4. ACCESS TO PROPERTY — Where taxable property is occupied by a person other than the taxpayer, the taxpayer shall make arrangements with the occupant to provide access to the assessor.

5. BUSINESS HOURS — Unless otherwise requested by the taxpayer, inspections shall be conducted during business hours.

6. ASSESSMENT WITHOUT INSPECTION — If, on attending at the taxable property under section 5, no adult occupant is present or permission to inspect the property is denied, the tax assessor may assess the value of the taxable property based on the best information available to the assessor.

Commentary

Note that no sanctions are embodied for a refusal to permit an assessment inspection. Implicit in the tax assessor's ability in s. 6 to use other information available, however, is the presumption that a taxpayer would not be able to appeal the assessment based on the fact that the information was incomplete, since the refusal of the taxpayer would itself have given rise to the situation complained of.

COMING INTO FORCE

7. COMING INTO FORCE DATE — These Regulations come into force on [the day on which they are registered/specified date].

Commentary

The regulations are expected to come into force on the same date on which the *First Nations Fiscal and Statistical Management Act* comes into force.

FIRST NATIONS RATES AND EXPENDITURE LAWS TIMING REGULATIONS

Introductory Commentary

The *First Nations Rates and Expenditure Laws Timing Regulations* are one of the set of regulations proposed to be made under the *First Nations Fiscal and Statistical Management Act*.[253] The regulations have not yet been made, but have been released by the government for consultation purposes.[254]

The regulations are made under s. 36(1)(*a*) of the *First Nations Fiscal and Statistical Management Act*, and set the dates on which certain types of laws must be made by First Nations under s. 10 of the Act.

The regulations essentially require that a First Nation taxing under the *First Nations Fiscal and Statistical Management Act* must set its annual tax rates and budgets on the same date as tax rates are set in neighbouring municipalities.

The regulations are expected to come into force on the same date on which the *First Nations Fiscal and Statistical Management Act* comes into force.

---

[253] S.C. 2005, c. 9.
[254] Available at First Nations Fiscal Initiative website at <http://www.fnfi.ca>.

FIRST NATIONS RATES AND EXPENDITURE LAWS TIMING REGULATIONS
(PROPOSED)

Her Excellency the Governor General in Council, on the recommendation of the Minister of Indian Affairs and Northern Development, pursuant to section 10 and paragraph 36(1)(a) of the *First Nations Fiscal and Statistical Management Act*, hereby makes the annexed *First Nations Rates and Expenditure Laws Timing Regulations*.

Commentary

The introductory Order in Council sets out the enabling authority for the *First Nations Rates and Expenditure Laws Timing Regulations*, which are ss. 10 and 36(1)(a) of the *First Nations Fiscal and Statistical Management Act*. Paragraphs 36(1)(a) is the general regulation-making power:

> 36. (1) The Governor in Council may, on the recommendation of the Minister made having regard to any representations by the Commission, make regulations
>
> > (a) *prescribing anything that is to be prescribed under* subparagraph 5(1)(a)(i), paragraph 5(1)(e) or (4)(a), subsection 5(7) or *section 10*; ...

Note that the regulations are to be made on the recommendation of the Minister of Indian Affairs and Northern Development, after consultation by the Minister with the First Nations Tax Commission.

The italicized text in paragraph (a) establishes the link to the requirement for regulations set out in s. 10 of the Act. Section 10 requires every First Nation that has a property taxation law to set the tax rates and establish a budget for expenditure of tax revenues at least once a year:

> 10. A council of a first nation that makes a property taxation law shall, at least once each year *at a time prescribed by regulation*, make
>
> > (a) a law under paragraph 5(1)(a) setting the rate of tax to be applied to the assessed value of each class of lands, interests or rights; and
> >
> > (b) a law under paragraph 5(1)(b) establishing a budget for the expenditure of revenues raised under the property taxation law.

The italicised wording provides the link to the First Nations Rates and Expenditure Laws Timing Regulations.

FIRST NATIONS RATES AND EXPENDITURE LAWS TIMING REGULATIONS

TIMING

1. TIMING OF LAWS — The council of a first nation that makes a property taxation law shall make the laws referred to in paragraphs 10(a) and (b) of the *First Nations Fiscal and Statistical Management Act* on the date, established by the province in which the reserve is located, for the setting of the tax rates applicable to lands subject to provincial jurisdiction that are adjacent to the reserve.

Commentary

The laws referred to in paragraph 10(a) are annual property taxation laws that set the rate of tax to be applied to the assessed value of each class of lands, interests or rights being taxed in the reserve. The laws referred to in paragraph 10(b) are annual budget laws for the expenditure of revenues raised under property taxation laws.

Although, read literally, this provision appears to require that these laws be *made* on the date in question, in practice the laws would be made by the council of the First Nation in advance of that date and would simply provide that they come into force (or take effect) on the prescribed date.

The prescribed date is the date on which annual tax rates and budgets are set in neighbouring municipalities.

2. CAVEAT — Nothing in section 1 precludes the amendment of a law made under paragraph 10(1)(*a*) or (*b*) of the Act, or the making of additional laws under either paragraph, at any other time.

Commentary

This provision simply confirms that the fact that the First Nation council is required to make an annual rates or budget law on a specified date does not mean that it cannot make further rates or budget laws, or amendments to such laws, at other times of the year.

COMING INTO FORCE

3. COMING INTO FORCE DATE — These Regulations come into force on [the day on which they are registered/specified date].

Commentary

The regulations are expected to come into force on the same date on which the *First Nations Fiscal and Statistical Management Act* comes into force.

FIRST NATIONS TAX COMMISSION REVIEW PROCEDURES REGULATIONS

Introductory Commentary

The *First Nations Tax Commission Review Procedures Regulations* are one of the set of regulations proposed to be made under the *First Nations Fiscal and Statistical Management Act*.[255] The regulations have not yet been made, but have been released by the government for consultation purposes.[256]

The regulations are to be made under s. 36(1)(b) and 36(3) of the *First Nations Fiscal and Statistical Management Act*. They establish procedures by which the First Nations Tax Commission is to review First Nation property taxation laws and laws respecting procedures by which the interests of taxpayers may be represented to the First Nation council.

The regulations also put in place procedures by which members of First Nations or taxpayers can request that the Commission conduct a review under s. 33(1) of the Act to determine

- whether the First Nation council has complied with Parts 1 and 2 of the Act and the regulations, or

- whether the First Nation has unfairly or improperly applied a property tax law.

The regulations establish procedures for the launching by the First Nations Tax Commission of its own review under s. 33(2) of the Act, to determine whether the First Nation council has complied with Parts 1 and 2 of the Act and the regulations, or has unfairly or improperly applied a property tax law.

The regulations set out the manner in which reviews of the affected First Nation laws are to be conducted, the way in which reviews of complaints from taxpayers under s. 33(1) of the Act are to be dealt with, and how the Commission can conduct its self-initiated reviews under s. 33(2) of the Act. Among other things, the regulations provide for:

- delegation of the Commission's responsibilities for review of First Nation laws and the conduct of complaint reviews to panels composed of from one to three Commissioners;

- reviews to be conducted without hearings;

- the filing of documents;

- how complaints are to be made;

- the manner in which a First Nation council can respond to a complaint;

- the role of intervenors;

---

[255] S.C. 2005, c. 9.

[256] Available at First Nations Fiscal Initiative website at <http://www.fnfi.ca>.

- attempts at settlement;
- the manner of conducting hearings; and
- the rendering of decisions by the Commission.

Note that although s. 31(2) of the Act contemplates the establishment of procedures "in accordance with any regulations made under paragraph 36(1)(b)" for review by the First Nations Tax Commission of representations made to it by taxpayers under s. 7(b) of the Act, these regulations do not set out any procedures in this regard.

The regulations are expected to come into force on the same date on which the *First Nations Fiscal and Statistical Management Act* comes into force.

FIRST NATIONS TAX COMMISSION REVIEW PROCEDURES REGULATIONS
(PROPOSED)

Her Excellency the Governor General in Council, on the recommendation of the Minister of Indian Affairs and Northern Development, pursuant to section 33 and paragraphs 36(1)(*b*) and subsection 36(3) of the *First Nations Fiscal and Statistical Management Act*, hereby makes the annexed *First Nations Tax Commission Review Procedures Regulations*.

Commentary

The introductory Order in Council sets out the enabling authorities for the *First Nations Tax Commission Review Procedures Regulations*, which are ss. 33, 36(1)(b) and 36(3) of the *First Nations Fiscal and Statistical Management Act*. Paragraph 36(1)(b) is the general regulation-making power:

> 36. (1) The Governor in Council may, on the recommendation of the Minister made having regard to any representations by the Commission, make regulations ...
>
> (b) establishing the procedures to be followed in reviewing laws submitted under section 7 and conducting reviews under section 33, including procedures
>
> (i) for requiring the production of documents from a first nation or person requesting a review under subsection 33(1),
>
> (ii) for conducting hearings, and
>
> (iii) authorizing the Commission to apply to a justice of the peace for a subpoena compelling a person to appear before the Commission to give evidence and bring any documents specified in the supoena, and to pay associated travel expenses;

Note that the regulations are to be made on the recommendation of the Minister of Indian Affairs and Northern Development, after consultation by the Minister with the First Nations Tax Commission.

The "laws submitted under section 7" that are referred to in the opening words of paragraph 36(1)(b) are property taxation laws and laws respecting procedures by which the interests of taxpayers may be represented to the council. The Commission is required under s. 31 of the Act to review all types of local revenue laws (laws made by a First Nation council under s. 5(1) of the Act), including property taxation laws and laws respecting procedures by which the interests of taxpayers may be represented to the council.

The rest of s. 36(1)(b) gives authority to make regulations to establish procedures for conducting reviews under section 33 of the Act:

33. (1) On the request in writing by a member of a first nation, or by a person who holds an interest in reserve lands or has a right to occupy, possess or use the reserve lands, who

(a) is of the opinion that the first nation has not complied with this Part or Part 1 or with a regulation made under either Part or section 141 or 142 or that a law has been unfairly or improperly applied,

(b) has requested the council of the first nation to remedy the situation, and

(c) is of the opinion that the council has not remedied the situation,

the Commission shall conduct a review of the matter *in accordance with the regulations.*

(2) If the Commission is of the opinion that a first nation has not complied with this Part or Part 1 or with a regulation made under either Part or section 141 or 142 or that a law has been unfairly or improperly applied, it shall conduct a review of the matter *in accordance with the regulations.*

The italicised wording in those provisions provides the link to the *First Nations Tax Commission Review Procedures Regulations.*

The additional enabling authority in s. 36(3) of the Act adds extra elements to the regulation-making powers in s. 36(1)(b):

(3) Regulations made under paragraph (1)(b) may authorize the Commission to

(a) vary the procedures to accommodate the customs or culture of a first nation in respect of which a hearing is being held;

(b) extend or shorten any period provided for in those regulations;

(c) dispense with compliance with any procedure provided for in the regulations in the interest of securing a just, expeditious and inexpensive hearing of a complaint; and

(d) delegate any of the powers of the Commission under section 31 or 33 to one or more commissioners.

This subsection gives authority to include provisions of this sort in the regulations that might otherwise be beyond the Governor in Council's regulation-making powers.

FIRST NATIONS TAX COMMISSION REVIEW PROCEDURES REGULATIONS

INTERPRETATION

1. (1) DEFINITIONS — The following definitions apply in these Regulations.

"Act"
« Loi »
"Act" means the *First Nations Fiscal and Statistical Management Act*.

"applicant"
« demandeur »
"applicant" means a person who requests a review under section 33 of the Act.

Commentary

An applicant would be a person who

- holds an interest in reserve lands or has a right to occupy, possess or use the reserve lands;

- believes that the First Nation council has not complied with Parts 1 and 2 of the Act or the regulations, or has unfairly or improperly applied a property tax law; and

- has requested the First Nation council to remedy the situation, without avail.

"business day"
« jour férié »
"business day" means a day other than a Saturday or holiday.

Commentary

Note that "holiday" is defined in s. 35(1) of the *Interpretation Act*:

"holiday" means any of the following days, namely, Sunday; New Year's Day; Good Friday; Easter Monday; Christmas Day; the birthday or the day fixed by proclamation for the celebration of the birthday of the reigning Sovereign; Victoria Day; Canada Day; the first Monday in September, designated Labour Day; Remembrance Day; any day appointed by proclamation to be observed as a day of general prayer or mourning or day of public rejoicing or thanksgiving; and any of the following additional days, namely,

(a) in any province, any day appointed by proclamation of the lieutenant governor of the province to be observed as a public holiday or as a day of general prayer or mourning or day of public rejoicing or thanksgiving within the province, and any day that is a non-juridical day by virtue of an Act of the legislature of the province, and

(b) in any city, town, municipality or other organized district, any day appointed to be observed as a civic holiday by resolution of the council or other authority charged with the administration of the civic or municipal affairs of the city, town, municipality or district.

"intervenor"
« *intervenant* »

"intervenor" means a person or organization added as an intervenor under section 16.

Commentary

An intervenor, in general terms, is a person or organization that requests permission of a court or tribunal to make representations in a legal proceeding carried on between two other parties.

"party"
« *partie* »

"party" means an applicant or a first nation that is the subject of a review.

"reply"
« *réponse* »

"reply" means a document used by a first nation to answer to a request for review.

"request for review"
« *demande d'examen* »

"request for review" means a request for a review under section 33 of the Act.

"review"
« *examen* »

"review" means a review by the Commission under section 33 of the Act.

REVIEW OF LOCAL REVENUE LAWS

2. (1) REFERRAL TO PANEL — On receipt of a property taxation law referred to in paragraph 10(a) of the Act that was submitted to the Commission for review under section 31 of the Act, the Commission may refer the local revenue law to a panel composed of one or more Commissioners to conduct the review.

Commentary

A property taxation law referred to in s. 10(a) of the Act is a property taxation law that sets the rate of tax to be applied to the assessed value of each class of lands, interests or rights, which every taxing First Nation is required to make annually.

(2) REFERRAL TO PANEL — On receipt of any other property taxation law, or a law made under paragraph 5(1)(c) of the Act, that was submitted to the Commission for review under section 31 of the Act, the Commission may refer the local revenue law to a panel composed of three or more Commissioners to conduct the review.

Commentary

A law made under s. 5(1)(c) of the Act is a law respecting procedures by which the interests of taxpayers may be represented to the council.

3. NON-CONFORMING LAWS — Where a panel constituted under subsection 2(1) or (2) is not completely satisfied that a law referred to in those subsections complies with the Act and any regulations and standards made under the Act, the panel shall refer the law for review by the Commission as a whole.

Commentary

Note that while under s. 31(3) the Commission must approve a local revenue law that complies with the Act, the regulations and any standards made by the Commission under s. 35(1) of the Act, s. 31(3) does not prevent the Commission from approving a local revenue law that does *not* comply with the Act, regulations and standards.[257] Section 3 of the regulations, however, prevents a panel from itself approving a law that it knows or suspects is non-conforming, requiring instead that any such law be referred to the Commission as a whole.

---

[257] Aside possibly for the approval of laws made under s. 5(1)(d) for financing capital infrastructure for the provision of local services on reserve lands, since s. 32(2) requires the Commission to issue a certificate after approving such a law stating that the law complies with the Act and regulations (but not its standards).

COMPLIANCE REVIEWS

Referral to panel

4. (1) REFERRAL TO PANEL — On receipt of a request for review of a matter under section 33 of the Act, the Commission may refer the request to a panel composed of one or more Commissioners.

(2) COMMISSION INCLUDES PANEL — A reference to the Commission in sections 5 to 42 includes a reference to a panel of Commissioners constituted under subsection (1).

Commentary

The effect of this provision is to make the rules set out in ss. 5 to 42 applicable to panels as well, even though they are not mentioned specifically.

Documents

5. DECISION WITHOUT HEARING — The Commission may make a decision in any review on the basis of written materials filed with the Commission without holding a hearing.

Commentary

This section confirms that there is no automatic right to a hearing on a complaint under s. 33 of the Act, and that the Commission can deal with the complaint on the basis of documentary evidence alone.

6. (1) DELIVERY OF DOCUMENTS — A document may be delivered by sending it by fax, registered mail or e-mail or by personal delivery.

(2) DEEMED DELIVERY — Documents sent by fax shall be considered to have been delivered on receipt of electronic confirmation of successful transmission.

(3) DEEMED DELIVERY — Documents sent by e-mail shall be considered to have been delivered on receipt of electronic confirmation that the e-mail has been opened.

7. (1) ADDRESS FOR DELIVERY — A document may be

(a) **filed with the Commission by delivering it to the Commission at:**

321-345 Yellowhead Highway
Kamloops, British Columbia
V2H 1H1
fax: (250) 828-9858
review@fntc.ca

(*b*)   delivered to an applicant or intervenor at the address for delivery indicated on the documents filed with the Commission; and

(*c*)   delivered to a first nation by delivering it to the administrative office of the first nation.

(2) REPRESENTATIVES — Where a party is represented by another person, a document required to be delivered to the party may be delivered to the representative.

8. (1) DELIVERY OF COPIES — When a document is filed with the Commission, the Commission shall deliver a copy of it to all parties and intervenors.

(2) STAMPED RECEIPT — Documents received by the Commission shall be stamped with the date of receipt.

(3) LATE FILING — A document received by the Commission after 5:00 pm shall be considered to have been filed on the next business day.

(4) FILING BY FAX OR E-MAIL — A party who files a document by fax or e-mail is not required to file the original document.

9. (1) AUTHORIZATION — Documents prepared on behalf of a party shall be signed by a person authorized by the party and shall state the nature of the person's authorization.

(2) PROOF OF CAPACITY — The Commission may at any time require a person acting on behalf of a party to provide proof of the person's authority to act in that capacity.

10. (1) FILING A REQUEST FOR REVIEW — A request for review shall set out

(a)   the full name, address, and telephone number, and any available fax number or e-mail address, of the applicant and of any representative acting on behalf of the applicant;

(b)   an address for delivery of documents, if different from the address of the applicant or representative;

(c)   the name of the first nation, and the title of any local revenue law, in respect of which the request for review is made;

(d)   the grounds for the request for review;

(e) a concise statement of the facts on which the applicant intends to rely;

(f) the remedy sought;

(g) any other information that the applicant believes the Commission requires in order to conduct the review; and

(h) if the review is requested on an expedited basis, the reasons for the urgency.

(2) ACCOMPANYING DOCUMENTATION — A request for review shall be accompanied by copies of the applicant's request for a remedy made to the council of the first nation pursuant to paragraph 33(1)(*b*) of the Act and any related correspondence with the council of the first nation.

Commentary

Paragraph 33(1)(b) of the Act requires that, before requesting a review under s. 33, an applicant must have first "requested the council of the first nation to remedy the situation". This provision of the regulations requires the applicant to provide the Commission with documentation to evidence that such a request has been made.

11. DEFICIENT DOCUMENTS — Where a request for review does not contain the information required under section 10, the Commission shall

(a) identify what information is missing; and

(b) advise the applicant that the information must be provided before the Commission will proceed with the request for review.

12. (1) REPLY — A first nation may reply to a request for review by filing with the Commission a written reply within 10 business days after delivery of the copy of the request for review by the Commission.

(2) CONTENT OF REPLY — A reply to a request for review shall identify the request for review to which the reply relates and set out

(a) the name of the first nation, and the name, address and telephone number, and any e-mail address or fax number, of any representative acting on behalf of the first nation;

(b) an address for delivery of documents, if other than that of the administrative office of the first nation or the office of its representative;

(c) an outline of the position the first nation takes in response to the request for review;

(d) an admission or denial of each allegation of fact contained in the request for review;

(e) a concise statement of any additional facts on which the first nation intends to rely;

(f) **any other information that the first nation believes the Commission requires in order to conduct the review; and**

(g) **if the review is requested on an expedited basis, the reasons for the urgency.**

13. FAILURE TO REPLY — Where a first nation fails to submit a reply, the Commission may conduct the review on the basis of the submissions of the applicant alone.

14. (1) FILING OF RESPONSE — The applicant may file a response to the first nation's reply with the Commission within 5 business days after delivery of the reply by the Commission.

(2) CONTENT OF RESPONSE — A response to the first nation's reply shall identify the request for review to which the response relates and admit or deny any additional statements of fact contained in the reply.

15. AFFECTED PERSONS — Within 10 business days after the filing of a request for review that meets the requirements of section 10, the Commission shall

(a) **publish a notice of the review on an Internet website maintained by the Commission; and**

(b) **deliver a copy of the request for review to the first nation and to the First Nations Financial Management Board.**

Commentary

The website currently maintained by the First Nations Tax Commission can be found at <http://www.fntc.ca/main.phtml>.

16. (1) ADDING INTERVENOR — Any person or organization may apply to the Commission to be added as an intervenor

(a) **where a hearing has been set down, at any time before the hearing commences; and**

(b) **in any other case, at any time before a decision on the review is rendered.**

Commentary

Note that a person or organization must *apply* to be added as an intervenor, and that the Commission has the discretion to accept or reject such an application.

(2) ADDING BOARD AS INTERVENOR — At the request of the First Nations Financial Management Board made under subsection (1), the Commission shall add the Board as an intervenor for the purpose of making representations as to the impact of any requested remedy.

Commentary

Note that, unlike other intervenors, the First Nations Financial Management Board has the *right* to be added as an intervenor if it makes such a request.

(3) ROLE OF INTERVENORS — An intervenor may make written submissions and, where a hearing is being held, oral argument to the Commission.

17. DELIVERY OF DOCUMENTS — On adding a person or organization as an intervenor, the Commission shall deliver to the person or organization copies of the request for review, any reply filed by the first nation and any response filed under section 14.

18. (1) STATUTORY DECLARATIONS — The Commission may require confirmation, by way of a statutory declaration, of any facts alleged in a request for review or reply that have not been admitted.

Commentary

A statutory declaration is defined in s. 35(1) of the *Interpretation Act* as:

> "statutory declaration" means a solemn declaration made pursuant to section 41 of the *Canada Evidence Act*;

Section 41 of the *Canada Evidence Act* provides as follows:

> 41. Any judge, notary public, justice of the peace, provincial court judge, recorder, mayor or commissioner authorized to take affidavits to be used either in the provincial or federal courts, or any other functionary authorized by law to administer an oath in any matter, may receive the solemn declaration of any person voluntarily making the declaration before him, in the following form, in attestation of the execution of any writing, deed or instrument, or of the truth of any fact, or of any account rendered in writing:
>
> I, ..., solemnly declare that (state the fact or facts declared to), and I make this solemn declaration conscientiously believing it to be true, and knowing that it is of the same force and effect as if made under oath.
>
> Declared before me .... at .... this .... day of .... 19.............

(2) **CROSS-EXAMINATION ON DECLARATION** — A party who has submitted a statutory declaration shall make the deponent of the declaration available for cross-examination on the content of the declaration by any other party.

19. AMENDMENTS TO REQUEST FOR REVIEW — An applicant may request to the Commission that a review already under way address additional issues that would otherwise be the subject of a separate review.

20. CONSOLIDATION — The Commission may hold a single hearing in respect of more than one review or direct that two or more reviews be consolidated.

21. REQUIRED ATTENDANCE — The Commission may require the parties to attend at any conferences or meetings necessary to the conduct of a review.

Settlement

22. (1) SETTLEMENT CONFERENCES — A settlement conference may be scheduled by the Commission or at the request of a party at any stage in a review.

(2) **PRESENCE OF APPLICANT** — Where a representative is acting for an applicant, the Commission may direct that the applicant be present at the settlement conference or available to instruct the representative at that time.

23. (1) INFORMAL RESOLUTION — The Commission may make settlement recommendations to the parties and may suspend the review to enable the parties to attempt to resolve the subject of the request for review informally.

(2) **REFERRAL TO MEDIATION** — The Commission may recommend to the parties that the request for review be referred to formal mediation, in which case the Commission shall provide to the parties a roster of mediators who are independent of the Commission.

24. CONSENT ORDER — Where the parties reach an agreement, the Commission may make an order under paragraph 33(3)(*a*) of the Act embodying that agreement.

Commentary

Paragraph 33(3)(*a*) of the Act gives the Commission the authority to order a First Nation to remedy a situation that gave rise to a request for a review.

25. RECOMMENCEMENT OF REVIEW — Where six months have elapsed since a review was referred to mediation or adjourned for other settlement discussions without a settlement being reached, the Commission shall recommence the review and notify the parties accordingly.

Hearings

26. (1) DIRECTED HEARING — The Commission may at any time direct that a request for review be set down for a hearing.

(2) NOTICE OF HEARINGS — Where the Commission directs that a hearing be held, the Commission shall fix the time, date and place for the hearing and deliver a notice of the hearing to all parties and intervenors.

27. (1) CONDUCT OF HEARINGS — The Commission may request that a brief written summary of the submissions of parties and intervenors be filed in advance of a hearing.

(2) EXPEDITING HEARING — With the agreement of the parties, the Commission may

(a)   proceed on the basis of an agreed statement of facts; or

(b)   limit the number of witnesses to be called at a hearing.

(3) TELE-CONFERENCING — The Commission may hear oral evidence or oral submissions by tele-conference.

(4) ADJOURNMENTS — The Commission may adjourn a hearing for such time and on such terms as it considers appropriate.

28. FAILURE TO ATTEND — Where a party or intervenor who has been given notice of a hearing fails to attend, the Commission may proceed with the hearing and complete its review in the absence of that party or intervenor.

29. (1) EVIDENCE AND INFORMATION — In conducting a review the Commission may

(a)   receive and accept written or oral submissions and evidence, whether or not the evidence was given on oath or is admissible in a court of law;

(b) at the request of a party, require another party to provide the Commission with any documents necessary to the conduct of its review; and

(c) direct that written submissions be filed.

(2) SUBPOENAS — A party may, at any time prior to the conclusion of a hearing, request the Commission to apply to a justice of the peace for a subpoena compelling a person to appear before the Commission to give evidence and to bring any documents specified in the subpoena.

(3) TRAVEL EXPENSES — The Commission shall pay travel expenses, in the amount set out in Tariff A of the *Federal Court Rules, 1998*, to every person compelled by subpoena to appear before it.

Commentary

Tariff A of the *Federal Court Rules, 1998* sets out the fees payable by parties to proceedings in the Federal Court of Canada. The tariff is available online at <http://laws.justice.gc.ca/en/F-7/SOR-98-106/107756.html>.

30. (1) PRE-HEARING CONFERENCES — Where a hearing is to be held, a pre-hearing conference shall be scheduled by the Commission to

(a) direct the pre-hearing production of documents by a party;

(b) determine whether a subpoena will be required in respect of any person who may be required as a witness;

(c) request a party to provide further information regarding its position;

(d) develop an agreed statement of facts or obtain admissions that might facilitate the hearing;

(e) attempt to simplify the matters in dispute between the parties, including the resolution of some or all of them; or

(f) discuss the conduct of the hearing, including the order in which the parties will proceed, the number and identity of witnesses, and the estimated time required.

(2) REQUIRE ATTENDANCE — Where a representative is acting for an applicant, the Commission may direct that the applicant be present at the pre-hearing conference.

(3) SINGLE COMMISSIONER — A pre-hearing conference may be conducted by a single Commissioner or an employee of the Commission.

31. (1) OFFICIAL REPORTERS — At the request of a party, the Commission may consent to the examination of a person outside a hearing, having regard to

(a) the expected absence of the person at the time of the hearing;

(b)   the age or any illness or infirmity of the person;

(c)   the distance the person resides from the place where the hearing will be held; and

(d)   the expense of having the person attend at the hearing.

(2) DIRECTIONS — In giving its consent under subsection (1), the Commission shall give directions regarding the time, place and manner of the examination, the notice to be given to the person being examined and to the other parties, the attendance of any other witnesses and the production of any requested documents or other material.

(3) CROSS-EXAMINATION — Other parties may cross-examine any person examined outside a hearing.

(4) COPIES OF TRANSCRIPT — A party submitting transcribed evidence shall provide a copy of the transcript, at its own expense, to the Commission and to all other parties.

32. (1) ADVERSE WITNESSES — Subject to subsection (4), a party may call another party as a witness at a hearing by delivering a subpoena and travel expenses to that party in accordance with subsections 29(2) and (3).

(2) CORPORATIONS — Where the other party is a corporation, the party shall provide as a witness an officer or director of the corporation who has knowledge of the facts in issue.

(3) FIRST NATION — Where the other party is a first nation, the party shall provide as a witness the person who administers the taxes of the first nation or another person who has knowledge of the facts in issue.

(4) NOTICE — A party shall give another party at least 5 business days' notice of its intention to call that party as a witness, unless the party, or a person referred to in subsection (2) or (3), is in attendance at the hearing.

General

33. (1) DECISIONS OF THE COMMISSION — All decisions and orders of the Commission in a review shall be issued in written form, and shall be accompanied by written reasons.

(2) PUBLICATION — A decision or order of the Commission, and the accompanying reasons, shall be published in the *First Nations Gazette* or on an Internet website maintained by the Commission.

Commentary

The *First Nations Gazette* is co-published by the Indian Taxation Advisory Board and the Native Law Centre of Canada at the University of Saskatchewan. Subscriptions for the 2005 year cost $72. Further information can be obtained, and subscriptions ordered, at the *First Nations Gazette* website at <http://www.usask.ca/nativelaw/publications/desc/fng.html>.

The website presently maintained by the First Nations Tax Commission can be found at <http://www.fntc.ca/main.phtml>.

(3) PROVISION OF COPIES — The Commission shall provide a copy of its decisions, orders and reasons to all parties and intervenors and make copies of them available for inspection by the public at its offices.

(4) COMPLIANCE PERIOD — An order made pursuant to paragraph 33(3)(a) of the Act shall set out the period within which the first nation shall implement the required remedy.

Commentary

Paragraph 33(3)(a) of the Act gives the Commission the authority to order a First Nation to remedy a situation that gave rise to a request for a review.

34. NON-COMPLIANCE — Where the applicant fails to comply with these Regulations, the Commission may dismiss the request for review.

35. TIME PERIODS VARIABLE — The Commission may, on the application of a party, extend or shorten any period provided for in these Regulations.

36. VARIANCES — Where it is necessary to secure the just, expeditious or inexpensive hearing of a request for review, or to accommodate the customs or culture of the first nation in respect of which a hearing is held, the Commission may vary any procedure provided for by these Regulations.

37. COSTS — No costs shall be awarded.

Commentary

On the completion of hearings before some tribunals, the tribunal may order the unsuccessful party to pay the costs of the successful party. This provision precludes any such order.

COMMISSION-INITIATED REVIEW

38. (1) NOTICE OF REVIEW — Where the Commission proposes to conduct a review pursuant to subsection 33(2) of the Act, it shall deliver a notice to the first nation advising it of the review.

Commentary

Subsection 33(2) of the Act authorizes the Commission to launch its own review to determine whether a First Nation council has complied with Parts 1 and 2 of the Act and the regulations, or has unfairly or improperly applied a property tax law.

(2) CONTENT OF NOTICE — The notice referred to in subsection (1) shall

(a) **where the Commission is of the opinion that the first nation has not complied with the Act or a regulation, identify the provision of the Act or regulation in question and the reason the Commission believes it has not been complied with; and**

(b) **where the Commission is of the opinion that the first nation has unfairly or improperly applied a law, identify the law in question and the reason the Commission believes it has been unfairly or improperly applied.**

39. PRODUCTION OF DOCUMENTS — A notice under section 38 may require a first nation to produce any documents set out in the notice relating to the subject of the review.

40. (1) NOTICE — Within 10 business days after the delivery of a notice under section 38, the Commission shall

(a) **publish a notice of the proposed review on an Internet website maintained by the Commission; and**

(b) **deliver a copy of the notice to the First Nations Financial Management Board.**

Commentary

The website presently maintained by the First Nations Tax Commission can be found at <http://www.fntc.ca/main.phtml>.

(2) ADDING BOARD AS INTERVENOR — At the request of the First Nations Financial Management Board, the Commission shall add it as an intervenor for the purpose of making representations as to the impact of any potential remedy.

Commentary

Note that, unlike other intervenors, the First Nations Financial Management Board has the *right* to be added as an intervenor if it makes such a request.

41. REPLY BY FIRST NATION — A reply to a notice shall identify the notice to which the reply relates and set out

(a) the name of the first nation, and the name, address and telephone number, and any e-mail address or fax number, of any representative acting on behalf of the first nation;

(b) an address for delivery of documents, if other than that of the administrative office of the first nation or the office of its representative;

(c) an outline of the position the first nation takes in response to the allegations set out in the notice;

(d) an admission or denial of each allegation of fact contained in the notice;

(e) a concise statement of any additional facts on which the first nation intends to rely; and

(f) any other information that the first nation believes the Commission requires in order to conduct the review.

42. (1) HEARING — The Commission may at any time direct that a review conducted pursuant to subsection 33(2) of the Act be set down for a hearing and, at the request of the first nation, shall hold a hearing.

Commentary

Unlike reviews requested by taxpayers or other parties under s. 33(1) of the Act, where the Commission can refuse to hold an oral hearing,[258] in a review under s. 33(2) of the Act the First Nation has a right to have an oral hearing held.

(2) PROCEDURES FOR HEARING — Subsection 26(2) and sections 27 to 31 apply, with such modifications as are necessary, to a hearing directed under subsection (1).

COMING INTO FORCE

43. COMING INTO FORCE DATE — These Regulations come into force on [the day on which they are registered/specified date].

---

[258] See s. 5 of the regulations.

Commentary

The regulations are expected to come into force on the same date on which the *First Nations Fiscal and Statistical Management Act* comes into force.

FIRST NATIONS TAXATION ENFORCEMENT REGULATIONS

Introductory Commentary

The *First Nations Taxation Enforcement Regulations* are one of the set of regulations proposed to be made under the *First Nations Fiscal and Statistical Management Act*.[259] The regulations have not yet been made, but have been released by the government for consultation purposes.[260]

The regulations are made under s. 36(1)(*a*) of the *First Nations Fiscal and Statistical Management Act*, and set out the procedures required under ss. 5(1)(e) and 5(7) of the Act to be incorporated in property taxation laws that provide for measures to collect unpaid taxes.

Paragraph 5(1)(e) of the Act sets out the law-making powers of First Nations in relation to collection of amounts owing under property taxation laws. This includes the power to create liens, to impose interest and penalties on unpaid amounts, to seize and assign interests or rights in reserve lands in accordance with s. 5(7) of the Act, to seize and sell personal property located on reserve lands and to discontinue certain services paid for by taxes. These powers are subject to any conditions and procedures required by regulation.

The regulations place conditions or limits on the exercise of a First Nation's powers under s. 5(1)(e).[261] They require that First Nation laws relating to the collection of unpaid taxes include particular provisions:

- requiring that various minimum periods of advance notice be given to tax debtors and, in some cases, published, prior to undertaking collection activities;[262]

- setting maximum interest rates;[263]

- requiring that a registry of liens be maintained;[264]

- providing for certain prescribed procedures to be followed in auctioning off property seized for payment of unpaid taxes, including providing redemption opportunities for tax debtors;[265]

- restricting the parties who can take an assignment of interests on auction, in order to avoid circumventing the protections on alienation of reserve lands contained in the *Indian Act*; and

---

[259] S.C. 2005, c. 9.

[260] Available at First Nations Fiscal Initiative website at <http://www.fnfi.ca>.

[261] s. 3. Unless otherwise noted, section references in the footnotes refer to the *First Nations Taxation Enforcement Regulations*.

[262] ss. 7, 13, 14, 22 and 25.

[263] s. 6(2).

[264] s. 11.

[265] ss. 14 to 18.

- restricting the extent to which a First Nation can discontinue municipal services where taxes remain unpaid.[266]

The regulations are expected to come into force on the same date on which the *First Nations Fiscal and Statistical Management Act* comes into force.

---

[266]   ss. 26 and 27.

FIRST NATIONS TAXATION ENFORCEMENT REGULATIONS
(PROPOSED)

Her Excellency the Governor General in Council, on the recomendation of the Minister of Indian Affairs and Northern Development, pursuant to paragraph 5(1)(e), subsection 5(7) and paragraph 36(1)(a) of the *First Nations Fiscal and Statistical Management Act*, hereby makes the annexed *First Nations Taxation Enforcement Regulations*.

Commentary

The introductory Order in Council sets out the enabling authority for the *First Nations Taxation Enforcement Regulations*, which are ss. 5(1)(e), 5(7) and 36(1)(a) of the *First Nations Fiscal and Statistical Management Act*. Paragraph 36(1)(a) is the general regulation-making power:

> 36. (1) The Governor in Council may, on the recommendation of the Minister made having regard to any representations by the Commission, make regulations
>
> (a) *prescribing anything that is to be prescribed under* subparagraph 5(1)(a)(i), *paragraph 5(1)(e)* or (4)(a), *subsection 5(7)* or section 10; ...

Note that the regulations are to be made on the recommendation of the Minister of Indian Affairs and Northern Development, after consultation by the Minister with the First Nations Tax Commission.

The italicized text in paragraph (a) establishes the link to the requirement for regulations set out in s. 5(1)(e). Paragraph 5(1)(e) authorizes First Nation councils to make property taxation laws incorporating measures to facilitate the collection of unpaid taxes, provided that those laws also incorporate the conditions and procedures prescribed by regulation:

> 5. (1) ... the council of a first nation may make laws ...
>
> (e) *subject to any conditions, and in accordance with any procedures, prescribed by regulation*, respecting the enforcement of laws made under paragraph (a) in respect of outstanding taxes or charges, including
>
> (i) the creation of liens on reserve lands and interests in reserve lands,
>
> (ii) the imposition and recovery of interest and penalties on an amount payable pursuant to a law made under that paragraph, where the amount is not paid when it is due, and the rate of interest or the amount of the penalty, as the case may be,
>
> (iii) subject to subsection (7), the seizure, forfeiture and assignment of interests or rights in reserve lands,

> (iv) the seizure and sale of personal property located on reserve lands, other than property located in a dwelling, and
>
> (v) the discontinuance of services;

The "laws made under paragraph (a)" referred to in the opening words of paragraph (e) are property taxation laws. The power to make laws under s. 5(1)(e)(iii) respecting the seizure, forfeiture and assignment of interests or rights in reserve lands is stipulated to be "subject to subsection (7)". Subsection 5(7) allows First Nation councils to transfer seized rights or interests (that would otherwise be prohibited under the *Indian Act*):[267]

> (7) Notwithstanding the *Indian Act* or any instrument conferring a right or interest in reserve lands, if there are outstanding taxes payable pursuant to a law made under paragraph (1)(a) for more than two years, the first nation may assign the right or interest *in accordance with the conditions and procedures prescribed by regulation.*

The italicised wording in ss. 5(1)(e) and 5(7) provides the link to the *First Nations Taxation Enforcement Regulations.*

FIRST NATIONS TAXATION ENFORCEMENT REGULATIONS

INTERPRETATION

1. DEFINITIONS — The following definitions apply in these Regulations.

"Act"
« Loi »
"Act" means the First Nations Fiscal and Statistical Management Act.

"Commission"
« Commission »
"Commission" means the First Nations Tax Commission.

"debtor"
« débiteur »
"debtor" means an taxpayer who is liable for unpaid taxes, interest or penalties imposed under a property taxation law.

---

[267]   For further explanation, see the Commentary following s. 5(7) of the FNFSMA.

"registered"
« enregistré »

"registered", in respect of an interest in reserve lands — other than a lien referred to in section 11 — or a right to occupy, possess or use reserve lands, means registered in the Reserve Land Register, the Surrendered and Designated Lands Register, the First Nations Land Register or a registry or land titles system of the province in which the lands are located.

Commentary

The Reserve Land Register is established under s. 21 of the *Indian Act*:

> 21. There shall be kept in the Department a register, to be known as the Reserve Land Register, in which shall be entered particulars relating to Certificates of Possession and Certificates of Occupation and other transactions respecting lands in a reserve.

The Surrendered and Designated Lands Register is established under s. 55(1) of the *Indian Act*:

> 55. (1) There shall be maintained in the Department a register, to be known as the Surrendered and Designated Lands Register, in which shall be recorded particulars in connection with any transaction affecting absolutely surrendered or designated lands.

The First Nations Land Register is established under s. 25(1) of the *First Nation Land Management Act*[268]:

> 25. (1) The Minister shall establish a register to be known as the First Nation Land Register.

Subsection 25(2) of that Act provides that, until regulations are made under that Act governing its operation, the First Nation Land Register is to be administered in essentially the same manner as the Reserve Land Register.

The definition of "registered" excepts out liens, since those are to be registered under s. 11 of the regulations in a local registry, maintained by the First Nation.

"taxable property"
«bien imposable »

"taxable property" means an interest in reserve lands, or a right to occupy, possess or use reserve lands, that is subject to taxation under a property taxation law.

---

[268] S.C. 1999, c. 24.

Commentary

The definition of taxable property follows the wording of s. 5(1)(a) of the Act that describes the types of rights and interests in reserve land that can be taxed.

"tax administrator"
« administrateur fiscal »

"tax administrator" means the person responsible for the administration of a property taxation law.

2. *INDIAN ACT* DEFINITIONS — Unless the context otherwise requires, words and expressions used in these Regulations that are not otherwise defined in these Regulations or the Act have the same meaning as in the *Indian Act*.

Commentary

This would include words such as "reserve" and "council".

APPLICABLE CONDITIONS AND PROCEDURES

3. CONDITIONS — Enforcement measures set out in a property taxation law are subject to the conditions, and shall be carried out in accordance with the procedures, prescribed in sections 4 to 27.

Commentary

Paragraph 5(1(e) and s. 5(7) of the Act provide that property taxation laws providing mechanisms for the collection of unpaid taxes and the assignment of seized rights and interests must include the conditions and procedures that are prescribed by regulation. Although the requirements of ss. 4 to 27 of the regulations do not refer to property taxation laws *per se*, by virtue of s. 3 the requirements set out in those sections are required to be incorporated into a First Nation's property taxation laws.

4. NOTICES — All notices referred to in these Regulations shall be in writing and shall be served on the debtor in the same manner as is provided for service of originating documents under the *Federal Court Rules, 1998*.

Commentary

The service requirements of the *Federal Court Rules, 1998* are set out in ss. 128 to 137 of those rules, the relevant portions of which are:

> 128. (1) **PERSONAL SERVICE ON INDIVIDUAL —** Personal service of a document on an individual, other than an individual under a legal disability, is effected

(a) by leaving the document with the individual;

(b) by leaving the document with an adult person residing at the individual's place of residence, and mailing a copy of the document to the individual at that address;

(c) where the individual is carrying on a business in Canada, other than a partnership, in a name or style other than the individual's own name, by leaving the document with the person apparently having control or management of the business at any place where the business is carried on in Canada;

(d) by mailing the document to the individual's last known address, accompanied by an acknowledgement of receipt form in Form 128, if the individual signs and returns the acknowledgement of receipt card or signs a post office receipt;

(e) by mailing the document by registered mail to the individual's last known address, if the individual signs a post office receipt; or

(f) in any other manner provided by an Act of Parliament applicable to the proceeding.

(2) **EFFECTIVE DAY OF SERVICE** — Service under paragraph (1)(b) is effective on the tenth day after the copy is mailed.

(3) **EFFECTIVE DAY OF SERVICE** — Service under paragraph (1)(d) or (e) is effective on the day of receipt indicated on the acknowledgement of receipt form or post office receipt, as the case may be.

129. **PERSONAL SERVICE ON INDIVIDUAL UNDER LEGAL DISABILITY** — Personal service of a document on an individual under a legal disability is effected by serving the individual in such a manner as the Court may order, having regard to the manner in which the interests of the person will be best protected.

130. (1) **PERSONAL SERVICE ON CORPORATION** — Subject to subsection (2), personal service of a document on a corporation is effected

(a) by leaving the document

(i) with an officer or director of the corporation or a person employed by the corporation as legal counsel, or

(ii) with the person apparently in charge, at the time of the service, of the head office or of the branch or agency in Canada where the service is effected;

(b) in the manner provided by any Act of Parliament applicable to the proceeding; or

(c) in the manner provided for service on a corporation in proceedings before a superior court in the province in which the service is being effected.

(2) **PERSONAL SERVICE ON MUNICIPAL CORPORATION** — Personal service of a document on a municipal corporation is effected by leaving the document with the chief executive officer or legal counsel of the municipality.

131. **PERSONAL SERVICE ON PARTNERSHIP** — Personal service of a document on a partnership is effected by leaving the document with

(a) where the partnership is a limited partnership, a general partner; and

(b) in any other case, a partner or the person who has the control or management of the partnership business at its principal place of business in Canada.

131.1 **PERSONAL SERVICE ON SOLE PROPRIETORSHIP** — Personal service of a document on a sole proprietorship is effected by leaving the document with

(a) the sole proprietor; or

(b) the person apparently in charge, at the time of the service, of the place of business of the sole proprietorship in Canada where the service is effected.

132. **PERSONAL SERVICE ON UNINCORPORATED ASSOCIATION** — Personal service of a document on an unincorporated association is effected by leaving the document with

(a) an officer of the association; or

(b) the person who has the control or management of the affairs of the association at any office or premises occupied by the association.

133. (1) **PERSONAL SERVICE OF ORIGINATING DOCUMENT ON THE CROWN** — Personal service of an originating document on the Crown, the Attorney General of Canada or any other minister of the Crown is effected by [transmitting the document]

(a) [in Ottawa] to the office of the Deputy Attorney General of Canada in Ottawa; and

(b) [elsewhere] to the Director of the regional office of the Department of Justice referred to in subsection 4(2) of the *Crown Liability and Proceedings (Provincial Court) Regulations.*

(3) [Inapplicable.]

134. **ACCEPTANCE OF SERVICE BY SOLICITOR** — Personal service of a document on a party may be effected by the acceptance of service by the party's solicitor.

135. Deemed personal service on a person outside Canada — Where a person

(a) is resident outside Canada and, in the ordinary course of business, enters into contracts or business transactions in Canada in connection with which the person regularly makes use of the services of a person resident in Canada, and

(b) made use of such services in connection with a contract or business transaction,

in a proceeding arising out of the contract or transaction, personal service of a document on the person resident outside Canada is effected by personally serving the person resident in Canada.

136. (1) **SUBSTITUTED SERVICE OR DISPENSING WITH SERVICE** — Where service of a document that is required to be served personally cannot practicably be effected, the Court may order substitutional service or dispense with service.

(2) **MOTION MAY BE MADE *EX PARTE*** — A motion for an order under subsection (1) may be made *ex parte*.

(3) **ORDER TO BE SERVED** — A document served by substitutional service shall make reference to the order that authorized the substitutional service.

137. (1) **SERVICE OUTSIDE CANADA** — Subject to subsection (2), a document to be personally served outside Canada may be served in the manner set out in rules 127 to 136 or in the manner prescribed by the law of the jurisdiction in which service is to be effected.

(2) **HAGUE CONVENTION** — Where service is to be effected in a contracting state to the Hague Convention, service shall be as provided by the Convention.

5. OTHER INTEREST HOLDERS — Copies of notices referred to in these Regulations shall be served on

(a) where the notice is in respect of taxable property, all holders of registered rights or interests in the taxable property and other persons named on the assessment roll in respect of that property; and

(b) **where the notice is in respect of personal property, all holders of security interests in the personal property registered under the laws of the province in which the property is located.**

Commentary

Note that the reference to registered rights or interests in paragraph (a) refers to those registered in the land registries set out in the definition of "registered" in s. 1.

6. (1) RECOVERY OF INTEREST AND PENALTIES — A property taxation law that provides for the imposition of interest or a penalty in respect of unpaid taxes shall include the rate of interest and the manner in which the amount of the penalty is calculated, as the case may be.

(2) MAXIMUM RATE OF INTEREST — The rate of interest on unpaid taxes shall not exceed 15% per annum.

Commentary

Similar restrictions are found in

- s. 345(3) of the Ontario *Municipal Act, 2001*;[269]
- s. 415 of the Vancouver Charter;[270]
- s. 5(2) of the New Brunswick General Regulations – Real Property Tax Act;[271] and
- s. 6 of the Manitoba Fees, Discounts and Penalties Regulation.[272]

(3) COMPOUNDING — Interest on unpaid taxes shall not be compounded.

Commentary

Similar restrictions are found in ss. 345(4) and (5) of the Ontario *Municipal Act, 2001*.[273]

(4) TOTAL PENALTIES — The total of any penalties imposed in respect of unpaid taxes shall not exceed 10% of the amount of the unpaid taxes.

---

[269] R.S.O. 2001, c. 25.
[270] R.S.B.C. 1953, c. 55.
[271] N.B. Reg. 84-210.
[272] Man. Reg. 50/97, made under *The Municipal Act*, C.C.S.M. c. M225.
[273] R.S.O. 2001, c. 25.

Commentary

Similar restrictions are found in

- s. 345(2) of the Ontario *Municipal Act, 2001*;[274] and
- s. 376 of the Vancouver Charter.[275]

7. (1) TAX ARREARS CERTIFICATE — Subject to subsection (2), a first nation's tax administrator shall issue a tax arrears certificate and personally deliver it or send it by registered mail to the taxpayer, at the taxpayer's address indicated on the assessment roll, and to all holders of registered rights or interests in the taxable property and other persons named on the assessment roll in respect of that property, before taking any enforcement measures or commencing any proceedings referred to in these Regulations.

Commentary

Note that the reference to registered rights or interests in paragraph 5(a) refers to those registered in the land registries set out in the definition of "registered" in s. 1.

(2) LIMITATION — A tax arrears certificate may not be issued before the expiration of six months after the day on which the taxes became due.

8. CONTENT OF CERTIFICATE — A tax arrears certificate shall include a description of the taxable property and state

(a)   the amount of taxes that are payable;

(b)   the amount of any penalty incurred; and

(c)   the amount of interest payable on the unpaid taxes, and the date by which all amounts owing may be paid without incurring further interest and penalties.

9. SUSPENSION DURING REVIEW — No proceedings referred to in any of sections 7, 13, 14, 22 and 25 shall be taken, and any time periods set out in those sections cease to run, while a request for review under section 33 of the Act relating to the liability of the taxpayer to pay unpaid taxes is being considered by the First Nations Tax Commission.

---

[274]   *Ibid.*
[275]   R.S.B.C. 1953, c. 55.

Commentary

Section 33 of the Act gives a right to members of first nations or taxpayers to request that the First Nations Tax Commission conduct a review to determine

- whether the first nation council has complied with Parts 1 and 2 of the Act and the regulations, or
- whether the first nation has unfairly or improperly applied a property tax law.

LIENS

10. CREATION OF LIENS — A lien may be created under a property taxation law only after a tax arrears certificate has been issued.

11. LOCAL REGISTRY OF LIENS — The tax administrator of a first nation shall maintain a local registry of liens, and shall register in it every lien created under a property taxation law of that first nation in that registry.

Commentary

The Act is silent as to the effect that registration of such a lien will have.

12. (1) MANNER OF DISCHARGE — A property taxation law that provides for the creation of a lien shall set out the manner in which the lien may be discharged.

(2) REGISTRATION OF DISCHARGE — On receiving payment of the taxes, interest and penalties in respect of which a lien was issued, the tax administrator of a first nation shall register a discharge of the lien without delay.

ASSIGNMENT OF TAXABLE PROPERTY

13. NOTICE OF SEIZURE — Where a property taxation law provides for the seizure and assignment of taxable property for unpaid taxes, interest or penalties, and the taxes, interest and penalties remain unpaid more than 9 months after a tax arrears certificate was issued, the first nation's tax administrator may serve on the debtor a notice describing the proceedings — referred to in sections 14 to 21 — that may be taken in respect of the property if the amounts owing are not paid.

Commentary

Note that because under s. 7(2) a tax arrears certificate cannot be issued until at least 6 months after taxes are payable, a notice under this section cannot be issued until at least 15 months after the date on which taxes became due.

14. (1) TIMING OF SALE — Subject to sections 18 and 19, the right to an assignment of taxable property may be sold, by public tender or auction, not less than 6 months after service of a notice on the debtor under section 13.

Commentary

Because in most cases rights or interests in reserve land that are subject to taxation are interests granted by the Crown under the *Indian Act*, the mechanism for the transfer of the right or interest will be an assignment of the lease, permit or other right or interest, rather than a sale of the property *per se*. The successful bidder will therefore end up holding the same lease, permit or other right or interest with the Crown, which will continue to administer it in the same manner as it was administered with the original holder.

Note that because under s. 7(2) a tax arrears certificate cannot be issued until at least 6 months after taxes are payable, and under s. 13 a notice cannot be issued until at least 9 months thereafter, an assignment may be auctioned off under this section no earlier than 21 months after the date on which taxes became due.

This provision is subject to ss. 18 and 19, which provide that

- an assignment auctioned off under this section does not take effect for a further 3 months (during which time the taxpayer can redeem the property); and

- an assignment can be made only to a person who would have been entitled to hold the property under the *Indian Act*.[276]

(2) PUBLICATION OF NOTICE — Notice of a public tender or auction shall be published in the local newspaper with the largest circulation at least once per week for four weeks in advance of the sale and shall be posted in a prominent place on the reserve not less than 10 days before the date of the auction.

(3) CONTENT OF NOTICE — A notice of public tender or auction shall set out

(a)   the upset price; and

(b)   any conditions that are attached to the acceptance of an offer.

Commentary

The upset price on an auction is the price below which bids will not be accepted.

---

[276]   For further information on this restriction, see the Commentary following s. 19(1).

15. UPSET PRICE — The upset price on a sale of the right to an assignment of taxable property shall not be less than the total of the amount of taxes, interest and penalties owing, together with interest to the end of the redemption period referred to in section 17.

Commentary

The redemption period adds another 3 months of interest.

16. PURCHASE BY FIRST NATION — Where there is no bid that is equal to or greater than the upset price, the first nation shall be deemed to have purchased the right to assignment for the amount of the upset price.

Commentary

While s. 5(1)(e)(iii) refers to the forfeiture of seized lands, this section provides the sole *de facto* mechanism by which seized lands would end up in the hands of the First Nation.

17. (1) REDEMPTION PERIOD — Within 3 months after the holding of a public tender or auction in respect of taxable property, the debtor may redeem the right to assignment of the taxable property by paying to the first nation the amount of the upset price plus 3%.

Commentary

Note that the redemption amount is based on the amount of the upset price, not the amount of the successful bid.

The addition of the 3-month redemption period to the 21-month period that must expire from the date on which taxes became due before the subject property can be auctioned off under s. 14[277] brings the total period before assignment to 24 months. This conforms to the restriction in s. 5(7) of the FNFSMA, which requires that taxes must have been outstanding for at least two years before an assignment can be made:

> (7) Notwithstanding the *Indian Act* or any instrument conferring a right or interest in reserve lands, if there are outstanding taxes payable pursuant to a law made under paragraph (1)(a) for more than two years, the first nation may assign the right or interest in accordance with the conditions and procedures prescribed by regulation.

---

[277] Under s. 7(2) of the regulations, a tax arrears certificate cannot be issued until at least 6 months after taxes are payable, under s. 13 a notice cannot be issued until at least 9 months thereafter, and under s. 14 an assignment may be auctioned off no earlier than a further 6 months after service of the notice, which brings the total to 21 months after the date on which taxes became due.

(2) REFUND TO PURCHASER — On the redemption of a right to assignment, where the right to assignment was sold to a bidder in accordance with section 14, the first nation shall without delay repay to that bidder the amount of the bid.

18. (1) EFFECTIVE DATE OF SALE AND ASSIGNMENT — A sale of a right to assignment of taxable property in accordance with section 14 or 16 is not complete, and no assignment of the taxable property shall be made, until the expiration of the redemption period provided for in section 17.

(2) ASSIGNMENT OF TAXABLE PROPERTY — Subject to section 19, on the expiration of the redemption period, the first nation shall assign the taxable property to the highest bidder in accordance with section 14, or to itself as the deemed purchaser in accordance with section 16.

Commentary

Note that it is the First Nation that makes the assignment, not the Minister of Indian Affairs and Northern Development. The power to make such an assignment, which would otherwise be prohibited by the *Indian Act*,[278] derives from s. 5(7) of the FNFSMA:

> (7) Notwithstanding the *Indian Act* or any instrument conferring a right or interest in reserve lands, if there are outstanding taxes payable pursuant to a law made under paragraph (1)(a) for more than two years, the first nation may assign the right or interest in accordance with the conditions and procedures prescribed by regulation.

19. (1) RESTRICTION ON ASSIGNMENT — Taxable property shall not be assigned to any person or entity who would not have been entitled under the *Indian Act* to obtain the interest or right constituting the taxable property.

Commentary

The categories of persons to whom taxable property can be assigned will depend on the type of interest that has been seized and is being auctioned off. Examples of limitations in this regard would be:

- under s. 24 of the *Indian Act*, interests of individual First Nation members allotted under s. 20 of that Act can be transferred only to the First Nation or to another member of the First Nation; and

---

[278] For further details on this, see the Commentary following s. 7(2) of the FNFSMA.

- a right or interest in designated lands will be subject to the terms of the designation, including any terms relating to who can hold the right or interest.[279]

(2) NOTIFICATION OF MINISTER — The council of the first nation shall without delay notify the Minister in writing of any sale of a right to assignment of taxable property in accordance with section 15 or 16.

(3) REGISTRATION OF ASSIGNMENT — An assignment of taxable property shall be registered

(a) where the property is subject to the *First Nations Land Management Act*, in the First Nations Land Register; and

(b) in any other case, in the Reserve Land Register or Surrendered and Designated Lands Register.

Commentary

The Reserve Land Register is established under s. 21 of the *Indian Act*. The Surrendered and Designated Lands Register is established under s. 55(1) of the *Indian Act*. The First Nations Land Register is established under s. 25(1) of the *First Nation Land Management Act*.[280]

Further information on these is set out in the Commentary following the definition of "registered" in s. 1.

20. (1) PROCEEDS OF SALE — The proceeds of sale of taxable property shall be paid to any holders of interests in the property and to the first nation in order of their priority at law.

Commentary

Note that this provision does not itself establish a priority at law, but only makes reference to priorities that otherwise exist by common law or statute.

(2) SURPLUS PROCEEDS — Any monies received from the sale of the debtor's interest that are in excess of amounts paid out in accordance with subsection (1) shall be paid to the debtor.

21. CERTIFICATE OF ASSIGNMENT — The tax administrator of a first nation shall register an assignment of any taxable property sold in

---

[279] For example, a designation that expressly provides that it is for the purposes of a housing development for First Nation members would preclude the transfer of possession of affected property to any person other than a First Nation member.
[280] S.C. 1999, c. 24.

accordance with section 18 in every registry in which the taxable property is registered at the time of the assignment.

SEIZURE AND SALE OF PERSONAL PROPERTY

22. (1) NOTICE — Where a property taxation law provides for the seizure and sale of personal property to pay for unpaid taxes, interest or penalties, and taxes, interest and penalties remain unpaid more than 30 days after a tax arrears certificate was issued, the first nation's tax administrator may serve on the debtor a notice of seizure and sale in respect of any personal property that is located on the reserve.

(2) CONTENT OF NOTICE — A notice of seizure and sale of personal property shall state that

    (a) if the debtor does not pay the unpaid taxes, interest and penalties within 7 days, the tax administrator may seize the personal property described in the notice; and

    (b) if, within 67 days following the seizure of the personal property, the debtor does not pay the unpaid taxes, interest and penalties, and the cost of seizure of the property, the tax administrator may sell the seized personal property.

(3) TIMING OF SEIZURE — Subject to section 24, not less than 7 days after service of a notice of seizure and sale of personal property, if the taxes, interest and penalties remain unpaid, the tax administrator may request a sheriff, bailiff or by-law enforcement officer to seize any personal property described in the notice that is in the possession of the debtor and is located on the reserve.

(4) PUBLICATION OF NOTICE OF SALE — Not less than the earlier of

    (a) 60 days after seizure of the personal property, and

    (b) where a challenge to the seizure was made in a court of competent jurisdiction and dismissed by that court, the day of the dismissal,

the tax administrator of the first nation shall publish a notice of the sale of the property in the local newspaper with the largest circulation, for each of at least 7 days in advance of the sale.

(5) PUBLIC AUCTION — A sale of personal property shall be conducted by public auction.

(6) LIMITATION — The application of subsections (1) to (5) in respect of personal property subject to a registered security interest is subject to any laws of the province in which the property is situated regarding the seizure and sale of such property.

Commentary

Provincial legislation such as the Ontario *Personal Property Security Act*[281] gives priority to holders of registered interests in personal property over other claimants.

23. (1) PROCEEDS OF SALE — The proceeds of sale of seized personal property shall be paid to any holders of security interests in the property and to the first nation in order of their priority under the laws applicable in the province in which the property was seized.

Commentary

Note that although the First Nation can seize and auction off personal property under the regulations, its right to payment of the proceeds of the auction is determined in accordance with the applicable provincial legislation, which is incorporated by reference into the regulations.

(2) SURPLUS PROCEEDS — Any monies received from the sale of the seized personal property that are in excess of amounts paid out under subsection (1) shall be paid to the debtor.

24. LIMITATION — Personal property of a debtor that would be exempt from seizure under a writ of execution issued by a superior court of the province in which the property is situated is exempt from seizure under a property taxation law.

Commentary

See, for example,

- the Nova Scotia *Value of Chattels Exempt from Seizure Regulations*, N.S. Reg. 112/85;
- section 3 of the British Columbia *Court Order Enforcement Act*, R.S.B.C. 1996, c. 78;
- section 2648 of the *Civil Code of Quebec*;
- the Northwest Territories *Exemptions Act*, R.S.N.W.T. 1988, c. E-9.

DISCONTINUANCE OF SERVICES

25. (1) NOTICE — Where

(a)   revenues from a property taxation law are used to provide services to taxpayers,

---

[281]   R.S.O. 1990, Ch. P.10,

(b)   the property taxation law provides for the discontinuance of services for unpaid taxes, interest or penalties, and

(c)   taxes, interest or penalties remain unpaid by a debtor more than 30 days after a tax arrears certificate was issued,

subject to sections 26 and 27, the first nation's tax administrator may serve on the debtor a notice of discontinuance of any services provided to the taxable property by or on behalf of the first nation.

Commentary

Because ss. 26 and 27 prohibit discontinuance of water, fire protection, police or garbage collection services, and discontinuance of electrical or natural gas services to residences during the winter months, notices of discontinuance could not be sent in respect of those services.

(2) 30-DAY NOTICE REQUIREMENT — Services provided to the taxable property shall not be discontinued before the expiration of 30 days after service of a notice of discontinuance.

Commentary

When added to the 30-day period that must pass before a notice of discontinuance is sent, under this subsection services could not be cut off until at least 60 days after the due date for the taxes in question.

26. LIMITATION — A first nation may not discontinue water, fire protection, police or garbage collection services to a debtor.

27. RESIDENTIAL SERVICES — A first nation may not discontinue electrical or natural gas services to a residential dwelling during the period from November 1 in any year to March 31 in the following year.

Commentary

A similar provision is set out in s. 31(5) of the Ontario *Electricity Act, 1998.*[282]

COMING INTO FORCE

28. COMING INTO FORCE DATE — These Regulations come into force on [the day on which they are registered or a specified date].

---

[282]   S.O. 1998, ch. 15, Sched. A.

Commentary

The regulations are expected to come into force on the same date on which the *First Nations Fiscal and Statistical Management Act* comes into force.

LOCAL REVENUE MANAGEMENT IMPLEMENTATION REGULATIONS

Introductory Commentary

The *Local Revenue Management Implementation Regulations* are one of the set of regulations proposed to be made under the *First Nations Fiscal and Statistical Management Act*.[283] The regulations have not yet been made, but have been released by the government for consultation purposes.[284]

The regulations are to be made under s. 56 of the *First Nations Fiscal and Statistical Management Act*, which provides for the making of regulations relating to the manner of implementing powers of the First Nations Financial Management Board under ss. 52 and 53 of the Act.

The regulations place duties on the First Nations Financial Management Board and on First Nations when the Board imposes a co-management arrangement or assumes third-party management of their property taxation system. The regulations provide for:

- assignment of a manager to act on behalf of the Board;
- the type of information to be conveyed to the manager and the manner in which it is to be conveyed;
- the relationship between the manager and outside parties, including financial institutions;
- notice and reporting requirements; and
- fees to be paid by a First Nation for co-management or third-party management services.

The regulations are expected to come into force on the same date on which the *First Nations Fiscal and Statistical Management Act* comes into force.

---

[283] S.C. 2005, c. 9.
[284] Available at First Nations Fiscal Initiative website at <http://www.fnfi.ca>.

LOCAL REVENUE MANAGEMENT IMPLEMENTATION REGULATIONS *(PROPOSED)*

Her Excellency the Governor in Council, on the recommendation of the Minister of Indian Affairs and Northern Development, pursuant to section 56 of the *First Nations Fiscal and Statistical Management Act*, hereby makes the annexed *Local Revenue Management Implementation Regulations*.

Commentary

The introductory Order in Council sets out the enabling authority for the regulations, which is s. 56 of the *First Nations Fiscal and Statistical Management Act*. Section 56 of the Act provides for regulations relating to the manner of implementing co-management and third-party management powers of the First Nations Financial Management Board under ss. 52 and 53 of the Act:

> 56. The Governor in Council may, on the recommendation of the Minister made having regard to any representations by the Board, make regulations
>
> (a) respecting the implementation of a co-management arrangement or third-party management of a First Nation's local revenues, including the obligations of affected First Nations to provide access to financial records; and
>
> (b) fixing fees that the Board may charge for services, including fees to First Nations for co-management and third-party management services, and the manner in which the fees may be recovered.

Note that the regulations are to be made on the recommendation of the Minister of Indian Affairs and Northern Development, having regard to any representations by the First Nations Financial Management Board.

LOCAL REVENUE MANAGEMENT IMPLEMENTATION REGULATIONS

INTERPRETATION

1. (1) DEFINITIONS — The following definitions apply in these Regulations.

"Act"
« Loi »
"Act" means the *First Nations Fiscal and Statistical Management Act*.

"certificate"
« certificat »
"certificate" means a certificate issued by the Board to a first nation under subsection 50(3) of the Act.

Commentary

Under s. 50(3) of the Act, the First Nations Financial Management Board issues a certificate to a First Nation if, after conducting a review at the request of the First Nation, it is of the opinion that the First Nation is in compliance with the Board's standards, which are established under s. 55(1) of the Act.

"financial institution"
« institution financière »
"financial institution" means the First Nations Finance Authority or a person — including a bank, credit union or caisse populaire — or trustee with whom local revenues are deposited or by or through whom local revenues are invested.

"law-making delegate"
« Version anglaise seulement »
"law-making delegate" means a person or body to which the council of a first nation has, under paragraph 5(1)(f) or 9(1)(b) of the Act, delegated any of the council's powers to make laws.

Commentary

Under s. 5(1)(f) of the Act, a First Nation can delegate any of its powers to make laws under ss. 5(1)(a) to (e) of the Act. This includes the power to make property taxation laws. Under s. 9(1)(b) of the Act, a First Nation can delegate the power to make laws respecting the financial administration of the First Nation. This definition is found only in the English version of the regulations.

"local revenue budget law"
« budget des dépenses de recettes locales »
"local revenue budget law" means a law made under paragraph 5(1)(b) of the Act establishing a budget for the expenditure of local revenues.

"local services capital infrastructure"
« immobilisations de services locaux »
"local services capital infrastructure" means improvements and works that are, or are intended to be, used wholly or in part for the delivery of

programs or services on a reserve, including buildings, water, sewer, gas, electrical and communications works, roads, walkways and other transportation systems, and parks.

"manager"
« administrateur »
"manager" means a person referred to in subsection 2(1).

Commentary

Under s. 2(1) of the Regulations, a manager can be an employee of the Board assigned to act as its agent, or an outside contractor engaged by the Board for that purpose.

"tax administrator"
«administrateur fiscal *»*

"tax administrator", in respect of a first nation, means the person responsible for the administration of the property taxation laws of the first nation.

"third-party local services agreement"
«entente de services locaux »

"third-party local services agreement" means an agreement, lease, instrument granting a right-of-way or easement, permit or other instrument to which a first nation or Her Majesty in right of Canada is a party that provides, wholly or in part, for the delivery of programs or services and under which payments may be made from local revenues.

(2) *INDIAN ACT* **DEFINITIONS** — Unless the context otherwise requires, words and expressions used in these Regulations and not otherwise defined have the same meaning as in the *Indian Act.*

APPOINTMENT OF MANAGER

2. (1) BOARD MAY APPOINT MANAGER — Subject to subsection **(2)** and section 3, where the Board requires a first nation to enter into a co-management arrangement or assumes third-party management, it shall assign an employee of the Board, or engage another person, to act as the agent of the Board for that purpose.

(2) DIRECTORS — A director of the Board shall not be assigned or engaged under subsection **(1).**

(3) DOCUMENT EVIDENCING ENGAGEMENT OR ASSIGNMENT — The scope of authority of a person assigned or engaged under subsection **(1)** to act for the Board shall be set out in writing and provided to the council of the first nation without delay.

3. (1) LIMITATION ON MANAGER'S AUTHORITY — A manager shall not

    (a)   give an order under paragraph 52(2)(e) of the Act;

Commentary

Paragraph 52(2)(*e*) of the Act permits the Board, when it has assumed third-party management of a First Nation's local revenues, to order that expenditures of those revenues be approved by, or paid with cheques co-signed by, the Board's manager.

    (b)   act in the place of a council of the first nation under paragraph 53(2)(a) of the Act; or

Commentary

Under s. 53(2)(a) of the Act, the Board may make laws under ss. 5(1)(a) to (f) of the Act in place of the First Nation council. This includes property taxation laws, local revenue budget laws, laws relating to taxpayer representation, borrowing laws, tax collection laws and laws delegating the First Nation council's powers.

    (c)   assign rights or interests under paragraph 53(2)(d) of the Act.

Commentary

This refers to the ability of the Board, on assuming third-party management, to auction off and assign seized rights or interests under s. 5(7) of the Act.

4. NOTICE OF REQUIRED INFORMATION — The Board or its manager may require information referred to in section 54 of the Act by an oral or written request to the council of the first nation, or to any of its councillors, employees or law-making delegates.

Commentary

Section 54 of the Act permits the Board to require from the First Nation any information about its financial management system and financial performance that the Board requires for a decision regarding a co-management arrangement or third-party management of the First Nation's local revenues.

5. (1) BASE-LINE RECORDS AND DOCUMENTS — At any time after receipt of a notice under subsection 52(1) or 53(1) of the Act and while a comanagement arrangement or third-party management is in effect, the first nation shall, on receipt of an oral or written request, give the Board and its manager access to, and copies — or the opportunity to make copies — of, all records and documents respecting the first nation's local revenue laws and their administration, including records and documents relating to

Commentary

The notices under ss. 52(1) and 53(1) of the Act referred to in the opening words of this section are notices requiring a First Nation to enter into a co-management arrangement in respect of its local revenues and notices that the Board is assuming management of a First Nation's local revenues, respectively.

   (a)   **communications between the first nation and the First Nations Tax Commission, the First Nations Finance Authority or the Minister;**

   (b)   **assessments for the calculation of local revenues, and the levying and collection of local revenues;**

   (c)   **budgets for the expenditure of local revenues;**

   (d)   **interests in reserve lands, or rights to occupy, possess or use reserve lands, that are subject to local revenue laws;**

   (e)   **the first nation's local revenue account and all expenditures of local revenues, including audit reports required under section 14 of the Act and any drafts of such reports;**

Commentary

Section 14 of the Act requires that a First Nation's local revenue account be audited at least once every calendar year.

   (f)   **any deposit, loan or investment, or any other agreement with a financial institution, relating to local revenues;**

   (g)   **representations made under paragraph 6(3)(c) of the Act;**

Commentary

This refers to representations made by taxpayers in response to proposed First Nation property taxation laws, budget laws, or laws relating to taxpayer representation.

   (h)   **the enforcement of local revenue laws;**

   (i)   **agreements and communications between the first nation and the First Nations Finance Authority, including those related to the borrowing of money from the Authority;**

   (j)   **agreements and communications between the first nation and any law-making delegate relating to the delegation of law-making powers;**

   (k)   **complaints made, or reviews carried out, under section 33 of the Act, including any agreements and communications with the First Nations Tax Commission in respect of such a complaint or review;**

Commentary

Under s. 33 of the Act, complaints can be made to the First Nations Tax Commission where it is alleged that a First Nation has not complied with the Act or regulations, or has unfairly or improperly applied a property taxation law.

(l) **each program or service funded wholly or in part out of local revenues;**

(m) **third-party local services agreements;**

(n) **local services capital infrastructure;**

(o) **any other agreements, obligations, commitments or other arrangements under which the first nation is or may be or become obligated to expend local revenues or is or may become entitled to receive local revenue; and**

(p) **drafts of records or documents referred to in any of paragraphs (*a*) to (*o*).**

(2) COPIES — A first nation shall, without delay, on receipt of any records or documents referred to in subsection (1) that are produced or obtained while a co-management arrangement or third-party management is in effect, provide the Board or its manager with a copy of the record or document.

6. (1) THIRD-PARTY COPIES OF RECORDS AND DOCUMENTS — At any time after the Board gives a notice under subsection 52(1) or 53(1) of the Act and while a co-management arrangement or third-party management is in effect, the Board or its manager may request copies of records or documents referred to in section 5 from any person who possesses or has control over them, including

Commentary

The notices under ss. 52(1) and 53(1) of the Act referred to in the opening words of this section are notices requiring a First Nation to enter into a co-management arrangement in respect of its local revenues and notices that the Board is assuming management of a First Nation's local revenues, respectively.

(a) **the First Nations Tax Commission;**

(b) **the First Nations Finance Authority;**

(c) **a financial institution;**

(d) **a law-making delegate;**

(e) **any party to a third-party local services agreement;**

(f) **any person who manages or controls local services capital infrastructure;**

(g)   the first nation's auditor; and

(h)   the person in charge of the Reserve Land Register, the Surrendered and Designated Lands Register, or the First Nations Land Register, or of any register maintained by or for the first nation, in which interests in reserve lands, or rights to occupy, possess or use reserve lands, are recorded.

Commentary

The Reserve Land Register is established under s. 21 of the *Indian Act*. The Surrendered and Designated Lands Register is established under s. 55(1) of the *Indian Act*. The First Nations Land Register is established under s. 25(1) of the *First Nation Land Management Act*.[285]

(2) FIRST NATION ASSISTANCE — The first nation shall cooperate with and assist the Board and its manager as required to enable them to obtain copies of records and documents under subsection (1).

7. (1) EXPLANATIONS — Where a first nation is required to provide records or documents under section 5, the councillors, employees, law-making delegates and agents of the first nation shall, at the request of the Board or its manager, provide an explanation of the records or documents.

(2) REQUIREMENT TO OBTAIN INFORMATION — Where a councillor, employee, law-making delegate or agent is not able to provide an explanation that the Board or its manager has required the first nation to provide under subsection (1), he or she shall make every effort without delay to obtain any information necessary to provide the explanation, and any records or documents necessary to provide the explanation, to the Board or its manager.

8. CARE AND RETURN OF RECORDS — Where the Board or a manager obtains records or documents from a first nation, or creates records or documents on behalf of the first nation, while a co-management arrangement or third-party management is in effect, the Board or manager

(a)   shall maintain care and control over them until they are returned to the first nation;

(b)   may make and retain copies of them; and

(c)   subject to paragraph (*b*), shall return the records to the first nation without delay on termination of the co-management arrangement or third-party management.

---

[285]   S.C. 1999, c. 24.

9. FIRST NATION ACCESS TO RECORDS — On receipt of a written request from the council of the first nation, the Board shall allow a representative of the council to inspect and copy records referred to in section 8, on such terms and conditions as will ensure security and safekeeping of the records.

CO-MANAGEMENT

10. (1) NOTICE TO FINANCIAL INSTITUTION — Where an order is made under paragraph 52(2)(*e*) of the Act requiring that expenditures be approved, or that cheques be co-signed by a manager, the manager shall provide a copy of the order to each financial institution with whom the first nation has any ongoing financial arrangements.

(2) REVOCATION OF ORDER — Where an order referred to in subsection (1) is revoked by the Board, the manager shall provide a copy of the revocation to each financial institution referred to in that subsection.

THIRD-PARTY MANAGEMENT

11. (1) APPLICATION OF ACT AND REGULATIONS TO BOARD — For greater certainty, in acting in the place of the council of a first nation under subsection 53(2) of the Act, the Board is subject to all of the requirements applicable to the council under the Act and any regulations made under the Act.

Commentary

Under s. 53(2) of the Act, on assuming third-party management, the Board can act in the place of the council of a First Nation to

(a) make laws under ss. 5(1)(a) to (e) of the Act or, with the consent of the council, under s. 5(1)(f);

(b) implement laws made under ss. 5(1)(a) to (e) of the Act and manage the First Nation's local revenue account, including any necessary borrowing;

(c) provide for the delivery of programs and services that are paid for out of local revenues;

(d) auction off and assign seized rights or interests to pay unpaid taxes; and

(e) exercise any powers delegated to the Board under a law of the First Nation or an agreement between the First Nation and the Board or between the First Nation and the First Nations Finance Authority.

(2) CERTIFICATE-GRANTING POWERS — For the purposes of paragraph 32(1)(*a*) of the Act, while acting in the place of the council of a first nation under subsection 53(2) of the Act, the Board may grant a certificate in respect of the first nation under subsection 50(3) of the Act.

Commentary

Paragraph 32(1)(*a*) of the Act prohibits the First Nations Tax Commission from approving a borrowing law of a First Nation unless the First Nation has received from the First Nations Financial Management Board a certificate under s. 50(3) of the Act stating that the Board is of the opinion that the First Nation is in compliance with the Board's standards, established under s. 55(1) of the Act. This provision of the Regulations essentially states that if the Board, acting on behalf of a First Nation council in respect of which it has assumed third-party management, requests such a certificate from itself, the First Nations Tax Commission must honour that certificate for the purposes of approving a borrowing law (presumably made by the Board acting on behalf of the First Nation council) under s. 32(1)(*a*) of the Act.

12. (1) NOTICE TO FINANCIAL INSTITUTIONS — Where the Board assumes third-party management, the Board or its manager shall provide, to each financial institution with whom the first nation has any ongoing financial arrangements, a copy of the notice of assumption of third-party management given by the Board to the council of the first nation.

(2) SIGNATORIES — The Board may by written notice to a financial institution authorize one or more individuals to act as signatory for the manager for the purposes of subsection (1) and establish the number of signatories required for any purpose.

(3) NOTICE OF TERMINATION OF THIRD-PARTY MANAGEMENT — Where third-party management is terminated by the Board, the Board or its manager shall provide a copy of the notice of termination to each financial institution referred to in subsection (1).

SHARING OF INFORMATION

13. SHARING OF INFORMATION — The Board or its manager may disclose any records and other information available to it, including records, documents and information obtained under these Regulations, that the Board or manager considers necessary to carry out co-management or third-party management effectively or to fulfil the objectives set out in section 14.

MANAGEMENT REPORTS

14. (1) COOPERATIVE MANAGEMENT— Where the Board assumes third-party management, it shall endeavour to work cooperatively with the council of the first nation, the first nation's tax administrator and any employee of the first nation designated by the council, to enable the first

nation and its administration to resume full responsibility for the management, control and administration of all local revenue laws.

(2) NO REDUCTION OF BOARD AUTHORITY — Subsection (1) shall not be construed to limit or otherwise affect the powers and discretion of the Board in respect of the implementation of third-party management.

15. (1) REMEDIAL MANAGEMENT PLAN — Within 60 days after assuming third-party management, the Board shall review the records, documents and information available to it relating to the first nation's local revenues and local revenue laws, and produce a remedial management plan, to address the matters that contributed to the assumption of third-party management.

(2) CONTENT OF PLAN — A remedial management plan may include a debt reduction plan, a budget and an expenditure plan.

(3) REGULAR REPORTING — Advice given by the Board under subsection 53(5) of the Act shall be set out in a written report.

Commentary

Subsection 53(5) of the Act requires the Board, after assuming third-party management, to review the need for third-party management at least once every six months and advise the First Nations Finance Authority, the First Nations Tax Commission and the council of the First Nation accordingly.

(4) EXPLANATION OF REPORT — A report prepared under subsection (1) and each report prepared under subsection 53(5) of the Act shall advise as to whether the Board is of the opinion that there is a continuing need for third-party management.

(5) FINAL REPORT — Where the Board has assumed third-party management, it shall, in addition to the requirements of subsection 53(5) of the Act, within six months after the termination of third-party management, provide the council of the first nation with a report summarizing any third-party management activities not previously reported on and include in the report

(a) a description or copy of all local revenue laws enacted;

(b) a description or copy of all agreements that the Board has entered into while acting in the place of the council of the first nation;

(c) a copy of the most recent local revenue account audit provided to the Board, and a statement of the revenues deposited to, and any expenditures from, the local revenue account, from the last day covered by the audit to the most recent date practicable; and

(d) an update to the management plan required under subsection (1).

(6) MEETINGS TO REVIEW REPORTS — At the written request of the council of the first nation, a manager shall, within 30 days after receipt

of the request, meet with the council to review any report submitted under subsection (1) or (5) or subsection 53(5) of the Act and respond to questions in respect of the report.

Commentary

The report under s. 53(5) of the Act is a report reviewing the need for third-party management, which is produced by the Board at least once every six months.

FEES FOR MANAGEMENT SERVICES

16. (1) BOARD RECORDS — The Board shall maintain records of the fees and disbursements paid or payable by the Board to a manager or other person in the course of implementing a co-management arrangement or third-party management.

(2) FREQUENCY OF INVOICES — The Board shall invoice a first nation, not more often than once each month, for the amount of fees and disbursements referred to in subsection (1) that were invoiced to the Board since the date of the last invoice rendered to the first nation under this subsection, plus 10% of that amount.

(3) INVOICING — After termination of a co-management arrangement or third-party management, a final invoice may be sent to the first nation under subsection (2) within 90 days after the date of termination.

(4) FORM OF INVOICES — An invoice sent under subsection (2) shall set out the nature and amounts of the fees and disbursements incurred since the date of the most recent invoice rendered to the first nation under this section and shall be accompanied by a copy of any invoices from any manager engaged by the Board in respect of the implementation of the co-management arrangement or third-party management.

NOTICES

17. (1) NOTICES AND ORDERS — The following notices and orders issued by the Board shall be in writing:

   (a) **a notice given by the Board to the council of a first nation requiring a first nation to enter into a co-management arrangement under subsection 52(1) of the Act, or terminating a co-management arrangement under subsection 52(3) of the Act;**

   (b) **a notice given by the Board to the council of a first nation assuming third-party management of a first nation's local revenues under subsection 53(1) of the Act or terminating third-party management under subsection 53(4) of the Act;**

   (c) **a notice required to be given to the Minister under subsection 53(1) of the Act; and**

Commentary

This refers to a notice of the Board's intention to assume third-party management of a First Nation's local revenue account.

> **(d) an order permitted to be given by the Board under paragraph 52(2)(e) of the Act and any revocation of such an order.**

Commentary

This refers to an order by the Board that expenditures of local revenues of a First Nation be approved by, or paid with cheques co-signed by, a manager appointed by the Board.

> **(2) NOTICE OF TERMINATION TO MINISTER — The Board shall provide the Minister with a copy of a notice terminating third-party management given under subsection 53(6) of the Act.**

> **18. (1) ADVICE TO AUTHORITY AND COMMISSION — Where the Board gives a notice to the council of the first nation under subsection 52(1) of the Act requiring a co-management arrangement or a notice under subsection 52(5) of the Act terminating a co-management arrangement, it shall provide a copy of the notice to the First Nations Finance Authority and First Nations Tax Commission.**

> **(2) COPIES OF REPORT — Where the Board gives a report under subsection 53(5) of the Act, it shall provide a copy of the report to the council of the first nation and to the First Nations Finance Authority and First Nations Tax Commission.**

Commentary

The report under s. 53(5) of the Act is a report reviewing the need for third-party management, which is produced by the Board at least once every six months.

> **(3) COPIES OF NOTICE — Where the Board gives a notice to the council of the first nation assuming third-party management under subsection 53(1) of the Act or terminating third-party management under subsection 53(6) of the Act, it shall provide a copy of the notice to the First Nations Finance Authority and First Nations Tax Commission.**

> **19. DELIVERY — Notices, copies, orders, reports, invoices, requests or other documents referred to in these Regulations may be delivered personally or by courier, transmitted by fax or e-mail or mailed by prepaid registered post in Canada.**

COMING INTO FORCE

20. COMING INTO FORCE DATE — These Regulations come into force on [the day on which they are registered/specified date].

Commentary

The regulations are expected to come into force on the same date on which the *First Nations Fiscal and Statistical Management Act* comes into force.

SHORT-TERM POOLED INVESTMENT FUND REGULATIONS

Introductory Commentary

The *Short-term Pooled Investment Fund Regulations* are one of the set of regulations proposed to be made under the *First Nations Fiscal and Statistical Management Act.*[286] The regulations have not yet been made, but have been released by the government for consultation purposes.[287]

The regulations are to be made under ss. 87(2)(f) and 89(a) of the *First Nations Fiscal and Statistical Management Act.*

Subsection 87(1) of the Act permits the Authority to establish short-term pooled investment funds. While the Act does not define what constitutes a short-term pooled investment fund, examples of the types of investment funds currently offered by the First Nations Finance Authority Inc. can be examined at the website of the First Nations Finance Authority. The current funds are described as funds that "offer high levels of protection of investor capital, combined with flexibility of subscription and redemption."[288]

Paragraphs 87(2)(a) to (e) set out the types of investments in which funds in a short-term pooled investment fund can be invested. Paragraph 87(2)(f) permits the Governor in Council to add other types of investments by regulation. The *Short-term Pooled Investment Fund Regulations* add, as a permitted investment, pooled investment funds established by the Municipal Finance Authority of British Columbia under section 16 of the British Columbia *Municipal Finance Authority Act.*[289]

The regulations are expected to come into force on the same date on which the *First Nations Fiscal and Statistical Management Act* comes into force.

---

[286] S.C. 2005, c. 9.

[287] Available at First Nations Fiscal Initiative website at <http://www.fnfi.ca>.

[288] First Nations Finance Authority website:<http://www.fnfa.ca/member/pooled_investments.htm>. or http://www.fnfa.ca/forms/pooled_invest_ funds.pdf.

[289] R.S.B.C. 1996, c.325.

SHORT-TERM POOLED INVESTMENT FUND REGULATIONS
(PROPOSED)

Her Excellency the Governor in Council, on the recommendation of the Minister of Indian Affairs and Northern Development, pursuant to paragraphs **87(2)(*f*)** and **89(*a*)** of the *First Nations Fiscal and Statistical Management Act*, hereby makes the annexed *Short-term Pooled Investment Fund Regulations*.

Commentary

The introductory Order in Council sets out the enabling authority for the regulations as ss. 87(2)(f) and 89(a) of the *First Nations Fiscal and Statistical Management Act*. Paragraph 89(a) reads as follows:

> 89. The Governor in Council may, on the recommendation of the Minister after consultation by the Minister with the Authority, make regulations
>
> > (a) *prescribing anything that is to be prescribed under* subsection 82(1) and *paragraphs* 85(3)(c) and (4)(b) and *87(2)(f)*;

Note that the regulations are to be made on the recommendation of the Minister of Indian Affairs and Northern Development, after consultation by the Minister with the First Nations Finance Authority. The italicized text in paragraph (a) establishes the link to s. 87(2)(f).

Subsection 87(2) limits the types of investments in which funds in a short-term pooled investment fund can be invested. While ss. 87(2)(a) to (e) set out specific types of investments, s. 87(2)(f) permits the Governor in Council to add other types of investments by regulation:

> (2) Funds in a short-term pooled investment fund may be invested only in ...
>
> > (f) *any other investments or class of investments prescribed by regulation.*

The italicised wording establishes the link to the *Short-term Pooled Investment Fund Regulations*.

SHORT-TERM POOLED INVESTMENT FUND REGULATIONS

PRESCRIBED INVESTMENTS

1. PERMITTED INVESTMENTS — For the purposes of paragraph **87(2)(*f*)** of the *First Nations Fiscal and Statistical Management Act*, funds in

a short-term pooled investment fund may be invested in pooled investment funds established by the Municipal Finance Authority of British Columbia under section 16 of the British Columbia *Municipal Finance Authority Act.*

Commentary

Subsection 87(1) of the Act permits the Authority to establish short-term pooled investment funds. While the Act does not define what constitutes a short-term pooled investment fund, examples of the types of investment funds currently offered by the First Nations Finance Authority Inc. can be examined at the website of the First Nations Finance Authority. The current funds are described as funds that "offer high levels of protection of investor capital, combined with flexibility of subscription and redemption."[290]

Subsection 87(2) limits the types of investments in which funds in a short-term pooled investment fund can be invested:

> (2) Funds in a short-term pooled investment fund may be invested only in
>
> (a) securities issued or guaranteed by Canada, a province or the United States;
>
> (b) fixed-term deposits, notes, certificates or other short-term paper of, or guaranteed by, a bank, trust company or credit union, including swaps in United States currency;
>
> (c) securities issued by the Authority or by a local, municipal or regional government in Canada;
>
> (d) commercial paper issued by a Canadian company that is rated in the highest category by at least two recognized security-rating institutions;
>
> (e) any class of investments permitted under an Act of a province relating to trustees; or
>
> (f) any other investments or class of investments prescribed by regulation.

Paragraphs 87(2)(a) to (e) set out the types of investments in which funds in a short-term pooled investment fund can be invested. Paragraph 87(2)(f) permits the Governor in Council to add other types of investments by regulation.

Section 1 of the regulations adds, as a permitted investment, pooled investment, funds established by the Municipal Finance Authority of British Columbia under section 16 of the British Columbia *Municipal Finance Authority Act.*[291]

---

[290] *Ibid.*
[291] R.S.B.C. 1996, c.325.

COMING INTO FORCE

2. COMING INTO FORCE DATE — These Regulations come into force on [the day on which they are registered/specified date].

Commentary

The regulations are expected to come into force on the same date on which the *First Nations Fiscal and Statistical Management Act* comes into force.

FIRST NATIONS LAND MANAGEMENT ACT

Introductory Commentary

The *First Nations Land Management Act*[292] ("the FNLMA" or "the Act") received royal assent on June 17, 1999. The Act ratified and brought into effect the Framework Agreement on First Nations Land Management ("the Framework Agreement") between the federal government and fourteen First Nations. The Framework Agreement had been signed by the parties on February 12, 1996, with ratification to follow.

The Act restates many of the provisions of the Framework Agreement, sometimes verbatim. It provides that a First Nation listed in the schedule to the Act can develop and approve a "land code" according to the procedures set out in the Act. When it does so and the land code is certified and comes into force, that First Nation is authorized to manage its first nation land (reserves under the *Indian Act*) autonomously. This represents a major step away from the paternalistic land management provisions of the *Indian Act*, where virtually every reserve land transaction must be granted, approved or consented to by, or on behalf of, the Minister of Indian Affairs and Northern Development ("the Minister") or by the Governor in Council. It should be noted that the vast majority of First Nations presently remain under the land management regime of the *Indian Act*.[293] Signing on to the Framework Agreement and coming under the FNLMA is entirely optional for a First Nation.

The FNLMA is considered to be legislation enabling First Nation sectoral governance. It does not offer a comprehensive aboriginal self-government regime.[294] The Act relates to the management and governance of land, leaving other subject areas to be governed according to the *Indian Act* for the participating First Nations. For example, the *Indian Act* provisions dealing with elections, by-laws, deceased estates, Indian registration and membership continue to apply to First Nations who are operating under the FNLMA in regard to land management.

---

[292]   S.C. 1999, c. 24.

[293]   There are currently 36 First Nation signatories to the Framework Agreement, of which 14 have approved land codes and individual agreements with the federal government. There are in excess of 600 Indian bands in Canada to which the *Indian Act* applies.

[294]   One First Nation has moved on from operations according to the Framework Agreement and FNLMA to a more comprehensive self-government arrangement. The Westbank First Nation, on the shores of Okanagan Lake in British Columbia, was one of the original First Nation signatories to the Framework Agreement, and had approved its own land code. On May 6, 2004, the *Westbank First Nation Self-Government Act* received Royal Assent and it came into force on April 1, 2005. That Act approved and gave force of law to the Westbank First Nation Self-Government Agreement signed on behalf of the Westbank First Nation and Her Majesty in right of Canada on October 3, 2003. As a result the FNLMA no longer applies to Westbank.

Constitutional Premises of the Act

As noted above, the key purpose of this Act is to enable First Nations to move past the restrictive and intrusive land management provisions of the *Indian Act* and to operate autonomously in the management of first nation lands and resources. This transition is not to affect title to the land.[295] Reserve land title under the *Indian Act* is vested in Her Majesty for the use and benefit of a band,[296] and this state of affairs is declared to continue under the FNLMA;[297] the coming into force of a First Nation's land code will not change that status. The Act states that first nation land will continue to be "land reserved for the Indians"[298] within the meaning of Class 24 of section 91 of the *Constitution Act, 1867*, meaning that the federal Parliament continues to have legislative jurisdiction in respect of these lands, rather than provinces.

The Framework Agreement is declared *not* to be a treaty or land claims agreement within the meaning of section 35 of the *Constitution Act, 1982*.[299] Some comprehensive land claims agreements (also described as "modern treaties") include self-government powers and, in some cases, certain of these are intended to be protected by section 35.[300] The First Nation government powers

---

[295]   S. 5 of the FNLMA provides as follows:

    5. For greater certainty, except for first nation land exchanged in accordance with section 27,

        (a) title to first nation land is not affected by the Framework Agreement or this Act;

        (b) first nation land continues to be set apart for the use and benefit of the first nation for which it was set apart; and

        (c) first nation land continues to be land reserved for the Indians within the meaning of Class 24 of section 91 of the *Constitution Act, 1867*.

[296]   R.S.C. 1985, c. I-5, s. 2(1).

[297]   Para. 5(b), FNLMA; see footnote 295 above.

[298]   Para. 5(c), FNLMA; *ibid.*

[299]   Subs. 2(3) of the FNLMA provides:

    (3) For greater certainty, neither the Framework Agreement nor this Act is a land claims agreement referred to in section 35 of the Constitution Act, 1982.

Clause 1.3 of the Framework Agreement provides:

    1.3 This Agreement is not a treaty and shall not be considered to be a treaty within the meaning of section 35 of the *Constitution Act, 1982*.

[300]   For example, the Nisga'a Final Agreement, paragraph 23 of Chapter 2 provides:
NISGA'A SECTION 35 RIGHTS

    23. This Agreement exhaustively sets out Nisga'a section 35 rights, the geographic extent of those rights, and the limitations to those rights, to which the Parties have agreed, and those rights are:

        a. the aboriginal rights, including aboriginal title, as modified by this Agreement, in Canada of the Nisga'a Nation and its people in and to Nisga'a Lands and other lands and resources in Canada;

        b. the jurisdictions, authorities, and rights of Nisga'a Government; and

        c. the other Nisga'a section 35 rights.

contained in the FNLMA and the Framework Agreement are not constitutionally protected in this way.

Land Codes

The land code is the foundational document adopted by a First Nation as a key step in taking on land management powers and responsibilities according to the Act. In the event of any conflict between the land code and a first nation law, the land code takes precedence.[301] First nation laws must be made in accordance with rules for enactment and any other guidance or limitations set out in the land code.[302] Once a land code is certified by the verifier and is in force, it has the force of law and judicial notice may be taken of it.[303]

The land code governs many ongoing aspects of land management by the First Nation. Subsection 6(1) of the Act sets out the mandatory contents of the land code.[304] A land code must include matters such as: a description of the land subject to the code; the rules and procedures applying to the use and occupation of land, including the rules for interests held by individual members of the First Nation; the procedures applying to the transfer of land from a deceased person's estate; requirements for accountability to members of the First Nation for the management of first nation land and the moneys derived from the land; rules applying to the enactment and publication of laws; rules applying to conflict of interest in the management of land; rules for the granting and expropriation of interests in land by the First Nation; and procedures for amending the code.[305]

The Act lists only the mandatory elements to be included in a land code. Clause 5.3 of the Framework Agreement goes on to list some other optional elements that a First Nation might choose to include in a land code, such as limits on the powers of the council to make laws, and any general reservations or limitations on interests to be granted in first nation land.

While it is assumed that a First Nation wanting to exercise autonomous land management powers according to the Act and Framework Agreement would want all of its reserve land to be governed by this regime, exceptions are possible under the Act. The basic unit of management is assumed to be a single reserve[306] (many First Nations have more than one reserve), but even this minimum unit of management may be reduced in exceptional circumstances (for example where part of a reserve is subject to litigation).[307]

---

[301] Subs. 20(4), FNLMA.
[302] Para. 6(1)(g) and subsection 20(1), FNLMA.
[303] Subs. 15(1), FNLMA.
[304] Subs. 6(1) of the FNLMA corresponds very closely with clause 5.2 and paragraph 5.4(a) of the Framework Agreement.
[305] See s. 6(1) for the entire list of mandatory elements.
[306] Subs. 6(2), FNLMA.
[307] S. 7, FNLMA.

A land code must be approved by a majority of the First Nation members who vote in the approval process.[308] As a minimum, more than 25% of all voters eligible to vote must vote to approve the code.[309]

"Individual Agreement" between a First Nation and the Minister

In addition to developing a land code, a scheduled First Nation must also negotiate a separate agreement with the federal government before it can exercise powers according to the Act. This "individual agreement", as it is called in the Act,[310] must describe the land to become subject to the land code, describe the existing interests in land that are to be the subject of the transfer to the First Nation by Her Majesty of Her rights and interests as grantor,[311] provide for the environmental assessment regime that will apply to first nation land in the interim period before first nation laws are enacted on the subject, and generally provide for any other terms relating to the transfer of administration. The individual agreement is to be approved in the same community process as for approval of the land code.

Procedures for Coming into Force of a Land Code

A scheduled First Nation may develop a land code and a process for its approval by the membership, and negotiate an individual agreement with the Minister. The First Nation and the Minister then jointly appoint a "verifier" from a list established in accordance with the Framework Agreement.[312] The verifier's primary role is to determine whether a proposed land code and the process for approving it conform to the requirements of the Act and the Framework Agreement. After the vote,[313] the verifier is to determine whether the conduct of the community approval process was consistent with the process previously confirmed. Finally the verifier is to certify the validity of an approved land code.[314] The verifier's role may also include making certain necessary determinations in regard to disputes between the First Nation and the Minister before a land code comes into force.[315]

---

[308] Subs. 12(1), FNLMA. This subsection provides for two specified options for the calculation of the necessary participation level at paragraphs (a) and (b). There is a third option which is essentially community approval by another method agreed by the First Nation and the Minister. All three options are subject to the more-than-25% minimum approval level rule.

[309] Subs. 12(2), FNLMA.

[310] Subs. 6(3), FNLMA. Also called an "individual First Nation agreement" in the heading to clause 6 of the Framework Agreement

[311] Para. 6(3)(b) and subsection 16(3), FNLMA.

[312] Subs. 8(1) of the FNLMA, which corresponds closely to clause 8 of the Framework Agreement. Clause 44.1 of the Framework Agreement provides that the Lands Advisory Board, jointly with the Parties, is responsible for establishing a list of acceptable verifiers, and clause 44.3 provides that the selection and assignment of verifiers will be arranged by the Minister, the First Nation and the Lands Advisory Board.

[313] The verifier publishes notice of the vote and observes the vote: section 11, FNLMA.

[314] Subs. 8(1), FNLMA.

[315] Subs. 8(2), FNLMA.

Law Making Powers

In addition to the power to make a land code, which has the force of law [316] once it has come into force, a First Nation may also make "first nation laws" in accordance with s. 20 of the Act. First Nations may make laws "respecting the development, conservation, protection, management, use and possession of first nation land"[317] — a very broad power! Others include the power to enact laws respecting:

- interests in, and licences in relation to First Nation land;
- regulation of land use and development including zoning;
- creation, acquisition and granting of interests in land; and
- environmental assessment and protection.[318]

The contours of the new regime in relation to land transactions

Underlying title held by Her Majesty

The Act does not change the fundamental nature of reserve land title holding. First nation lands are reserves that are subject to a land code. Legal title to them is still held by Her Majesty for the use and benefit of the First Nation for which it was set apart.[319] However, in this Act, Parliament has exercised its powers to give effect to a management scheme agreed to in the Framework Agreement, which is very different from the *Indian Act*. The FNLMA provides that the First Nation may exercise the powers, rights and privileges of owner, grant interests in, and licences in relation to, first nation lands, and manage the resources in those lands,[320] subject to certain restrictions set out in the Act and Framework Agreement, in the land code, and in the First Nation's laws. The First Nation council exercises the powers on behalf of, and for the benefit of, the First Nation.[321]

Third Party Interests

Third party interests, such as business and residential leases, pipelines and other utility rights of way, may already exist on reserve land under the *Indian Act* regime. These may have been entered into by Her Majesty as grantor, acting for the benefit of, and on the directions of, the First Nation on whose land the development lies. They may, alternatively, have been established through expropriation. The FNLMA and Framework Agreement provide that existing interests and licences continue according to their terms.[322] When a land code comes into force, the rights and obligations of Her Majesty, as grantor of those existing

[316] Subs. 15(1), FNLMA.
[317] Para. 20(1)(b), FNLMA.
[318] This law-making power is subject to the requirements of section 21, FNLMA
[319] S. 5, FNLMA.
[320] S. 18(1), FNLMA.
[321] S. 18(3), FNLMA. The council may delegate these powers to another person or body.
[322] S. 16(2), FNLMA.

interests, are transferred to the First Nation by operation of the Act.[323] From that point on, no interest in or licence in relation to First Nation land can be acquired or granted except in accordance with the First Nation's land code.[324] One legal practitioner has commented that the challenges of offering long-term stability and certainty, as well as security of tenure, are critical for encouraging lease-holders and other third parties to invest in First Nation land, and that over-coming these challenges will serve First Nations' economic interests well as they seek to attract and maintain investment.[325]

Limits on Alienation

The scope of First Nation power under the Act is very broad, but a First Nation cannot sell its land outright. The principle found at clause 13.2 of the Framework Agreement explains the thinking underpinning these aspects of the regime: "The Parties declare that it is of fundamental importance to maintain the amount and integrity of First Nation land." The only means for alienation of title or the right of full ownership of land[326] are voluntary land exchange, or expropriation by the federal government. An exchange requires community approval and must pass through the hands of Her Majesty in right of Canada.[327] Expropriation is very limited under the Act. Only the federal government may expropriate, not provinces, municipalities or utility corporations. Expropriation is to be used only as a last resort, after consideration of other approaches and attempted negotiation. If expropriation proceeds, the government must take the minimum amount of land and the minimum interest in the land necessary to fulfill the purpose.[328] Even then, compensation must be (at least in part) in the form of land that may be added as first nation land.[329]

Expropriation by FN

First Nations have the power to expropriate interests in their land necessary for community works and other community purposes.[330] Rules for this purpose are to be contained in the land code. Compensation is to be paid based on the rules in the federal *Expropriation Act*.[331] Interests taken pursuant to s. 35 of the *Indian Act* (which sets out powers to expropriate reserve land) cannot be expropriated by a First Nation.[332]

---

[323]   S. 16(3) and para. 6(3)(b), FNLMA.

[324]   S. 16(1), FNLMA.

[325]   Isaac, Thomas; *First Nations Land Management Act and Third Party Interests*, (2005) Alta. L. Rev. 1047, at pp. 1048 and 1060.

[326]   Or transfer of full and complete administration and control, in the case of transfer to Her Majesty in right of Canada or a province.

[327]   Ss. 27 and 28, FNLMA; clause 14, Framework Agreement.

[328]   S. 29, FNLMA.

[329]   S. 31, FNLMA.

[330]   S. 28, FNLMA.

[331]   R.S.C. 1985, c. E-21.

[332]   s. 28(2), FNLMA.

Interaction between the Act and the Framework Agreement

The long title of the FNLMA is *An Act providing for the ratification and the bringing into effect of the Framework Agreement on First Nation Land Management.* The Framework Agreement is not a schedule to the Act, but it is referred to in the long title and in the preamble. In certain cases it is also referred to in the body of the Act in relation to rules governing particular activities. For example, in relation to a voluntary land exchange by the First Nation, s. 26 of the Act provides that "land may not be alienated except where it is exchanged for other land in accordance with the Framework Agreement and this Act."

At the very least, the Framework Agreement might be used in the interpretation of the Act to help resolve ambiguity in the Act. It should be kept in mind that the Act does ratify and bring into effect the Framework Agreement in accordance with its terms.[333] One legal practitioner, in making a presentation on the Framework Agreement and on the early days of First Nations operating according to their land codes, made the following comment:

> The emphasis here is on the Agreement, because the First Nations regard it as the basis of their land management initiative. In broad terms, there is nothing in the First Nations Land Management Act (Bill C-49) that is not in the Agreement; but there are things in the Agreement which are not in the Act.[334]

First Nations in the Schedule, and those with Land Codes in force

While originally limited to the fourteen First Nation signatories, the Act included a provision which enabled more First Nations to sign on. That provision was brought into force by Order in Council[335] in 2003, and there are now 36 First Nations listed in the schedule to the Act. First Nations listed in the schedule are able to develop and ratify a land code according to procedures set out in the Act and Framework Agreement, and are thereby eligible to become "operational". Fourteen First Nations have ratified land codes and individual agreements under the Act and Framework Agreement.[336]

---

[333]   s. 4(1), FNLMA.

[334]   Henderson, Bill; *Framework Agreement on First Nation Land Management*; paper presented at a May 25-26, 2000 conference presented by Insight Information Co.; conference title Aboriginal Land Management and Property Development Strategies. Mr. Henderson devotes a significant portion of the written paper to an argument against the First Nations Land Management initiative being seen as a delegation of federal powers to First Nations.

[335]   SI/2003-108.

[336]   The list of fourteen First Nations currently operational under the Act is **not** the same as the list of the original fourteen signatories to the Framework Agreement. Seven of the original fourteen have ratified land codes and individual agreements, and seven other First Nations, which are more recent signatories to the Framework Agreement, are also operating according the Act. See the Schedule at the end of the Act for the names of the First Nations on it, and the commentaries there for the list of First Nations with approved land codes.

It is important to note that jurisprudence mentioning the Act or Framework Agreement by name is extremely limited to date, and the importance of those few existing cases to the understanding and interpretation of the Act and the new land management regime is minimal. Readers will find reference to these cases, and to other decisions rendered in relation to the *Indian Act* that may apply by analogy, in the Commentaries and Case Law references following particular provisions of the Act.

FIRST NATIONS LAND MANAGEMENT ACT

S.C. 1999, C. 24

ASSENTED TO JUNE 17, 1999

An Act providing for the ratification and the bringing into effect of the Framework Agreement on First Nation Land Management

PREAMBLE

Commentary

This preamble, like most, sets out statements of fact related to the context in which the Act was enacted and statements of intention as to what it is intended to achieve. The preamble forms part of the statute and can be used to assist in determining its purpose.[337]

WHEREAS Her Majesty in right of Canada and a specific group of first nations concluded the Framework Agreement on First Nation Land Management on February 12, 1996 in relation to the management by those first nations of their lands;

Commentary

The text of the Framework Agreement on First Nation Land Management (referred to herein as the "Framework Agreement"), as amended, is set out in full following the text of the Act. Certain provisions of the Framework Agreement will be quoted directly or cross-referenced in commentaries or footnotes. The Act has many provisions that are very similar, and in some cases identical, to the provisions of the Framework Agreement.

AND WHEREAS the ratification of the Agreement by Her Majesty requires the enactment of an Act of Parliament;

Commentary

Clause 48 of the Framework Agreement provides for its ratification by Canada and the First Nation.[338]

---

[337]   R. Sullivan, *Sullivan and Driedger on the Construction of Statutes*, 4th ed., (Toronto: Butterworths, 2002) at p. 296; P.A. Côté, *The Interpretation of Legislation in Canada*, 3rd ed., (Carswell, Toronto, 2000) at p. 59.

[338]   Clause 48 of the Framework Agreement reads as follows:

     48.1 The Parties agree that they will seek to ratify this Agreement and implement it in the following manner:

NOW, THEREFORE, Her Majesty, by and with the advice and consent of the Senate and House of Commons of Canada, enacts as follows:

SHORT TITLE

1. SHORT TITLE — This Act may be cited as the *First Nations Land Management Act*.

DEFINITIONS

2. (1) INTERPRETATION — The definitions in this subsection apply in this Act.

"council"
« conseil »

"council", in relation to a first nation, has the same meaning as the expression "council of the band" in subsection 2(1) of the *Indian Act*.

Commentary

The definition of "council of the band" in the *Indian Act* reads as follows:

"council of the band" means

> (a) in the case of a band to which section 74 applies, the council established pursuant to that section,

> (b) in the case of a band to which section 74 does not apply, the council chosen according to the custom of the band, or, where there is no council, the chief of the band chosen according to the custom of the band;

Section 74 of the *Indian Act*, referred to in the definition of "council of the band", permits the Minister of Indian Affairs and Northern Development to declare that the council of a band is to be selected by elections held in accordance with the *Indian Act*.

"eligible voter"
« électeur »

"eligible voter" means a first nation member who is eligible to vote under subsection 10(2).

> (a) each First Nation agrees to develop a land code and to seek community approval; and

> (b) following community approval by two First Nations, Canada agrees to recommend to Parliament the enactment of legislation.

48.2 This Agreement will be considered to have been ratified by a First Nation when the First Nation approves a land code, and to have been ratified by Canada when the federal legislation comes into force.

"first nation"
« première nation »
"first nation" means a band named in the schedule.

Commentary

A reference to a First Nation in this Act is a reference to an *Indian Act* band that has been named in the schedule to the Act by the Governor in Council according to the conditions set in s. 45 of the Act.

"first nation land"
« terres de la première nation »
"first nation land" means reserve land to which a land code applies and includes all the interests in and resources of the land that are within the legislative authority of Parliament.

Commentary

Subsection 2(1) of the Indian Act defines "reserve" as:

"reserve"

(a) means a tract of land, the legal title to which is vested in Her Majesty, that has been set apart by Her Majesty for the use and benefit of a band, and

(b) except in subsection 18(2), sections 20 to 25, 28, 36 to 38, 42, 44, 46, 48 to 51, 58 to 60 and the regulations made under any of those provisions, includes designated lands.

The part of the definition of "first nation land" referring to the "legislative authority of Parliament" may recognize limitations that have been set by the courts regarding Parliament's power to legislate in respect of lands reserved for the Indians[339] and the federal government's executive power over reserve land in such cases as *St. Catherines Milling & Lumber Co. v. Ontario*,[340] *Attorney-General for Quebec v. Attorney-General for Canada* (the "Star Chrome" decision)[341] and *Smith v. Canada*[342], as these limitations have been adjusted by federal-provincial agreement such as the 1924 Ontario agreement[343] and the three Natural Resources Transfer Agreements[344] with the prairie provinces.

---

[339] Section 91(24) of the *Constitution Act, 1867* gives the federal government exclusive legislative authority over "24. Indians, and Lands reserved for the Indians."
[340] (1888), 14 A.C. 46 (P.C.).
[341] [1921] 1 A.C. 401 (P.C.).
[342] [1983] 1 S.C.R. 554.
[343] Agreement between Canada and Ontario dated March 24, 1924, confirmed by S.C. 14-15 George V, c. 48, and S.O. 14 George V, c. 15.
[344] NRTAs, *Constitution Act, 1930*.

"first nation law"
« texte législatif »

"first nation law" means a law referred to in section 20.

"first nation member"
« membre de la première nation »

"first nation member" means a person whose name appears on the band list of a first nation or who is entitled to have their name appear on that list.

Commentary

For a First Nation under this Act, this is effectively the same as the definition of "member of a band" in the Indian Act.[345]

"Framework Agreement"
« accord-cadre »

"Framework Agreement" means the Framework Agreement on First Nation Land Management concluded between Her Majesty in right of Canada and the first nations on February 12, 1996, and includes any amendments to the Agreement made pursuant to its provisions.

"individual agreement"
« accord spécifique »

"individual agreement" means an agreement with a first nation entered into under subsection 6(3).

Commentary

An individual agreement (i.e. an agreement between the Minister and an individual First Nation) must be approved by the members along with its land code as a prerequisite to a First Nation becoming operational under this Act.

"interest"
«intérêts»

"interest", in relation to first nation land, means any estate, right or interest of any nature in or to the land but does not include title to the land.

Commentary

The defined term "interest" is used in the Act to describe what may be granted by a First Nation to other parties (see ss. 18(1)(a) and (b) of the Act), and is also important in the determination of what may be 'registered'. "Title to

---

[345]   The definition in s. 2(1) of the *Indian Act* is as follows:
        "member of a band" means a person whose name appears on a Band List
        or who is entitled to have his name appear on a Band List;

the land" is excluded from the definition of "interest." This limitation supports the general proposition that title to First Nation land[346] may only be alienated in exceptional circumstances: expropriation by the federal government[347] and voluntary land exchange.[348] Both of these require the involvement of the federal government.

Because "interest" is defined so broadly, and includes "right ... of any nature in or to the land", the question of overlap in the respective meanings of the defined terms "licence" and "interest" arises. See the commentary below under the definition of "licence" for a brief discussion of this question.

The defined term "interest" is used extensively throughout the Act. Notable uses include: s. 6 dealing with content of land codes; s. 16 dealing with effects on coming into force of land codes; s. 18(1) dealing with First Nation powers; s. 20 dealing with First Nation laws; s. 25(3) dealing with registration; and ss. 28 to 32 inclusive, dealing with expropriation.

The corresponding definition found in the Framework Agreement is as follows:

> "interest", in relation to First Nation land, means any interest, right or estate of any nature in or to that land, including a lease, easement, right of way, servitude, or profit à prendre, but does not include title to that land

"land code"
« code foncier »

"land code" means a land code of a first nation referred to in subsection 6(1).

Commentary

The land code is a foundational document under this Act, akin to a constitutional instrument but in relation primarily to land management. While the First Nation council may make laws on certain matters related to land management, the land code must be ratified by the First Nation membership, and

---

[346] Section 37 of the *Indian Act* uses the phrase "title to lands" in making a distinction between transactions that may be authorized by means of designation (a surrender that is not absolute) in contrast to the types of transactions that may be authorized by absolute surrender (such as sale of land or transfer of fee simple title).

> 37. (1) Lands in a reserve shall not be sold nor title to them conveyed until they have been absolutely surrendered to Her Majesty pursuant to s. 38(1) by the band for whose use and benefit in common the reserve was set apart.

> (2) Except where this Act otherwise provides, lands in a reserve shall not be leased nor an interest in them granted until they have been surrendered to Her Majesty pursuant to s. 38(2) by the band for whose use and benefit in common the reserve was set apart.

[347] Ss. 29 to 33, FNLMA.

[348] Paragraph 6(1)(l) and s. 27, FNLMA.

can only be amended in accordance with the rules for amendment contained in the code itself. Subsection 6(1) of the Act sets out the required content of a land code.

"licence"
« permis »

"licence", in relation to first nation land, means any right of use or occupation of the land other than an interest in that land.

Commentary

By excluding any instrument that falls under the definition of "interest" above, the definition of "licence" effectively avoids what might otherwise have been a potentially significant overlap in the meaning of the two defined terms. However, this likely means that, because of the relatively broad meaning of "interest", there is little scope left for the meaning of the term "licence". This point appears to be most significant in relation to registration at s. 25(3) of the Act, where only interests are registrable, and only interests can be given a priority under a registry system established by the regulations. The corresponding definition of "licence" in the Framework Agreement is identical to this one.

"Minister"
« ministre »

"Minister" means the Minister of Indian Affairs and Northern Development.

"project"
« projet d'exploitation »

"project" has the same meaning as in subsection 2(1) of the *Canadian Environmental Assessment Act*.

Commentary

The *Canadian Environmental Assessment Act* defines "project" as:

> (a) in relation to a physical work, any proposed construction, operation, modification, decommissioning, abandonment or other undertaking in relation to that physical work, or
>
> (b) any proposed physical activity not relating to a physical work that is prescribed or is within a class of physical activities that is prescribed pursuant to regulations made under paragraph 59(b).[349]

---

[349]   S.C. 1992, c. 37, s. 2(1).

(2) WORDS AND EXPRESSIONS IN *INDIAN ACT* — **Unless the context otherwise requires, words and expressions used in this Act have the same meaning as in the** *Indian Act.*

Commentary

Examples of terminology used in the *First Nations Land Management Act* that take its meaning from the *Indian Act* include "band" and "reserve". Certain terms, such as "first nation", "council" and "first nation land", are defined using expressions from the *Indian Act*. It is worth noting that the majority of provisions of the *Indian Act* still apply to First Nations coming under this Act. The land management provisions of the *Indian Act* cease to apply when a First Nation's land code comes into force under this Act. *Indian Act* provisions relating to Indian registration, deceased estates, capital moneys and band council by-law-making powers continue to apply, among others.

(3) NOT LAND CLAIMS AGREEMENT — **For greater certainty, neither the Framework Agreement nor this Act is a land claims agreement referred to in section 35 of the** *Constitution Act, 1982.*

Commentary

This statement clarifies that neither the Framework Agreement nor the Act itself are intended to be constitutionally entrenched or protected by s. 35 of the *Constitution Act, 1982*. Article 1.3 of the Framework Agreement makes the same point, as a matter of contractual intention, where it says: "This Agreement is not a treaty and shall not be considered to be a treaty within the meaning of s. 35 of the *Constitution Act, 1982*."

Treaty rights given protection in s. 35 include rights established in modern "land claims" agreements. Subsection 35(1) provides:

> 35. (1) The existing aboriginal and treaty rights of the aboriginal peoples of Canada are hereby recognized and affirmed.

Subsection 35(3) goes on to state:

> (3) For greater certainty, in subsection (1) "treaty rights" includes rights that now exist by way of land claims agreements or may be so acquired.

HER MAJESTY

3. BINDING ON HER MAJESTY — **This Act is binding on Her Majesty in right of Canada and any reference in this Act to Her Majesty means Her Majesty in right of Canada.**

Commentary

Section 17 of the federal *Interpretation Act*[350] requires this type of provision to be in the Act if it is to bind the Crown:

> 17. No enactment is binding on Her Majesty or affects Her Majesty or Her Majesty's rights or prerogatives in any manner, except as mentioned or referred to in the enactment.

GENERAL

4. (1) RATIFICATION AND EFFECT — The Framework Agreement is hereby ratified and brought into effect in accordance with its provisions.

Commentary

This is consistent with clause 48 of the Framework Agreement, which provides that the agreement will be considered to have been ratified by Canada when the Act (the "federal legislation") comes into force. The following is the text of that clause of the Framework Agreement:

> 48. RATIFICATION OF AGREEMENT
>
> 48.1 The Parties agree that they will seek to ratify this Agreement and implement it in the following manner:
>
> > (a) each First Nation agrees to develop a land code and to seek community approval; and
> >
> > (b) following community approval by two First Nations, Canada agrees to recommend to Parliament the enactment of legislation.
>
> 48.2 This Agreement will be considered to have been ratified by a First Nation when the First Nation approves a land code, and to have been ratified by Canada when the federal legislation comes into force.

(2) DEPOSIT OF COPIES — The Minister shall cause a copy of the Framework Agreement and of any amendment made to the Agreement, certified by the Minister to be a true copy, to be deposited in the library of the Department of Indian Affairs and Northern Development situated in the National Capital Region and in such regional offices of that Department and other places as the Minister considers advisable.

Commentary

The Framework Agreement on First Nations Land Management, as amended, is reproduced in this volume beginning at page 297.

---

[350] R.S.C. 1985, c.- I-21, s.17

5. TITLE TO FIRST NATION LAND — For greater certainty, except for first nation land exchanged in accordance with section 27,

    (a) title to first nation land is not affected by the Frame-work Agreement or this Act;

Commentary

The meaning of the phrase "title to first nation land" is consistent with its usage elsewhere in this Act and in the *Indian Act*. It appears to denote the full right of ownership, fee simple title or the full administration and control in Her Majesty, rather than the impact of any lesser estates or interests upon title. This is consistent with the use of this phrase in the definition of "interest" in s. 2(1) of this Act. Subsection 37(1) of the *Indian Act* also employs essentially the same phrase:

> 37. (1) Lands in a reserve shall not be sold *nor title to them conveyed* until they have been absolutely surrendered to Her Majesty pursuant to subsection 38(1) by the band for whose use and benefit in common the reserve was set apart.

The stated exception to the general rule that title is not affected by the Act is in relation to land exchanged in accordance with s. 26(1).

Paragraphs 5(a) and (b) of the Act relate closely to the definition of "reserve" in the *Indian Act*.[351] It is useful to note that the FNLMA later declares the First Nation able to exercise the "powers, rights and privileges of an owner" in relation to this land,[352] notwithstanding the fact that legal title remains vested in Her Majesty.

    (b) first nation land continues to be set apart for the use and benefit of the first nation for which it was set apart; and

    (c) first nation land continues to be land reserved for the Indians within the meaning of Class 24 of section 91 of the *Constitution Act, 1867*.

Commentary

This statement of Parliament's intent with respect to the constitutional status of first nation land is similar to a statement found in the *Sechelt Indian Band*

---

[351]   *Indian Act*, s. 2(1):
      "reserve"

        (a) means a tract of land, the legal title to which is vested in Her Majesty, that has been set apart by Her Majesty for the use and benefit of a band, and

        (b) except in s. 18(2), ss. 20 to 25, 28, 36 to 38, 42, 44, 46, 48 to 51, 58 to 60 and the regulations made under any of those provisions, includes designated lands;

[352]   c.f paragraph 18(1)(a) of the *First Nations Land Management Act*, below.

Self-Government Act,[353] which provides for comprehensive self-government for the Sechelt Band in British Columbia.

ESTABLISHMENT OF LAND MANAGEMENT REGIME

Land Code and Individual Agreement

6. (1) ADOPTION OF LAND CODE — A first nation that wishes to establish a land management regime in accordance with the Framework Agreement and this Act shall adopt a land code applicable to all land in a reserve of the first nation, which land code must include the following matters:

(a) a legal description of the land that will be subject to the land code;

Commentary

This provision aims at achieving certainty as to the boundaries of land governed by the land code and the FNLMA, and therefore also as to the boundaries of any reserve land of the same First Nation remaining under the land management provisions of the *Indian Act.*

(b) the general rules and procedures applicable to the use and occupancy of first nation land, including use and occupancy under

(i) licences and leases, and

(ii) interests in first nation land held pursuant to allotments under subsection 20(1) of the *Indian Act* or pursuant to the custom of the first nation;

Commentary

This provision is linked to s. 16(4), below. The occupation of reserve land by individual First Nation members according to the custom of the band is capable of being governed by the land code and by First Nation laws. The *Indian Act* does not recognize such traditional or customary holdings, even though their practical or *de facto* existence is known.[354] Subsection 20(1) of the *Indian Act* provides that:

> 20. (1) No Indian is lawfully in possession of land in a reserve unless, with the approval of the Minister, possession of the land has been allotted to him by the council of the band.[355]

---

[353]   S.C. 1986, c. 27, s. 31. "For greater certainty, Sechelt lands are lands reserved for the Indians within the meaning of Class 24 of s. 91 of the *Constitution Act, 1867*."
[354]   For an extensive discussion of customary property rights on Indian reserves see Alcantara and Flanagan; "Individual Property Rights on Canadian Indian Reserves" (2004), 29 Queen's L.J. 489 to 532 at paras. 9 to 33.
[355]   R.S.C. 1985, c. I-6, s. 20(1).

(c) **the procedures that apply to the transfer, by testamentary disposition or succession, of any interest in first nation land;**

Commentary

Note that the part of the *Indian Act* dealing with wills and estates of deceased Indians (ss. 42 to 48) continues to apply after the coming into force of a land code. However, a land code must provide for the procedure by which interests in land are to be transferred from the estate of a deceased person.

Among those provisions ceasing to apply are ss. 49 and 50(4) of the *Indian Act*, which require the approval by the Minister for any transfer of lawful possession or occupation by "devise or descent" (by will or intestacy upon death of the holder), and approval of any sale under s. 50(2). Paragraph 6(1)(c) of the FNLMA provides First Nations with the opportunity to replace the Minister's role in these provisions of the *Indian Act* with another form of approval, or with a different scheme entirely.

(d) **the general rules and procedures respecting revenues from natural resources obtained from first nation land;**

Commentary

Subsection 58(5) of the *Indian Act* will no longer apply to a First Nation operating under the FNLMA. That subsection deals with a division of revenue from resources such as fallen timber, sand, gravel and clay between the band and a member in possession of land. A First Nation operating under the FNLMA can deal with this issue through its land code. This provision is linked to s. 16(4).

(e) **the requirements for accountability to first nation members for the management of first nation land and moneys derived from first nation land;**

Commentary

Band councils have traditionally been responsible to their members for their decisions in relation to land and moneys under the *Indian Act*. In some cases, the courts have categorized this as a fiduciary obligation, not dissimilar to the fiduciary obligation owed to bands by the government when it is placed in the position of managing band resources and assets for the benefit of the band.

(f) **a community consultation process for the development of general rules and procedures respecting, in cases of breakdown of marriage, the use, occupation and possession of first nation land and the division of interests in first nation land;**

Commentary

This provision is linked to s. 17, which requires First Nations to establish general rules and procedures respecting the use and possession of land, and the division of interests, upon marriage breakdown. See commentary under that section for a discussion of the gap in the *Indian Act*, and of Parliamentary committee reports on this subject.

> **(g) the rules that apply to the enactment and publication of first nation laws;**

Commentary

The *Statutory Instruments Act* does not apply to land codes or First Nation laws,[356] nor are these required to be published in the *Canada Gazette*. Process and publication rules are required for inclusion in the land code, although the FNLMA does not state any specific standards for these.

> **(h) the rules that apply to conflicts of interest in the management of first nation land;**
>
> **(i) the establishment or identification of a forum for the resolution of disputes in relation to interests in first nation land;**
>
> **(j) the general rules and procedures that apply in respect of the granting or expropriation by the first nation of inter-ests in first nation land;**
>
> **(k) the general rules and procedures for the delegation, by the council of the first nation, of its authority to manage first nation land;**

Commentary

Note that s. 6(1)(k) provides statutory authority for the land code to regulate the power of the council to delegate its land management authority.

> **(l) the procedures that apply to an approval of an exchange of first nation land; and**

Commentary

This provision is linked to ss. 5, 26 and 27. Exchange is the only stated exception (s. 26(1)) to the rule found in s. 5 that title to First Nation land is not to be affected by this Act. (Expropriation by the federal government must also be compensated by other land: para. 31(1)(a).) The procedures established in the

---

[356] S. 44, FNLMA.

land code might be expected to require membership approval for a voluntary exchange.

(m) the procedures for amending the land code.

Commentary

As the land code is a foundational document akin to a constitution (in relation primarily to land management), First Nations will likely provide a relatively stringent process for amending it, possibly including requirements for a membership vote. See ss. 10 to 12 inclusive and the commentaries under them in relation to the voting majority and process requirements for the original adoption of a land code by a First Nation.

(2) LAND MANAGEMENT REGIME — For greater certainty, if more than one reserve has been set apart for the use and benefit of a first nation, the first nation may establish a land management regime for any or all of its reserves.

Commentary

This provision is linked to the opening portion of s. 6(1), and to the whole of s. 7, dealing with conditions under which part of a reserve may be excluded from the application of a land code.

(3) INDIVIDUAL AGREEMENT — A first nation that wishes to establish a land management regime shall, in accordance with the Framework Agreement, enter into an individual agreement with the Minister describing the land that will be subject to the land code and providing for

(a) the terms of the transfer of administration of that land;

(b) a description of the interests and licences that have been granted by Her Majesty in or in relation to that land, and the date and other terms of the transfer to the first nation of Her Majesty's rights and obligations as grantor of those interests and licences;

(c) the environmental assessment process that will apply to projects on that land until the enactment of first nation laws in relation to that subject; and

(d) any other relevant matter.

Commentary

Subsection 6(3) allows the First Nation and the federal government to come to grips with some of the specifics of the transition to operation under the Act and the land code, before it takes place. For example, s. 6(3)(b) enables the government and the First Nation to consider, examine and agree on the existing interests in the land to become subject to the land code. Paragraph 6(3)(b) links to s. 16(3) of the Act.

7. (1) EXCLUDED LAND — Notwithstanding subsection 6(1), a portion of a reserve may be excluded from the application of a land code if it has been surveyed under Part II of the *Canada Lands Surveys Act* and if

> **(a)** **it is in an environmentally unsound condition that cannot be remedied by measures that are technically and financially feasible before the date that the land code is to be submitted for community approval under subsection 10(1);**
>
> **(b)** **it is the subject of litigation that is unlikely to be resolved before the date referred to in paragraph (a);**
>
> **(c)** **it is uninhabitable or unusable as a result of a natural disaster; or**
>
> **(d)** **the first nation and the Minister agree that, for any other reason, its exclusion is justifiable.**

(2) CONDITION — A portion of a reserve may not be excluded from a land code if the exclusion would have the effect of placing the administration of a lease or other interest in land in more than one land management regime.

(3) EXCLUSION NO LONGER VALID — A first nation shall amend the legal description of first nation land in its land code to include a portion excluded under subsection (1) if the first nation and the Minister agree that the condition that justified the exclusion no longer exists, and the individual agreement shall be amended accordingly.

Commentary

It is likely that a First Nation wanting the autonomy to operate under its own land code and this Act will want all of its reserve land to make the transition, rather than leaving some reserve land under the land management regime of the *Indian Act*. While this may be a reasonable perspective, the Act permits some flexibility. A working assumption underlying the opening portion of s. 6(1) is that whole reserves are the minimum unit of land for inclusion in a land code: "a land code applicable to all land in a reserve of the First Nation ...". In case it was not fully apparent from what went before, s. 6(2) clarifies that "the First Nation may establish a land management regime for any or all of its reserves." Section 7 goes on to furnish even greater flexibility by providing that in certain exceptional circumstances, such as environmental contamination or litigation, portions of a reserve may be surveyed and excluded from the land to become subject to a land code when originally adopted. However, s. 7(3) brings us back to the original assumption by providing that the excluded land will eventually be included under the land code once "the condition that justified the exclusion no longer exists."

Verification

8. (1) APPOINTMENT OF VERIFIER — The Minister and a first nation shall jointly appoint a verifier, to be chosen from a list established in accordance with the Framework Agreement, who shall

- **(a) determine whether a proposed land code and the proposed process for the approval of the land code and an individual agreement are in accordance with the Framework Agreement and this Act and, if they are in accordance, confirm them;**
- **(b) determine whether the conduct of a community approval process is in accordance with the process confirmed under paragraph (a); and**
- **(c) certify the validity of a land code that has been approved in accordance with the Framework Agreement and this Act.**

Commentary

Clause 8.4 of the Framework Agreement corresponds directly to s. 8(1) of the Act.

Clause 44 of the Framework Agreement provides for the establishment of a list of verifiers as follows:

44. PANELS OF ARBITRATORS, ETC.

44.1 The Parties and the Lands Advisory Board will jointly establish lists of mutually acceptable persons willing to act as mediators, arbitrators, verifiers and neutral evaluators.

44.2 Parties who become involved in a dispute may select mediators, arbitrators and neutral evaluators from the appropriate list, or may agree to the appointment of an individual who is not on the list.

44.3 The selection and assignment of verifiers and the procedure to be followed by verifiers will be arranged by the Lands Advisory Board, Canada and the First Nation.

44.4 Individuals appointed to act as mediators, arbitrators, verifiers or neutral evaluators must be unbiased and free from any conflict of interest relative to the matter in issue and have knowledge or experience to act in the appointed capacity.

Note that the Lands Advisory Board (referred to in clause 44.3 and elsewhere in the Framework Agreement) is not directly mentioned in the Act.

(2) DISPUTES — The verifier shall determine any dispute arising between a first nation and the Minister before a land code comes into force regarding the terms of the transfer of administration of land or the exclusion of a portion of a reserve from the application of a land code.

Commentary

Clause 8.5 of the Framework Agreement corresponds directly to s. 8(2) of the Act.

9. (1) NOTICE OF DETERMINATION — The verifier shall, within thirty days after receiving a first nation's documents, as required by the Framework Agreement, make a determination under paragraph 8(1)(a) and give notice of the determination to the first nation and the Minister.

Commentary

Clause 8.8 of the Framework Agreement corresponds directly with s. 9(1) of the Act. The documents to be provided by the First Nation to the verifier are set out at clause 8.3 of the Framework Agreement:

> 8.3 The First Nation will submit the following information to the verifier:
>
> (a) a copy of the proposed land code;
>
> (b) an initial list of the names of every First Nation member who, according to the First Nation's records at that time, would be eligible to vote on whether to approve the proposed land code; and
>
> (c) a detailed description of the community approval process that the First Nation proposes to use under clause 7.

(2) REASONS — If the verifier determines that a proposed land code or a proposed community approval process is not in accordance with the Framework Agreement or this Act, the verifier shall give written reasons to the first nation and the Minister.

Community Approval and Certification

10. (1) SUBMISSION TO MEMBERS — If the verifier determines that a proposed land code and a proposed community approval process of a first nation are in accordance with the Framework Agreement and this Act, the council of the first nation may submit the proposed land code and the individual agreement to the first nation members for their approval.

(2) ELIGIBILITY TO VOTE — Every person who is eighteen years of age or over and a first nation member, whether or not resident on the reserve of the first nation, is eligible to vote in the community approval process.

Commentary

The *Indian Act* also provides that band members eighteen years of age or older may vote in band elections and in designation and surrender votes. However, the *Indian Act* did provide that only members living on reserve were eligible to vote. This restriction was challenged in the 1999 Supreme Court of Canada decision in *Corbiere v. Canada* (Minister of Indian and Northern Affairs),[357] and the Court struck it down as discriminating against the equality rights of members resident off-reserve. The court established the analogous ground of "aboriginality-residence" under s. 15 of the *Canadian Charter of Rights and Freedoms*. The Framework Agreement, signed in February 1996, and the FNLMA, which received royal assent in June 1999, therefore avoid the pitfall of being too narrow in their voting provisions by specifying that members "whether or not resident on the reserve of the first nation" may vote to approve or reject a proposed land code and individual First Nation agreement.

Clauses 7.6 and 7.7 of the Framework Agreement set out certain commitments on the part of First Nations to inform voters, and provide some possible methods for doing so. These are not specifically replicated in the Act.

(3) INFORMATION TO BE PROVIDED — The council shall, before proceeding to obtain community approval, take reasonable measures, such as those described in the Framework Agreement, to locate voters and inform them of their right to vote, the means of exercising that right and the content of the Framework Agreement, this Act, the proposed land code and the individual agreement.

Commentary

Clause 7.6 of the Framework Agreement corresponds to s. 10(3) of the Act. Clause 7.7 of the Framework Agreement sets out some possible methods by which First Nations may locate and inform voters. These are not replicated in the Act.

> 7.7 Reasonable steps to locate and inform eligible voters may include the following:
>
> (a) mailing out information to eligible voters at their last known addresses;
>
> (b) making enquiries of family members and others to locate eligible voters whose addresses are not known or are uncertain;
>
> (c) making follow up contact with eligible voters by mail or telephone;

357 [1999] S.C.J. No. 24, [1999] 2 S.C.R. 203.

(d) placing advertisements in newspapers circulating in the community and in newspapers circulating in other localities where the number of eligible voters warrants;

(e) posting notices in the community;

(f) holding information meetings in the community and in other places where appropriate; and

(g) making copies of the documents referred to in clause 7.6(b) available at the administration office of the First Nation and in other places where appropriate.

(4) THIRD PARTIES — If other persons have an interest in the land that is to be subject to the proposed land code, the council shall, within a reasonable time before the vote, take appropriate measures to inform those persons of the proposed land code, this Act and the date of the vote.

11. (1) PUBLICATION OF NOTICE — The verifier shall publish a notice of the date, time and place of a vote.

(2) ROLE OF THE VERIFIER — The verifier, and any assistants that the verifier may appoint, shall observe the conduct of a vote.

(3) REPORT — Within fifteen days after the conclusion of a vote, the verifier shall send to the first nation and the Minister the verifier's report on the conduct of the vote.

12. (1) APPROVAL BY MEMBERS — A proposed land code and an individual agreement that have been submitted for community approval are approved if

(a) a majority of eligible voters participated in the vote and a majority of those voters voted to approve them;

(b) all those eligible voters who signified, in a manner determined by the first nation, their intention to vote have been registered and a majority of the registered voters voted to approve them; or

(c) they are approved by the community in any other manner agreed on by the first nation and the Minister.

(2) MINIMUM PARTICIPATION — Notwithstanding subsection (1), a proposed land code and an individual agreement are not approved unless more than twenty-five per cent of the eligible voters voted to approve them.

(3) INCREASED PERCENTAGE — A council may, by resolution, increase the percentage of votes required under subsection (2).

Commentary

Subsection 12(1) offers some flexibility in the level of voter participation required to approve a land code. Subsection 12(2) requires, as a minimum for any method chosen, that more than 25 per cent of eligible voters vote to approve the code.[358] There are three essential options offered in s. 12(1):

    (a) a majority of eligible voters participate in the vote, and a majority of those participating vote in favour (herein referred to as a "majority of a majority" for ease of reference): this method naturally achieves the minimum approval level set out in s. 12(2);

    (b) a majority of those eligible voters who register to vote, vote in favour: this method may well require the separate application of the minimum approval level set in s. 12(2);

    (c) approval by another method agreed between the First Nation and the Minister: clearly this will be subject to the minimum approval level set in s. 12(2).

The final touch of flexibility arrives with s. 12(3), which provides that the council can increase the minimum percentage of voters required to approve above the 25 per cent provided in s. 12(2).

The surrender and designation voting provisions found at s. 39 of the *Indian Act* provide for a complicated scheme, which has been judicially considered. This means that the already complex legislative provisions are not likely to be fully understood without reference to the *Cardinal* and *King* cases described below. In first votes, a "majority of a majority" approach is used to determine whether the band membership has assented to a designation or surrender under the *Indian Act*. In essence this is the same approach offered in s. 12(1)(a) of the FNLMA.

Case Law

Cardinal v. Canada, [1982] 3 C.N.L.R. 3 (S.C.C.)

The plaintiffs sought a declaration that a surrender taken in 1908 was invalid because it was assented to by only a majority of the eligible voters who attended the surrender meeting, and not a majority of the eligible voters of the band as a whole.

In the Supreme Court of Canada decision in that case, the court looked at the wording of s. 49(1) of the 1906 *Indian Act*,[359] a substantially similar predecessor

---

[358]   Note that s. 12(2) requires that, as a minimum, more than 25 per cent of all eligible voters must vote to approve the land code and individual agreement. This is really a "minimum approval level". The marginal note to this subsection refers to "minimum participation" which appears to be somewhat misleading.

[359]   R.S.C. 1906, c. 81, s. 49:

    49. Except as in this Part otherwise provided, no release or surrender of a reserve, or a portion of a reserve, held for a [sic] the use of the Indians of any band, or of any individual Indian, shall be valid or binding, unless the release or surrender shall be assented to by a majority of the male members of the band of the full age of twenty-one years, at a meeting or council thereof summoned for that purpose, according to the rules

to s. 39(1) of the present Act. It determined that the key issue was whether the phrase "at a general meeting of the band"[360] modified "majority", narrowing its application so as to refer only to *a majority of those attending the meeting* (a majority of a majority), or whether the phrase was merely descriptive of the location where the vote of *a majority of all electors of the band* was to take place (an absolute majority).

In reaching this interpretation of "majority" in *Cardinal*, the court construed the wording of s. 49(1) of the 1906 Act as requiring that a quorum composed of a majority of eligible voters be present at a surrender meeting. It reached this conclusion by considering the wording of s. 49(2) of that Act, which stated that no band member shall be eligible to attend or vote at a surrender meeting unless he habitually resides on or near the reserve in question. Since s. 49(2) limits the number of band members who are eligible to vote at a surrender meeting, the court felt that this militated against an interpretation of "majority" as meaning an absolute majority of band members; otherwise, s. 49(2) would have the effect of giving a negative vote to those band members who were ineligible to attend (because they would still be counted in determining the total number of votes required to achieve a majority).[361]

Since the court considered this to be an untenable result unintended by the legislature, it read the two subsections together as requiring "that there be a meeting of eligible members of the band and that in attendance at that meeting there must be a majority of [eligible voters]".[362]

In determining how the required assent was to be ascertained, the court in *Cardinal* applied the following reasoning:

> There remains to determine only the requirement for the expression of assent, in the sense of that term in s. 49(1), at the meeting attended by the prescribed majority. In the common law and, indeed, in general usage of the language, a group of persons may, unless specially organized, express their view only by an agreement by the majority. A refinement arises where all members of a defined group present at a meeting do not express a view. In that case, as we shall see, the common law expresses again the ordinary sense of our language that the group viewpoint is that which is expressed by the majority of those declaring or voting on the issue in question. Thus, by this rather simple line of reasoning, the section is construed as meaning that *an assent, to be valid, must be given by a majority of a majority of eligible band members in attendance*

---

of the band, and held in the presence of the Superintendent General, or of an officer duly authorized to attend such council, by the Governor in Council or by the Superintendent General.

[360] Found in subparagraph 39(1)(b)(i) of the present Act.

[361] [1982] 3 C.N.L.R. 3 at 10, quoting Gillanders J.A. in *Glass Bottle Blowers Association of United States v. Dominion Glass Co.*, [1943] O.W.N. 652 at 656.

[362] *Ibid.*, at p. 9.

at a meeting called for the purpose of giving or withholding assent.[363]

Canada v. King, [1986] F.C.J. No. 136, [1986] 4 C.N.L.R. 74 (T.D.).

The plaintiffs were seeking to force the Governor in Council to approve a surrender that had been assented to by only a majority of the band's electors who had attended the meeting — a majority of a majority. The court applied the reasoning in *Cardinal* to find that s. 39(1) of the 1970 *Indian Act*,[364] identical in all relevant respects to the present s. 39(1), also required only a majority of a majority.

The court buttressed its application of the "majority of a majority" interpretation by referring to the incongruity that would otherwise be presented by s. 39(2) of the *Indian Act*:

> Since Parliament has thus declared that where the majority of the electors does vote, no second referendum will be held, it is by inference declaring that such a vote is valid. In turn, where the majority of those votes favour the surrender, the surrender is valid. Had Parliament intended that no surrender would be valid unless it was assented to by an absolute majority of the electors of the band it would have employed that precise language in the section.[365]

13. (1) COPY AND DECLARATION — If a first nation votes to approve a land code and an individual agreement, its council shall, after the conclusion of the vote and without delay, send to the verifier a copy of the approved code and a declaration that the code and agreement were approved in accordance with section 12.

(2) REPORT OF IRREGULARITY — The Minister or an eligible voter may, within five days after the conclusion of a vote, report any irregularity in the voting process to the verifier.

14. (1) CERTIFICATION — The verifier shall, after receiving a copy of the land code and the declaration, certify the validity of the land code unless the verifier, after giving the first nation and the Minister a reasonable opportunity to make submissions on the matter but within ten days after the conclusion of the vote, is of the opinion that

(a) the community approval process confirmed under paragraph 8(1)(a) was not followed or the community approval was otherwise irregular; and

---

[363] (Emphasis added.) *Ibid.*, at p. 9.

[364] R.S.C. 1970 c. I-6.

[365] [1986] F.C.J. No. 136, [1986] 4 C.N.L.R. 74 at 78 (T.D.).

(b)   the land code might not have been approved but for that irregularity.

(2) TRANSMITTAL — The verifier shall, without delay, send a copy of the certified land code to the first nation and the Minister.

(3) PRESUMPTION — A certified land code is deemed to have been validly approved by the first nation.

Coming into Force of Land Code

15. (1) COMING INTO FORCE — A land code comes into force and has the force of law on the day it is certified or on any other later date that may be specified in or under the land code and judicial notice shall thereafter be taken of the land code in any proceedings.

(2) ACCESS TO LAND CODE — A copy of the land code of a first nation shall be maintained by the council for public inspection at a place designated by the council.

16. (1) EFFECT — After the coming into force of a land code, no interest in or licence in relation to first nation land may be acquired or granted except in accordance with the land code of the first nation.

Commentary

Subsection 16(1), in combination with s. 18 and s. 38(1), which provides that *Indian Act* land management powers no longer apply, makes it clear that the Minister will no longer have authority to grant interests in First Nation land, and that these may only be granted by a First Nation authority (the council or a delegated body) after the coming into force of the land code.

(2) INTERESTS OF THIRD PARTIES — Subject to subsections (3) and (4), interests in and licences in relation to first nation land that exist on the coming into force of a land code continue in accordance with their terms and conditions.

(3) TRANSFER OF RIGHTS OF HER MAJESTY — On the coming into force of the land code of a first nation, the rights and obligations of Her Majesty as grantor in respect of the interests and licences described in the first nation's individual agreement are transferred to the first nation in accordance with that agreement.

Commentary

One law review commentator has raised questions about security of tenure for third-party interests under the FNLMA from the perspective that law-making powers might be used to limit third-party contractual rights, and that First Nation expropriation powers might be used in unusual ways, among others.

However, he does allow that this is a relatively untested regime, and that "many of these challenges may not be borne out in practice."[366]

Case Law

Chapman v. Canada; Westwick v. Canada, [2003] B.C.J. No. 2742, 2003 BCCA 665.

The British Columbia Court of Appeal dismissed an appeal from a decision to strike certain pleadings. The chambers judge declined to strike the claims in their entirety, but pruned the pleadings of certain challenges to the validity of leases on the Musqueam Reserve and of certain allegations based upon the *First Nations Land Management Act.* In particular the pleadings alleged that the Crown, the First Nation and the Council wrongfully agreed to "impose" on the Plaintiffs the *First Nations Land Management Act* which would breach the terms of the plaintiffs' leases. The Court of Appeal determined that the *First Nations Land Management Act* was enabling legislation, allowing for the exercise of a range of powers by a First Nation upon satisfaction of certain criteria. It found that the allegations contained in these pleadings were, at that stage, speculative, that no damages could then possibly be proven, and that these allegations were appropriately struck from the pleadings.

(4) INTERESTS OF FIRST NATION MEMBERS — Interests in first nation land held on the coming into force of a land code by first nation members pursuant to allotments under subsection 20(1) of the *Indian Act* or pursuant to the custom of the first nation are subject to the provisions of the land code governing the transfer and lease of interests in first nation land and sharing in natural resource revenues.

Case Law

Many Guns v. Siksika Nation Tribal Administration [2003] A.J. No. 1182, [2004] 1 C.N.L.R. 176 (Prov. Ct.).

The defendant was found negligent in having failed to install a Texas gate at an entrance to the community pasture, a factor resulting in the destruction of the plaintiff's horse following a collision with a fire truck. In its reasons for judgment the court considered the reference in s. 16(4) of the FNLMA[367] to customary holdings of First Nation members. This was part of the court's determination that the federal government bore no liability in this case, but rather that the use of the land as community pasture fell into the broad category of the First Nation's customary use of land.

---

[366]   Isaac; "First Nations Land Management Act and Third Party Interests" Alta. L. Rev. (2005) at 1047.

[367]   *Ibid.*, paras. 83-84.

Rules on Breakdown of Marriage

17. (1) OBLIGATION OF FIRST NATION — A first nation shall, in accordance with the Framework Agreement and following the community consultation process provided for in its land code, establish general rules and procedures, in cases of breakdown of marriage, respecting the use, occupation and possession of first nation land and the division of interests in first nation land.

(2) ESTABLISHMENT OF RULES AND PROCEDURES — The first nation shall, within twelve months after its land code comes into force, incorporate the general rules and procedures into its land code or enact a first nation law containing the general rules and procedures.

(3) DISPUTES — The first nation or the Minister may refer any dispute relating to the establishment of the general rules and procedures to an arbitrator in accordance with the Framework Agreement.

Commentary

Section 17 should be read in conjunction with paragraph 6(1)(f) of the Act, requiring the inclusion in the land code of a community consultation process for the development of these rules and procedures.

Provincial laws relating to the division of property on marriage breakdown apply to registered Indians and First Nation members. However, those laws have been held not to apply when they would affect the use or occupation of real property on reserves and conflict with the *Indian Act* provisions relating to allotment of land to members. While courts can make unequal divisions of other assets in order to compensate for their inability to deal with real property on reserve, this is not a fully satisfactory solution, as the matrimonial home is often the most valuable asset of a couple.

Section 17 of the FNLMA and the corresponding provisions of the Framework Agreement require the First Nation to make rules and procedures to deal with use and occupation of land and division of interests in the case of marriage breakdown, targeted toward filling the gap remaining even now in the *Indian Act*. Senate and House of Commons committees have considered and reported on the gap in the *Indian Act* relating to matrimonial real property in 2003, 2004 and 2005.[368]

---

[368]   "A Hard Bed To Lie In: Matrimonial Real Property On Reserve" – An Interim Report of the Standing Senate Committee on Human Rights; November 2003. A copy of this report can be found on the Parliament of Canada website at <http://www.parl.gc.ca/common/Committee_SenRep.asp?Language=E&parl=37&Ses=2&comm_id=77>

"On-Reserve Matrimonial Real Property: Still Waiting" – A Report of the Standing Senate Committee on Human Rights; December 2004. A copy of this report can be found on the Parliament of Canada website at <http://www.parl.gc.ca/38/1/parlbus/commbus/senate/com-e/huma-e/rep-e/rep04dec04e.htm.>

"Walking Arm-In-Arm To Resolve The Issue Of On-Reserve Matrimonial Real Property" – A Report of the House of Commons Standing Committee on Aboriginal Affairs

Case Law

Derrickson v. Derrickson, [1986] S.C.J. No. 16, [1986] 1 S.C.R. 285.

The Supreme Court of Canada determined that the British Columbia *Family Relations Act* when dealing with the ownership and possession of real property did not apply to reserve lands. It concluded that when provincial legislation of general application extends to a matter of federal exclusive jurisdiction, it is to be given a limited meaning that will confine it within the limits of the provincial jurisdiction. Because the court was of the opinion that the right to possession of reserve lands was at the essence of the federal government's exclusive legislative power under s. 91(24) of the *Constitution Act, 1867,* it held that provincial legislation cannot apply to alter rights to possession of reserve lands.

It held further that the provisions of the *Family Relations Act* in question were not referentially incorporated by s. 88 of the *Indian Act*, since they were in conflict with the provisions of the *Indian Act.*

British Columbia Native Women's Society v. Canada, [1999] F.C.J. No. 1296, [2000] 1 F.C. 304.

The Federal Court Trial Division dismissed an application to strike portions of a statement of claim relating to the alleged failure of the Framework Agreement on First Nations Land Management to make provision for Indian women on reserves who, according to the claim, unlike all other Canadian women, had in law and in practice no matrimonial property rights. The statement of claim sought declarations that the Framework Agreement breached the Crown's fiduciary duty and the plaintiffs' Charter rights, together with interim injunctive relief to prevent the Crown from executing either the Framework Agreement or any derivative agreement with a First Nation. The defendant sought to have references to the Framework Agreement struck out for want of a reasonable cause of action and as vexatious, frivolous and abusive. However, the defendant's application was dismissed as the court found that the portions of the claim concerning the Framework Agreement were not plainly, obviously and beyond doubt pleadings which could not possibly succeed.

Commentators have written[369] that it was in response to this challenge that the federal government and participating First Nations added a clause to the Framework Agreement allowing First Nations to formulate their own matrimonial property laws. Clause 5.4 of the Framework Agreement corresponds closely to section 17 and paragraph 6(1)(f) of the Act.

---

and Northern Development; June 2005. A copy of this report can be found on the Parliament of Canada website at <http://www.parl.gc.ca/committee/CommitteePublication.aspx?SourceId =119922>

[369] Alcantara and Flanagan; "Individual Property Rights on Canadian Indian Reserves" (2004), 29 Queen's L.J. 489 – 532 at para. 48

LAND MANAGEMENT REGIME

First Nation Powers

18. (1) POWER TO MANAGE — A first nation has, after the coming into force of its land code and subject to the Framework Agreement and this Act, the power to manage first nation land and, in particular, may

(a) exercise the powers, rights and privileges of an owner in relation to that land;

(b) grant interests in and licences in relation to that land;

(c) manage the natural resources of that land; and

(d) receive and use all moneys acquired by or on behalf of the first nation under its land code.

(2) LEGAL CAPACITY — For any purpose related to first nation land, a first nation has the legal capacity necessary to exercise its powers and perform its duties and functions and, in particular, may

(a) acquire and hold real and personal property;

(b) enter into contracts;

(c) borrow money;

(d) expend and invest money; and

(e) be a party to legal proceedings.

(3) EXERCISE OF POWER — The power of a first nation to manage first nation land shall be exercised by the council of a first nation, or by any person or body to whom a power is delegated by the council in accordance with the first nation's land code, and that power shall be exercised for the use and benefit of the first nation.

(4) MANAGEMENT BODY — A body established to manage first nation land is a legal entity having the capacity, rights, powers and privileges of a natural person.

Commentary

Section 18 of the Act contains a statement of the key powers necessary for a First Nation to grant interests in first nation land (reserve land) upon the coming into force of its land code, and generally to exercise a broad range of powers to engage in contractual and other transactions in the management of land as a government.

The legal status of bands and band councils under the *Indian Act* has been the subject of considerable debate and has arisen many times in litigation over the last three decades. While the courts have generally arrived at the conclusion that *Indian Act* bands and their councils have sufficient capacity to conduct necessary business, the capacity of a band has never been made explicit in the *Indian Act* itself. Instead, the courts have generally found it to be implicit in the powers available under the *Indian Act*.

Section 18 of the FNLMA goes further than the *Indian Act,* by setting out general and specific powers in s. 18(1) and elements of legal status and capacity of a First Nation in s. 18(2), and by clarifying in s. 18(3) that it is the council of the First Nation that can exercise these powers to manage land on behalf of the First Nation. Finally s. 18(4) clarifies that another body delegated by the council to exercise these powers will also have legal capacity. Note that the powers of the First Nation in ss. 18(1) and 18(2) are described by general and more specific listed subject areas, whereas in s. 18(4) a delegated body is described as "having the capacity, rights, powers and privileges of a natural person."

The case law below illustrates the *Indian Act* legal capacity questions, and provides the backdrop for the more explicit approach to legal powers and capacities found in the FNLMA.

Case Law

PSAC v. Francis, [1982] 2 S.C.R. 72.

The Supreme Court of Canada held that, while the *Indian Act* did not establish a band or band council as a corporate body, it did grant the band council certain powers which, if exercised, rendered the band council subject to the same liabilities as the law imposes on natural persons exercising those powers. The band council's status as an entity with legal capacity to act as an employer therefore arose by necessary implication.

Mintuck v. Valley River Band No. 63A (1977), 75 D.L.R. (3d) 589 (Man. C.A.).

In an earlier decision the Manitoba Court of Appeal had held that a band can be sued in tort for the actions of its council, and that it was appropriate to name the chief and council as representatives of the band for that purpose. It also ruled that a judgement obtained in such an action could be executed against the assets of the band. Similarly, in a recent decision in *Horseman v. Horse Lake First Nation,*[370] the Alberta Court of Appeal confirmed that a band is a public body and that if it acts either maliciously or in abuse of its powers it will be liable for the tort of breach of public authority.

R. v. Cochrane, [1977] M.J. No. 301, [1977] 3 W.W.R. 660 (Co. Ct.).

The court held that while a band may be a suable entity, it is neither a natural person nor a corporation.

Cache Creek Motors Ltd. v. Porter, [1979] B.C.J. No. 1602, 14 B.C.L.R. 13 (Co. Ct.).

The court confirmed that band can be sued in its own right without the involvement of the Minister of Indian Affairs and Northern Development.

---

[370]   [2005] A.J. No. 24, 248 D.L.R. (4th) 505 (C.A.).

Joe v. Findlay, [1987] B.C.J. No. 20, 12 B.C.L.R. (2d) 166 (S.C.).

It was held that a band council's authority to bring and defend legal proceedings on behalf of the band, although not expressly provided for in the *Indian Act*, must be inferred as a necessary adjunct to give effect to the band council's powers under s. 81 of the Act. The court also confirmed that it was not necessary for the council to seek the consent of the band to do so.

King v. Gull Bay Indian Band, [1983] O.J. No. 2152, 38 C.P.C. 1 (Dist. Ct.).

The court found that Indian bands are not unincorporated associations, but are instead legal entities that are therefore capable of being sued. This ruling was followed in *Bannon v. Pervais,*[371] *Springhill Lumber Ltd. v. Lake St. Martin Indian Band*[372] and *Clow Darling Ltd. v. Big Trout Lake Band.*[373]

Kucey v. Peter Ballantyne Band Council, [1987] S.J. No. 193, [1987] 3 W.W.R. 438 (C.A.).

The court followed the Supreme Court of Canada decision in *PSAC v. Francis,*[374] and held that because Indian band councils are given significant rights to contract and incur legal obligations in the course of fulfilling their statutory mandate, they may sue or be sued in their own name: that they have an existence in law that goes beyond that of their individual members.

Wewayakum Indian Band v. Canada, [1991] F.C.J. No. 213, [1991] 3 F.C. 420 (T.D.).

The court concluded that Indian bands have a special status enabling them to institute, prosecute and defend a court action. It observed that a band has the same power to sue as a corporation, and would consequently be subject to any resulting obligations.[375]

William v. Lake Babine Indian Band, [1999] B.C.J. No. 842, [2000] 1 C.N.L.R. 233 (S.C.).

The British Columbia Supreme Court, in determining how an Indian band could be served with a legal process, commented on the reasoning in *Wewayakum Indian Band v. Canada.* It noted that although an Indian band may have similar obligations and rights to a corporation, that does not mean that it functions as, or assumes the legal status of, a corporation. It concluded instead that a band is more analogous to an unincorporated entity than to a corporation.

---

[371]   [1989] O.J. No. 426, 68 O.R. (2d) 276 (Dist. Ct.).
[372]   [1985] M.J. No. 425, [1986] 2 C.N.L.R. 179 (Q.B.).
[373]   70 O.R. (2d) 56 (Dist.Ct.).
[374]   [1982] 2 S.C.R. 72.
[375]   [1991] F.C.J. No. 213, [1991] 3 F.C. 420 (T.D.) at 429.

Otineka Dev Corp. Ltd. v. Canada, [1994] T.C.J./A.C.I. No. 23, [1994] 2 C.N.L.R. 83 (F.C.).

The Tax Court of Canada determined that, for the purposes of the tax exemptions granted by s. 149(1)(d) of the *Income Tax Act*, a band engaging in particular governmental activities is a municipality.

Montana Band v. Canada, [1997] F.C.J. No. 1486, [1998] 2 F.C. 3 (T.D.)

The Federal Court held that a band's capacity to sue or be sued arises by implication from its statutory powers, but has uncertain boundaries. It confirmed that a band or band council does not have the legal powers of a natural person in the same way a corporation does. It also confirmed that the naming of a band as a party to a legal action, followed by certain named band members (usually the elected councillors) acting on their own behalf as well as on behalf of all other members of the band, was sufficient to resolve any uncertainties about legal status that might exist.[376]

Nelson House Indian Band v. Frost, [1999] M.J. No. 63, 169 D.L.R. (4th) 606 (C.A.).

The court held that an Indian band empowered to control and manage revenue moneys under s. 69 of the *Indian Act* has the capacity to sue for the recovery of revenue moneys that had allegedly been misappropriated.

19. TRANSFER OF MONEYS — On the coming into force of the land code of a first nation, all revenue moneys collected, received or held by Her Majesty for the use and benefit of the first nation or its first nation members cease to be Indian moneys and shall be transferred to the first nation.

Commentary

This is a reference to the transfer of the "revenue moneys" category of "Indian moneys", a defined term in the *Indian Act*.[377] Sections 61 to 69 of the *Indian Act* govern the administration of Indian moneys. Section 62 establishes the two categories of capital moneys and revenue moneys, and ss. 66 and 69 deal with administration of revenue moneys under that Act. According to s. 38(1)(a) of the FNLMA, ss. 66 and 69 of the *Indian Act* cease to apply to a First Nation and its lands under the FNLMA.

The website of the Framework Agreement on First Nations Land Management (maintained by the Lands Advisory Board) offers the following comment in respect of s. 19:

> *Transfer of Revenue* The Act provides that revenue moneys of the First Nation previously collected and held by Canada will

---

[376] [1997] F.C.J. No. 1486, [1998] 2 F.C. 3 (T.D.) at para. 32.
[377] R.S.C. 1985, c. I-5, s. 2(1)

be transferred to the First Nation when its land code comes into effect.[378]

First Nation Laws

20. (1) POWER TO ENACT LAWS — The council of a first nation has, in accordance with its land code, the power to enact laws respecting

(a)   **interests in and licences in relation to first nation land;**

(b)   **the development, conservation, protection, management, use and possession of first nation land; and**

(c)   **any matter arising out of or ancillary to the exercise of that power.**

Commentary

Note the scope and breadth of these powers, particularly those set out in paragraph (b).

(2) PARTICULAR POWERS — Without restricting the generality of subsection (1), first nation laws may include laws respecting

(a)   **the regulation, control or prohibition of land use and development including zoning and subdivision control;**

(b)   **subject to section 5, the creation, acquisition and granting of interests in and licences in relation to first nation land and prohibitions in relation thereto;**

(c)   **environmental assessment and environmental protection;**

Commentary

Note the limitations on the use of this law-making power set out at s. 21 of this Act. Environmental protection laws are not to be enacted until an agreement is reached under s. 21(1), and those laws must meet the requirements of s. 21(2). Environmental assessment laws must meet the requirements of s. 21(3). The individual agreement must contain a statement of transitional arrangements relating to environmental assessments on First Nation land.[379]

(d)   **the provision of local services in relation to first nation land and the imposition of equitable user charges for those services; and**

---

[378]   from the Executive Summary of the First Nations Land Management Act Bill C-49 found at: <http://www.fafnlm.com/LAB.NSF/vSysSiteDoc/C-49+Legislation+Summary?OpenDocument>.

[379]   Paragraph 6(3)(b), FNLMA

(e)   the provision of services for the resolution of disputes in relation to first nation land.

Commentary

There is some potential for overlap between what a First Nation might choose to place in its land code (see s. 6 of the Act), and the subjects upon which a council may enact laws.

Note that a First Nation operating under the FNLMA may still make use of the list of by-law making powers in ss. 81 (e.g. "provide for the health of residents on the reserve ...") and 83 (real property taxation, business licensing, and appropriation and expenditure of funds) of the *Indian Act*. While no part of s. 81 or 83 of the *Indian Act* ceases to apply upon the coming into force of a land code,[380] it seems apparent that some by-laws capable of being made under s. 81(1) of that Act could also be achieved under s. 20 of the FNLMA. For example, s. 81(1)(g) of the *Indian Act* provides for "the dividing of the reserve into zones and the prohibition of construction or maintenance of any class of buildings ... ," while s. 20(2)(a) of the FNLMA provides law-making power for the "regulation, control or prohibition of land use and development including zoning and subdivision control." By-laws made under s. 81(1) of the *Indian Act* are subject to ministerial disallowance under s. 82(2), whereas there is no ministerial oversight in the FNLMA.

(3) ENFORCEMENT MEASURES — A first nation law may provide for enforcement measures, consistent with federal laws, such as the power to inspect, search and seize and to order compulsory sampling, testing and the production of information.

(4) INCONSISTENCY — In the event of any inconsistency or conflict between the land code of a first nation and the provisions of a first nation law or of a by-law made by its council under section 81 of the *Indian Act*, the land code prevails to the extent of the inconsistency or conflict.

21. (1) ENVIRONMENTAL PROTECTION — Before enacting any first nation law respecting environmental protection, a first nation shall enter into an agreement with the Minister and the Minister of the Environment in relation to environmental protection in accordance with the Framework Agreement.

(2) MINIMUM STANDARDS — For the purposes of an agreement entered into under subsection (1), the standards of environmental protection established by first nation laws and the punishments imposed for failure to meet those standards must be at least equivalent in their effect to any standards established and punishments imposed by the laws of the province in which the first nation land is situated.

---

[380]   See s. 38, FNLMA.

(3) ENVIRONMENTAL ASSESSMENT — First nation laws respecting environmental assessment must provide for the establishment, in accordance with the Framework Agreement, of an environmental assessment process applicable to all projects carried out on first nation land that are approved, regulated, funded or undertaken by the first nation.

22. (1) OFFENCES AND PUNISHMENT — A first nation law may create offences punishable on summary conviction and provide for the imposition of fines, imprisonment, restitution, community service and any other means for achieving compliance.

(2) INCORPORATION BY REFERENCE — A first nation law may adopt or incorporate by reference the summary conviction procedures of Part XXVII of the *Criminal Code*, as amended from time to time.

Commentary

Part XXVII of the *Criminal Code* deals with summary conviction offences and procedures generally. This Part of the *Criminal Code* applies to "proceedings" defined in s. 785 as:

> (a) proceedings in respect of offences that are declared by an Act of Parliament or an enactment made thereunder to be punishable on summary conviction, and

> (b) proceedings where a justice is authorized by an Act of Parliament or an enactment made thereunder to make an order;

Consequently, it appears that Part XXVII of the *Criminal Code* may apply to offences established under a First Nation law whether that Part is incorporated by reference in the First Nation law or not.

Subsection 22(2) of the FNLMA is linked with Framework Agreement clause 19.2, which reads:

> 19.2 First Nation laws may adopt or incorporate by reference the summary conviction procedures of the *Criminal Code* for the purpose of enforcement.

(3) PROSECUTION — A first nation may, in relation to prosecutions of contraventions of first nation laws,

(a) retain its own prosecutors;

(b) enter into an agreement with Her Majesty and a provincial government for the use of provincial prosecutors; or

(c) enter into an agreement with Her Majesty for the use of agents engaged by Her Majesty.

23. EVIDENCE — In any proceedings, a copy of a first nation law appearing to be certified as a true copy by an officer of the first nation is,

without proof of the officer's signature or official character, evidence of its enactment on the date specified in the law.

24. (1) APPOINTMENT OF JUSTICES OF THE PEACE — A first nation or, if Her Majesty and the first nation have entered into an agreement for that purpose in accordance with the Framework Agreement, the Governor in Council, may appoint justices of the peace to ensure the enforcement of first nation laws including the adjudication of offences for contraventions of first nation laws.

(2) JUDICIAL INDEPENDENCE — A justice of the peace appointed for a first nation shall have tenure and remuneration, and be subject to conditions of removal, that reflect the independence of the office of justice of the peace in the province in which the first nation land is situated.

(3) POWERS — Justices of the peace have all the powers necessary for the performance of their duties and functions.

(4) APPEALS — An appeal lies from a decision of a justice of the peace in the manner in which an appeal lies in summary conviction proceedings under Part XXVII of the Criminal Code and the provisions of that Part relating to appeals apply to appeals under this section.

(5) COURTS OF A PROVINCE — If no justices of the peace are appointed for a first nation, its first nation laws shall be enforced through a court of competent jurisdiction of the province in which its first nation land is situated.

First Nation Land Register

25. (1) ESTABLISHMENT — The Minister shall establish a register to be known as the First Nation Land Register.

(2) ADMINISTRATION OF REGISTER — The First Nation Land Register is to be administered, subject to this section, in the same manner as the Reserve Land Register established under the *Indian Act*.

Commentary

The Reserve Land Register is established by s. 21 of the *Indian Act*:

> 21. There shall be kept in the Department a register, to be known as the Reserve Land Register, in which shall be entered particulars relating to Certificates of Possession and Certificates of Occupation and other transactions respecting lands in a reserve.[381]

Subsection 55(1) of the *Indian Act* establishes the Surrendered and Designated Lands Register, which is administered by the Minister in addition to

---

[381]   R.S.C. 1985, c. I-5, s. 21.

the Reserve Land Register. These are dealt with by the Department of Indian Affairs and Northern Development under a single administration known as the Indian Lands Registry Office. The procedure manual titled "Indian Lands Registration Manual – 2003" is found on the Indian and Northern Affairs Canada website.[382]

(3) REGULATIONS — The Governor in Council may, on the recommendation of the Minister and in accordance with the Framework Agreement, make regulations respecting the administration of the First Nation Land Register, the registration of interests in it and the recording of any other matter, including but not limited to regulations respecting

    (a)   the effects of registering interests, including priorities;

    (b)   the payment of fees for the registration of interests and for any other service in relation to the Register;

    (c)   the appointment, remuneration, powers, functions and duties of officers and employees who administer the Register; and

    (d)   the keeping, by officers and employees, of documents that are not registrable.

Commentary

Regulations under this provision have not been made at the time of publication. Regulations would have the potential to offer the advantage of a legislated system of priorities for registered interests, something generally lacking under the *Indian Act*.[383]

Limitations on Alienation of First Nation Land

26. (1) ALIENATION OF LAND — First nation land may not be alienated except where it is exchanged for other land in accordance with the Framework Agreement and this Act.

(2) EXPROPRIATION — Interests in first nation land may not be expropriated except by Her Majesty or a first nation in accordance with the Framework Agreement and this Act.

27. (1) RESTRICTIONS ON EXCHANGE — A first nation may exchange first nation land only if

---

[382]   <http://www.ainc-inac.gc.ca/ps/lts/ilr98toc_e.html>.
[383]   The only semblance of a statutory priority system for registered interests in the *Indian Act* is a very limited one set out at s. 55(4):

    Effect of registration

      (4) An assignment registered under this section is valid against an unregistered assignment or an assignment subsequently registered.

R.S.C., 1985, c. I-5, subs. 55(4).

(a) compensation for the first nation land includes land that Her Majesty has agreed will be set apart as a reserve and that is to become first nation land; and

(b) the Minister has approved the form of the exchange.

(2) ADDITIONAL COMPENSATION — In addition to land referred to in subsection (1), other compensation may be provided including land that will not become first nation land.

(3) TERMS AND CONDITIONS — An exchange of first nation land may be made subject to other terms and conditions.

(4) COMMUNITY APPROVAL — The exchange of first nation land must be approved by first nation members in accordance with the land code of the first nation and must be completed in accordance with the Framework Agreement.

Commentary

Clause 14 of the Framework Agreement contains more detail than the Act respecting the process to be followed to complete a voluntary land exchange. Points of interest include the following:

The First Nation will authorize the federal government to make the exchange (clauses 14.5 and 14.6 of the Framework Agreement). Title to the land to be received in exchange will be transferred to the federal government, which will set it apart as reserve (clause 14.4 of the Framework Agreement).

28. (1) EXPROPRIATION BY A FIRST NATION — A first nation may, in accordance with the general rules and procedures contained in its land code, expropriate any interest in its first nation land that, in the opinion of its council, is necessary for community works or other first nation community purposes.

Commentary

Subsection 18(2) of the *Indian Act* provides the Minister with a power to authorize use of reserve land for specified purposes such as health projects, or with consent of the council, for other purposes for the general welfare of the Band. That provision includes a power to take land in the lawful possession of a member, upon payment of compensation. The expropriation powers available in s. 28(1) of the FNLMA are exercisable by the council in its discretion if so authorized in the land code, without any involvement of the Minister. A First Nation may expropriate not just the interests of its own members — expropriation can extend, for example, to leasehold interests held by non-members.

(2) EXCEPTION — An interest in first nation land obtained under section 35 of the *Indian Act* or held by Her Majesty is not subject to expropriation by a first nation.

Commentary

Section 35 of the *Indian Act* provides for expropriation (or a grant in lieu of expropriation) of reserve land by provinces, municipalities and other corporations with expropriation powers, upon consent of the Governor in Council. When less than a full interest in land has been expropriated in this way (for example, an easement), the land remains part of the reserve. Subsection 28(2) of the FNLMA does not permit the First Nation to re-appropriate or expropriate back such an interest taken under section 35 of the *Indian Act.*

(3) EFFECTIVE DATE — An expropriation takes effect from the day on which a notice of expropriation is registered in the First Nation Land Register or the thirtieth day after the day on which the notice is served on the person whose interest is expropriated, whichever is the earlier.

(4) EFFECT OF EXPROPRIATION — An expropriated interest becomes the property of the first nation free of any previous claim or encumbrance.

(5) COMPENSATION — A first nation shall pay fair compensation to the holder of an expropriated interest and, in determining that compensation, the first nation shall apply the rules set out in the *Expropriation Act*, with such modifications as the circumstances require.

(6) RESOLUTION OF DISPUTES — Any dispute concerning compensation shall be determined according to the system for the resolution of such disputes established by a first nation in accordance with the Framework Agreement.

29. (1) EXPROPRIATION BY HER MAJESTY — An interest in first nation land may be expropriated by Her Majesty for the use of a federal department or agency and with the consent and by order of the Governor in Council.

Commentary

This expropriation power represents a significant change from s. 35 of the *Indian Act.* There, it is provinces, municipalities and corporations having their own statutory powers of expropriation, who, with consent from the Governor in Council, are explicitly enabled to expropriate reserve land. Here it is only the federal government. The restrictions in the following subsections and sections also make it a very limited power. This is consistent with clause 13.2 of the Framework Agreement which provides:

13.2 The Parties declare that it is of fundamental importance to maintain the amount and integrity of First Nation land.

(2) CONSENT OF GOVERNOR IN COUNCIL — The Governor in Council may consent to an expropriation only if it is justifiable and necessary for a federal public purpose that serves the national interest.

(3) MATTERS TO BE CONSIDERED — The Governor in Council may consent to an expropriation only if the Governor in Council is satisfied that, in addition to any other legal requirements that may apply, the following requirements have been met:

(a)   there is no other reasonably feasible alternative to the expropriation, such as the use of land that is not first nation land;

(b)   reasonable efforts have been made to acquire the interest through agreement with the first nation;

(c)   the most limited interest necessary is expropriated for the shortest time possible; and

(d)   information relevant to the expropriation is provided to the first nation.

Commentary

These provisions bear a resemblance to some of the principles set out in the Sparrow case[384] for justification of infringement of aboriginal rights. There the Supreme Court of Canada required: that there be a "valid public purpose" such as fishery conservation (compare "justifiable and necessary for a federal public purpose that serves the national interest" in s. 29(2)); that consultation with the aboriginal group occur in regard to the proposed infringement (compare "reasonable efforts have been made to acquire the interest through agreement with the first nation" and "information relevant to the expropriation is provided to the first nation" in s. 29(3)); and that a principle of minimal impairment be observed (compare "the most limited interest necessary is expropriated for the shortest time possible" in s. 29(3)).

It is also interesting to note that in 2001 the Supreme Court of Canada in *Osoyoos Indian Band v. Oliver (Town)*[385] found for the first time a duty to minimally impair the reserve as part of the Crown's fiduciary obligation to First Nations in the context of expropriation under s. 35 of the *Indian Act*.

(4) REPORT TO BE MADE PUBLIC — Before the Governor in Council consents to the expropriation, the department or agency referred to in subsection (1) shall provide to the first nation, and make available to the

---

[384]   *Sparrow v. R.*, [1990] S.C.J. No. 49, [1990] 1 S.C.R. 1075.
[385]   [2001] S.C.J. No. 82, [2001] 3 S.C.R. 746.

public, a report stating the justifications for the expropriation and describing the steps taken to satisfy the requirements of subsection (3).

(5) DISPUTES — If a first nation objects to a proposed expropriation, it may, within sixty days after the report has been made public, refer the matter to a neutral evaluator in accordance with the Framework Agreement.

(6) TIME OF CONSENT — The Governor in Council may not consent to the expropriation before the expiration of the period referred to in subsection (5) or, if the first nation has referred the matter to a neutral evaluator, before the neutral evaluator has reported on the matter.

30. PARTIAL EXPROPRIATION — If less than the full interest of a first nation in first nation land is expropriated by Her Majesty,

(a)   the land in which an interest is expropriated continues to be first nation land and subject to the provisions of the land code and first nation laws that are not inconsistent with the expropriation; and

(b)   the first nation continues to have the right to use and occupy that land except to the extent that the use and occupation is inconsistent with the expropriation.

31. (1) COMPENSATION — Where an interest in first nation land is expropriated by Her Majesty, compensation shall be provided to the first nation consisting of

(a)   land that, when accepted by that first nation, will become first nation land; and

(b)   any additional compensation required to achieve the total compensation determined under subsection (3).

(2) LAND OF A LESSER AREA — Land provided to a first nation as compens-ation may be of an area that is less than the area of the land in which an interest has been expropriated if the total area of the land comprised in a reserve of the first nation is not less following the expropriation than at the coming into force of its land code.

(3) DETERMINATION OF COMPENSATION — The total compensation shall be determined taking into account the following factors:

(a)   the market value of the expropriated interest or of the land in which an interest has been expropriated;

(b)   the replacement value of any improvement to the land;

(c)   any expenses or losses resulting from a disturbance attributable to the expropriation;

(d)   any reduction in the value of any interest in first nation land that is not expropriated;

(e) any adverse effect on any cultural or other special value of the land to the first nation; and

(f) the value of any special economic advantage arising out of or incidental to the occupation or use of the land to the extent that that value is not otherwise compensated.

(4) INTEREST — Interest is payable on compensation from the effective date of an expropriation at the prejudgment interest rate that is paid in civil proceedings in the superior court of the province in which the land is situated.

(5) DISPUTE — If an agreement on compensation cannot be reached, the first nation or the expropriating department or agency may refer the matter to an arbitrator in accordance with the Framework Agreement.

(6) LIMIT — Any claim or encumbrance in respect of an interest expropriated by Her Majesty may only be made or discharged against the compensation paid under this section.

32. (1) RESTITUTION — An interest in first nation land expropriated by Her Majesty that is no longer required for the purpose for which it was expropriated shall revert to the first nation and, if the full interest of the first nation was expropriated, it shall be returned to the first nation in accordance with terms and conditions negotiated by the first nation and the expropriating department or agency.

(2) IMPROVEMENTS — When an interest reverts or is returned to a first nation, the minister responsible for the expropriating department or agency shall determine the disposition of any improvements made to the land.

(3) DISPUTE — If the first nation and the expropriating department or agency cannot agree on the terms and conditions of the return of the full interest, the first nation or the department or agency may, in accordance with the Framework Agreement, refer the matter to an arbitrator.

Commentary

The expression "full interest" is used in ss. 30 and 32. In context, it seems clear that this means all of the Indian interest in the land. However, the use of the term "interest", especially in the phrase "full interest" in the expropriation sections (ss. 29 to 33), seems to be somewhat inconsistent with the way it is defined in s. 2(1). Despite this apparent inconsistency, the contextual use in the expropriation provisions seems clear enough.

33. *EXPROPRIATION ACT* — Without limiting the generality of section 37, in the event of any inconsistency or conflict between this Act and the *Expropriation Act* in relation to the expropriation of interests in first nation

land by Her Majesty, this Act prevails to the extent of the inconsistency or conflict.

LIABILITY

34. (1) FIRST NATION NOT LIABLE — A first nation is not liable in respect of anything done or omitted to be done before the coming into force of its land code by Her Majesty or any person or body authorized by Her Majesty to act in relation to first nation land.

Case Law

Many Guns v. Siksika Nation Tribal Administration, [2003] A.J. No. 1182, [2004] 1 C.N.L.R. 176 (Prov. Ct.) paras. 66 to 92.

The defendant was found negligent in failing to have installed a Texas gate at the entrance to the community pasture, a factor resulting in the destruction of the plaintiff's horse following a collision with the defendant's emergency vehicle. The defendant's liability flowed from its own interest in and administration of the land. In reasons for judgment the court noted the defendant's unsuccessful argument that, in the event negligence was found, it should be relieved of liability by operation of the *Indian Act* and the *First Nations Land Management Act* (as the accident occurred before responsibility for the reserve lands passed from the Crown to the Siksika Nation).

(2) INDEMNIFICATION OF FIRST NATION — Her Majesty shall indemnify a first nation for any loss suffered by the first nation as a result of an act or omission described in subsection (1).

(3) HER MAJESTY NOT LIABLE — Her Majesty is not liable in respect of anything done or omitted to be done after the coming into force of the land code of a first nation by the first nation or any person or body authorized by the first nation to act in relation to first nation land.

(4) INDEMNIFICATION OF HER MAJESTY — The first nation shall indemnify Her Majesty for any loss suffered by Her Majesty as a result of an act or omission described in subsection (3).

Commentary

Section 34 provides a scheme for allocation of risk relating to the transition from government control of reserve land transactions under the *Indian Act* to First Nation control under this Act. There appears to be a basic recognition that, with legal control come responsibility and certain liabilities.

IMMUNITY AND JUDICIAL REVIEW

35. IMMUNITY — No criminal or civil proceedings lie against an arbitrator, mediator, neutral evaluator or verifier appointed under the Framework Agreement or this Act or any member of a board established

by section 38 of the Framework Agreement who is, in good faith, exercising a power or performing a duty or function in accordance with the Framework Agreement or this Act for anything done or omitted to be done during the course of the exercise or purported exercise of any power or the performance or purported performance of any duty or function of that person in accordance with the Framework Agreement or this Act.

36. (1) DETERMINATIONS FINAL — Every determination under this Act or the Framework Agreement by a verifier or arbitrator is final, and no order shall be made, process entered or proceedings taken in any court, whether by way of injunction, *certiorari*, prohibition, *mandamus*, *quo warranto* or otherwise, to question, review or prohibit such a determination.

(2) ACTIONS FINAL — No order shall be made, process entered or proceedings taken in any court, whether by way of injunction, *certiorari*, prohibition, *mandamus*, *quo warranto* or otherwise, to question, review or prohibit any other action under this Act or the Framework Agreement by a verifier or arbitrator or any action under the Framework Agreement by a neutral evaluator.

(3) REVIEW BY FEDERAL COURT — Notwithstanding subsections (1) and (2), the Attorney General of Canada or anyone directly affected by the matter in respect of which relief is sought may make an application under the *Federal Courts Act* on any of the grounds referred to in paragraph 18.1(4)(a) or (b) of that Act for any relief against a verifier, arbitrator or neutral evaluator by way of an injunction or declaration or by way of an order in the nature of *certiorari*, prohibition, *mandamus* or *quo warranto*.

Commentary

This provision, sometimes known as a "privative clause", limits review by the courts of the actions and decisions of certain independent actors: verifiers; arbitrators; and neutral evaluators. While ss. 36(1) and (2) are very extensive in their exclusion of the courts' powers of review, s. 36(3) provides for an exception when one of those actors has acted without or beyond its jurisdiction, or has refused to exercise its jurisdiction (s. 18.1(4)(a) of the *Federal Courts Act*[386]), or has failed to observe a principle of natural justice or procedural fairness or other required procedure (s. 18.1(4)(b) of the *Federal Courts Act*.[387])

---

[386] R.S.C. 1985, c. F-7.

[387] Set out below are ss. 18.1(3) and (4) of the *Federal Courts Act*, R.S.C. 1985, c. F-7 :

(3) On an application for judicial review, the Federal Court may

(a) order a federal board, commission or other tribunal to do any act or thing it has unlawfully failed or refused to do or has unreasonably delayed in doing; or

(b) declare invalid or unlawful, or quash, set aside or set aside and refer back for determination in accordance with such directions as

OTHER ACTS

37. OTHER ACTS — In the event of any inconsistency or conflict between this Act and any other federal law, this Act prevails to the extent of the inconsistency or conflict.

38. (1) *INDIAN ACT* **— On the coming into force of the land code of a first nation, the following cease to apply to the first nation, first nation members and first nation land:**

(a)   **sections 18 to 20, 22 to 28, 30 to 35, 37 to 41 and 49, subsection 50(4) and sections 53 to 60, 66, 69, 71 and 93 of the** *Indian Act***;**

(b)   **any regulations made under section 57 of that Act; and**

(c)   **to the extent of any inconsistency or conflict with the Framework Agreement, the land code or first nation laws, any regulations made under sections 42 and 73 of that Act.**

Commentary

Subsection 38(1) provides that the land management provisions of the *Indian Act* cease to apply on the coming into force of a land code. This removes the significant ministerial powers and controls over reserve land transactions, making way for the exercise of First Nation powers found in the FNLMA.

(2) LEASEHOLD INTERESTS — Subsection 89(1.1) of the *Indian Act* **continues to apply to leasehold interests in any first nation land that was designated land on the coming into force of a first nation's land code.**

---

it considers to be appropriate, prohibit or restrain, a decision, order, act or proceeding of a federal board, commission or other tribunal.

(4) The Federal Court may grant relief under subsection (3) if it is satisfied that the federal board, commission or other tribunal

(a)   acted without jurisdiction, acted beyond its jurisdiction or refused to exercise its jurisdiction;

(b)   failed to observe a principle of natural justice, procedural fairness or other procedure that it was required by law to observe;

(c)   erred in law in making a decision or an order, whether or not the error appears on the face of the record;

(d)   based its decision or order on an erroneous finding of fact that it made in a perverse or capricious manner or without regard for the material before it;

(e)   acted, or failed to act, by reason of fraud or perjured evidence; or

(f)   acted in any other way that was contrary to law.

(Note that only grounds contained in paragraphs (a) and (b) of subsection (4) above are specified in FNLMA s. 36(3) as being available in a challenge to decisions of the verifier, arbitrator or neutral evaluator.)

(3) APPLICATION — **A land code may extend the application of subsection 89(1.1) of the Indian Act, or any portion of it, to other leasehold interests in first nation land.**

Commentary

Subsection 38(2) of the FNLMA maintains the exception provided by s. 89(1.1) of the *Indian Act*, allowing leasehold interests on (formerly) designated lands to be mortgaged, notwithstanding the leaseholder/mortgagee being a First Nation member.

Subsection 38(3) enables a First Nation in its land code to extend the application of s. 89(1.1) of the *Indian Act* to other leasehold interests in First Nation land; for example, leases of land in the lawful possession of a First Nation member.

Subsections 89(1) and (1.1) of the *Indian Act* provide as follows:

89. (1) Subject to this Act, the real and personal property of an Indian or a band situated on a reserve is not subject to charge, pledge, mortgage, attachment, levy, seizure, distress or execution in favour or at the instance of any person other than an Indian or a band.

(1.1) Notwithstanding subsection (1), a leasehold interest in designated lands is subject to charge, pledge, mortgage, attachment, levy, seizure, distress and execution.

A mortgage of leasehold interest in reserve land is a form of security for business financing used under the *Indian Act*. Subsection 38(3) of the FNLMA provides an opportunity for First Nations to expand somewhat the availability of this financing and security option. In the event of loan default, the lender seeks to be in position to take over the lease or assign its interest in it.

39. (1) *INDIAN OIL AND GAS ACT* — **The** *Indian Oil and Gas Act*

(a) **continues to apply in respect of any first nation land that was subject to that Act on the coming into force of the land code of a first nation; and**

(b) **applies in respect of an interest in first nation land that is granted to Her Majesty for the exploitation of oil and gas pursuant to a land code.**

Commentary

Note that the *Indian Oil and Gas Act*[388] applies only to "Indian lands" as defined in that Act, which are limited to lands that have been surrendered or designated under s. 38 of the *Indian Act*:

---

[388]   R.S.C. 1985, c. I-7.

"Indian lands" means lands reserved for the Indians, including any interests therein, surrendered in accordance with the *Indian Act* and includes any lands or interests in lands described in any grant, lease, permit, licence or other disposition referred to in section 5;

(2) ROYALTIES — For greater certainty, the provisions of the *Indian Oil and Gas Act* respecting the payment of royalties to Her Majesty in trust for a first nation apply, notwithstanding any other provision of this Act, in respect of first nation land referred to in subsection (1).

40. (1) ENVIRONMENTAL LAWS — For greater certainty, in the event of any inconsistency or conflict between a land code or a first nation law and any federal law that relates to environmental protection, the federal law prevails to the extent of the inconsistency or conflict.

(2) MIGRATORY BIRDS, ENDANGERED SPECIES, FISHERIES — For greater certainty, this Act does not extend or limit any right or power in relation to migratory birds, endangered species or fisheries.

Commentary

Note the potential for conflict between any aboriginal and treaty rights to hunt, fish and use land, and certain federal statutes: the *Migratory Birds Convention Act, 1994;*[389] the *Species at Risk Act;*[390] and the *Fisheries Act.*[391]

41. *CANADIAN ENVIRONMENTAL ASSESSMENT ACT* — Section 10 of the *Canadian Environmental Assessment Act* does not apply to a project carried out on first nation land.

Commentary

Section 10 of the *Canadian Environmental Assessment Act*[392] reads as follows:

10. (1) If a project is to be carried out in whole or in part on a reserve that has been set apart for the use and benefit of a band and that is subject to the Indian Act, the council of the band for whose use and benefit the reserve has been set apart shall, if regulations that apply to the band have been made under paragraph 59(1) and have come into force, ensure that an environmental assessment of the project is conducted in

[389] S.C. 1994, c. 22.
[390] S.C. 2002, c. 29.
[391] R.S.C 1985, c. F-14.
[392] S.C. 1992, c. 37.

accordance with those regulations before the band council exercises one of the following powers or performs one of the following duties or functions in respect of the project, namely, where the band council

(a) is the proponent of the project and does any act or thing that commits it to carrying out the project in whole or in part;

(b) makes or authorizes payments or provides a guarantee for a loan or any other form of financial assistance to the proponent of the project for the purpose of enabling the project to be carried out in whole or in part, including financial assistance in the form of any reduction, avoidance, deferral, removal, refund, remission or other form of relief from the payment of any tax; or

(c) takes any action under a provision prescribed under paragraph 59(1.001) for the purpose of enabling the project to be carried out in whole or in part.

(2) Where an environmental assessment of a project is required under subsection (1), the band council shall ensure that the assessment is conducted as early as is practicable in the planning stages of the project and before irrevocable decisions are made.

42. EMERGENCIES ACT — The *Emergencies Act*[393] continues to apply to first nation land except that any appropriation, requisition or use of first nation land required under that Act must be expressly authorized by order of the Governor in Council.

43. (1) ACTS RESPECTING NUCLEAR ENERGY — Subject to subsection (2), nothing in this Act limits the application of the *Nuclear Safety and Control Act*[394] and the *Nuclear Energy Act*[395] to first nation lands.

(2) EXPROPRIATION PROVISIONS — In the event of any inconsistency or conflict between the provisions of this Act relating to expropriation and the *Nuclear Energy Act*,[396] the provisions of this Act prevail to the extent of the inconsistency or conflict.

---

[393]   R.S.C., 1985, c. 22 (4th Supp.).
[394]   S.C. 1997, c. 9.
[395]   *Ibid.*
[396]   R.S.C 1985, c. A-16.

Commentary

While s. 37 is a general rule giving precedence to the FNLMA over other federal statutes in the event of conflict or inconsistency, ss. 39, 40, 42 and 43 provide for certain exceptions where the named statutes will prevail to the extent described in each of these sections.

44. NON-APPLICATION OF *STATUTORY INSTRUMENTS ACT* — The *Statutory Instruments Act*[397] **does not apply in respect of a land code or first nation laws.**

AMENDMENT OF SCHEDULE

45. ADDITION OF BAND TO SCHEDULE — The Governor in Council may, by order, add the name of a band to the schedule if the Governor in Council is satisfied that the signing of the Framework Agreement on behalf of the band has been duly authorized and that the Framework Agreement has been so signed.

Commentary

The Schedule to the Act has been amended once, by SOR/2003-178, to add an additional 22 First Nations to the Schedule, bringing the number to 36. Although the Act no longer applies to the Westbank First Nation,[398] it has not yet been removed from the Schedule.

TRANSITIONAL PROVISION

46. (1) VALIDITY — Any action taken or determination or decision made under the Framework Agreement before the coming into force of sections 6 to 14, 35 and 36 is deemed, to the extent that it would have been valid under those sections, to have been validly taken or made under this Act.

(2) COMING INTO FORCE OF LAND CODE — Notwithstanding subsection (1), a land code may not come into force before the coming into force of this section.

CONDITIONAL AMENDMENT

47. [Amendment]

---

[397]   R.S.C 1985, c. S-22.

[398]   By virture of s. 7 of the *Westbank First Nation Self-Government Act*, S.C. 2004, c. 17.

Commentary

Section 47 provided for the eventual amendment of s. 43 of the FNLMA when the *Nuclear Safety and Control Act*[399] came into force in 1997. This section is now spent.

COMING INTO FORCE

48. ORDER OF GOVERNOR IN COUNCIL — Section 45 comes into force on a day to be fixed by order of the Governor in Council after the completion of a review of the Framework Agreement in accordance with its provisions and any consultations that the Governor in Council may require.

Commentary

Section 45 was brought into force on May 20, 2003 by SI/2003-108.

SCHEDULE
(Sections 2 and 45)

FIRST NATIONS

1. Westbank

Commentary

The *Westbank First Nation Self-Government Act*[400] came into force on April 1, 2005 and provided the Westbank First Nation with a more comprehensive self-government arrangement in respect to its reserve lands. Section 7 of that Act provides that the FNLMA does not apply to the Westbank First Nation. At the date of publication, however, item 1 of the Schedule had not been amended to remove the reference to the Westbank First Nation.

2. Musqueam

3. Fort George (also known as Lheit-Lit'en and Lheidli T'enneh)

4. Anderson Lake (also known as N'Quatqua)

5. Squamish

6. Siksika Nation

7. John Smith (also known as Muskoday)

8. Cowessess

9. The Pas (also known as Opaskwayak Cree)

10. Nipissing Band of Ojibways (also known as Nipissing)

---

[399] S.C 1997, c. 9.
[400] S.C. 2004, c. 17.

11. **Scugog (also known as Mississaugas of Scugog Island)**

12. **Chippewas of Rama (also known as Chippewas of Mnjikaning)**

13. **Chippewas of Georgina Island**

14. **Saint Mary's**

15. **Garden River**

16. **Moose Deer Point**

17. **Whitecap No. 94**

18. **Kinistin**

19. **Mississauga**

20. **Whitefish Lake**

21. **Songhees**

22. **Beecher Bay**

23. **Pavilion**

24. **Tsawwassen**

25. **Tsawout**

26. **Kingsclear**

27. **Skeetchestn**

28. **Muskeg Lake**

29. **Burrard**

30. **Sliammon**

31. **Osoyoos**

32. **Chippewas of Kettle and Stony Point**

33. **Dokis**

34. **Chippewas of the Thames**

35. **Kitselas**

36. **McLeod Lake**

Commentary

This schedule contains the names of all First Nations whose representatives have signed the Framework Agreement and met the conditions contained in s. 45. Being listed on the schedule does not denote that a First Nation has approved a land code. Only when a land code has been approved under s. 12 of the Act and has come into force may the First Nation exercise the powers set out in the FNLMA.

According to the website of the Framework Agreement on First Nations Land Management,[401] operated by the Lands Advisory Board, there are 14 First

---

[401]   <http://www.fafnlm.com/LAB.NSF/vSysSiteDoc/Members+Communities? OpenDocument>.

Nations who have land codes in force. That list of "operational" First Nations is reproduced below:[402]

Nipissing
Opaskwayak
Lheidli T'enneh
Westbank
Scugog Island
Muskoday
Georgina Island
Beecher Bay
Tsekani (Mcleod Lake)
Ts'kw'aylaxw (Pavilion)
Sliammon
Tsawwassen
Kinistin
Whitecap Dakota Sioux

The Lands Advisory Board website also lists five additional First Nations as recent signatories to the Framework Agreement and participants in the developmental stage, although these have not yet been added to the Schedule:

Flying Dust
Swan Lake
Leq'a:mel (formerly Lakahahmen)
T'Sou-ke
Skway

---

[402] Note however that the list still includes Westbank. See the commentary in the schedule above.

FRAMEWORK AGREEMENT ON FIRST NATION LAND MANAGEMENT

Agreement made this 12th day of February, 1996.

BETWEEN:

THE FOLLOWING FIRST NATIONS:

WESTBANK, MUSQUEAM, LHEIDLI T'ENNEH (formerly known as "LHEIT-LIT'EN"), N'QUATQUA, SQUAMISH, SIKSIKA, MUSKODAY, COWESSESS, OPASKWAYAK CREE, NIPISSING, MISSISSAUGAS OF SCUGOG ISLAND, CHIPPEWAS OF MNJIKANING, CHIPPEWAS OF GEORGINA ISLAND, SAINT MARY'S, as represented by their Chiefs

AND

HER MAJESTY THE QUEEN IN RIGHT OF CANADA, as represented by the Minister of Indian Affairs and Northern Development

WHEREAS:

The First Nations have a profound relationship with the land that is rooted in respect for the Spiritual value of the Earth and the gifts of the Creator and have a deep desire to preserve their relationship with the land;

The First Nations should have the option of withdrawing their lands from the land management provisions of the *Indian Act* in order to exercise control over their lands and resources for the use and benefit of their members;

The Parties wish to enter into a government to government agreement, within the framework of the constitution of Canada, to deal with the issues of land management;

The Parties understand that this Agreement must be ratified;

NOW THEREFORE,

In consideration of the exchange of promises contained in this Agreement and subject to its terms and conditions, the Parties agree that the First Nations shall have the option of exercising control over their lands and resources.

PART I

PRELIMINARY MATTERS

1. INTERPRETATION

1.1 In this Agreement,

"Canada" or "Crown" means Her Majesty the Queen in right of Canada;

"eligible voter" means a member of a First Nation who is eligible, pursuant to clause 7.2, to vote under this Agreement;

"federal law" means a law enacted by Canada and does not include a land code or a First Nation law;

"federal legislation" means the legislation to be enacted by Canada under Part X;

"First Nation" means a band that is a Party to this Agreement;

"First Nation land", in respect of a First Nation, means all or part of a reserve that the First Nation describes in its land code;

"First Nation law" means a law enacted by a First Nation in accordance with its land code;

"First Nation Lands Register" means the register established pursuant to clause 51 to register interests in First Nation land;

"interest", in relation to First Nation land, means any interest, right or estate of any nature in or to that land, including a lease, easement, right of way, servitude, or profit à prendre, but does not include title to that land;

"land code" means a code, approved by a First Nation in accordance with this Agreement, that sets out the basic provisions regarding the exercise of the First Nation's rights and powers over its First Nation land (although each First Nation can select its own name for the land code);

"Lands Advisory Board" means the board referred to in clause 38;

"licence", in relation to First Nation land, means any right of use or occupation of First Nation land, other than an interest in that land;

"member", in respect of a First Nation, means

    (a) a person whose name appears on the Band List, or

    (b) a person who is entitled to have his or her name appear on the Band List;

"Minister" means the Minister of Indian Affairs and Northern Development, or such other member of the Queen's Privy Council as is designated by the Governor in Council for the purposes of this Agreement;

"verifier" means the person appointed pursuant to clauses 8 and 44 to monitor and verify the opting in process for a First Nation.

1.2 Terms that are defined or used in the *Indian Act* have the same meaning in this Agreement, unless the context otherwise requires.

1.3 This Agreement is not a treaty and shall not be considered to be a treaty within the meaning of section 35 of the *Constitution Act, 1982*.

1.4 The Parties acknowledge that the Crown's special relationship with the First Nations will continue.

1.5 This Agreement does not affect any lands, or any rights in lands, that are not subject to this Agreement.

1.6 This Agreement is not intended to define or prejudice inherent rights, or any other rights, of First Nations to control their lands or resources or to preclude other negotiations in respect of those rights.

2. FIRST NATION LAND

2.1 Land that is a reserve of a First Nation is eligible to be managed by that First Nation under a land code as First Nation land.

2.2 First Nation land includes all the interests, rights and resources that belong to that land, to the extent that these are under the jurisdiction of Canada and are part of that land.

2.3 The Parties agree that First Nation lands are lands reserved for Indians within the meaning of section 91(24) of the *Constitution Act, 1867*.

3. INDIAN OIL AND GAS

3.1 The *Indian Oil and Gas Act* will continue to apply to any First Nation lands, or interests in First Nation land, that are "Indian lands" within the meaning of that Act.

3.2 Any interest in First Nation land that is granted to Canada for the exploitation of oil and gas under a land code will be deemed to be "Indian lands" within the meaning of the *Indian Oil and Gas Act*.

3.3 Section 4 of the *Indian Oil and Gas Act* will continue to apply to revenues and royalties from oil or gas on First Nation land, despite anything to the contrary in clause 12.

4. RESERVES

4.1 Any reserve managed by a First Nation under a land code will continue to be a reserve within the meaning of the *Indian Act*.

4.2 Any reserve, title to which is vested in Canada, and managed by a First Nation under a land code, will continue to be vested in Canada for the use and benefit of the respective First Nation for which it was set apart.

4.3 Where a First Nation wishes to manage a reserve, the whole of the reserve will be included as First Nation land to avoid disjointed administration of the reserve, subject to clauses 4.4 and 4.5.

4.4 A portion of a reserve may be excluded from a land code only if

(a)   the portion of the reserve is in an environmentally unsound condition and the condition cannot be remedied by measures that are technically and financially feasible before the land code is expected to be submitted for community approval;

(b)   the portion of the reserve is the subject of ongoing litigation that is unlikely to be resolved before the land code is expected to be submitted for community approval;

(c)   the portion of the reserve is uninhabitable or unusable as a result of a natural disaster; or

(d)   there exist one or more other reasons which the First Nation and the Minister agree justify excluding a portion of a reserve.

4.5 A portion of a reserve which is to be excluded from a land code must be surveyed under Part II of the *Canada Lands Survey Act* and the exclusion must not have the effect of placing the administration of a lease or other interest in land under different land management systems.

4.6 The First Nation will make provision to amend the description of its First Nation land in its land code to include the excluded portion of the reserve when the First Nation and the Minister agree that the condition justifying the exclusion no longer exists and the individual agreement will be amended accordingly.

PART II

OPTING IN PROCEDURE

5. DEVELOPMENT OF A LAND CODE

5.1 A First Nation that wishes to manage one or more of its reserves will first develop a land code.

5.2 The land code of a First Nation will

(a)   describe the lands that are subject to the land code;

(b)   set out the general rules and procedures that apply to the use and occupancy of First Nation land, including use and occupancy under

(i)   licenses and leases, and

(ii)   interests in First Nation land held pursuant to allotments under subsection 20(1) of the *Indian Act* or pursuant to the custom of the First Nation;

(b.1) set out the procedures that apply to the transfer, by testamentary disposition or succession, of any interest in First Nation land;

(c)   set out the general rules and procedures that apply to revenues from natural resources belonging to First Nation land;

(d)   set out the requirements for accountability to First Nation members for the management of moneys and First Nation lands under the land code;

(e)   set out the procedures for making and publishing its First Nation laws;

(f)   set out the conflict of interest rules for land management;

(g)   identify or establish a forum for the resolution of disputes in relation to interests in First Nation lands, including the review of land management decisions where a person, whose interest in First Nation land is affected by a decision, disputes that decision;

(h)   set out the general rules and procedures that apply to the First Nation when granting or expropriating interests in First Nation land, including provisions for notice and the service of notice;

(i)   set out the general authorities and procedures whereby the First Nation council delegates administrative authority to manage First Nation land to another person or entity; and

(j)   set out the procedure by which the First Nation can amend its land code or approve an exchange of its First Nation land.

5.3 A land code could also contain the following provisions:

(a)   any general conditions or limits on the power of the First Nation council to make First Nation laws;

(b)   any general exceptions, reservations, conditions or limitations to be attached to the rights and interests that may be granted in First Nation land;

(c)   any provisions respecting encumbering, seizing, or executing a right or interest in First Nation land as provided in clause 15; and

(d)   any other matter respecting the management of First Nation land.

5.4 In order to clarify the intentions of the First Nations and Canada in relation to the breakdown of a marriage as it affects First Nation land:

(a)   a First Nation will establish a community process in its land code to develop rules and procedures, applicable on the breakdown of a marriage, to the use, occupancy and possession of First Nation land and the division of interests in that land;

(b)   for greater certainty, the rules and procedures referred to in clause (a) shall not discriminate on the basis of sex;

(c)   the rules and procedures referred to in clause (a) shall be enacted in the First Nation's land code or First Nation laws;

(d)   in order to allow sufficient time for community consultation during the community process referred to in clause (a), the First Nation shall have a period of 12 months from the date the land code takes effect to enact the rules and procedures;

(e)   any dispute between the Minister and a First Nation in respect of this clause shall, notwithstanding clause 43.3, be subject to arbitration in accordance with Part IX;

(f)   for greater certainty, this clause also applies to any First Nation that has voted to approve a land code before this clause comes into force.

6. DEVELOPMENT OF INDIVIDUAL FIRST NATION AGREEMENT

6.1 The Minister and each First Nation that intends to manage its First Nation land will also enter into an individual agreement to settle the actual level of operational funding for the First Nation and the specifics of the transfer of administration between Canada and the First Nation.

6.2 The First Nation and the Minister will each choose a representative to develop the individual agreement and to assist in transferring administration of the First Nation land.

6.3 Upon the request of a First Nation that is developing a land code, the Minister will provide it with the following information, as soon as practicable:

(a)   a list of all the interests and licences, in relation to the proposed First Nation land, that are recorded in the Reserve Land Register and the Surrendered and Designated Lands Register under the *Indian Act*;

(b)   all existing information, in Canada's possession, respecting any actual or potential environmental problems with the proposed First Nation land; and

(c)   any other information in Canada's possession that materially affects the interests and licences mentioned in clause 6.3(a).

6.4 An amendment to an individual agreement with the Minister must be made in accordance with the procedure in that agreement.

7. COMMUNITY APPROVAL

7.1 Both the First Nation's land code and its individual agreement with the Minister need community approval in accordance with this clause.

7.2 Every person who is a First Nation member, whether resident on or off-reserve, who is at least 18 years of age, is eligible to vote on whether to approve their First Nation's proposed land code and its individual agreement with the Minister.

7.3 The land code and individual agreement will be considered approved by the community if

(a)   a majority of eligible voters participate in the vote and at least a majority of the participating voters vote to approve them;

(b)   the First Nation registers all eligible voters who signified, in a manner determined by the First Nation, their intention to vote, and a majority of the registered voters vote to approve them; or

(c)   the community approves them in such other manner as the First Nation and the Minister may agree upon.

7.4 The land code and individual agreement will not be considered approved if less than 25% plus one of all eligible voters voted to approve them.

7.5 The First Nation council may, by resolution, increase the minimum percentage for community approval otherwise required under this clause.

7.6 A First Nation will take reasonable steps to locate its eligible voters and inform them of

(a)   their right to participate in the approval process and the manner in which that right can be exercised; and

(b)   the content of this Agreement, the individual agreement with the Minister, the proposed land code and the federal legislation.

7.7 Reasonable steps to locate and inform eligible voters may include the following:

(a)   mailing out information to eligible voters at their last known addresses;

(b)   making enquiries of family members and others to locate eligible voters whose addresses are not known or are uncertain;

(c)   making follow up contact with eligible voters by mail or telephone;

(d)   placing advertisements in newspapers circulating in the community and in newspapers circulating in other localities where the number of eligible voters warrants;

(e)   posting notices in the community;

(f)   holding information meetings in the community and in other places where appropriate; and

(g)   making copies of the documents referred to in clause 7.6(b) available at the administration office of the First Nation and in other places where appropriate.

7.8 A First Nation will, within a reasonable time before the vote, also take appropriate measures to inform other persons having an interest in its lands of the federal legislation, the proposed land code and the date of the vote.

7.9 Where the federal legislation has not yet been enacted when a First Nation proceeds under this clause, Canada will provide the First Nation with a draft copy of its proposed legislation which the First Nation will use to inform its eligible voters and other persons.

7.10 An amendment to a land code must be made in accordance with the procedure in the First Nation's land code.

8. VERIFICATION PROCESS

8.1 Where a First Nation develops a proposed land code and resolves to submit it to the community for approval, an independent person will be appointed as a verifier to monitor and verify the opting in process. The verifier will be chosen in accordance with clause 44.

8.2 The representatives of the First Nation and the Minister, who have been assisting in the process of transferring administration of the land, will meet with the verifier and provide information and advice to the verifier, after consulting with their respective Parties.

8.3 The First Nation will submit the following information to the verifier:

(a)   a copy of the proposed land code;

(b)   an initial list of the names of every First Nation member who, according to the First Nation's records at that time, would be eligible to vote on whether to approve the proposed land code; and

(c)   a detailed description of the community approval process that the First Nation proposes to use under clause 7.

8.4 The verifier will

(a)   decide whether the proposed land code conforms with the requirements of clause 5;

(b)   decide whether the proposed community approval process conforms with the requirements of clause 7;

(c)   determine whether the community approval process is conducted in accordance with the process that was confirmed; and

(d)   certify as being valid a First Nation's land code that is properly approved by the First Nation.

8.5 The verifier also has the power to make a final decision to resolve

(a)   any dispute regarding whether a portion of a reserve may be excluded from a land code pursuant to clause 4.4; and

(b)   any dispute regarding the specifics of the transfer of administration between Canada and the First Nation.

8.6 A verifier will make decisions that are consistent with clauses 4.4 and 4.5.

8.7 A verifier will not deal with disputes over funding.

8.8 Within 30 days of receiving the First Nation's information pursuant to clause 8.3, the verifier will issue a written notice to the First Nation and the Minister stating whether the proposed land code and community approval process are consistent with this Agreement.

8.9 The verifier will provide written reasons to the First Nation and the Minister in any case where he or she decides that the proposed land code and community approval process are not consistent with this Agreement.

9. CONDUCT OF COMMUNITY VOTE

9.1 Once the verifier confirms that the proposed land code and community approval process are consistent with this Agreement, the First Nation may proceed to submit its proposed land code, and the individual agreement with the Minister, for community approval.

9.2 The verifier will publish one or more notices advising the community of the date, time and place of the First Nation's approval vote.

9.3 The verifier may designate one or more assistants to help observe the conduct of the vote.

9.4 The verifier and any assistant observers will have complete authority to observe the approval process.

9.5 Within 15 days of the conclusion of the vote, the verifier will issue a written report to the First Nation and to the Minister on whether the community approval process was conducted in accordance with the process as previously confirmed.

10. CERTIFICATION OF LAND CODE

10.1 Where a First Nation approves a land code and its individual agreement with the Minister, the First nation council must, without delay, send a true copy of the land code to the verifier together with a statement from the First Nation council that the land code and the individual agreement were properly approved.

10.2 Upon receiving a copy of a First Nation's land code and statement, the verifier will, subject to clause 11, certify the land code as being valid.

10.3 The verifier will immediately provide the First Nation, the Lands Advisory Board and the Minister with a copy of any certified land code.

10.4 The Lands Advisory Board will, in such manner as it considers advisable, publish a notice announcing the certification of a land code and the date the land code takes effect and advising the public of the means of obtaining copies of it.

10.4.1 Certified copies of the land code will be made available to the public at such places deemed necessary by the First Nation.

10.5 Once a land code is certified by a verifier and takes effect, the land code has the force of law and will be given judicial notice.

10.6 A land code that has been certified pursuant to this Agreement is deemed to have been validly approved by the First Nation.

10.7 A land code takes effect on the day that it is certified by the verifier or on such later date as may be specified in the land code.

11. DISPUTED VOTE

11.1 The Minister or any eligible voter may, within five days after the conclusion of the vote, report any irregularity in the voting process to the verifier.

11.2 A verifier will not certify a land code if he or she is of the opinion that the following two conditions exist:

(1) the process by which the land code was approved varied from the process previously confirmed by the verifier or was otherwise irregular; and

(2) the land code might not have been approved but for the irregularity in the process.

11.3 Before making a decision under this clause, the verifier will provide the First Nation and the Minister with a reasonable opportunity to make submissions on the issue.

11.4 Any decision by a verifier under this clause must be made within 10 days of the conclusion of the vote.

PART III

FIRST NATION LAND MANAGEMENT RIGHTS AND POWER

12. LAND MANAGEMENT POWERS

12.1 A First Nation with a land code in effect will, subject to clause 13, have the power to manage its First Nation land and exercise its powers under this Agreement.

12.2 This power includes

(a) all the rights, powers and privileges of an owner, in relation to its First Nation land; and

(b) the authority to grant interests and licences in relation to its First Nation land and to manage its natural resources, subject to clauses 3, 18.5 and 23.6.

12.3 An interest or licence granted in relation to First Nation land is subject to any exception, reservation, condition or limitation established by the First Nation in its land code.

12.4 For any purpose related to First Nation land, a First Nation will have legal capacity to acquire and hold property, to borrow, to contract, to expend and invest money, to be a party to legal proceedings, to exercise its powers and to perform its duties.

12.5 First Nation land, revenues, royalties, profits and fees in respect of that land will be managed by the First Nation council or its delegate for the use and benefit of the First Nation.

12.6 If a First Nation establishes an entity for the purpose of administering its First Nation land, the entity shall be deemed to be a legal entity with the capacity, rights, powers and privileges of a natural person.

12.7 A First Nation has the right, in accordance with its land code, to receive and use all moneys acquired by or on behalf of the First Nation under its land code.

12.8 Once a First Nation's land code takes effect, all revenue moneys collected, received or held by Canada for the use and benefit of the First Nation or its members before that date, and from time to time thereafter, shall cease to be Indian moneys under the *Indian Act*, except for the purposes of paragraph 90 (1) (a), and shall be transferred by Canada to the First Nation.

13. PROTECTION OF FIRST NATION LAND

13.1 Title to First Nation land is not changed when a First Nation's land code takes effect.

13.2 The Parties declare that it is of fundamental importance to maintain the amount and integrity of First Nation land.

13.3 First Nation land will not be sold, exchanged or conveyed, except for any exchange or expropriation of First Nation land made in accordance with this Agreement.

14. VOLUNTARY EXCHANGE OF FIRST NATION LAND

14.1 A First Nation has the right to exchange a parcel of First Nation land for another parcel of land, if that other parcel of land becomes First Nation land. An exchange of First Nation land may provide for additional compensation, including land that may not become First Nation land, and may be subject to any other terms and conditions.

14.2 Any exchange of First Nation land will require community approval in accordance with the process established in the land code.

14.3 First Nation land will only be exchanged for land that Canada consents to set apart as a reserve. In addition, the agreement of Canada is required on the technical aspects of the exchange.

14.4 The title to the land to be received in exchange for that First Nation land will be transferred to Canada and will be set apart by Canada as a reserve, as of the date of the land exchange or such later date as the First Nation may specify. This does not apply to land that is received by the First Nation as additional compensation and that is not intended to become First Nation land.

14.5 Where an exchange of First Nation land is approved by a First Nation in accordance with its land code, the First Nation can execute an authorization to Canada to transfer title to the land.

14.6 Upon the issuance to Canada of an authorization to transfer title to First Nation land under clause 14.5, Canada will transfer title to the land in accordance with the authorization and the applicable terms and conditions of the exchange.

14.7 A copy of the instruments transferring title to First Nation land will be registered in the First Nation Lands Register.

14.8 As of the date of the land exchange, or such later date as the First Nation may specify, the description of First Nation land in the land code will be deemed to be amended to delete the description of the First Nation land that was exchanged and to add the description of the First Nation land received in exchange.

14.9 For greater certainty, the First Nation land that was exchanged will cease to be a reserve.

15. IMMUNITY FROM SEIZURE, ETC.

15.1 The Parties confirm that section 29 and subsections 89(1) and (2) of the *Indian Act* will continue to apply to any reserve that is First Nation land.

15.2 Subsection 89(1.1) of the *Indian Act* will continue to apply to all leasehold interests that existed when the land code took effect if the First Nation land was designated land at that time.

15.3 A land code may provide that some or all of the provisions of subsection 89(1.1) of the *Indian Act* are also applicable to other leasehold interests in any First Nation lands.

15.4 The Parties confirm that section 87 of the *Indian Act* continues to apply to First Nation land, so that

(a)   the interest of an Indian or a First Nation in a reserve that is First Nation land remains exempt from taxation, subject to section 83 of the *Indian Act*; and

(b)   the personal property of an Indian or a First Nation, situated on a reserve that is First Nation land, remains exempt from taxation.

16. THIRD PARTY INTERESTS

16.1 Interests or licences held by third parties or Canada in First Nation land, that exist at the time the land code takes effect, continue in force according to their terms and conditions.

16.2 Any rights of locatees in possession of First Nation land, either by custom or by allotment under the *Indian Act*, to transfer, lease and share in natural resource revenues will be defined in the land code.

16.3 Once a land code takes effect, no interest or licence in relation to First Nation land may be acquired or granted except in accordance with the land code.

16.4 For greater certainty, disputes in relation to third party interests shall be dealt with in the forum identified or established in a land code pursuant to clause 5.2(g).

17. EXPROPRIATION BY FIRST NATIONS

17.1 A First Nation with a land code in effect has the right to expropriate interests in First Nation lands without consent if deemed by the First Nation council to be necessary for community works or other First Nation purposes.

17.2 A First Nation's power of expropriation will be exercised in accordance with the rules and procedures specified in its land code, its laws and this Agreement.

17.3 An interest in First Nation land that a First Nation expropriates becomes the property of the First Nation free of any previous claim or encumbrance in respect of the interest.

17.4 A First Nation that expropriates an interest in First Nation land will give fair compensation based on the heads of compensation set out in the *Expropriation Act* (Canada).

17.5 A First Nation will establish a mechanism to resolve disputes over compensation it pays for expropriation.

17.6 Any interest in First Nation land that was obtained pursuant to section 35 of the *Indian Act* or any interest that has been acquired by Canada, or that is acquired after this Agreement comes into force by Canada in accordance with this Agreement, is not subject to First Nation expropriation.

17.7 A First Nation is not precluded from entering into an agreement with a utility or public body for the purpose of granting it an interest in First Nation land that is exempt from expropriation by the First Nation.

17.8 No expropriation of an interest in First Nation land by a First Nation takes effect earlier than either of the following days:

(a)   the date the notice of expropriation is registered in the First Nation Lands Register; or

(b)   the 30th day after the day the last copy of the notice is served.

PART IV

FIRST NATION LAW MAKING

18. LAW MAKING POWERS

18.1 The council of a First Nation with a land code in effect will have the power to make laws, in accordance with its land code, respecting the development, conservation, protection, management, use and possession of First Nation land and interests and licences in relation to that land. This includes laws on any matter necessary or ancillary to the making of laws in relation to First Nation land.

18.2 The following examples illustrate some of the First Nation laws contemplated by the Parties:

(a)   laws on the regulation, control and prohibition of zoning, land use, subdivision control and land development;

(b)   laws on the creation, regulation and prohibition of interests and licences in relation to First Nation land;

(c)   laws on environmental assessment and protection;

(d)   laws on the provision of local services in relation to First Nation land and the imposition of equitable user charges; and

(e)   laws on the provision of services for the resolution, outside the courts, of disputes in relation to First Nation land.

18.3 A land code will not address the taxation of real or personal property. Section 83 of the *Indian Act* will continue to apply.

18.4 In any proceeding, a copy of a First Nation law, appearing to be certified as a true copy by an officer of the First Nation is, without proof of the officer's signature or official character, evidence of its enactment on the date specified in the law.

18.5 This Agreement does not affect or extend existing rights and powers, or create additional rights and powers, related to fisheries.

19. ENFORCEMENT OF FIRST NATION LAWS

19.1 To enforce its land code and its First Nation laws, a First Nation will have the power to

(a)   establish offences that are punishable on summary conviction;

(b)   provide for fines, imprisonment, restitution, community service, and alternate means for achieving compliance; and

(c)   establish comprehensive enforcement procedures consistent with federal law, including inspections, searches, seizures and compulsory sampling, testing and the production of information.

19.2 First Nation laws may adopt or incorporate by reference the summary conviction procedures of the *Criminal Code* for the purpose of enforcement.

19.3 Persons may be appointed by the First Nation or the Governor in Council to act as justices of the peace for the purposes of enforcement. If no justice of the peace is appointed, then First Nation laws will be enforced through the provincial courts.

19.4 A person appointed as a justice of the peace under this clause will have jurisdiction to try offences established by or under a land code or a First Nation law.

19.5 Decisions made by a justice of the peace appointed under this clause may be appealed to a court of competent jurisdiction.

19.6 The First Nation will protect the independence of each justice of the peace it appoints in a way similar to that in a province, for example tenure, removal and remuneration.

19.7 The First Nation and Canada may enter into agreements for the training, supervision and administrative support for justices of the peace appointed by the First Nation. Provinces may also be parties to such agreements with First Nations.

19.8 The First Nation and Canada will enter into an agreement for the appointment, training, supervision and administrative support for any justice of the peace appointed under this clause by the Governor in Council. The affected province will be invited to participate in the development of and be a party to such agreement.

19.9 For the purpose of prosecuting offences, the First Nation will follow one or more of these options:

(a)   retain its own prosecutor;

(b)   enter into an agreement with Canada and the government of the province to arrange for a provincial prosecutor; or

(c)   enter into an agreement with Canada to arrange for a federal agent to prosecute these offenses.

20. APPLICATION OF FEDERAL LAWS

20.1 Federal laws applicable on First Nation land will continue to apply, except to the extent that they are inconsistent with the federal legislation.

20.2 Notwithstanding any inconsistency with the federal legislation, the *Emergencies Act* will apply on First Nation land, but any appropriation of an interest in First Nation land under the *Emergencies Act* shall be authorized expressly by an order in council.

20.3 For greater certainty, and subject to Part VII, the *Atomic Energy Control Act* or any successor legislation continue to apply to First Nation lands.

21. INAPPLICABLE SECTIONS OF INDIAN ACT AND REGULATIONS

21.1 Once a land code takes effect, the First Nation, its members and its First Nation land will not be subject to the following:

(a) sections 18 to 20 and 22 to 28 of the *Indian Act*;

(b) sections 30 to 35 of the *Indian Act*;

(c) sections 37 to 41 of the *Indian Act*;

(d) sections 49, 50(4) and 53 to 60 of the *Indian Act*;

(e) sections 66, 69 and 71 of the *Indian Act*;

(f) section 93 of the *Indian Act*;

(g) regulations made under section 57 of the *Indian Act*; and

(h) regulations made under sections 42 and 73 of the *Indian Act* to the extent that they are inconsistent with this Agreement or the land code or the laws of the First Nation.

22. EXISTING FIRST NATION BY-LAWS

22.1 A First Nation will continue to have the authority under the *Indian Act* to make by-laws.

PART V

ENVIRONMENT

23. GENERAL PRINCIPLES

23.1 The council of a First Nation with a land code in effect will have the power to make environmental laws relating to First Nation land.

23.2 The Parties intend that there should be both an environmental assessment and an environmental protection regime for each First Nation.

23.3 The principles of these regimes are set out below, while specific details of environmental protection will be set out in an environmental management agreement between the Minister and the Minister of the Environment and each First Nation.

23.4 The environmental assessment and protection regimes will be implemented through First Nation laws.

23.5 The Parties agree to harmonize their respective environmental regimes and processes, with the involvement of the provinces where they agree to participate, to promote effective and consistent environmental regimes and processes and to avoid uncertainty and duplication.

23.6 This Agreement is not intended to affect rights and powers relating to migratory birds or endangered species. These matters may be dealt with in the context of other negotiations. This Agreement is not intended to determine or prejudice the resolution of these issues.

24. ENVIRONMENTAL MANAGEMENT AGREEMENT

24.1 The Minister and the Minister of the Environment and each First Nation with a land code in effect, or a group of such First Nations, will negotiate an environmental management agreement.

24.2 The Parties wish to involve the appropriate provinces in the development of the environmental management agreements. The Parties agree to harmonize environmental management, with the involvement of the provinces where they agree to participate. A province could become a party to an environmental management agreement or there could be separate agreements among the First Nation, Canada and the province.

24.3 An environmental management agreement in essence will be a plan on how the First Nation will enact environmental protection laws deemed essential by the First Nation and the Minister and the Minister of the Environment. It will also include timing, resource, inspection and enforcement requirements.

24.4 The Parties will identify areas they consider essential for environmental protection for particular First Nations. At the time of this Agreement, the Parties have identified the following areas as essential for all First Nations:

(a) solid waste management;

(b) fuel storage tank management;

(c) sewage treatment and disposal; and

(d) environmental emergencies.

24.5 For those areas identified as essential by the Parties, First Nation environmental protection standards and punishments will have at least the same effect as those in the laws of the province in which the First Nation is situated.

24.6 For greater certainty, if there is an inconsistency between the provision of a federal law respecting the protection of the environment and a provision in a land code or First Nation law respecting the protection of the environment, the federal provision will prevail to the extent of the inconsistency.

24.7 The parties to each environmental management agreement will make best efforts to sign the agreement within one year after the First Nation's land code takes effect, or within such longer period as they may agree to.

24.8 Each environmental management agreement will include a mechanism for its periodic review and updating by the parties to that agreement.

25. ENVIRONMENTAL ASSESSMENT

25.1 Subject to clause 27, a First Nation will, with the assistance of the Lands Advisory Board and the appropriate federal agencies, make best efforts to develop an environmental assessment process within one year after the First Nation's land code takes effect, or within such longer period as the Minister and the First Nation may agree to.

25.2 The First Nation and the Minister will, in the individual agreement referred to in clause 6, address how to conduct the environmental assessment of projects on First Nation land during the interim period until the First Nation's environmental assessment process is developed.

25.3 The First Nation's environmental assessment process will be consistent with requirements of the *Canadian Environmental Assessment Act*.

25.4 The First Nation's environmental assessment process will be triggered in appropriate cases where the First Nation is approving, regulating, funding or undertaking a project on First Nation land. The assessment will occur as early as possible in the planning stages of the project before an irrevocable decision is made.

25.5 The Parties agree that section 10 of the *Canadian Environmental Assessment Act* will not apply to projects located on First Nation land.

25.6 The Parties agree to use their best efforts to implement the principle that the First Nation's environmental assessment process be used where an environmental assessment of a project on First Nation land is required by the *Canadian Environmental Assessment Act*.

25.7 The Parties agree to develop a plan to harmonize their respective environmental assessment processes, with the involvement of the provinces where they agree to participate.

26. OTHER AGREEMENTS

26.1 The First Nation and Canada recognize that it may be advisable to enter into other agreements with each other and other jurisdictions to deal with environmental issues like harmonization, implementation, timing, funding and enforcement.

26.2 Where matters being negotiated pursuant to clause 26.1 normally fall within provincial jurisdiction, or may have significant impacts beyond the boundaries of First Nation land, the parties will invite the affected province to be a party to such negotiations and resulting agreements.

27. RESOURCES

27.1 The Parties understand that the obligation of a First Nation to establish environmental assessment and environmental protection regimes depends on adequate financial resources and expertise being available to the First Nation.

PART VI

FUNDING

28. APPROPRIATION

28.1 Any amounts provided by Canada to the First Nations pursuant to funding arrangements in relation to First Nation land shall be paid out of such moneys as may be appropriated by Parliament for this purpose.

29. DEVELOPMENTAL FUNDING

29.1 Canada and the Lands Advisory Board will enter into a funding arrangement to allow the First Nations to develop land codes and community approval processes for their land codes, to negotiate the individual agreements mentioned in clause 6 and to seek community approval under clause 7.

30. OPERATIONAL FUNDING

30.1 An individual agreement between the Minister and a First Nation will determine the resources to be provided by Canada to the First Nation to manage First Nation lands and make, administer and enforce its laws under a land code. The agreement will determine specific funding issues, for example period of time, and terms and conditions.

30.2 A method for allocating such operating funds as may have been appropriated by Parliament will be developed by the Parties and the Lands Advisory Board.

30.3 Unless a First Nation and Canada agree otherwise, an individual agreement respecting the provision of funding under this clause will have a maximum term of five years and will include provisions for its amendment and renegotiation.

31. LANDS ADVISORY BOARD FUNDING

31.1 Canada will enter into a funding arrangement with the Lands Advisory Board for the five year period following the coming into force of this Agreement.

PART VII

EXPROPRIATION OF FIRST NATION LAND BY CANADA

32. RESTRICTIONS

32.1 In accordance with the principle stated in clause 13.2, the Parties agree, as a general principle, that First Nation lands will not be subject to expropriation.

32.2 Despite the general principle against expropriation, First Nation land may be expropriated by Canada

(a)   only with the consent of the Governor in Council; and

(b)   only by and for the use of a federal department or agency.

32.3 The Governor in Council will only consent to an expropriation of First Nation land if the expropriation is justifiable and necessary for a federal public purpose that serves the national interest.

32.4 When making a decision to expropriate First Nation land, the Governor in Council, in addition to other steps that may be required before making such a decision, will at a minimum follow these steps:

(a)   it will consider using means other than expropriation and will use those other means where reasonably feasible;

(b)   it will use non-First Nation land, where such land is reasonably available;

(c)   if it must use First Nation land, it will make reasonable efforts to acquire the land through agreement with the First Nation, rather than by expropriation;

(d)   if it must expropriate First Nation land, it will expropriate only the smallest interest necessary and for the shortest time required; and

(e)   in every case, it will first provide the First Nation with information relevant to the expropriation.

32.5 Prior to the Governor in Council issuing an order consenting to the expropriation of First Nation land, the federal department or agency will make public a report on the reasons justifying the expropriation and the steps taken in satisfaction of this clause and will provide a copy of the report to the First Nation.

32.6 Where a First Nation objects to a proposed expropriation it may refer the issue to an independent third party for a neutral evaluation under Part IX, within 60 days of the release of the report referred to in clause 32.5.

32.7 An order of the Governor in Council consenting to the expropriation will not be issued earlier than

(a)   the end of the 60 day period referred to in clause 32.6; or

(b)   the day the opinion or recommendation of the neutral evaluator is released, where the First Nation referred the proposed expropriation to an independent evaluator under clause 32.6.

33. COMPENSATION BY CANADA

33.1 In the event of the expropriation of First Nation land by Canada under this Part, Canada will provide compensation to the First Nation in accordance with this clause.

33.2 The compensation will include alternate land of equal or greater size or of comparable value. If the alternate land is of less than comparable value, then additional compensation will be provided. The alternate land may be smaller than the land being expropriated only if that does not result in the First Nation having less land area than when its land code took effect.

33.3 The total value of the compensation provided by Canada under this clause will be based on the following:

(a)   the market value of the land or interest that is acquired;

(b)   the replacement value of any improvement to the land that is acquired;

(c)   the damages attributable to disturbance;

(d)   the value of any special economic advantage arising out of or incidental to the occupation or use of the affected First Nation land to the extent that this value is not otherwise compensated;

(e)   damages for any reduction in the value of a remaining interest; and

(f)   damages for any adverse effect on any cultural or other special value of the land.

33.4 If the value and nature of the compensation cannot be agreed upon by the federal department or agency and the affected First Nation, either party may refer a dispute on compensation to arbitration under Part IX.

33.5 Any claim or encumbrance in respect of the interest expropriated by Canada may only be claimed against the amount of compensation that is otherwise payable to the person or entity whose interest is being expropriated.

33.6 Interest on the compensation is payable from the date the expropriation takes effect, at the same rate as for prejudgment interest in the superior court of the province in which the First Nation land is located.

34. STATUS OF LANDS

34.1 Where less than the full interest of the First Nation in First Nation land is expropriated by Canada,

(a)   the land retains its status as First Nation land;

(b)   the land remains subject to the land code and to any law of the First Nation that is otherwise applicable, except to the extent the land code or law is inconsistent with the expropriation; and

(c)   the First Nation may continue to use and occupy the land, except to the extent the use or occupation is inconsistent with the expropriation.

34.2 Alternate land accepted by the First Nation as part of the compensation will become both a reserve and First Nation land.

35. REVERSION OF INTEREST IN FIRST NATION LAND

35.1 Where an expropriated interest in First Nation land, which is less than the full interest of the First Nation in the land, is no longer required by Canada for the purpose for which it was expropriated, the interest in land will revert to the First Nation.

35.2 The Minister responsible for the expropriating department or agency, without the consent of the Governor in Council, may decide that the interest is no longer required and determine the disposition of any improvements.

36. RETURN OF FULL INTEREST IN FIRST NATION LAND

36.1 Where the full interest of a First Nation in First Nation land was expropriated but is no longer required by Canada for the purpose for which it was expropriated, the land will be returned to the First Nation on terms negotiated by the First Nation and the federal department or agency, at the time of the expropriation or at a later date as agreed to by them.

36.2 Where the terms and conditions of the return cannot be agreed upon by the First Nation and the federal department or agency, either party may refer the dispute to arbitration under Part IX.

36.3 The Minister responsible for the expropriating department or agency, without the consent of the Governor in Council, may decide that the land is no longer required and determine the disposition of any improvements.

37. APPLICATION OF EXPROPRIATION ACT

37.1 Any provisions of the *Expropriation Act*, (Canada) that are applicable to an expropriation of First Nation land by Canada continue to apply, unless inconsistent with this Agreement.

PART VIII

LANDS ADVISORY BOARD

38. LANDS ADVISORY BOARD

38.1 The Lands Advisory Board shall consist of at least three members appointed:

(a)   Prior to September 1, 2003, by the Councils of the original First Nation parties to this Agreement; and

(b)   After September 1, 2003, by the Councils of the First Nations that have ratified this Agreement, whether they ratify the Agreement on, before or after that date.

38.2 The Lands Advisory Board will have all necessary powers and capacity to properly perform its functions under this Agreement.

38.3 The Lands Advisory Board will [sic] a chairperson to preside over the Board and, subject to the direction of the Board, to act on its behalf.

39. FUNCTIONS OF THE LANDS ADVISORY BOARD

39.1 In addition to any other functions specifically assigned to it by the Parties, the Lands Advisory Board will be responsible for the following functions:

(a)   developing model land codes, laws and land management systems;

(b)   developing model agreements for use between First Nations and other authorities and institutions, including public utilities and private organizations;

(c)   on request of a First Nation, assisting the First Nation in developing and implementing its land code, laws, land management systems and environmental assessment and protection regimes;

(d)   assisting a verifier when requested by the verifier;

(e)   establishing a resource centre, curricula and training programs for managers and others who perform functions pursuant to a land code;

(f)   on request of a First Nation encountering difficulties relating to the management of its First Nation lands, helping the First Nation in obtaining the expertise necessary to resolve the difficulty;

(g)   proposing regulations for First Nation land registration;

(h)   proposing to the Minister such amendments to this Agreement and the federal legislation as it considers necessary or advisable;

(i)   in consultation with First Nations, negotiating a funding method with the Minister; and

(j)   performing such other functions or services for a First Nation as are agreed to between the Board and the First Nation.

39.2 The Lands Advisory Board will have authority to adopt rules for the procedure at its meetings and generally for the conduct of its affairs.

40. RECORD KEEPING

40.1 The Lands Advisory Board will maintain a record containing

(a)   the name of each First Nation that approves a land code;

(b)   a copy of that land code;

(c)   a copy of each amendment to a land code; and

(d)   the dates on which each was approved and certified.

40.2.1 The Lands Advisory Board shall, in consultation with the Minister prescribe procedures for a First Nation to authorize the signing of this Agreement and for the formal signature of First Nations to this Agreement, and shall advise the Minister when a First Nation has completed the procedures.

40.2.2 Subject to sub-clause **40.2.1**, a First Nation may only become a signatory under this section with the consent of Canada, and Canada shall advise the Lands Advisory Board if and when such consent is given.

40.2.3 The Lands Advisory Board shall receive and record the adhesion of a First Nation party to this Agreement, made after January 1, 2001, and advise the Minister that the said First Nation has signed the Framework Agreement.

41. ANNUAL REPORT

41.1 Within 90 days following the end of each year of operation, the Lands Advisory Board will deliver to the Parties an annual report, in both official languages, on the work of the Board for that year.

41.2 The Minister will cause a copy of the Lands Advisory Board's annual report to be laid before each House of Parliament within the first 30 sitting days of that House after the Minister receives it.

42. LANDS ADVISORY BOARD NO LONGER IN EXISTENCE

42.1 In the event that the Lands Advisory Board is no longer in existence, the functions of the Lands Advisory Board under this Agreement will be performed by the Parties, except as follows:

(a)   the functions set out in clauses 29 and 39, except clause **39.1(g)**, will be performed by the First Nations; and

(b)   the functions set out in clauses 10 and 40 will be assumed by the First Nations Lands Register.

PART IX

DISPUTE RESOLUTION

43. GENERAL PRINCIPLES

43.1 The Parties are committed to resolving any dispute that may arise out of this Agreement among themselves, amicably and in good faith. Where they cannot resolve a dispute through negotiation, the Parties agree to establish and participate in the out-of-court processes referred to in this Part to resolve the dispute.

43.2 Nothing in this Agreement is to be construed as preventing the Parties from using mediation to assist them in reaching an amicable agreement in respect of any issue in dispute. Where a Party has referred a dispute to mediation, the other Party is obliged to attend an initial meeting with the mediator. However, either Party can end a mediation process any time after the initial meeting.

43.3 Subject to clause 43.4, any dispute arising from the implementation, application or administration of this Agreement, the federal legislation, an individual agreement or an environmental management agreement may be resolved in either of two ways:

(a)   Neutral evaluation – it may be referred to neutral evaluation by one party to the dispute; or

(b)   Arbitration – it may be referred to arbitration by both parties to the dispute.

43.4 Any dispute respecting compensation for First Nation land expropriated by Canada or the terms and conditions for the return of the full interest in First Nation land will be referred to arbitration.

43.5 Any objection by a First Nation to a proposed expropriation under Part VII that has been referred to neutral evaluation will be evaluated and a report submitted by the neutral evaluator to the First Nation and Canada within 60 days of the referral to the neutral evaluator.

44. PANELS OF ARBITRATORS, ETC.

44.1 The Parties and the Lands Advisory Board will jointly establish lists of mutually acceptable persons willing to act as mediators, arbitrators, verifiers and neutral evaluators.

44.2 Parties who become involved in a dispute may select mediators, arbitrators and neutral evaluators from the appropriate list, or may agree to the appointment of an individual who is not on the list.

44.3 The selection and assignment of verifiers and the procedure to be followed by verifiers will be arranged by the Lands Advisory Board, Canada and the First Nation.

44.4 Individuals appointed to act as mediators, arbitrators, verifiers or neutral evaluators must be unbiased and free from any conflict of interest relative to the matter in issue and have knowledge or experience to act in the appointed capacity.

45. NEUTRAL EVALUATION

45.1 Where a dispute is referred to neutral evaluation, the evaluator will where appropriate,

(a)   identify the issues in the dispute;

(b)   assess the strengths of each party's case;

(c)   structure a plan for the progress of the case;

(d)   encourage settlement of the dispute; and

(e)   provide the parties with a non-binding opinion or recommendation to resolve the dispute.

46. ARBITRATION

46.1 Unless otherwise agreed by the Parties, each arbitration will be conducted in accordance with this clause.

46.2 The procedure will follow the Commercial Arbitration Code, which is a schedule to the *Commercial Arbitration Act.*

46.3 If no appropriate procedural provision is in that Code, the parties in dispute may adopt the Commercial Arbitration Rules in force from time to time of the British Columbia International Commercial Arbitration Centre.

46.4 The arbitrator will establish the procedures of the arbitration, subject to this clause.

47. RELATED ISSUES

47.1 The parties to a dispute will divide the costs of the dispute resolution process equally between themselves.

47.2 Any person whose interests will be adversely affected by a dispute that is referred to a dispute resolution process may participate in the process, if

(a)   all parties to the process consent; and

(b)   the person pays the costs of his or her participation, unless otherwise agreed by the other parties to the dispute.

47.3 The decision of a verifier and a decision or award of an arbitrator will be final and binding on the participating parties.

47.4 No order shall be made, processed, entered or proceeding taken in any court, whether by way of injunction, *mandamus*, *certiorari*, prohibition or *quo warranto* to contest, review, impeach or limit the action of a person acting as a verifier, an arbitrator or a neutral evaluator under this Agreement.

47.5 Despite clause 47.4, judicial review may be taken under the *Federal Court Act* within 30 days of a decision of a person acting as a verifier, an arbitrator or a neutral evaluator under this Agreement in respect of such person exceeding his or her jurisdiction, refusing to exercise his or her jurisdiction or failing to observe a principal of natural justice.

PART X

RATIFICATION AND ENACTMENTS BY THE PARTIES

48. RATIFICATION OF AGREEMENT

48.1 The Parties agree that they will seek to ratify this Agreement and implement it in the following manner:

(a)   each First Nation agrees to develop a land code and to seek community approval; and

(b)   following community approval by two First Nations, Canada agrees to recommend to Parliament the enactment of legislation.

48.2 This Agreement will be considered to have been ratified by a First Nation when the First Nation approves a land code, and to have been ratified by Canada when the federal legislation comes into force.

49. ENACTMENTS BY THE PARTIES

49.1 Canada agrees that the federal legislation that it recommends to Parliament will be consistent with and will ratify this Agreement.

49.2 In the event of an inconsistency or conflict between the federal legislation and any other federal enactment, the federal legislation will prevail to the extent of the inconsistency or conflict.

49.3 In the event of any inconsistency or conflict between the land code of a First Nation and the provisions of a First Nation law or of a by-law made by its council under section 81 of the *Indian Act*, the land code will prevail to the extent of the inconsistency or conflict.

PART XI

OTHER MATTERS

50. LIABILITY

50.1 The First Nation will not be liable for acts or omissions of Canada or any person or entity authorized by Canada to act in relation to First Nation land that occurred before the First Nation's land code takes effect.

50.2 Canada will not be liable for acts or omissions of the First Nation or any person or entity authorized by the First Nation to act in relation to First Nation land that occur after the First Nation's land code takes effect.

50.3 Canada will indemnify a First Nation for any loss arising from an act or omission by Canada, or any person or entity acting on behalf of Canada, in respect of First Nation land that occurred before the First Nation's land code takes effect.

50.4 The First Nation will indemnify Canada for any loss arising from an act or omission by the First Nation, or any person or entity acting on behalf of the First Nation, in respect of First Nation land that occurs after the land code takes effect.

50.5 No action or other proceeding lies or shall be commenced against a person acting as a member of the Lands Advisory Board, a mediator, verifier, neutral evaluator or arbitrator for or in respect of anything done, or omitted to be done, in good faith, during the course of and for the purposes of carrying out his or her functions under this Agreement.

51. FIRST NATION LANDS REGISTER

51.1 Canada will establish a First Nation Lands Register to record documents respecting First Nation land or interests in First Nation land. It will be administered by Canada as a subsystem of the existing Reserve Land Register.

51.2 A separate register will be maintained for each First Nation with a land code in effect.

51.3 The Governor in Council will be authorized in the federal legislation to make regulations respecting the First Nation Lands Register. These regulations will be developed by the Lands Advisory Board and the Minister.

52. STATUS OF DOCUMENTS

52.1 The *Statutory Instruments Act*, or any successor legislation, will not apply to a land code or to First Nation laws.

53. PROVINCIAL RELATIONS

53.1 Where Canada and a First Nation intend to enter into an agreement that is not referred to in this Agreement but is required to implement this Agreement and where it deals with matters that normally fall within provincial jurisdiction, or may have significant impacts beyond the boundaries of First Nation land, Canada and the First Nation will invite the affected province to be a party to the negotiations and resulting agreement.

54. TIME LIMITS

54.1 The time limits in this Agreement for the doing of anything may be waived on consent.

55. OTHER REGIMES

55.1 Nothing in this Agreement prevents a First Nation, at any time, from opting into any other regime providing for community decisionmaking and community control, if the First Nation is eligible for the other regime and opts into it in accordance with procedures developed for that other regime.

55.2 Sub-clause 38.1 and clause 57 do not apply to a First Nation to which sub-clause 55.1 applies.

56. REVIEW PROCESS

56.1 The Lands Advisory Board will, on a continuing basis, consult with representatives of the Parties for the purpose of assessing the effectiveness of this Agreement and the federal legislation.

56.2 Within four years of the federal legislation coming into force, the Minister and the Lands Advisory Board or their representatives will jointly conduct a review of this Agreement. It will focus on the following issues, among others:

(a)   the functioning of land management under this Agreement;

(b)   the adequacy and appropriateness of the funding arrangements;

(c)   the role of the Lands Advisory Board;

(d)   whether there is a demand by other First Nations to use this Agreement;

(e)   changes that may improve the functioning of First Nation land management;

(f)   the dispute resolution processes; and

(g)   such other issues as may be agreed to by the Parties.

56.3 Canada and the First Nations will make best efforts to complete this review within one year. Following completion of the review, the Minister will meet with representatives of the First Nations to discuss the results of the review.

57. AMENDMENTS

57.1 Until September 1, 2003, this Agreement may be amended by agreement of the parties, provided that the amendments to Part VIII may be made with the consent of Canada and 2/3 of the original First Nation parties to this Agreement.

57.2 No amendment affecting the powers, authorities, obligations, operations or operational funding of a First Nation that has ratified this agreement is effective with respect to that First Nation without the consent of that First Nation.

57.3 After September 1, 2003, this Agreement, may, subject to 57.2, be amended with the consent of Canada and 2/3 of the First Nations which have ratified the Agreement, before, on or after that day.

58. RECITALS

58.1 The recitals form part of this Agreement.

59. COMING INTO FORCE

59.1 This Agreement will come into force in respect of Canada and a First Nation when Canada and that First Nation both ratify this Agreement under Part X.

59.2 Despite clause 59.1, such provisions of this Agreement as are necessary to allow a First Nation to ratify this Agreement before Canada ratifies this Agreement will have effect as of the day Canada and that First Nation both sign this Agreement.

SPECIFIC CLAIMS RESOLUTION ACT

Introductory Commentary

Over the decades, First Nations' complaints about how the Crown was discharging its responsibilities under treaties and agreements multiplied. In the past, there were few avenues for redress. For example, between 1927 and 1951, the Indian Act hindered First Nations by requiring them to get government permission if they wanted to use their own money to advance their claims. That effectively barred First Nations from making claims against Canada. As a result, grievances accumulated and the relationship between First Nations and the federal government suffered. In recent times, federal governments have acknowledged that ways of settling these problems had to be found. We recognize that Aboriginal people have legitimate and long-standing grievances that, as a just society, it was our responsibility to address. … We have set out, in Bill C-6, to create a more independent process for resolving claims, a more neutral system that will level the playing field for negotiation, to resolve claims more efficiently and, more important, honourable senators, a system that will allow First Nations to capitalize on their increasing opportunities for economic development by fostering a climate of trust, cooperation and certainty.

Hon. Jack Austin at the 2nd reading of Bill C-6

The *Specific Claims Resolution Act*[403] ("the Act" or the "SCRA") received royal assent and became law on November 7, 2003. Although it has been enacted by Parliament, at the date of publication it is not yet in force and has yet to take effect. Indeed, according to media sources,[404] the federal government has expressed the intention of not bringing the Act into force, which would require an Order in Council under s. 85 of the Act.[405]

Irrespective of the government's intention to bring or not to bring the Act into force, the following commentary and annotations may serve to inform future endeavours to reform the Specific Claims process. As outlined by the Honourable Jack Austin in the introductory quote, the reform to this process has been a long time in coming. Whether by means of the SCRA or by some other means, change to a process known for its large and growing inventory of

---

[403] S.C. 2003, c. 23.

[404] See, for example, *First Nations Strategic Bulletin, vol.3, issue 9, September 2005,* available at: <http://www.cmaq.net/fr/upload/22368.pdf>.

[405] This order could bring all of the statute into force at the same time, or different parts at different times.

outstanding claims seems inevitable. Therefore, the commentary set out below is offered not for the purpose of considering "whether" but "how".

Background

In 1974, responding to First Nations' frustration at having to go to the courts to settle their historic grievances, the Government of Canada established the Office of Native Claims within the Department of Indian Affairs and Northern Development. Later, in 1982, the government established the current Specific Claims Policy, *Outstanding Business: A Native Claims Policy — Specific Claims* (*"Outstanding Business"*).[406]

The introduction to that policy states:

> The federal government's policy on Native claims finds its genesis in a statement given in the House of Commons on August 8, 1973 by the Minister of Indian Affairs and Northern Development. Since that time experience and consultations with Indian bands and other Native groups and associations have prompted the government to review and clarify its policies with respect to the two broad categories of claims: comprehensive claims and specific claims.
>
> The term "comprehensive claims" is used to designate claims which are based on traditional Native use and occupancy of land. Such claims normally involve a group of bands or Native communities within a geographic area and are comprehensive in their scope including, for example, land, hunting, fishing and trapping rights and other economic and social benefits.
>
> The government has already made public its policy on comprehensive claims in a booklet entitled *In All Fairness*, published in December 1981. The term "specific claims" with which this booklet deals refers to those claims which relate to the administration of land and other Indian assets and to the fulfillment of treaties.

In keeping with the distinction between Comprehensive Claims and Specific Claims, the policy defines "specific claims" as follows:

> The government's policy on specific claims is that it will recognize claims by Indian bands which disclose an outstanding "lawful obligation", *i.e.*, an obligation derived from the law on the part of the federal government.
>
> A lawful obligation may arise in any of the following circumstances:
>
> > i) The non-fulfillment of a treaty or agreement between Indians and the Crown.

---

[406] Throughout the introductory note and the commentary on the text of the Act, the term "current Specific Claims Policy" is used to refer to Canada's specific claims policy document that has been in use since 1982: Canada, Minister of Indian Affairs and Northern Development, *Outstanding Business: A Native Claims Policy – Specific Claims*, Ottawa, 1982.

ii) A breach of an obligation arising out of the *Indian Act* or other statutes pertaining to Indians and the regulations thereunder.

iii) A breach of an obligation arising out of government administration of Indian funds or other assets.

iv) An illegal disposition of Indian land.

2) Beyond Lawful Obligation

In addition to the foregoing, the government is prepared to acknowledge claims which are based on the following circumstances:

i) Failure to provide compensation for reserve lands taken or damaged by the federal government or any of its agencies under authority.

ii) Fraud in connection with the acquisition or disposition of Indian reserve land by employees or agents of the federal government, in cases where the fraud can be clearly demonstrated.

Under the process established to implement *Outstanding Business,* claims are accepted for negotiation when it is determined that Canada has an outstanding "lawful obligation" to a First Nation. If a lawful obligation is found, specific claims settlements are negotiated between First Nations, Canada and (where applicable) the relevant province or territory.

Criticisms of the Process

The process established under *Outstanding Business* has been criticized for several reasons:

- By retaining control over such matters as the approval of funding for research of claims and potential claims, the government is perceived as being able to assert control over which claims are brought forward for consideration.

- By retaining control over "research funding" and "negotiation funding",[407] the government is perceived as being able to control which claims are able to move through the process.

- The Minister is viewed as being both the defendant in Specific Claims and, in the absence of a mechanism for adjudication or binding arbitration, as the final arbiter of Specific Claims. Some have referred to this as a conflict of interest.

---

[407] The Act refers to funding for the "research, preparation and conduct" of claims. Under the current process the government provides grant funding to First Nations for research and loan funding for participation in negotiations. Such funding is intended to offset costs of hiring legal counsel and other experts, travel expenses etc.

- Despite all of the efforts to settle claims, the number of claims settled under *Outstanding Business* has been overshadowed by the number of claims that are waiting to be addressed under the process.

Efforts to Address the Criticisms: The Indian Claims Commission

In response to complaints, such as those outlined above, in 1991, the government established a Commission of Inquiry under the *Inquiries Act* to complement the claims process. The mandate of the Indian Claims Commission ("ISCC") was stated as follows:

> AND WE DO HEREBY advise that our Commissioners on the basis of Canada's Specific Claims Policy published in 1982 and subsequent formal amendments or additions as announced by the Minister of Indian Affairs and Northern Development (hereinafter "the Minister"), by considering only those matters at issue when the dispute was initially submitted to the Commission, inquire into and report upon:
>
> (a) whether a claimant has a valid claim for negotiation under the Policy where that claim has already been rejected by the Minister; and
>
> (b) which compensation criteria apply in negotiation of a settlement, where a claimant disagrees with the Minister's determination of the applicable criteria.[408]

The reports and recommendations of the ICC are not binding on the Crown; they are submitted to the Minister for consideration and the Minister can choose to accept or reject the ICC's recommendations.

The ICC was established as in "interim measure" — a stop-gap for the situation that preceded its creation, including a growing backlog of claims and concerns about the Specific Claims process itself. Presumably the ICC was created pending a more comprehensive review of the Specific Claims policy and process.

Since the creation of the ICC, the inventory of Specific Claims has continued to grow and calls for change to the Specific Claims process have remained.[409]

After the creation of the ICC, Canada worked with First Nations in two separate processes, the Joint Working Group and the Joint Task Force, to consider possible changes to the Specific Claims Process. The Joint Task Force produced a detailed report that recommended key changes to the process:

- that it have a statutory basis;
- that there be a mechanism for binding decisions on the validity of claims; and
- that the emphasis be on alternative dispute resolution.

---

[408] Order in Council PC 1992-1730

[409] The Indian Specific Claims Commission was established pursuant to order-in-council P.C. 1991-1329 (as amended by P.C. 1992-1730). The Commission operates and is generally known as the Indian Claims Commission or ICC.

Bill C-60 (later Bill C-6) followed the work of the Joint Task Force and the Joint Task Force Report. It is beyond doubt that the JTF report formed the starting place for work on the SCRA.

Goals of the Act

> The new independent body envisioned in this legislation will oversee a streamlined process for resolving specific claims that reflects the preference of both Canada and First Nations to right the wrongs of the past through constructive and co-operative negotiations. (Minister Nault)

To this end the SCRA creates the Canadian Centre for the Independent Resolution of First Nations Specific Claims (the Centre). The Centre is composed of two Divisions, the Commission Division and the Tribunal. As will be outlined in more detail below, the Centre is designed to meet the goals of the SCRA and to address the criticisms outlined above in the following ways:

The Centre:

° The Centre operates independently from the Minister of Indian Affairs and Northern Development and the Department of Indian Affairs and Northern Development ("DIAND"). It is a "separate employer" headed by a "deputy head". While it submits reports to Parliament through the Minister, it does not otherwise "answer to" the Minister.

° The appointments under the Act (Chief Executive Officer, Chief Commissioner, Vice-Chief Commissioner, Chief Adjudicator, Vice-Chief Adjudicator, Commissioners and Adjudicators) reflect the criteria of independence established by the case law.[410]

The Commission Division:

° The Commission will administer the provision of research funding and funding for the conduct of claims. This authority includes the power to establish the rules and criteria applicable to such funding.

° The Commission is mandated to ensure the parties exhaust all reasonable attempts to resolve claims through alternative dispute resolution, including negotiation, mediation, arbitration, and — with the consent of the parties — binding arbitration.

° The Commission will assist the parties to ensure that claims move expeditiously through the process by conducting "preparatory meetings" to ensure that claims are properly researched and that all issues have been raised as early in the process as possible.

---

[410] The requirements for institutional independence are set out by the Supreme Court of Canada in *Canadian Pacific Ltd. v Matsqui*, [1995] 1 S.C.R. 3 at 57, in relation to tribunals established by bands themselves:

> Thus, to conform to the requirements of institutional independence, the appellant bands' by-laws will have to guarantee remuneration and stipulate periods of tenure for tribunal members.

The Tribunal Division

    ° The Tribunal Division is mandated, where certain criteria are met,[411] to adjudicate, among other things, the issue of validity and the issue of compensation with respect to all claims under $10 million. The decisions of the Tribunal are binding on the Crown.

    ° Access to the Tribunal is designed to maximize the opportunities for the parties to negotiate claims rather than to have them adjudicated. The Tribunal may be viewed as a mechanism of last resort under the Act.

Once established, the Centre will replace the current Indian Specific Claims Commission (ISCC), which was set up in 1991 as an interim measure to make non-binding recommendations on specific claims that have not been accepted by Canada for negotiation.

Legislative History

Bill C-60, now the SCRA, was originally introduced in the House of Commons on June 13, 2002. Although it died on the order paper, it was re-introduced to the house as Bill C-6 on October 9, 2002. It was read a second time and deemed referred to the Standing Committee on Aboriginal Affairs, Northern Development and Natural Resources on the same date.

The Bill was sent back to the House on December 6, 2002, with several technical amendments and one process-related amendment: that the report required under s. 76(1) be referred by each House of Parliament "to the appropriate committee of that House". The Bill was adopted by the House, as amended, on March 18, 2003.

Bill C-6 was given first reading by the Senate on March 19, 2003. Following second reading, the Standing Senate Committee on Aboriginal Peoples reviewed the bill and returned it to the Senate on June 12, 2003, with a number of amendments, including:

- the raising of the claim limit specific in s. 56 from $7 million to $10 million;

- in s. 76(1), a requirement for the Minister to give First Nations an opportunity to make representations in the context of the review of the SCRA required under the same subsection;

- the addition of s. 76.1 which requires the Minister to provide claimants[412] with an opportunity to make representations regarding the appointment of the Chief Executive Officer, Chief Executive Officer, Chief Commissioner, Vice-Chief Commissioner, Chief Adjudicator, Vice-Chief Adjudicator, Commissioners and Adjudicators; and

---

[411]   SCRA, s. 32

[412]   For a period of one year after the Act comes into force, the work "claimant" in s. 76 is to be read as including, per s. 77.1 (also added by the Senate), claimants under the *Outstanding Business* policy.

- the addition of s. 76.2(1), which prohibits any appointee to the Centre from acting for a party with respect to a claim that the appointee learned about or worked on while an appointee to the Centre.

- the addition of s. 76.2(2), which prohibits any appointee to the Centre from accepting any employment with DIAND or a First Nation that had a claim pending before the centre during the appointee's term of office.

In accordance with Parliamentary procedure, the Bill was returned to the House of Commons to consider the amendments made by the Senate.[413] The bill was adopted as amended on November 4, 2003, and received Royal Assent on November 7, 2003.

The Act has not, as yet, come into force.

The Canadian Centre for the Independent Resolution of First Nations Specific Claims

Part 1 — The Centre

The Centre is comprised of the Chief Executive Officer (CEO), the Commission and the Tribunal.

The CEO, the Chief and Vice-Chief Commissioners, the Chief and Vice-Chief Adjudicators, the Commissioners and Adjudicators, are all appointed by the Governor in Council, on recommendation of the Minister. Pursuant to s. 76.1, the Minister is required to provide an opportunity for claimants under the Act[414] to make representations with respect to these appointments.

The CEO will be responsible for administering the affairs of the Commission and, except where otherwise assigned to the Tribunal, the affairs of the Tribunal. The CEO will be responsible for the overall management of the Centre, including preparing and submitting annual reports to the Minister, and providing interpretation, translation services and public education activities.

As noted above, the Centre will operate independently from the Minister and from Indian and Northern Affairs Canada.

The Centre is a separate employer. Consequently, the Centre, rather than the Treasury Board of Canada, is responsible for personnel management and employer/employee relations. Section 11 sets out a broad range of matters for which the Centre is responsible in this regard.

---

[413] According to the parliamentary website, LEGISINFO, "[i]n an unusual development, on September 25, 2003, the bill was referred back to the Senate Committee "for the purpose of studying the impact on Bill C-6 of the recent Supreme Court decision recognizing the Metis people as a distinct Aboriginal Nation." Additional hearings were held from September 30 to October 2, 2003. Bill C-6 was reported back to the Senate without further amendment on October 7, and the bill was adopted, as amended, on October 21, 2003."
See: <http://www.parl.gc.ca/common/Bills_ls.asp?lang=E&source=library_prb&Parl=37&Ses=2&ls=C6>.

[414] Pursuant to s. 77.1, for the period of one year after the SCRA comes into force, the Minister is also obliged to provide an opportunity for claimants under the *Outstanding Business* policy to make representations on appointments under ss. 5, 21(1) and 41(1).

The operations of the Centre are subject to audit by the Auditor General of Canada who, under s. 17, has responsibility for submitting a report on any such audit to both the Centre and to the Minister.

The Centre is responsible for reporting quarterly to the Minister on the compensation payable with respect to claims resolved "other than by a decision of the Tribunal" as well as the total amount of compensation payable as the result of Tribunal decisions.

Part 2 — The Commission

A Chief Commissioner, assisted by a Vice-Chief Commissioner, will be responsible for the management of the Commission. The post of Chief Commissioner may be held by the CEO of the Centre. The Commission will include up to five Commissioners in addition to the Chief and Vice-Chief Commissioners. The three "functions" specific in the SCRA are:[415]

- to administer funding for the research, preparation and conduct of specific claims;

- to assist parties in the use of ADR processes to resolve specific claims; and

- to refer the issues of validity and compensation to the Tribunal.

Accordingly, the Commission will be responsible for certain activities currently undertaken by DIAND. For example, the Commission will administer the filing of specific claims,[416] as well as the research funding and funding provided to claimants for the preparation and conduct of specific claims.[417]

The Commission will not review the claim for validity, nor review the reasons for the claim having been rejected, as does the ISCC currently. However, the Commission will oversee the use of alternative dispute resolution processes ("ADR processes") to resolve claims, which replaces the ISCC's function of providing mediation services.

The Commission is mandated (see s. 24(e)) to foster the use of a broad range of ADR processes, including — on the consent of the parties — binding arbitration. All specific claims, regardless of value, will have access to the Commission and, consequently, a broad range of ADR processes.

In carrying out its functions, the Commission may:

- establish rules of procedure for the conduct of specific claims under the SCRA, except with respect to the proceedings before the Tribunal (s. 24(a));

---

[415] s. 23

[416] There is no specific provision in the Act allowing the Commission to refuse to file a claim that does not meet the definition of Specific Claim, or for any other reason. Section 50 permits a party, "at any time" to apply to the Tribunal to have the claim struck out on the basis that the claim, on its face, is not admissible under s. 26. Other grounds for such a motion include: the claimant is not a "first nation" (*e.g.* has been filed by an individual); the claim is "frivolous, vexatious or premature" or may not, under s. 74, be allowed to continue.

[417] s. 24(b)

- set criteria for the provision of funding for the research, preparation or conduct of a specific claim (s. 24(b));

- arrange for research or technical studies agreed to by the parties (s. 24(c)); and

- foster the use of a broad range of ADR processes to resolve claims (s. 24(e)).

The Commission is required to convene a preparatory meeting of the parties, prior to the claim being referred to the Minister for consideration, to allow the parties to identify issues in the claim, to clarify the basis of the claim, and to identify further research that may be required to investigate the claim. On the request of a party, the Commission may hold further preparatory meetings.[418]

The Commission may also convene meetings with the claimant community to allow members of the community to be involved in the claims process. If the current practice of the ISCC serves as any guide, such meetings may provide an opportunity for the parties to the claim to hear from elders and other community members with respect to the history of the claim. Such meetings may also be used to allow parties to visit specific sites that may be in issue in the claim.[419]

On the completion of preparatory meetings and, presumably, on the completion of any further research identified in the course of such meetings, the Commission is required to suspend proceedings in relation to the claim until the Minister provides a decision on whether the Crown will agree to negotiate the claim. While the Minister is obliged to provide regular reports with respect to when a decision is required and any reasons for delay, the Commission may not consider the passage of time prior to the Minister providing an answer as a decision not to negotiate the claim.[420]

On receipt of a decision by the Minister not to negotiate a claim, the Commission is required, should the claimant wish to proceed, to assist the parties to resolve the issue of validity of the claim through the use of ADR processes.[421]

Should the parties not resolve the issue of validity, the Commission may refer the matter to the Tribunal for a decision on validity provided the following criteria have been met:

- all matters of fact and law arising from the claim have been fully researched, clearly articulated, and considered by the Minister (s. 32(1)(a));

- all appropriate ADR processes have been exhausted (s. 32(1)(b)); and

- the claimant has waived compensation for any amount exceeding the claim limit established under s. 56 (currently $10 million).

---

[418] s. 28
[419] *Ibid.*
[420] s. 30
[421] s. 31

Where the Minister agrees to negotiate a claim, or where the Tribunal decides that a claim is valid, the Commission is required to assist the parties to resolve the issue of compensation, again using a broad range of ADR processes as necessary.

Referral of a claim to the Tribunal on the matter of compensation is similar to referral of a claim on the issue of validity. The criteria that must be satisfied are:

- the claimant's position on compensation, including all supporting facts and law must have been clearly identified, adequately researched and considered by the Minister in course of ADR between the parties (s. 35(1)(a));

- all appropriate ADR processes have been exhausted (s. 35(1)(b));

- no compensation other than monetary compensation is being sought (s. 35(1)(c));

- the claimant has waived any compensation in excess of the claim limit established under s. 56 (currently $10 million); and

- in accordance with the calculation set out in s. 35(1)(e), compensation ordered to be paid by the Tribunal in the fiscal year could not — even if the "claim limit" amount were awarded in all outstanding claims — exceed the budget allocated by the government for the payment of Tribunal awards for that fiscal year.

Part 3 — The Tribunal

A Chief Adjudicator, assisted by a Vice-Chief Adjudicator, will be responsible for managing the business of the Tribunal. The Tribunal may have up to five Adjudicators in addition to the Chief and Vice-Chief.[422]

The Chief Adjudicator is responsible for the management of the affairs of the Tribunal, including the striking of panels of Adjudicators to conduct hearings and decide issues before the Tribunal.[423]

The Tribunal has authority to establish its own process through rules of procedure (s. 45(1)). The items listed in s. 45 in this regard are generally reflective of the rules that apply to many courts and tribunals. The rules of the Tribunal are to be available to the public and, if possible, published in the *First Nations Gazette* or similar publication.

The Tribunal is not bound by the rules of evidence in the same way as a court of law (s. 46(f)). It is also authorized to apply its own rules in a manner that is culturally sensitive (s. 46(g)). In keeping with the focus of the SCRA on promoting negotiated settlements, the Tribunal is explicitly authorized to suspend proceedings to allow the parties to make further efforts at resolving the claim (s. 46(d)(ii)).

The jurisdiction of the Tribunal is to consider:

---

[422] s. 41
[423] s. 43

- the issue of validity on claims up to $10 million (ss. 52, 53, 56);
- the issue of compensation on claims up to $10 million (ss. 52, 53, 56);
- whether the claim is, together with any other specific claim, subject to one claim limit under subsection 56(2) (s. 51(1));
- any application brought under s. 47 ("interlocutory issues"); and
- any application to strike brought under s. 50.

The Tribunal's jurisdiction under ss. 47 and 50 does not appear to be limited to claims below the claim limit established by s. 56. Subsection 51(b) provides a residual power to the Tribunal to "decide ... any other issue, if all parties consent".

The imposition of a claim limit on the jurisdiction of the Tribunal has been a matter of debate and commentary as Bill C-6 progressed through the legislative process. According to DIAND's information:

> Past experience has shown that the value of the majority of specific claims does not exceed [the claim limit] ... Of the 251 specific claims settled as of March 31, 2003, over 80 per cent were valued at under $10 million.

Other aspects of the SCRA

- The *SCRA* clarifies and modernizes the definition of a specific claim – translating policy language into legislative terms and incorporating changes to the law since the definition was created. The legislative definition also clarifies various aspects of the policy as it was set out in *Outstanding Business*.

1. Comparison of the definitions of Specific Claim set out in s. 26 of the SCRA and the Outstanding Business policy:

SCRA	Outstanding Business	Commentary
s. 26(1)(a) breach of — or failure to fulfil — a legal obligation of the Crown, including a fiduciary obligation, -that relate to the provision of lands or other assets and that arises from an agreement between the first nation and the Crown or from a treaty, (ii) under any legislation — pertaining to Indians or lands reserved for the Indians — of Canada or of a colony of Great Britain of which at least	The government's policy on specific claims is that it will recognize claims by Indian bands which disclose an outstanding "lawful obligation", i.e., an obligation derived from the law on the part of the federal government. – The non-fulfillment of a treaty or agreement between Indians and the Crown. – A breach of an obligation arising out of the Indian Act or other statutes pertaining to Indians	The SCRA specifies that the definition of specific claim includes breaches of fiduciary obligation. Outstanding Business is silent on the matter, although "fiduciary obligation" has been "read in" to the policy for several years. The SCRA specifies that treaty claims are to relate to the provision of land or assets. *Outstanding Business* appeared to contemplate any non-fulfillment of a treaty or agreement. The SCRA language clarifies that claims arising prior to

some portion now forms part of Canada, (iii) that arises out of the Crown's administration of reserve lands, Indian moneys or other assets of the claimant;	and the regulations thereunder. – A breach of an obligation arising out of government administration of Indian funds or other assets.	Confederation are included in the definition. While not included in the text of *Outstanding Business*, pre-Confederation claims have been considered under that policy since 1991. The SCRA specifies that administration of reserve land is also intended to be included in the definition.
s. 26(b) an illegal lease or disposition by the Crown of reserve lands;	– An illegal disposition of Indian land.	The SCRA specifies that "lease" is to be included in the notion of "disposition".
s. 26(c) failure to provide compensation for reserve lands taken or damaged by the Crown or any of its agencies under legal authority;	i) Failure to provide compensation for reserve lands taken or damaged by the federal government or any of its agencies under authority.	– no difference
s. 26(d) fraud by employees or agents of the Crown in connection with the acquisition, leasing or disposition of reserve lands.	Fraud in connection with the acquisition or disposition of Indian reserve land by employees or agents of the federal government, in cases where the fraud can be clearly demonstrated.	The SCRA does not include the proviso "where the fraud can be clearly demonstrated".
Exceptions (not found in *Outstanding Business*) s. 26(2) A first nation may not file a claim that (a) is based on events that occurred within the 15 years immediately preceding the filing of the claim; (b) is based on a land claims agreement entered into after December 31, 1973, or any related agreement or Act of Parliament; (c) is based on an Act of Parliament or agreement that is mentioned in the schedule, or an Act of Parliament or agreement for the implementation of such an Act or agreement; (d) concerns the delivery or funding of programs or services related to policing, regulatory enforcement, corrections, education, health, child protection or social assistance, or of any similar public programs or services;		See comments under title: *Laches and limitations and the 15 year rule,* below see commentary under s. 26(2)(a) The SCRA specifies that treaty claims are to be based on historic treaties rather than modern land claims. The SCRA specifies that certain agreements and Acts of Parliament are not to give rise to specific claims. The agreements listed in the schedule are Self Government Agreements

(e) is based on any agreement between the first nation and the Crown that provides for another mechanism for the resolution of disputes arising from the agreement; or (f) is based on, or alleges, aboriginal rights or title.	and the Acts are Self Government Acts. As the government enters an ever broader set of arrangements with First Nation communities, it is possible that an ever broader range of claims and issues could be submitted under the SCRA. The prohibition against claims based on "delivery and funding of programs or services" is undoubtedly intended to limit the scope of the Specific Claims process. As an alternative to litigation, the SCRA process is not also intended to become an alternative to dispute resolution processes negotiated with First Nations in other contexts. The Crown has consistently taken the view that the Specific Claims process was not intended to address claims of aboriginal rights and title. That policy is now expressed in statutory language.

2. Joining claims

One of the implications of imposing a claim limit on the jurisdiction of the Tribunal is that one must then determine how to define a claim for the purpose of the claim limit. Section 56(2) attempts to do so. It states:

> (2) Two or more specific claims shall, for the purposes of the application of the claim limit under paragraph (1)(a), be treated as one claim if they
>
> (a) are made by the same claimant and are based on the same or substantially the same facts; or
>
> (b) are made by different claimants, are based on the same or substantially the same facts and relate to the same assets.

Section 65 specifies that, unless the parties agree otherwise, claims that are subject to a single claim limit under s. 56(2) are to be heard together by the Tribunal. Section 65 also requires, unless the parties agree otherwise, that claims that "present common issues of law or fact that create a risk that decisions on the claims will be irreconcilable" also be heard together.

Finally, s. 66 states:

> 66. If a panel, in considering a specific claim, determines that a first nation has a specific claim or a potential specific claim based on the same or substantially the same facts and relating to the same assets as the specific claim, or that there is any other specific claim or potential specific claim by a first nation that must be before the Tribunal to enable a full resolution of the specific claim, it shall suspend proceedings with respect to the specific claim until, in the case of another specific claim, it is before the Tribunal or, in the case of a potential specific claim, it has been filed under this Act and is before the Tribunal.

The SCRA does not specify what is to happen if the other potential claimant referred to in s. 66 does not file a claim under the Act. One answer may be that there is a considerable onus on a claimant First Nation to ensure that all overlapping claims are brought forward at the time that First Nation files its claim. A second answer may be that First Nations who have claims that are subject to the type of overlapping claims set out in s. 66 are, from a practical point of view, excluded from the Tribunal process. It would appear that the rationale underlying s. 66 is to protect the Crown from having to pay one claimant First Nation, pursuant to an order of the Tribunal, for liability arising with respect to a particular set of facts pertaining to a particular asset and then having subsequently to pay a different First Nation for the same liability.

a) Laches and limitations and the 15 year rule

In keeping with the policy established under *Outstanding Business*, neither the Minister nor the Tribunal may take into account laches or limitation periods in assessing the validity of a claim. To the contrary, the Act specifies that:

> 26(2) A first nation may not file a claim that
>
> (a) is based on events that occurred within the 15 years immediately preceding the filing of the claim;

Where limitation periods are meant to ensure claims are brought in a timely fashion while witnesses can still be found and evidence located, the SCRA places priority on ensuring that Specific Claims are not modern or recent complaints against the Crown. The Act makes no provision for claims that are too old to take to court but not yet old enough to be resolved under this Act. The policy underlying this section may be to simply limit the volume of possible claims that can be brought under the SCRA process.

3. Release and indemnity/Extinguishment of rights

The decisions of the Tribunal on the issues of validity and compensation are intended to be final and binding. They are not, with the exception of Judicial Review, subject to appeal. A Tribunal decision that a claim is not valid or a decision on compensation are conclusive between the parties in all proceedings in any court or tribunal arising out of the same or substantially the same facts.[424] However, subsection 71(3) specifies that a decision that a claim is valid is conclusive only for purposes of the SCRA; it cannot be relied upon in subsequent court proceedings, save for judicial review. This rule appears to prevent a claimant from obtaining a favourable ruling from the Tribunal and then turning to the courts to have compensation decided.

Where the Tribunal decides that a specific claim is invalid or awards compensation on the claim, the effect of that order is to release the respondents from any further cause of action or liability with respect to that claim and to any other claim that could be brought based on the same facts. This release applies to the claimant and to members of the claimant.[425] In addition to releasing the respondents from future liability, the order, in effect, commits the claimant to indemnify the respondents against any future liability related to the same facts that arises as the result of future legal actions or proceedings brought by the claimant or any of its members against a third party.[426] The indemnity clause is designed to protect the respondents who have settled the claim with the claimant but are added to subsequent litigation on the same matter.

Further, if compensation is awarded under the Act for an unlawful disposition of "all of the interests or rights of a claimant in or to land and the interests or rights have never been restored to the claimant", then, by operation of the statute, all the claimant's interests in, and rights to, the land are extinguished.[427] This extinguishment of rights does not prejudice the claimant's ability to pursue a province with respect to the unlawful disposition. The extinguishment of the claimant's rights occurs "despite" s. 39 of the *Indian Act*,[428] which requires, *inter alia,* that a surrender or rights to reserve land be "assented to by a majority of the band" and approved by the Governor in Council. The question that remains is whether extinguishment of First Nation rights to land by operation of statute will be upheld by the courts in the absence of assent by a majority of band members.

Similarly, despite s. 39 of the *Indian Act*, if compensation is awarded to a claimant for the unexpired term of a lease of land that was entered into by Canada in a manner inconsistent with the claimant's rights to the land, then, for the duration of the lease, the lessee is deemed to have the rights to the land provided for in the lease.[429]

Protection of third-party rights and interests is at the core of s. 57(2). Subsection 56(1) requires that claims heard by the Tribunal be claims for compensation only; however, this section demonstrates that in some cases the effect of a Tribunal ruling will be to determine rights in land. It ensures that third parties in possession of lands subject to a leasehold to which a First Nation may have a continuing right or claim, will remain in possession of those lands at least for the term of the lease.

---

[424]   s. 71(2)
[425]   s. 72(a)
[426]   s. 72(b)
[427]   s. 57(1)
[428]   R.S.C. 1985, c. I-5.
[429]   s. 57(2)

Review of the Act

Section 76 specifies that, "[n]ot earlier than three years and not later than five years after the coming into force of this section" the Minister is to conduct a complete a review of the mandate and structure of the Centre and "of any other matters related to this Act that the Minister considers appropriate." Pursuant to an amendment introduced by the Senate, First Nations are to be consulted as part of the review.

The review may present an opportune time to assess issues such as:

- the claim limit established by s. 56;
- the bifurcation of the process into a validity stage and a compensation stage;
- the requirement to suspend claims (s. 66) where there is a potential overlap; and
- the requirement that the Tribunal be limited by the size of its compensation budget, to a certain number of decisions in any given year (s. 35).

Provinces and other First Nations

The Commission must ensure that Provinces or First Nations that may be affected by the outcome of a claim are provided notice of the claim (s. 36). The Commission may, on the request of the parties, allow a province or other First Nation to participate as a party to the claim (s. 37). In addition, the Tribunal may add as a party a province that has agreed to submit to the jurisdiction of the Tribunal (s. 60). The consent of the parties is not required under s. 60.

Apportioning claims

Where claims by different claimants are subject to a single claim limit, s. 56(3) allows the Tribunal to apportion any compensation ordered fairly between the claimants.

Similarly, under s. 35(3) the Commission is required, on the request of a party, to ask that Tribunal to determine the issue of the extent of each respondent party's liability with respect to each claimant for a claim.[430] Paragraph 56(1)(c) also specifies that the Tribunal shall, in awarding compensation, "award compensation against each respondent party proportional to the party's responsibility ..."

---

[430] See also s. 55.

SPECIFIC CLAIMS RESOLUTION ACT

S.C. 2003, C. 23

ASSENTED TO NOVEMBER 7, 2003

[Editor's note: The shaded text indicates that this statute has not been proclaimed and likely will not be proclaimed.]

An Act to establish the Canadian Centre for the Independent Resolution of First Nations Specific Claims to provide for the filing, negotiation and resolution of specific claims and to make related amendments to other Acts

Her Majesty, by and with the advice and consent of the Senate and House of Commons of Canada, enacts as follows:

SHORT TITLE

1. SHORT TITLE — This Act may be cited as the *Specific Claims Resolution Act*.

INTERPRETATION

2. DEFINITIONS — The following definitions apply in this Act.

Commentary

The definitions below are set out alphabetically, and apply to all Parts of the Act.[431] Note that the definitions in the French version of s. 2(1) are also set out alphabetically and, unlike other sections of the Act, are not therefore equivalent to the English definitions printed across from them on the page. To assist in locating the equivalent French definition of a particular term, the French equivalent is listed in italics in the marginal note to the definition (e.g., *Centre* in the first definition below).

"Centre"
« *Centre* »
"Centre" means the Canadian Centre for the Independent Resolution of First Nations Specific Claims established under section 4.

"claim limit"
« *indemnité maximale* »
"claim limit" means the maximum under paragraph 56(1)(a).

---

[431] By contrast, the definitions set out in ss. 16, 37, 57 and 90 of the Act apply only to the Part of the Act in which they are located.

Commentary

The claim limit operates as a limit on the jurisdiction of the Tribunal. Arguably, the legislated process results in fewer options for claimants with claims that exceed the claim limit, given that under the current policy, all claims, irrespective of size or value, have access to the Indian Claims Commission ("ICC"). However, this difference may be illusory, as there is no prohibition under the statute from the use of non-binding arbitration for any claim, which is essentially the service provided by the ICC. The contrary view is that the ICC provides specialized expertise that will not be available to parties to a claim under the new process.

"claimant"
« revendicateur »
"claimant" means a first nation whose specific claim has been filed.

Commentary

"First nation" is also a defined term for the purposes of this Act.

See also s. 77.1, which provides that for a period of one year after the coming into force of this Act, the term "claimant", for the purposes of s. 76.1, also includes claimants under the current Specific Claims process.

"Commission"
« Commission »
"Commission" means the Commission Division of the Centre described in Part 2.

"Crown"
« Sa Majesté »
"Crown" means Her Majesty in right of Canada.

"first nation"
« première nation »
"first nation" means

Commentary

The term First Nation, while in common use in the media and in many legal contexts, does not have an agreed-upon or fixed meaning. In the SCRA and in the *First Nations Fiscal and Statistical Management Act*, the principal point of reference for the definition is the definition of "band" set out in the *Indian Act*.

(a)   a band as defined in subsection 2(1) of the *Indian Act*;

Commentary

"Band" is defined by the *Indian Act*[432] as follows:

"band" means a body of Indians

(a) for whose use and benefit in common, lands, the legal title to which is vested in Her Majesty, have been set apart before, on or after September 4, 1951,

(b) for whose use and benefit in common, moneys are held by Her Majesty, or

(c) declared by the Governor in Council to be a band for the purposes of this Act;

(b) a group of persons that was, but is no longer, a band within the meaning of paragraph (a) and that has, under a land claims agreement, retained the right to bring a specific claim; and

(c) a group of persons that was a band within the meaning of paragraph (a), that is no longer a band by virtue of an Act or agreement mentioned in the schedule and that has not released its right to bring a specific claim.

Commentary

Under modern land claim and self-government agreements, it is possible for a First Nation community not to retain status as a "band" under the *Indian Act*, but to retain the right to have specific grievances or claims addressed through the Specific Claims process. The SCRA was not designed to limit rights so retained.

"interlocutory issue"
« question interlocutoire »

"interlocutory issue" means an issue in relation to which an application may be made to the Tribunal under section 47.

"land claims agreement"
« accord sur des revendications territoriales »

"land claims agreement" has the same meaning as in subsection 35(3) of the *Constitution Act, 1982*.

"Minister"
« ministre »

"Minister" means the Minister of Indian Affairs and Northern Development or such other member of the Queen's Privy Council for Canada as

---

[432] R.S.C. 1985, c. I-5, s. 2 "band".

may be designated by the Governor in Council as the Minister for the purposes of this Act.

"party"
« partie »
"party", in respect of a specific claim, means any claimant and the Crown, and any province added as a party under section 37 or 60.

Commentary

"Crown" is a defined term for the purposes of this Act to mean the Crown in right of Canada. Under section 37, on the request of the parties, the Commission shall allow a province to participate as a party for the purposes of Part II of the Act.

"specific claim"
« revendication particulière »
"specific claim" means a claim that is filed under section 26.

Commentary

The introductory commentary to the Act includes a chart comparing the definition of "specific claim" found in the current Specific Claims policy, *"Outstanding Business: A Native Claims Policy – Specific Claims"* and the definition found in s. 26. See also the commentary under s. 26.

"Tribunal"
« Tribunal »
"Tribunal" means the Tribunal Division of the Centre described in Part 3.

PURPOSE

3. PURPOSE — The purpose of this Act is to establish the Centre, including the Commission to help first nations and the Crown resolve specific claims and the Tribunal to decide certain issues arising from those claims.

Commentary

Until the coming into force of this Act, the Specific Claims Process will continue to be managed in part by the Department of Indian and Northern Development ("DIAND"), and in part by the Indian Claims Commission ("ICC"). This Act removes the administrative aspects of DIAND's involvement in that process, essentially reducing DIAND's direct role to that of defendant. For example, DIAND currently administers research funding provided to claimants and potential claimants. This function will be transferred to the Commission (see ss. 23 and 24).

The ICC is mandated to review the validity of Specific Claims with respect to which the Minister has taken a decision not to negotiate. The ICC makes non-binding recommendations and reports to the Minister. It also provides mediation services to the parties, on a purely voluntary basis, once a claim has been validated. The review of rejected claims (at least for claims up to the claim limit established under s. 56(1)) will fall within the mandate and jurisdiction of the Tribunal. The coordination and oversight of alternative dispute resolution processes will fall to the Commission.

This Act does not specify whether the Indian Claims Commission will continue to operate either for an interim transition period or in the longer term, once the SCRA is brought into force. Presumably the purpose of the SCRA is to create a structure and process that would, eventually if not immediately, completely replace the current structures and processes.

PART 1

CANADIAN CENTRE FOR THE INDEPENDENT RESOLUTION OF FIRST NATIONS SPECIFIC CLAIMS

Establishment, Composition and Functions

4. ESTABLISHMENT — The Canadian Centre for the Independent Resolution of First Nations Specific Claims is hereby established.

Commentary

The Centre created in this section will be responsible for a broad range of activities, many of which are currently the responsibility of either the Department of Indian Affairs and Northern Development ("DIAND"), or the Indian Claims Commission ("ICC").[433]

5. COMPOSITION — The Centre consists of the Chief Executive Officer — to be appointed by the Governor in Council on the recommendation of the Minister — and the Commission and the Tribunal.

Commentary

While the ultimate decision on the appointment of a Chief Executive Officer lies with the Governor in Council, the government is obliged to seek input from First Nations who are claimants under the Act (and, for a period of one year

---

[433] For further information, refer to the introductory commentary to the Act.

after the coming into force of the Act, with claimants under the current Specific Claims policy).[434]

> **6. FUNCTIONS — The Centre is responsible for**
>
> **(a) administering the affairs of the Commission and, with the exception of any matters assigned under this Act to the Tribunal or its Chief Adjudic ator, those of the Tribunal;**

Commentary

The Centre is composed of both a Commission and a Tribunal. Certain aspects of the Tribunal's mandate and authority have been removed from the purview of the Centre's management structure to maintain the independence of the Tribunal in the exercise of its adjudicative functions: see ss. 43-46.

In particular, s. 43 states:

> 43. (1) The Chief Adjudicator is responsible for the management of the business and affairs of the Tribunal, including the following responsibilities:
>
> > (a) to strike panels to conduct hearings and decide issues before the Tribunal;
> >
> > (b) to lead the Tribunal in the exercise of its power to make rules under subsection 45(1); and
> >
> > (c) to provide guidance and assistance to panels.

Accordingly, the scope of affairs pertaining to the Tribunal, but within the responsibility of the Centre (meaning, under the responsibility of the Chief Executive Officer), is rather narrow.

> **(b) providing, at its expense, appropriate translation and interpretation services in connection with the resolution of specific claims under this Act; and**

Commentary

This paragraph specifies that translation and interpretation costs, whether they arise from the use of Canada's officials languages or from the use of First Nation languages, will be borne by the Centre rather than by the claimant, the Department of Indian Affairs and Northern Development, or any other party.

> **(c) obtaining, developing and distributing educational materials for public information in respect of specific claims and fostering public understanding of this Act, including an understanding of the role and activities of the Commission and the Tribunal.**

---

[434] See s. 76.1.

Commentary

The Indian Specific Claims Commission currently has a mandate to provide public information and educational materials related to the current Specific Claims process. This section specifies that the Centre will continue this function.[435]

Chief Executive Officer

7. FUNCTIONS, POWERS AND DUTIES — The Chief Executive Officer has supervision over and direction of the work and staff of the Centre.

Commentary

The Centre is composed of two divisions: the Commission and the Tribunal.

8. (1) TERM AND TENURE — The Chief Executive Officer shall hold office during good behaviour for a term of not more than five years and may be removed for cause by the Governor in Council.

(2) RE-APPOINTMENT — The Chief Executive Officer is eligible for re-appointment on the expiration of any term of office.

(3) REMUNERATION — The Chief Executive Officer shall be paid the remuneration that is fixed by the Governor in Council.

Commentary

A person who holds office during good behaviour can be removed in one of two ways:

- by order of the Governor in Council, on the recommendation of the Canadian Judicial Council,[436] made following an inquiry requested by the Minister of Justice under s. 69 of the *Judges Act*;[437] or

- by an order of the Governor in Council, following any other process that provides the person with an opportunity to be heard in accordance with the principles of natural justice.

In the latter instance, allegations of misfeasance would normally be provided to the Governor in Council, which would then provide the appointee with an opportunity to answer them. The Governor in Council would then make its decision whether to remove the appointee based on the written material before it.[438]

---

[435] See: <http://www.indianclaims.ca/english/pub/pub.html>.
[436] Established under s. 59(1) of the *Judges Act*, R.S.C. 1985, c. J-1.
[437] R.S.C. 1985, c. J-1.
[438] A similar procedure was followed, and received judicial approval, in *Weatherill v. Canada (Attorney General)*, [1999] 4 F.C. 107; [1999] F.C.J. No. 787 (F.C.T.D.).

Case Law

Weatherill v. Canada (Attorney General), [1999] 4 F.C. 107; [1999] F.C.J. No. 787 (F.C.T.D.).

The Federal Court upheld the dismissal by the Governor in Council of the Chairman of the former Canada Labour Relations Board, who held office during good behaviour, for incurring unreasonable hospitality and travel expenses. The applicant had been offered an opportunity to make submissions in response to a report on his expenses and in response to the application to the Governor in Council for his removal, but chose not to do so. The court concluded that the requirements of natural justice had been satisfied, and that a further inquiry under s. 69 of the *Judges Act* was not required.

Wedge v. Canada (Attorney General), [1997] F.C.J. No. 872 (F.C.T.D.); (1997), 4 Admin. L.R. (3d) 153; 133 F.T.R. 277.

The Federal Court upheld the dismissal by the Governor in Council of a member of the Veterans Appeal Board, who held office during good behaviour, for allegedly having participated in election irregularities. The court found that there had been no breach of procedural fairness in the way in which the applicant had been treated. The applicant had been informed of the allegations against him by letter, and had been given copies of an investigation report and copies of the final report to the Governor in Council. The applicant had had the opportunity to respond orally, and his written responses to the investigation report and final report were submitted to the Governor in Council. The court held that the applicant was not entitled to cross-examine witnesses interviewed, or to a full, formal, court-like hearing. The court also concluded that the standard of good behaviour to which an appointee will be held is in the discretion of the Governor in Council, which extends to its judgment as to whether the appointee's conduct could undermine public confidence in the federal institution with which he had been appointed to serve.

Subsection 8(1), together with s. 8(3), parallels the requirements for institutional independence set out by the Supreme Court of Canada in *Canadian Pacific Ltd. v Matsqui* in relation to tribunals established by bands themselves:

> Thus, to conform to the requirements of institutional independence, the appellant bands' by-laws will have to guarantee remuneration and stipulate periods of tenure for tribunal members.[439]

(4) FULL-TIME — If the Chief Executive Officer is appointed full-time, he or she shall devote the whole of his or her time to the performance of the duties of the office and is entitled to be paid reasonable travel and living expenses incurred in the course of carrying out his or her duties under this Act while absent from his or her ordinary place of work, but the payment

---

[439]   [1995] 1 S.C.R. 3 at 59.

may not exceed the maximum limits for those expenses authorized by the Treasury Board for employees of the Government of Canada.

Commentary

Work-related travel for government employees is governed by a set of Treasury Board policies.[440]

(5) PART-TIME — If the Chief Executive Officer is appointed part-time, he or she is entitled to be paid reasonable travel and living expenses incurred in the course of carrying out his or her duties under this Act while absent from his or her ordinary place of residence, but the payment may not exceed the maximum limits for those expenses authorized by the Treasury Board for employees of the Government of Canada.

Commentary

Work-related travel for government employees is governed by a set of Treasury Board policies.[441]

(6) CONFLICTING RESPONSIBILITIES AND ACTIVITIES PROHIBITED — The Chief Executive Officer shall not accept or hold any office or employment or carry on any activity inconsistent with the duties and functions of that office, but, for greater certainty, the Chief Executive Officer may also hold the office of Chief Commissioner of the Commission.

Commentary

Although authorized to hold the office of Chief Commissioner, there is no parallel provision permitting the Chief Executive Officer to hold the office of Chief Adjudicator. The Act appears designed to create distance between the CEO and the Tribunal that will not exist between the CEO and the Commission (see s. 6(a), for example, which specifies that certain administrative matters related to the Tribunal do not fall within the responsibilities of the CEO). With overarching responsibility for the administration of the Centre, including such matters as administration of research funding for claimants and potential claimants, the intention may be to limit the amount of administrative of financial influence the CEO could exert on the independent decision making functions of the Tribunal.

(7) COMPENSATION — The Chief Executive Officer is deemed to be employed in the public service of Canada for the purposes of the

---

[440] Available at: <http://www.tbs-sct.gc.ca/pubs_pol/hrpubs/TBM_113/menu-travel-voyage_e.asp>.

[441] *Ibid.*

Government Employees Compensation Act **and any regulations made under section 9 of the** *Aeronautics Act.*

Commentary

Both the *Government Employees Compensation Act*[442] and s. 9 of the *Aeronautics Act*[443] provide for compensation to be paid to government employees and their families for injuries or death resulting from activities undertaken in the course of duty. For example, subsection 9(1) of the *Aeronautics Act* states:

> 9. (1) The Governor in Council may make regulations establishing the compensation to be paid and the persons to whom and the manner in which such compensation shall be payable for the death or injury of any person employed in the public service of Canada or employed under the direction of any department of the public service of Canada that results directly from a flight undertaken by that person in the course of duty in the public service of Canada.

9. (1) DEPUTY HEAD — The Chief Executive Officer has the rank and status of a deputy head for the purposes of the *Financial Administration Act.*

Commentary

The Chief Executive Officer position is generally equivalent with Deputy Ministers, who are also deputy heads under the *Financial Administration Act.*[444]

(2) ABSENCE OR INCAPACITY — In the event of the absence or incapacity of the Chief Executive Officer, or if the office of Chief Executive Officer is vacant, the Chief Commissioner of the Commission — or if the offices of Chief Executive Officer and Chief Commissioner are held by the same person, the Vice-Chief Commissioner of the Commission — has the powers and duties of the Chief Executive Officer.

Personnel Management

10. SEPARATE EMPLOYER — The Centre is a separate employer under the *Public Service Staff Relations Act.*[445]

---

[442]   R.S.C. 1985, c. G-5.
[443]   R.S.C. 1985, c. A-2.
[444]   R.S.C. 1985, c. F-11.
[445]   R.S.C. 1985, c. P-35.

Commentary

One of the criticisms of the current Specific Claims Process is an appearance that there is no independence in the taking of final decisions on claims. The Minister may take advice from government officials and from the Indian Specific Claims Commission, but the final decision to negotiate a claim lies with the Minister. The Minister, of course, may also reasonably be thought to be the respondent or defendant in Specific Claims.

One of the key goals of the SCRA is to address concerns over the appearance of conflict of interest. The creation of the Centre as a separate employer is one feature of the legislation that addresses the concern: the Centre is separate from the Department of Indian Affairs and Northern Development ("DIAND") and, at least in some key aspects, from the Treasury Board. The Centre will submit its reports to Parliament via the Minister of Indian Affairs and Northern Development, but is not part of DIAND for any other purpose.

Generally, employees of the government are employed by the Treasury Board rather than by specific Departments. One implication of this structure is that a single union can represent employees working in various departments and negotiate collective agreements that apply to employees in several departments. In the case of a "separate employer" it is the separate employer, rather than Treasury Board, that is the employer. The employee's union bargains with management of the separate employer (in this case, the Centre) rather than with the Treasury Board of Canada. As a separate employer, the Centre, subject to the terms of this Act, has control over its classification, collective bargaining, pay and compensation systems.

The Centre, being designated a "separate employer" under the *Public Service Staff Relations Act*, will be subject to the provisions of that Act.

11. PERSONNEL MANAGEMENT — The Centre has exclusive authority in respect of personnel management and employer and employee relations, including the right to hire any staff it considers necessary for the proper conduct of the work of the Commission and of the Tribunal, to determine the terms and conditions of their employment and to terminate their employment, and may, in the exercise of that authority,

    (a) determine its requirements with respect to human resources and provide for the allocation and effective utilization of human resources;

    (b) implement an employment equity program;

Commentary

Given the business of the Centre and its mandate, one would expect an employment equity program to be established to give preference in the hiring of Aboriginal people to work at the Centre.

(c) determine requirements for the training and development of its personnel and fix the terms and conditions on which that training and development may be carried out;

(d) provide for the classification of positions and employees;

(e) determine and regulate its employees' pay, hours of work, leave and any related matters;

(f) provide for the awards that may be made to its employees for outstanding performance of their duties, for other meritorious achievement in relation to those duties and for inventions or practical suggestions for improvements;

(g) establish standards of discipline for its employees and fix the financial and other penalties, including termination of employment and suspension, that may be applied for breaches of discipline or misconduct and the circumstances and manner in which and the authority by which or by whom those penalties may be applied, or be varied or rescinded in whole or in part;

(h) provide for the termination of employment or the demotion to a position at a lower maximum rate of pay, for reasons other than breaches of discipline or misconduct, of its employees and establish the circumstances and manner in which and the authority by which or by whom those measures may be taken, or be varied or rescinded in whole or in part;

(i) determine and regulate the payments that may be made to its employees by way of reimbursement for travel or other expenses and by way of allowances in respect of expenses and conditions arising out of their employment; and

(j) provide for any other matters that the Centre considers necessary for effective personnel management.

Commentary

In the case of a "separate employer" it is the separate employer, rather than Treasury Board, that is the employer. The employee's union bargains with management of the separate employer (in this case, the Centre) rather than with the Treasury Board of Canada. As a separate employer, the Centre, subject to the terms of this Act, has control over its classification, collective bargaining, pay and compensation systems.

In establishing a separate employer and thus taking the new organization outside the normal regime governing employment in the federal government, it is normal for Parliament to address such matters as the establishment of benefit and insurance programs (see s. 12 below), the mobility rule for employees of the new organization to move into other government departments and agencies, and the mobility rules for public servants to become employees of the new organization (see s. 13 below).

For comparison purposes, see ss. 50-55 of the *Canada Customs and Revenue Agency Act.*[446]

12. (1) GROUP INSURANCE AND BENEFIT PROGRAMS — The Centre may establish benefit programs, including group insurance programs, for its employees, may set any terms and conditions in respect of those programs, including those relating to contributions, premiums, expenditures to be made from those contributions and premiums, benefits and the management, control and audit of the programs, may make contributions and pay premiums in respect of those programs and may enter into contracts for those purposes.

(2) *FINANCIAL ADMINISTRATION ACT* DOES NOT APPLY — The *Financial Administration Act* does not apply to any contributions made or premiums paid by the Centre or the members of any program established under subsection (1) in respect of the program or any benefits received by those members.

Commentary

Section 7 of the *Financial Administration Act* empowers the Treasury Board to address matters of group insurance and group benefits. As a separate employer, the Centre will have authority over such matters with respect to employees of the Centre.

13. (1) MOBILITY TO DEPARTMENTS — For the purpose of deployments or appointments made, or closed competitions held, under the *Public Service Employment Act*, employees of the Centre shall be treated as if they were employees within the meaning of the *Public Service Employment Act* and had the rights of recourse provided by that Act.

Commentary

As a general rule, public service staffing actions give priority to employees of the public service over members of the general public. Employees of the Centre will also enjoy this preferential treatment. Although this subsection is not stated to be "subject to" s. 13(2), preferential access to deployments[447] may be restricted in accordance with s. 13(2).

(2) WHEN DEPLOYMENTS MADE SUBJECT TO TERMS — The Public Service Commission may, in consultation with the Treasury Board and the Centre, set terms and conditions for the deployment of Centre

---

[446] S.C. 1999, c.17.
[447] "Deployment" refers to an employee being posted to a job of similar level without the use of a competitive staffing process.

employees to departments and agencies under the *Public Service Employment Act* if, in its opinion, the principles governing the Centre's staffing program are incompatible with those governing staffing under that Act.

Commentary

Should the Public Service Commission determine that the principles governing the Centre's staffing program (authorized under s. 12) are "incompatible" with the principles governing staffing for the public service, it may set terms and conditions for the deployment[448] of the Centre's employees into public service jobs.

Presumably, in the absence of any such terms or conditions, access to deployment opportunities would be governed by s. 13(1).

The Public Service Commission is obliged to consult with the Centre and the Treasury Board in establishing any such terms or conditions.

(3) MOBILITY TO THE CENTRE — When the Centre considers employees within the meaning of the *Public Service Employment Act* for employment within the Centre, it shall treat them as if they were employees of the Centre.

Commentary

By treating Public Servants as employees of the Centre for purposes of staffing actions, public servants would be on an equal footing with staff of the Centre in terms of any preferential treatment accorded the employees of the Centre in terms of closed competitions, deployments and the like.

14. PUBLIC SERVICE COMMISSION REVIEWS — The Public Service Commission may periodically review the compatibility of the principles governing the Centre's staffing program with those governing staffing under the *Public Service Employment Act* and, in that case, shall report its findings to the Centre.

Commentary

There is no formal requirement under this Act for the Centre to adopt the principles governing staffing under the *Public Service Employment Act*[449] ("PSEA"). However, for the purpose of ensuring that access to public service jobs under ss. 13(1) and (2) is governed by the same principles as would apply under the PSEA, a periodic review is necessary.

---

[448]   *Ibid.*
[449]   R.S.C. 1985 c. P-33, ss. 12 and 13(2).

15. POLITICAL PARTISANSHIP — Sections 32 to 34 of the *Public Service Employment Act* apply to the Chief Executive Officer, commissioners, adjudicators and employees of the Centre as if the Chief Executive Officer, commissioners and adjudicators were deputy heads, and the employees were employees, as defined in subsection 2(1) of that Act.

Commentary

The referenced sections of the *Public Service Employment Act* address the issue of political partisanship and political activity by deputy heads and public servants.

General Provisions

16. OFFICES — The offices of the Centre shall be in the National Capital Region as described in the schedule to the *National Capital Act.*

Commentary

The National Capital Region is generally the area comprised of Ottawa, Ontario and Gatineau, Quebec.

17. AUDIT — The accounts and financial transactions of the Centre shall be audited annually by the Auditor General of Canada, and a report of the audit shall be made to the Centre and to the Minister.

18. (1) ANNUAL REPORT — The Centre shall submit a report on the work of the Centre in a fiscal year to the Minister within six months after the end of that fiscal year, including the financial statements of the Centre and the report on them of the Auditor General of Canada.

(2) TABLING OF REPORT — The Minister shall cause a copy of the report to be laid before each House of Parliament on any of the first 30 days on which that House is sitting after the report is submitted to the Minister.

(3) AVAILABLE TO FIRST NATIONS AND THE PUBLIC — The Centre shall make the report available for public scrutiny at its offices and shall provide a copy of the report to a first nation on request.

Commentary

One of the ongoing concerns about the current Specific Claims Policy is that the Minister is perceived to be both defendant in the claims and the final decision maker. The SCRA is designed to address this concern and, accordingly, the Centre operates independently from both the Department of Indian Affairs and Northern Development and from the Minister. The Minister's responsibility to receive the Centre's annual reports under s. 18(1) and submit those reports to the Houses of Parliament under s. 18(2) does not detract from the principle of independence as it has been implemented by this Act.

19. QUARTERLY REPORT — Every three months, on the dates that the Minister specifies, the Centre shall report to the Minister

  (a) the total amount of compensation payable in respect of specific claims resolved other than by a decision of the Tribunal during that quarter; and

Commentary

Quarterly reports of this nature allow the government to manage budgets that may be created for the payment of compensation related to Specific Claims and to monitor ongoing commitments for claims that are not paid in a single lump sum (see s. 73(1)).

  (b) the total amount of compensation payable in respect of specific claims resolved by a decision of the Tribunal during that quarter.

Commentary

Reporting the total amount of compensation payable in respect of decisions of the Tribunal in a given quarter may be compared with the number of claims pending before the Tribunal and the remaining allocation of funds for payment of Tribunal orders (see s. 35(1)(b)). Taken together, these provisions provide the Minister with a means to forecast and manage compensation that may be ordered by the Tribunal.

PART 2

COMMISSION

Composition and Role

Composition

20. (1) COMPOSITION — The Commission Division of the Centre consists of a Chief Commissioner, a Vice-Chief Commissioner and up to five other commissioners to be appointed by the Governor in Council on the recommendation of the Minister.

Commentary

While the ultimate decision on the appointment of a Chief Executive Officer lies with the Governor in Council, the government is obliged to seek input from First Nations who are claimants under this Act (and, for a period of one year after the coming into force of the Act, with claimants under the current Specific Claims policy).[450]

(2) MODIFICATION OF NUMBER OF COMMISSIONERS — The Governor in Council may, on the recommendation of the Minister, at any time increase or reduce the number of commissioners.

(3) FULL-TIME AND PART-TIME — The Chief Commissioner and Vice-Chief Commissioner shall be appointed as full-time commissioners, and other commissioners may be appointed as full-time or part-time commissioners.

Commentary

There is a tension between this provision, which stipulates that the Chief Commissioner must be appointed on a full-time basis, and ss. 8(4) and (5), which suggest that the Chief Executive Officer may be either full or part-time but may also hold the office of Chief Commissioner. The two positions, taken together, appear to add up to more than a single full-time position.

(4) TERM AND TENURE — The Chief Commissioner and the Vice-Chief Commissioner shall hold office during good behaviour for a term of not more than five years and may be removed for cause by the Governor in Council.

(5) TERM AND TENURE — The other commissioners shall hold office during good behaviour for a term of not more than three years and may be removed for cause by the Governor in Council.

Commentary

The tenure (ss.20(4) and (5)) that applies to the Chief Commissioner and Vice-Chief Commissioner, as well as those that apply to Commissioners, parallel those that apply to the Chief Adjudicator, Vice-Chief Adjudicator and Adjudicators, respectively (ss. 41(5) and (6)).

A person who holds office during good behaviour can be removed in one of two ways:

---

[450]   See s. 76.1.

- by order of the Governor in Council, on the recommendation of the Canadian Judicial Council,[451] made following an inquiry requested by the Minister of Justice under s. 69 of the *Judges Act*;[452] or

- by an order of the Governor in Council, following any other process that provides the person with an opportunity to be heard in accordance with the principles of natural justice.

In the latter instance, allegations of misfeasance would normally be provided to the Governor in Council, which would then provide the appointee with an opportunity to answer them. The Governor in Council would then make its decision whether to remove the appointee based on the written material before it.[453]

Case Law

Weatherill v. Canada (Attorney General), [1999] 4 F.C. 107; [1999] F.C.J. No. 787 (F.C.T.D.).

The Federal Court upheld the dismissal by the Governor in Council of the Chairman of the former Canada Labour Relations Board, who held office during good behaviour, for incurring unreasonable hospitality and travel expenses. The applicant had been offered an opportunity to make submissions in response to a report on his expenses and in response to the application to the Governor in Council for his removal, but chose not to do so. The court concluded that the requirements of natural justice had been satisfied, and that a further inquiry under s. 69 of the *Judges Act* was not required.

Wedge v. Canada (Attorney General), [1997] F.C.J. No. 872 (F.C.T.D.), (1997), 4 Admin. L.R. (3d) 153; 133 F.T.R. 277.

The Federal Court upheld the dismissal by the Governor in Council of a member of the Veterans Appeal Board, who held office during good behaviour, for allegedly having participated in election irregularities. The court found that there had been no breach of procedural fairness in the way in which the applicant had been treated. The applicant had been informed of the allegations against him by letter, and had been given copies of an investigation report and copies of the final report to the Governor in Council. The applicant had had the opportunity to respond orally, and his written responses to the investigation report and final report were submitted to the Governor in Council. The court held that the applicant was not entitled to cross-examine witnesses interviewed, or to a full, formal, court-like hearing. The court also concluded that the standard of good behaviour to which an appointee will be held is in the discretion of the Governor in Council, which extends to its judgment as to whether the appointee's conduct could undermine public confidence in the federal institution with which he had been appointed to serve.

---

[451] Established under s. 59(1) of the *Judges Act*, R.S.C. 1985, c. J-1.
[452] R.S.C. 1985, c. J-1.
[453] A similar procedure was followed, and received judicial approval, in *Weatherill v. Canada (Attorney General)*, [1999] 4 F.C. 107; [1999] F.C.J. No. 787 (F.C.T.D.).

Subsections 21(4) and (5) together with s. 21(1) parallel the requirements for institutional independence set out by the Supreme Court of Canada in *Canadian Pacific Ltd. v Matsqui* in relation to tribunals established by bands themselves:

> Thus, to conform to the requirements of institutional independence, the appellant bands' by-laws will have to guarantee remuneration and stipulate periods of tenure for tribunal members.[454]

(6) RE-APPOINTMENT — A commissioner is eligible for reappointment on the expiration of any term of office in the same or another capacity.

REMUNERATION

21. (1) FULL-TIME COMMISSIONERS — Full-time commissioners shall devote the whole of their time to the performance of the duties of their office and shall be paid the remuneration that is fixed by the Governor in Council. They are entitled to be paid reasonable travel and living expenses incurred by them in the course of carrying out their duties under this Act while absent from their ordinary place of work, but the payment may not exceed the maximum limits for those expenses authorized by the Treasury Board for employees of the Government of Canada.

Case Law

This subsection, together with ss. 20(4) and (5) above, parallel the requirements for institutional independence set out by the Supreme Court of Canada in *Canadian Pacific Ltd. v Matsqui* in relation to tribunals established by bands themselves:

> Thus, to conform to the requirements of institutional independence, the appellant bands' by-laws will have to guarantee remuneration and stipulate periods of tenure for tribunal members.[455]

(2) PART-TIME COMMISSIONERS — Part-time commissioners shall be paid the remuneration that is fixed by the Governor in Council. They are entitled to be paid reasonable travel and living expenses incurred by them in the course of carrying out their duties under this Act while absent from their ordinary place of residence, but the payment may not exceed the maximum limits for those expenses authorized by the Treasury Board for employees of the Government of Canada.

---

[454]   [1995] 1 S.C.R. 3 at 59.
[455]   [1995], 1 S.C.R. 3 at 59.

Commentary

This subsection, together with ss. 20(4) and (5) parallels the requirements for institutional independence set out by the Supreme Court of Canada in *Canadian Pacific Ltd. v Matsqui* in relation to tribunals established by bands themselves:

> Thus, to conform to the requirements of institutional independence, the appellant bands' by-laws will have to guarantee remuneration and stipulate periods of tenure for tribunal members.[456]

(3) CONFLICTING RESPONSIBILITIES AND ACTIVITIES PROHIBITED — Commissioners shall not accept or hold any office or employment or carry on any activity inconsistent with their duties and functions as commissioner.

(4) COMPENSATION — Commissioners are deemed to be employed in the public service of Canada for the purposes of the *Government Employees Compensation Act* and any regulations made under section 9 of the *Aeronautics Act*.

Commentary

Both the *Government Employees Compensation Act*[457] and s. 9 of the *Aeronautics Act*[458] provide for compensation to be paid to government employees and their families for injuries or death resulting from activities undertaken in the course of duty. For example, subsection 9(1) of the *Aeronautics Act* states:

> 9. (1) The Governor in Council may make regulations establishing the compensation to be paid and the persons to whom and the manner in which such compensation shall be payable for the death or injury of any person employed in the public service of Canada or employed under the direction of any department of the public service of Canada that results directly from a flight undertaken by that person in the course of duty in the public service of Canada.

Management

22. (1) CHIEF COMMISSIONER — The Chief Commissioner is responsible for the management of the business and affairs of the Commission.

---

[456] *Ibid.*
[457] R.S.C. 1985, c. G-5.
[458] R.S.C. 1985, c. A-2.

(2) ABSENCE OR INCAPACITY — In the event of the absence or incapacity of the Chief Commissioner, or if the office of Chief Commissioner is vacant, the Vice-Chief Commissioner has the powers and duties of the Chief Commissioner.

Functions, Powers and Duties

23. FUNCTIONS — The Commission is responsible for

(a) administering funding for the research, preparation and conduct by first nations of specific claims;

Commentary

One of the criticisms of the current Specific Claims Process is an appearance that the Minister is both the defendant in the claims and also the final decision maker on claims. The Minister may take advice from the Indian Specific Claims Commission ("ISCC"), but it is the Minister and not the ISCC that decides the validity of claims. The impression that Canada has an unfair position with respect to the conduct of claims is exacerbated by the fact that the Department of Indian Affairs and Northern Development ("DIAND") administers research and negotiation funding provided to claimants and potential claimants.

Could discretion over research money not be exercised to delay certain claims? One of the key goals of the SCRA is to address concerns over the appearance of conflict of interest and, accordingly, it provides that the Commission will administer research funding.

While moving the administration of research funding to the Centre will undoubtedly alleviate concern over DIAND being both defendant and "banker" in the claims process, it will not necessarily alleviate more fundamental practical problems. Specific Claims are large claims requiring extensive, expensive research. Research budgets can easily be fully allocated early in any given fiscal year (to maximize the rate at which claims are brought forward). The Commission's administration of such funding will be especially important in the context of preparatory meetings under s. 28(1) – the parties and Commission will jointly review the claim and may identify at that time outstanding issues that require further research. This function will be further complicated by the requirement to join related claims (s. 56(2)).

(b) assisting the parties in the effective use of appropriate dispute resolution processes at any time to facilitate the resolution of specific claims under this Act; and

Commentary

The SCRA, like the current Specific Claims Policy, places a greater emphasis on negotiated outcomes than on adjudicated or litigated outcomes. The structure of the SCRA, which separates the issue of validity of the claim from the issue of compensation, is designed to maximize opportunities to negotiate outstanding issues. The preference given to negotiation is also reflected in the requirement that all reasonable efforts at dispute resolution be exhausted prior to a claim being submitted to the Tribunal. Arguably it also underlies the claim limit, which requires the parties to negotiate resolution of the largest claims.

The emphasis that the SCRA places on negotiation is reflected in the following comments of the Minister of Indian Affairs and Northern Development that were set out in a departmental New Release dated November 7, 2003:

> "The *Specific Claims Resolution Act* is a key step toward a better process for addressing longstanding First Nation grievances," said Robert D. Nault, Minister of Indian Affairs and Northern Development. "The new independent body envisioned in this legislation will oversee a streamlined process for resolving specific claims that reflects the preference of both Canada and First Nations to right the wrongs of the past through constructive and co-operative negotiations."[459]

Case law:

Delgamuukw v. British Columbia [1997] S.C.J. No. 108, [1997] 3 S.C.R. 1010, at para. 186.

While stated in a different context, Mr. Justice Laforest's comments regarding the importance of negotiation in settling Aboriginal claims are no less apt in the Specific Claims context:

> Ultimately, it is through negotiated settlements, with good faith and give and take on all sides, reinforced by the judgments of this Court, that we will achieve ... the reconciliation of the pre-existence of aboriginal societies with the sovereignty of the Crown. Let us face it, we are all here to stay.

(c)   referring to the Tribunal issues of validity or compensation.

Commentary

The authority to refer the issue of the validity of a claim to the Tribunal is found in s. 32. The authority to refer issues of compensation is found in s. 35. In both cases, it is the Commission that must assess whether the criteria for such a referral have been met.

---

[459]   The full text of the News Release may be viewed at: <http://www.ainc-inac.gc.ca/nr/prs/s-d2003/2-02433_e.html>.

24. POWERS AND DUTIES — The Commission, in carrying out its functions, may

(a) make rules of procedure for specific claims under this Act, except with respect to proceedings before the Tribunal;

Commentary

Prompted, undoubtedly, by the SCRA's silence on the issue, commentators have posed the question as to whether s. 24(a) will be used to impose timelines on the conduct of Specific Claims. Any such timelines would be subject to s. 30, which appears to suspend the claims process while the claim is under consideration by the Minister. Section 30 appears to prevent the Commission from compelling the Minister to provide a decision on whether to negotiate a claim.

While the SCRA does not address the matter directly, it is possible that the Minister would be subject to judicial review with respect to providing a decision.

(b) establish, in accordance with any appropriation or allotment of funds to the Centre for these purposes, criteria for the provision of funding to first nations for research, preparation and conduct of specific claims, and allocate the funds in accordance with those criteria;

(c) arrange for any research, or expert or technical studies, agreed to by the parties;

(d) assist the parties to resolve any interlocutory issues; and

Commentary

"Interlocutory issues" are defined in s. 2 as the matters referred to in s. 47. That section authorizes the Tribunal:

1. in relation to a specific claim that is before the Commission, to summon witnesses or to order production of documents;

2. to determine whether the claim and any other specific claim should be heard together or consecutively, or decided together; or

3. to determine any other issue that needs to be resolved for a dispute resolution process in relation to the specific claim to proceed, if all other parties consent.

(e) foster, at all times, the effective use of appropriate dispute resolution processes — including facilitated negotiation, mediation, non-binding arbitration and, with the consent of the parties, binding arbitration — for the resolution of specific claims.

Commentary

The SCRA, like the current Specific Claims Policy, places a greater emphasis on negotiated outcomes than on adjudicated or litigated outcomes. The structure of the SCRA, which separates the issue of validity of the claim from the issue of compensation, is designed to maximize opportunities to negotiate outstanding issues. The preference given to negotiation is also reflected in the requirement that all reasonable efforts at dispute resolution be exhausted prior to a claim being submitted to the Tribunal. This paragraph sets out in detail examples of the range of dispute resolution mechanisms that are to be considered under the SCRA process.

Of interest is the reference to binding arbitration. The Tribunal, with its limited jurisdiction, is a formalized process of binding arbitration. If parties are permitted to agree to binding arbitration with respect to any claim, irrespective of the monetary value, query whether the Tribunal would be permitted under this Act to provide such services to the parties on a contract basis. If not, the result would appear to be a somewhat anomalous situation: the expert tribunal set up to address the very issues raised in Specific Claims would be precluded, in favour of other arbiters, from applying its expertise to the claims of highest value. One might infer from this that the government might consider the use of binding arbitration on discrete issues, but perhaps not for the resolution of a high-money value claim.

Restriction

25. PARTICIPATION IN FUNDING ADMINISTRATION — No person who participates or has participated in the administration of funding for the research, preparation or conduct of a specific claim may, in respect of the claim, attend a preparatory meeting under section 28 or participate in any capacity in a dispute resolution process.

Commentary

The functions undertaken by the Commission include both the administrative functions, such as provision of research funding to potential claimants, and the oversight of dispute resolution processes. Section 25 works to ensure that the Commission's independence and impartiality in the latter are not undermined or compromised by the former.

Process Relating to Specific Claims

Filing of Claims

26. (1) ADMISSIBLE CLAIMS — Subject to subsections (2) and (3), a first nation may file with the Commission a claim based on any of the following grounds, for compensation for its losses arising from those grounds:

(a) **breach of — or failure to fulfil — a legal obligation of the Crown, including a fiduciary obligation,**

    (i) **that relates to the provision of lands or other assets and that arises from an agreement between the first nation and the Crown or from a treaty,**

    (ii) **under any legislation — pertaining to Indians or lands reserved for the Indians — of Canada or of a colony of Great Britain of which at least some portion now forms part of Canada, or**

    (iii) **that arises out of the Crown's administration of reserve lands, Indian moneys or other assets of the claimant;**

(b) **an illegal lease or disposition by the Crown of reserve lands;**

(c) **failure to provide compensation for reserve lands taken or damaged by the Crown or any of its agencies under legal authority; or**

(d) **fraud by employees or agents of the Crown in connection with the acquisition, leasing or disposition of reserve lands.**

Commentary

The definition of Specific Claim set out here is largely consistent with the definition found in *Outstanding Business: A Native Claims Policy — Specific Claims*, the current Specific Claims policy:

> … As noted earlier, the term "specific claims" refers to claims made by Indians against the federal government which relate to the administration of land and other Indian assets and to the fulfillment of Indian treaties.
>
> 1) Lawful Obligation
>
> The government's policy on specific claims is that it will recognize claims by Indian bands which disclose an outstanding "lawful obligation", i.e., an obligation derived from the law on the part of the federal government.
>
> A lawful obligation may arise in any of the following circumstances:
>
>   i)   The non-fulfillment of a treaty or agreement between Indians and the Crown.
>
>   ii) A breach of an obligation arising out of the *Indian Act* or other statutes pertaining to Indians and the regulations thereunder.
>
>   iii) A breach of an obligation arising out of government administration of Indian funds or other assets.
>
>   iv) An illegal disposition of Indian land.

2)   Beyond Lawful Obligation

In addition to the foregoing, the government is prepared to acknowledge claims which are based on the following circumstances:

i)   Failure to provide compensation for reserve lands taken or damaged by the federal government or any of its agencies under authority.

ii)   Fraud in connection with the acquisition or disposition of Indian reserve land by employees or agents of the federal government, in cases where the fraud can be clearly demonstrated.

Outstanding Business does not specify that claims based on fiduciary obligation are permitted. In practical terms, this issue has largely been overcome, at least with respect to fiduciary obligations owed by Canada to First Nation communities with respect to land and other assets.

The SCRA makes it clear that claims arising before Confederation are included in the definition of "specific claim", including claims arising under colonial legislation.

The criterion addressing breach of treaty and breach of agreement is now tied specifically to matters related to the provision of land or other assets. As stated, the criterion appears to reflect experience to date under *Outstanding Business* (witness, for example, decisions of the Indian Specific Claims Commission which, when addressing treaty issues, focus largely on the provision of land and other assets). However, the criterion will clearly prevent the expansion of the Specific Claims process to cover other types of treaty claims.

The SCRA does not address the possibility of claims having been researched and filed under the *Outstanding Business* policy that may not be eligible under this Act. Nor does this Act address whether files currently in process under the *Outstanding Business* policy will continue to be processed under that policy or will be required to proceed under the Act.

It is also worth noting that the definition of Specific Claim does not place a monetary limit on the claims that may be filed with the Commission. Consistent with statements by the Department of Indian Affairs and Northern Development, all claims, irrespective of size, may be filed with the Commission.

Claims must also be "for compensation" for "losses". The SCRA is not equipped to address claims for declarations of rights or for claims for specific performance (e.g. the return of land). While it is open to the parties to come to a broad range of negotiated resolutions, the claim as it is filed with the Commission must be for compensation.

(2) EXCEPTIONS — A first nation may not file a claim that

(a)   is based on events that occurred within the 15 years immediately preceding the filing of the claim;

Commentary

The reason for this provision is not evident and it appears to be at odds with the policy underlying limitations of actions provisions found in provincial and federal limitations legislation. Where limitation periods are meant to ensure claims are brought in a timely fashion while witnesses can still be found and evidence located, the SCRA places priority on ensuring that Specific Claims are not modern or recent complaints against Canada. Query what is the status of claims that are too old to take to court, but are not yet old enough to be resolved under this Act.

The policy underlying this section may be to simply limit the volume of possible claims that can be brought under the SCRA process.

(b) is based on a land claims agreement entered into after December 31, 1973, or any related agreement or Act of Parliament;

Commentary

The possible bases for excluding modern land claims agreements from the SCRA process include:

> 1) most modern land claims have dispute resolution mechanisms; and

> 2) modern land claims are carefully negotiated agreements with relative parity of bargaining position as between the various parties. Arguably, there is little sense in permitting these claims to access a process that, with limited resources, was originally designed to address historic claims.

(c) is based on an Act of Parliament or agreement that is mentioned in the schedule, or an Act of Parliament or agreement for the implementation of such an Act or agreement;

Commentary

The Acts and Agreements set out in the Schedule are all related to self-government. Self-government issues would represent a new category of claim in the SCRA process, may touch on Aboriginal rights, and implicate the Inherent Right to Self-Government[460] policy of the Government of Canada. The SCRA is clearly not intended to expand the Specific Claims program in these directions.

(d) concerns the delivery or funding of programs or services related to

---

[460] Implementation of the Inherent Right and the Negotiation of Aboriginal Self-Government, established in 1995. A copy of it can be found on the website of Indian and Northern Affairs Canada at <http://www.ainc-inac.gc.ca/pr/pub/sg/plcy_e.html>.

> policing, regulatory enforcement, corrections, education, health, child protection or social assistance, or of any similar public programs or services;

Commentary

This section appears intended to prevent the expansion of the Specific Claims process to cover matters that were not previously part of the Specific Claims policy framework under *Outstanding Business: A Native Claims Policy – Specific Claims.*

> **(e) is based on any agreement between the first nation and the Crown that provides for another mechanism for the resolution of disputes arising from the agreement; or**

Commentary

Specific Claims, whether under the current Specific Claims policy or the SCRA, is a program that is intended to be an alternative to litigation. It is also intended to allow claims to be heard that might otherwise be time-barred. This paragraph makes clear that the SCRA process is not intended to replace other alternatives to litigation nor to disrupt or frustrate carefully negotiated agreements between First Nations and Canada.

> **(f) is based on, or alleges, aboriginal rights or title.**

Commentary

According to Canada, Aboriginal rights and title do not fall within the scope of the *Outstanding Business* Policy. The SCRA transforms that policy position to a law.

The Joint Task Force Report, which predated the SCRA, raised "site-specific" Aboriginal rights as an example of claims that cannot be brought under the Specific Claims process nor under the comprehensive claim process (which is not designed to address discrete infringements of specific rights). The JTF report notes that such rights "can suffer damage due to infringement on such rights, but they do not have access to comprehensive claim negotiations ..."[461]

However, there is at least one key point that weighs against the inclusion of Aboriginal rights or title, or any new category of claim, under the SCRA. The existing process is known for the excessively long time it takes for claims to be processed; adding new categories of claims to the new process will reduce the likelihood that the SCRA process will be more expeditious than the current process.

---

[461]   See: Assembly of First Nations and Specific Claims Branch, DIAND, *Report of the Joint Frist Nations-Canada Task Force on Specific Claims Policy Reform*, Ottawa, 1998, p.12

(3) WHEN OTHER PROCEEDINGS — A first nation may not file a claim if

(a) there are proceedings before a court or tribunal other than the Tribunal that relate to the same assets and could result in a decision irreconcilable with that of the claim, or that are based on the same or substantially the same facts;

(b) the first nation and the Crown are parties to those proceedings; and

(c) the proceedings have not been adjourned.

Commentary

The SCRA represents an alternative to litigation and, as such, it is not surprising that the Act does not allow Specific Claims to proceed in the face of active litigation on the same matters. This section is consistent with s. 74, which prevents a filed claim from proceeding in the face of active (or re-activated) litigation.

It is interesting to note that s. 26(3)(b) requires that both the First Nation and Canada be party to the litigation. If the claimant First Nation were pursuing a claim against a province in the courts on the same issues, there would still be considerable risk of irreconcilable decisions being rendered on the same set of facts.

(4) EXTENDED MEANING OF "CROWN" — OBLIGATIONS — In the application of paragraph (1)(a) in respect of any legal obligation that was to be performed in an area within Canada's present boundaries before that area became part of Canada, a reference to the Crown includes the Sovereign of Great Britain to the extent that the legal obligation or any liability relating to its breach or non-fulfilment became — or would, apart from any rule or doctrine that had the effect of limiting claims or prescribing rights against the Crown because of passage of time or delay, have become — the responsibility of the Crown in right of Canada.

(5) EXTENDED MEANING OF "CROWN" — ILLEGAL LEASE OR DISPOSITION — In the application of paragraph (1)(b) in respect of an illegal lease or disposition of reserve land located in an area within Canada's present boundaries before that area became part of Canada, a reference to the Crown includes the Sovereign of Great Britain to the extent that liability for the illegal lease or disposition became — or would, apart from any rule or doctrine that had the effect of limiting claims or prescribing rights against the Crown because of passage of time or delay, have become — the responsibility of the Crown in right of Canada.

Commentary

The careful wording of this section appears to confirm:

- that claims arising prior to Confederation are permissible under this Act;
- that pre-Confederation liabilities to be addressed under this Act pertain only to those that can be traced back to the British Crown; and
- that Canada does not intend, by operation of this Act, to accept responsibility for claims that became the responsibility of the various provinces on their joining confederation.

(6) EXTENDED MEANING OF "CROWN" — OTHER — In the application of paragraphs (1)(c) and (d) in respect of reserve lands located in an area within Canada's present boundaries, a reference to the Crown includes the Sovereign of Great Britain for the period before that area became part of Canada.

Commentary

It is important to keep in mind that the matters set out in s. 26(1)(c) and s. 26(1)(d) are set out in the current Specific Claims policy[462] under the heading: Beyond Lawful Obligation. This designation may mean that, strictly speaking, the matters set out in those paragraphs have given rise to grievances against Canada but do not give rise to legal liability on the part of Canada. Consequently, s. 26(6) does not need to use the careful language of s. 26(5) in ensuring that provincial liabilities do not attach to Canada: the matters in question may be viewed as not giving rise to liability on the part of either order of government.

This subsection confirms that claims based on pre-Confederation matters that can be traced back to the British Crown are permissible under this Act.

27. COPY TO MINISTER ON FILING — On the filing of a specific claim, the Commission shall provide a copy of it and its supporting documentation to the Minister.

Commentary

The role of the Commission in reviewing claims prior to consideration of the claim by the Minister is not clear. Whether the Commission will undertake no review; a cursory review of form, such as might be undertaken by a court registry; or a more thorough review against the criteria set out in section 26, remains to be clarified after the creation of the Commission.

Pursuant to s. 50, a party may apply to the Tribunal to strike the claim on the basis that the claim does not fall within the parameters of s. 26 (see s. 50(a)).

---

[462]   Canada, Minister of Indian Affairs and Northern Development, *Outstanding Business: A Native Claims Policy – Specific Claims, Ottawa, 1982..*

Preparatory Meetings

28. (1) INITIAL MEETING — The Commission shall, on the filing of a specific claim, convene a preparatory meeting of the parties for the purpose of identifying and clarifying the basis of the claim and the matters of fact or law on which the claimant relies in support of the claim, any additional research required and any other issue relevant to the preparation of the claim for consideration by the Minister.

Commentary

The initial meeting or meetings convened by the Commission are critical to everything that follows. The Commission will presumably assist the parties in coming to agreement on the appropriate scope of the claim, how to focus the efforts of the parties on the most essential elements of the claim and also with respect to the scope of the research required to allow each party to properly assess and advocate its own view of the claim. These meetings will start to frame the evidentiary record that will be used in all ADR processes required under this Act, as well as for any matters that are eventually referred to the Tribunal for a decision.

The scope or breadth of issues to be considered will be critical given ss. 56, 66 and 72, which require that claims arising from substantially the same facts be joined for the purposes of the SCRA and s. 72 which, on certain orders of the Tribunal, renders *res judicata* all claims arising from substantially the same facts.

(2) ADDITIONAL MEETINGS — The Commission, on the request of a party, may convene additional preparatory meetings and, when appropriate, community meetings in order to permit the involvement of other interested persons including elders, members of the claimant and relevant public officials.

Commentary

The authority to convene additional preparatory meetings is permissive – the Commission retains the discretion to call the meetings or not.

The current practice of the Indian Claims Commission is to convene "community sessions" that involve members of the claimant First Nation, representatives from the government, and Commissioners. These meetings allow the ICC to obtain evidence from claimant witnesses, including elders. It is not clear if the community meetings referred to in s. 28(2) are envisioned to be along the same lines, or if there would also be "community meetings" to allow "relevant public officials" to provide Canada's evidence.

The current practice of Community Sessions are outlined as follows by the ICC:

Stage 3: Community Session

This is a unique and important aspect of the Commission's inquiry process. At this stage, Commissioners and staff attend a session in the First Nation's community to hear directly from elders and other members of the First Nation. The community session encourages a much greater level of participation on the part of the First Nation and is carried out in a manner that is respectful of the First Nation's language, culture and traditions. The testimony and oral tradition of the elders is recorded and transcribed. These transcripts are an important source of information used to supplement the historical documents and promote a broader understanding of the claim from the First Nation's perspective. Questions are posed by the Commissioners or their legal counsel only and no cross-examination of elders is permitted. However, counsel for the Commission consults with both parties before and during the session to identify relevant questions and lines of inquiry. In some cases, expert witnesses may present evidence in a separate session, provided they have furnished a written report in advance and the Commissioners have requested their attendance in person. Experts may be subject to cross-examination.[463]

29. AMENDMENTS — At any time during or on the completion of the preparatory meetings, the claimant may make any amendments to its specific claim that it desires in order to fully and clearly set out the basis for its claim and the matters of fact or law on which it relies in support of the claim. The Commission shall provide a copy of any such amendments to the Minister.

Commentary

If the preparatory meetings are to be effective in assisting the parties to properly "scope" the claim and to ensure that all claims arising from "substantially the same facts" are identified and properly considered by the parties, it is necessary for the claimant to be able to amend the claim up to the time the claim is referred to the Minister for review (see section 30).

30. (1) PROCESS SUSPENDED FOR MINISTER'S DECISION — On the completion of the preparatory meetings relating to a specific claim and receipt of any amendments under section 29, the Commission shall suspend proceedings in relation to the claim until it receives in writing the Minister's decision on whether the Minister will negotiate the claim.

---

[463]   From the ISCC's website: <http://www.indianclaims.ca/english/about/claimsprocess.html>.

Commentary

Section 30 reflects the current practice under the Specific Claims Process, which is premised on Canada having an opportunity to fully consider a claim prior to entering into negotiations with a claimant.

(2) DELAY NOT TO BE CONSIDERED FOR VALIDITY — The Minister, in making a decision on whether to negotiate a claim, shall not consider any rule or doctrine that would have the effect of limiting claims or prescribing rights against the Crown because of passage of time or delay.

Commentary

This stipulation is consistent with the claim-assessment policy set out in the current Specific Claims policy, *Outstanding Business: A Native Claims Policy – Specific Claims:*

> 3) Statutes of Limitation and the Doctrine of Laches
>
> Statutes of Limitation are federal or provincial statutes which state that if one has a legitimate grievance, yet fails to take action in the courts within a prescribed length of time, the right to take legal action is lost. The right to take action on a valid civil claim, therefore, will expire after a certain length of time unless legal proceedings have been started.
>
> The doctrine of laches is a practice which has come into observance over the years. It is, therefore, a common law rule as opposed to a specific piece of legislation passed in Parliament. The doctrine is based on actual cases whereby people lose certain rights and privileges if they fail to assert or exercise them over an unreasonable period of time.
>
> With respect to Canadian Indians, however, the government has decided to negotiate each claim on the basis of the issues involved. Bands with longstanding grievances will not have their claims rejected before they are even heard because of the technicalities provided under the statutes of limitation or under the doctrine of laches. In other words, the government is not going to refrain from negotiating specific claims with Native people on the basis of these statutes or this doctrine. However, the government does reserve the right to use these statutes or this doctrine in a court case.

The SCRA does not state explicitly that should matters raised in a Specific Claim later become the subject of a court proceeding, Canada retains the right to rely on all defences, including laches and limitations. However, this is essentially beyond doubt.

(3) REPORT OF MINISTER — The Minister shall, at least every six months after the completion of the preparatory meetings, report to the Commission on the status of the review, the expected date of the Minister's decision and, if applicable, the reasons why more time is required than previously expected.

Commentary

It is interesting to note that the Minister's obligation to report on the status of the review of a claim starts at the completion of the preparatory meetings rather than from the time the claim is submitted to the Minister for review.

In advising that the decision will take longer than "previously expected", the Minister provides reasons for the delay but is not required to seek the concurrence of either Commission or the claimant. The following subsection, s. 30(4), directs that delay on the Minister's part cannot be deemed to be a rejection of the claim by the Commission.

(4) NO DEEMED DECISION — No passage of time in relation to the decision on whether to negotiate a claim may be considered as constituting a decision not to negotiate the claim.

Commentary

Whatever means may be available to the Commission to apply pressure on the government to provide a decision within a certain period of time, the Commission cannot deem a decision to have been rendered on the basis that the government has taken too long.

Prompted, undoubtedly, by the SCRA's silence on the issue, commentators have posed the question as to whether s. 24(a) will be used to impose timelines on the conduct of Specific Claims. Any such timelines would be subject to s. 30, which appears to suspend the claim process while the claim is under consideration by the Minister. Section 30 appears to prevent the Commission from compelling the Minister to provide a decision on whether to negotiate a claim.

While the SCRA does not address the matter directly, it is possible that the Minister would be subject to judicial review with respect to providing a decision.

Validity of Claims

31. AFTER DECISION NOT TO NEGOTIATE — On receipt of the Minister's decision not to negotiate a specific claim, the Commission shall, on the request of the claimant, assist the parties to attempt to resolve the issue of validity using any appropriate dispute resolution process.

Commentary

The Act does not appear to require the Minister to provide written reasons for a decision to negotiate or not to negotiate a claim, perhaps because the Minister does not finally dispose of or affect the rights of the claimant. The Act does not require the Minister to provide a defence to the claim. However, in light of the focus that is placed on negotiations and the use of alternative dispute resolution by the SCRA, it is difficult to see how the parties could hope to "resolve the issue of validity" unless Canada were to provide at least an overview of its reasons for having rejected the claim.

Under the current policy, *Outstanding Business*, a rejected claim could be re-submitted "should new evidence be located or additional legal arguments produced."[464] The SCRA does not address the question of whether a claim that has not been accepted for negotiation may be re-submitted to the Commission at a later date.

On the request of the claimant, the Commission is mandated to assist the parties, through the use of appropriate alternative dispute resolution processes, in resolving the issue of validity. Paragraph 24(a), above, states that the Commission is to "foster, at all times, the effective use of appropriate dispute resolution processes — including facilitated negotiation, mediation, non-binding arbitration and, with the consent of the parties, binding arbitration — for the resolution of specific claims." The SCRA, like the current Specific Claims Policy, places a greater emphasis on negotiated outcomes than on adjudicated or litigated outcomes. The preference given to negotiation is also reflected in the requirement that all reasonable efforts at dispute resolution be exhausted prior to a claim being submitted to the Tribunal. Given this pre-condition to access to the Tribunal, the Commission may expect that claimants will make such a request almost as often as the Canada may reject claims.[465]

---

32. (1) REFERRAL TO TRIBUNAL — On the request of the claimant, the Commission shall refer the issue of the validity of a specific claim to the Tribunal if it is satisfied that

  (a)   **the basis for the claim and all matters of fact and law on which the claimant relies in support of the claim have been fully and clearly identified and adequately researched and have been considered by the Minister;**

  (b)   **all dispute resolution processes appropriate for resolving the issue have been exhausted without the issue having been resolved; and**

  (c)   **the claimant has, in prescribed form, waived any compensation for the claim that is in excess of the claim limit as it applies to the claim in accordance with section 56.**

---

[464]   Canada, Minister of Indian Affairs and Northern Development, *Outstanding Business: A Native Claims Policy – Specific Claims, Ottawa, 1982.*

[465]   See s. 32(1)(b).

Commentary

At first instance, the Commission may refer and the Tribunal may hear only issues related to the validity of, rather than compensation related to, a claim. In the event that the Tribunal decides the issue of validity in favour of the claimant, the parties are obliged (see s. 33) to return to the negotiation table to attempt to resolve all issues related to compensation.

The criteria for referral of the issue of validity to the Tribunal clearly place responsibilities on both the claimant and Canada. These responsibilities point to the primacy given to negotiations as the preferred means of resolving specific claims under the Act. It will be incumbent on the claimant to ensure that a claim is well developed, clearly articulated and adequately researched. The Minister will be required to give due consideration to all aspects of a claim. Both parties bear responsibility to ensure that all appropriate dispute resolution mechanisms are utilized.

The requirement set out in paragraph (c) ensures that the limits on the jurisdiction of the Tribunal (under s. 56(1)) are maintained. Depending on the form of the waiver, it could prevent not only further recourse under this Act, but also further recourse to the courts, for compensation in addition to any order of the Tribunal. Subsection 71(3) also ensures that a decision by the Tribunal establishing the validity of a claim is not admissible as evidence before any other court or tribunal.

It is noteworthy that the limitation on the jurisdiction of the Tribunal is applied with respect to determinations of both validity and compensation.

(2) DOCUMENTS ON REFERRAL — When it refers the issue of validity to the Tribunal, the Commission shall provide to the Tribunal a copy of all documents that it has provided to the Minister under sections 27 and 29.

(3) ISSUE OF ALLOCATION OF RESPONSIBILITY — On the request of a party, the Commission shall, together with the issue of validity, refer to the Tribunal the issue of the extent, if any, of each respondent party's responsibility with regard to each claimant for the claim.

Compensation

33. AFTER FAVOURABLE DECISION ON VALIDITY — After the Minister decides to negotiate a specific claim, or the Tribunal decides that a specific claim is valid, the Commission shall assist the parties to resolve the issue of compensation using any appropriate dispute resolution process.

Commentary

The bill makes no further mention of the s. 32(1) waiver on compensation that a claimant must have completed in order to gain access to the Tribunal at the validity phase, leaving open a question of how or whether this waiver might influence the compensation phase before the Commission.

34. AMENDMENTS RE COMPENSATION — At any time after the decision of the Minister or Tribunal referred to in section 33, the claimant may make any amendments to its specific claim that it desires in order to fully and clearly set out its position with respect to compensation and the matters of fact or law on which it relies in support of that position. The Commission shall provide a copy of any such amendments to the Minister.

Commentary

Notwithstanding that it seems odd at first glance for a claim to be amended after it has been accepted for negotiation or found to be valid by the Tribunal, s. 34 is consistent with the principle that claims ought to be well developed, fully researched and clearly articulated – even if that means amendments at various stages of the process.

Consider two scenarios:

> 1) The Tribunal, in finding that a claim is valid, comments on a certain aspect of the claim that may have been unclear or difficult to resolve. This section would allow the claimant to remove that aspect of the claim or to re-articulate its views of the pertinent facts or law.

> 2) The Tribunal, in deciding that certain aspects of a claim are valid, may make findings of fact inconsistent with the version of the claim articulated by the claimant. Alternately, the Tribunal may find parts of the claim not to be valid.

This section provides the claimant with an opportunity to articulate a theory of compensation consistent with the findings of the Tribunal.

35. (1) REFERRAL TO TRIBUNAL — On the request of the claimant, the Commission shall refer the issue of compensation for a specific claim to the Tribunal if it is satisfied that

(a) the claimant's position with respect to compensation and all matters of fact or law on which the claimant relies in support of that position have been fully and clearly identified and adequately researched and have been considered by the Minister in the course of a dispute resolution process under section 33;

(b) all dispute resolution processes appropriate for resolving the issue have been exhausted without the issue having been resolved;

(c) no compensation other than monetary compensation is being claimed;

d) the claimant has, in prescribed form, waived any compensation for the claim that is in excess of the claim limit as it applies to the claim in accordance with section 56; and

    (e)   the result of the following calculation is an amount not less than the claim limit:

$$A - B - (C \times D)$$

where

A is the maximum amount of compensation that may be awarded by the Tribunal in a fiscal year as published by the Minister from time to time in the *Canada Gazette* on the recommendation of the Minister of Indian Affairs and Northern Development and with the approval of the Treasury Board,

B is the total amount of compensation awarded by the Tribunal in the current fiscal year,

C is the claim limit, and

D is the number of specific claims in respect of which the issue of compensation has been referred to the Tribunal but has not been decided.

Commentary

The criteria for a matter to be referred to the Tribunal for the purposes of a determination on compensation are designed to ensure that all possible efforts at a negotiated resolution have been exhausted; that compensation sought is restricted to money; that the limit on the jurisdiction of Tribunal is maintained without the possibility of recourse to the courts for additional compensation related to the same claim; and that sufficient funds are available to pay any order of compensation.

The criterion in paragraph (e) ensures that the number of claims that have been referred to the Tribunal for a determination on the issue of compensation could not result in total orders that could exceed the funds allocated by Canada for payment of Tribunal orders in any given fiscal year.

(2) DOCUMENTS ON REFERRAL — When it refers the issue of compensation to the Tribunal, the Commission shall provide to the Tribunal a copy of the documents that it has provided to the Minister under sections 27, 29 and 34.

(3) ISSUE OF ALLOCATION OF RESPONSIBILITY — On the request of a party, the Commission shall, together with the issue of compensation, refer to the Tribunal the issue of the extent, if any, of each respondent party's responsibility with regard to each claimant for the claim.

General

36. (1) NOTICE — The Commission shall give notice of the filing of a specific claim to each province, first nation or person whose interests a

party indicates in writing to the Commission might be significantly affected by the claim.

Commentary

Specific Claims raise issues that may implicate the interests of provinces or territories, corporations, landowners, or other First Nations. While this Act does not provide either the Commission or Tribunal with the jurisdiction to order that third parties be added to the proceeding, third parties will be notified of a claim in order to give them a chance to participate in accordance with s. 37.

(2) EFFECT OF FAILURE TO NOTIFY — Failure to provide notice does not invalidate any resolution of a specific claim under this Part.

37. PARTICIPATION — On the request of the parties, the Commission shall allow a province, first nation or person to be consulted during a dispute resolution process under this Part, or a province or first nation to participate as a party.

Commentary

Section 37 would appear to place restrictions on the Commission that do not currently apply to the Indian Claims Commission, in that the ICC oversees negotiations that involve First Nations, Canada and third parties such as railway companies, municipal corporations, etc.. This section provides that, in dispute resolution processes under the auspices of the Commission, such third parties may be "consulted". Query whether agreement by the parties will be sufficient to expand negotiations to include third parties.

38. (1) NO DISCLOSURE, PRODUCTION OR TESTIMONY WITHOUT CONSENT — CHIEF EXECUTIVE OFFICER, COMMISSIONER OR EMPLOYEE — Subject to section 75, the Chief Executive Officer, a commissioner or an employee of the Centre who obtains any document or information related to a specific claim in the course of their appointment or employment, unless the parties to the claim consent, may not be compelled to, and shall not, disclose, produce or give evidence about the document or information.

(2) NO DISCLOSURE, PRODUCTION OR TESTIMONY WITHOUT CONSENT — CONTRACTOR — Subject to section 75, a person whose services are engaged by the Centre in respect of a specific claim and who obtains any document or information in the course of their engagement, unless the parties to the claim consent, may not be compelled to, and shall not, disclose, produce or give evidence about the document or information.

Commentary

Section 38 must be read in conjunction with ss. 75 and 40.

Section 75 stipulates that, subject to measures imposed to preserve confidentiality of sensitive documents, "documents filed with the Commission or with the Tribunal are public documents."

Section 40 states that:

> Evidence of anything said, any position taken or any admission made by any person in the course of a dispute resolution process under this Part is not admissible, without the consent of all parties, before the Tribunal or in any other proceeding.

Nothing in s. 40 indicates that it does not apply to employees of the Centre or to Commissioners.

This section extends the protections set out in s. 40, by indicating that any information, whether obtained in the course of dispute resolution or not, is not the Commission's information to disclose. Subsection 38(2) extends the prohibition on disclosure to contractors and other persons whose "services are engaged" by the Commission.

The information referred to in s. 38 is also protected from disclosure under s. 24 of the *Access to Information Act*.

39. (1) PROHIBITION ON REPRESENTING PARTIES — CHIEF EXECUTIVE OFFICER, COMMISSIONER OR EMPLOYEE — The Chief Executive Officer, a commissioner or an employee of the Centre may not represent a party at a Tribunal hearing.

(2) PROHIBITION ON REPRESENTING PARTIES — CONTRACTOR — A person whose services are engaged by the Centre in respect of a specific claim may not represent a party at a Tribunal hearing in respect of the claim or any other claim based on the same or substantially the same facts.

40. EVIDENCE NOT ADMISSIBLE IN OTHER PROCEEDINGS — Evidence of anything said, any position taken or any admission made by any person in the course of a dispute resolution process under this Part is not admissible, without the consent of all parties, before the Tribunal or in any other proceeding.

Commentary

Any uncertainty concerning the existence of a negotiation privilege with respect to efforts at dispute resolution under this Part are clarified by s. 40. It stands in contrast to s. 75(1), which states, "Subject to subsection (2), documents filed with the Commission or with the Tribunal are public documents."

Certainty between the parties as to a prohibition on the future use before the Tribunal or other proceedings of positions taken in the context of negotiations serves to encourage the achievement of a negotiated resolution of the claim.

PART 3

TRIBUNAL

Composition and Role

Composition

41. (1) COMPOSITION — The Tribunal Division of the Centre consists of a Chief Adjudicator, a Vice-Chief Adjudicator and up to five other adjudicators to be appointed by the Governor in Council on the recommendation of the Minister.

Commentary

While the ultimate decision on the appointment of a Chief Executive Officer lies with the Governor in Council, the government is obliged to seek input from First Nations who are claimants under this Act (and, for a period of one year after the coming into force of the Act, with claimants under the current Specific Claims policy).[466]

(2) ELIGIBILITY — The majority of the adjudicators, including one of the Chief Adjudicator or the Vice-Chief Adjudicator, must be members in good standing of the bar of a province or the Chambre des notaires du Québec.

Commentary

Given the nature of the decisions required of the Tribunal under the SCRA and the extensive use of law and legal principles, it is to be expected that the Tribunal would be composed of a significant number of legal professionals. That said, it is also not surprising that the statute leaves room for persons with many other types of expertise other than legal training to be appointed to the Tribunal. The Tribunal will rely heavily on many disciplines including historical analysis, financial and economic data, and scientific and technical data.

---

[466] See s. 76.1.

(3) MODIFICATION OF NUMBER OF ADJUDICATORS — The Governor in Council may, on the recommendation of the Minister, at any time increase or reduce the number of adjudicators.

(4) FULL-TIME AND PART-TIME — The Chief Adjudicator and Vice-Chief Adjudicator shall be appointed as full-time adjudicators, and other adjudicators may be appointed as full-time or part-time adjudicators.

(5) TERM AND TENURE — The Chief Adjudicator and the Vice-Chief Adjudicator shall hold office during good behaviour for a term of not more than five years and may be removed for cause by the Governor in Council.

(6) TERM AND TENURE — The other adjudicators shall hold office during good behaviour for a term of not more than three years and may be removed for cause by the Governor in Council.

(7) RE-APPOINTMENT — An adjudicator is eligible for re-appointment on the expiration of any term of office in the same or another capacity.

Commentary

A person who holds office during good behaviour can be removed in one of two ways:

- by order of the Governor in Council, on the recommendation of the Canadian Judicial Council,[467] made following an inquiry requested by the Minister of Justice under s. 69 of the *Judges Act*;[468] or

- by an order of the Governor in Council, following any other process that provides the person with an opportunity to be heard in accordance with the principles of natural justice.

In the latter instance, allegations of misfeasance would normally be provided to the Governor in Council, which would then provide the appointee with an opportunity to answer them. The Governor in Council would then make its decision whether to remove the appointee based on the written material before it.[469]

Case Law

Weatherill v. Canada (Attorney General), [1999] 4 F.C. 107; [1999] F.C.J. No. 787 (F.C.T.D.).

The Federal Court upheld the dismissal by the Governor in Council of the Chairman of the former Canada Labour Relations Board, who held office during good behaviour, for incurring unreasonable hospitality and travel expenses. The applicant had been offered an opportunity to make submissions in response to a report on his expenses and in response to the application to the Governor in

---

[467]   Established under s. 59(1) of the *Judges Act*, R.S.C. 1985, c. J-1.
[468]   R.S.C. 1985, c. J-1.
[469]   A similar procedure was followed, and received judicial approval, in *Weatherill v. Canada (Attorney General)*, [1999] 4 F.C. 107; [1999] F.C.J. No. 787 (F.C.T.D.).

Council for his removal, but chose not to do so. The court concluded that the requirements of natural justice had been satisfied, and that a further inquiry under s. 69 of the *Judges Act* was not required.

Wedge v. Canada (Attorney General), [1997] F.C.J. No. 872 (F.C.T.D.), (1997), 4 Admin. L.R. (3d) 153; 133 F.T.R. 277.

The Federal Court upheld the dismissal by the Governor in Council of a member of the Veterans Appeal Board, who held office during good behaviour, for allegedly having participated in election irregularities. The court found that there had been no breach of procedural fairness in the way in which the applicant had been treated. The applicant had been informed of the allegations against him by letter, and had been given copies of an investigation report and copies of the final report to the Governor in Council. The applicant had had the opportunity to respond orally, and his written responses to the investigation report and final report were submitted to the Governor in Council. The court held that the applicant was not entitled to cross-examine witnesses interviewed, or to a full, formal, court-like hearing. The court also concluded that the standard of good behaviour to which an appointee will be held is in the discretion of the Governor in Council, which extends to its judgment as to whether the appointee's conduct could undermine public confidence in the federal institution with which he had been appointed to serve.

Subsections 40(3), together with ss. 40(5), 40(6) and 42(1), parallel the requirements for institutional independence set out by the Supreme Court of Canada in *Canadian Pacific Ltd. v Matsqui* in relation to tribunals established by bands themselves:

> Thus, to conform to the requirements of institutional independence, the appellant bands' by-laws will have to guarantee remuneration and stipulate periods of tenure for tribunal members.[470]

Remuneration

42. (1) FULL-TIME ADJUDICATORS — Full-time adjudicators shall devote the whole of their time to the performance of the duties of their office and shall be paid the remuneration that is fixed by the Governor in Council. They are entitled to be paid reasonable travel and living expenses incurred by them in the course of carrying out their duties under this Act while absent from their ordinary place of work, but the payment may not exceed the maximum limits for those expenses authorized by the Treasury Board for employees of the Government of Canada.

---

[470] [1995] 1 S.C.R. 3 at 59.

Case Law

This subsection, together with ss. 40(3), 40(5) and 40(6), parallels the requirements for institutional independence set out by the Supreme Court of Canada in *Canadian Pacific Ltd. v Matsqui* in relation to tribunals established by bands themselves:

> Thus, to conform to the requirements of institutional independence, the appellant bands' by-laws will have to guarantee remuneration and stipulate periods of tenure for tribunal members.[471]

(2) PART-TIME ADJUDICATORS — Part-time adjudicators shall be paid the remuneration that is fixed by the Governor in Council. They are entitled to be paid reasonable travel and living expenses incurred by them in the course of carrying out their duties under this Act while absent from their ordinary place of residence, but the payment may not exceed the maximum limits for those expenses authorized by the Treasury Board for employees of the Government of Canada.

(3) CONFLICTING RESPONSIBILITIES AND ACTIVITIES PROHIBITED — Adjudicators shall not accept or hold any office or employment or carry on any activity inconsistent with their duties and functions as adjudicator.

(4) COMPENSATION — Adjudicators are deemed to be employed in the public service of Canada for the purposes of the *Government Employees Compensation Act* and any regulations made under section 9 of the *Aeronautics Act*.

Commentary

Both the *Government Employees Compensation Act*[472] and s. 9 of the *Aeronautics Act*[473] provide for compensation to be paid to government employees and their families for injuries or death resulting from activities undertaken in the course of duty. For example, subsection 9(1) of the *Aeronautics Act* states:

> 9. (1) The Governor in Council may make regulations establishing the compensation to be paid and the persons to whom and the manner in which such compensation shall be payable for the death or injury of any person employed in the public service of Canada or employed under the direction of any department of the public service of Canada that results directly from a flight undertaken by that person in the course of duty in the public service of Canada.

---

[471] *Ibid.*
[472] R.S.C. 1985, c. G-5.
[473] R.S.C. 1985, c. A-2.

Management

43. (1) CHIEF ADJUDICATOR — The Chief Adjudicator is responsible for the management of the business and affairs of the Tribunal, including the following responsibilities:

(a) to strike panels to conduct hearings and decide issues before the Tribunal;

(b) to lead the Tribunal in the exercise of its power to make rules under subsection 45(1); and

(c) to provide guidance and assistance to panels.

(2) ABSENCE OR INCAPACITY — In the event of the absence or incapacity of the Chief Adjudicator or if the office of Chief Adjudicator is vacant, the Vice-Chief Adjudicator has the powers and duties of the Chief Adjudicator.

Functions, Powers and Duties

44. FUNCTIONS — The Tribunal is responsible to hold hearings into and decide issues before it relating to specific claims.

45. (1) POWERS OF THE TRIBUNAL — The Tribunal may make rules governing the proceedings, practice and procedures of panels, including rules governing

(a) giving of notice;

(b) presentation of the positions of the parties with respect to issues before the Tribunal and of matters of fact or law on which the parties rely in support of their positions;

(c) summoning of witnesses;

(d) production and service of documents;

(e) discovery proceedings;

(f) taking and preservation of evidence before the start of a hearing;

(g) pre-hearing conferences;

(h) introduction of evidence;

(i) imposition of time limits; and

(j) costs, which rules shall accord with the rules of the Federal Court, with any modifications that may be required.

(2) PUBLICATION OF RULES — The Tribunal shall make its rules available to the public and, if possible, publish them in the *First Nations Gazette* or a similar publication.

Commentary

The *First Nations Gazette* is co-published by the Indian Taxation Advisory Board and the Native Law Centre of Canada at the University of Saskatchewan. Subscriptions for the 2005 year cost $72. Further information can be obtained and subscriptions ordered at the *First Nations Gazette* website.[474]

46. POWERS OF A PANEL — A panel of the Tribunal may

(a) determine any questions of law or fact in relation to any matter within its jurisdiction under this Act;

Commentary

The issues that the Tribunal may address include:

- the issue of validity on claims up to $10 million (ss. 52, 53, 56);

- the issue of compensation on claims up to $10 million (ss. 52, 53, 56);

- whether the claim is, together with any other specific claim, subject to one claim limit under subsection 56(2) (s. 51(1));

- any application brought under s. 47 ("interlocutory issues"); and

- any application to strike brought under s. 50.

The Tribunal's jurisdiction under ss. 47 and 50 does not appear to be limited to claims below the claim limit established by s. 56. Finally, the Tribunal appears to have residual jurisdiction to decide any issue "if all other parties consent" under s. 51(1).

(b) order that specific claims be heard together or consecutively if they have issues of law or fact in common;

Commentary

This section must be read in light of ss. 56(2), 65 and 66, all of which bear on the question of when claims are to be heard together.

Subsection 56(2) requires that certain claims are to be treated as one claim for the purposes of the claim limit established in s. 56(1).

Section 65 specifies that, unless the parties agree otherwise, claims that are subject to a single claim limit under s. 56(2) are to be heard together by the Tribunal.

Section 65 also requires, unless the parties agree otherwise, that claims that "present common issues of law or fact that create a risk that decisions on the claims will be irreconcilable" also be heard together.

Section 66 requires that if a panel determines:

---

[474] <http://www.usask.ca/nativelaw/publications/desc/fng.html>.

1) that a First Nation has a specific claim or a potential specific claim based on essentially the same set of facts and relating to the same land or assets as a claim under consideration, or

2) that there is any other specific claim or potential specific claim by a First Nation that must be before the Tribunal to enable a proper and comprehensive resolution of a claim under consideration,

the panel must suspend proceedings with respect to the specific claim under consideration until, "in the case of another specific claim, it is before the Tribunal or, in the case of a potential specific claim, it has been filed under this Act and is before the Tribunal."

> **(c)   order that specific claims be decided together if decisions of the claims could be irreconcilable or if they are subject to one claim limit under subsection 56(2);**

Commentary

The Tribunal's discretion to order that matters be heard separately or together must be read in light of s. 56(2) and s. 65, which require that certain related claims be subject to a single claim limit and that certain related claims be heard together.

It is interesting to note that s. 46(c) does not specifically authorize a panel to determine if two or more claims are subject to a single claim limit; this authorization is set out in s. 51(a).[475]

> **(d)   delay or suspend a hearing or delay its decision of an issue**
>
> **(i)   to await any court decision that the panel reasonably expects will assist it in its hearing or decision,**
>
> **(ii)   to allow the parties to make further efforts to resolve an issue,**
>
> **(iii)   to permit further preparations by a party, or**
>
> **(iv)   for any other reason that the panel considers appropriate;**
>
> **(e)   in the same manner and to the same extent as a superior court of record, summon and enforce the attendance of witnesses and compel them to give oral or written evidence on oath and to produce the documents and things that the panel considers necessary to a full hearing and consideration of the matter before it;**

Commentary

The power of the Tribunal to compel witnesses reflects the power of the current Indian Claims Commission, under the *Inquiries Act*,[476] to also compel

---

[475]   See also s. 66.
[476]   R.S.C. 1985, c. I-11.

witnesses. The qualifier "in the same manner and to the same extent" as a superior court indicates that the Tribunal has the power to subpoena witnesses on pain of contempt, with the attendant power to obtain a warrant for the arrest of a witness that does not comply with the subpoena.

(f)   **receive and accept any evidence, including oral history, and other information, whether on oath or by affidavit or otherwise, that it sees fit, whether or not that evidence or information is or would be admissible in a court of law, unless it would be inadmissible in a court by reason of any privilege under the law of evidence;**

(g)   **in applying the Tribunal's rules of practice and procedure, take into consideration cultural diversity;**

(h)   **lengthen or shorten any time limit established by the Tribunal's rules of practice and procedure; and**

(i)   **award costs in accordance with the Tribunal's rules of practice and procedure.**

Panels, Hearings and Decisions

47. APPLICATIONS — On application by a party to a specific claim, the Tribunal may, at any time, determine

(a)   **in relation to a specific claim that is before the Commission, to summon witnesses or to order production of documents;**

(b)   **whether the claim and any other specific claim should be heard together or consecutively, or decided together; or**

Commentary

This section must be read in light of ss. 56(2), 65 and 66, all of which bear on the question of when claims are to be heard together.

Subsection 56(2) requires that certain claims are to be treated as one claim for the purposes of the claim limit established in s. 56(1).

Section 65 specifies that, unless the parties agree otherwise, claims that are subject to a single claim limit under s. 56(2) are to be heard together by the Tribunal.

Section 65 also requires, unless the parties agree otherwise, that claims that "present common issues of law or fact that create a risk that decisions on the claims will be irreconcilable" also be heard together.

Section 66 requires that if a panel determines:

1)   that a First Nation has a specific claim or a potential specific claim based on essentially the same set of facts and relating to the same land or assets as a claim under consideration, or

2) that there is any other specific claim or potential specific claim by a First Nation that must be before the Tribunal to enable a proper and comprehensive resolution of a claim under consideration,

the panel must suspend proceedings with respect to the specific claim under consideration until, "in the case of another specific claim, it is before the Tribunal or, in the case of a potential specific claim, it has been filed under this Act and is before the Tribunal."

(c) **any other issue that needs to be resolved for a dispute resolution process in relation to the specific claim to proceed, if all other parties consent.**

48. PANEL FOR INTERLOCUTORY ISSUE — On an application to determine an interlocutory issue, the Chief Adjudicator shall strike a panel of one adjudicator who must be a member in good standing of the bar of a province or the Chambre des notaires du Québec, or of three adjudicators, at least one of whom must be such a member, to decide the issue. If a panel of three adjudicators has been struck, the Chief Adjudicator shall designate one of them to chair the panel, but the Chief Adjudicator shall chair the panel if he or she is a member of it.

49. HEARING AND DECISION— A panel shall, after providing notice to the parties, hold a hearing, at the time and place that the panel considers most appropriate, into the interlocutory issue in respect of which the panel was struck, and make a decision on it.

50. APPLICATION TO STRIKE — On application by a party to a specific claim, the Tribunal may, at any time in whole or in part, order that the claim be struck out, with or without leave to amend, on the ground that it

(a) **is, on its face, not admissible under section 26;**

(b) **has not been filed by a first nation;**

(c) **is frivolous, vexatious or premature; or**

(d) **may not, under section 74, be continued.**

Commentary

As with motions to strike that are brought in court, it is reasonable to assume that the Tribunal panel will hear motions to strike under paragraph (a) without reference to evidence other than the claim itself. Evidence may be required, however, in order to decide motions brought under the other three paragraphs.

The jurisdiction set out in s. 50 does not appear to be subject to the claim limit established under s. 56(1).

51. DECISION OF ISSUE — On application by a party to a specific claim, the Tribunal may, at any time, decide

(a) whether the claim is, together with any other specific claim, subject to one claim limit under subsection 56(2); or

(b) any other issue, if all other parties consent.

Commentary

The Tribunal's jurisdiction under s. 51(b) seems to be residual in nature, although it is dependent on all other parties consenting to the application. This residual power appears to leave open the possibility of the Tribunal considering and deciding applications in the nature of a "trial of an issue" that would, by way of example, allow parties to resolve an impasse in negotiations.

52. PANEL FOR FINAL DECISION — On an application under section 50 or 51, or the referral to the Tribunal of an issue of validity or compensation, the Chief Adjudicator shall strike a panel of three or five adjudicators, at least one of whom must be a member in good standing of the bar of a province or the Chambre des notaires du Québec. The Chief Adjudicator shall designate one of them to chair the panel, but the Chief Adjudicator shall chair the panel if he or she is a member of it.

53. HEARING AND DECISION — A panel shall, after providing notice to the parties, hold a hearing, at the time and place that the panel considers most appropriate, into the issue in respect of which the panel was struck, and make a decision on it.

54. LIMITATION — In deciding an issue of the validity of a specific claim, a panel shall not consider any rule or doctrine that would have the effect of limiting claims or prescribing rights against the Crown because of passage of time or delay.

Commentary

Consistent with the constraint on the Minister against relying on limitation periods or legal rules against delay in bring claims (s. 30(2)), a Tribunal panel may not, when deciding on the validity of a specific claim, take into account limitation periods or delay in bringing a claim forward. Otherwise, Canada is entitled to raise any defence that would be available to it in court proceedings (s. 64).

This rule reflects the current Specific Claims Policy, which states:

> 3) Statutes of Limitation and the Doctrine of Laches
>
> Statutes of Limitation are federal or provincial statutes which state that if one has a legitimate grievance, yet fails to take action in the courts within a prescribed length of time, the

right to take legal action is lost . The right to take action on a valid civil claim, therefore, will expire after a certain length of time unless legal proceedings have been started.

The doctrine of laches is a practice which has come into observance over the years. It is, therefore, a common law rule as opposed to a specific piece of legislation passed in Parliament. The doctrine is based on actual cases whereby people lose certain rights and privileges if they fail to assert or exercise them over an unreasonable period of time.

With respect to Canadian Indians, however, the government has decided to negotiate each claim on the basis of the issues involved. Bands with longstanding grievances will not have their claims rejected before they are even heard because of the technicalities provided under the statutes of limitation or under the doctrine of laches. In other words, the government is not going to refrain from negotiating specific claims with Native people on the basis of these statutes or this doctrine. However, the government does reserve the right to use these statutes or this doctrine in a court case.

The Specific Claims process, whether under the current policy[477] or under this Act, is designed to address claims that might otherwise be time barred. In fact, the SCRA process is subject to the rule set out in s. 26(2)(a) requiring that a claim be at least 15 years old prior to being submitted under this Act (see commentary under s. 26(2)).

55. DECISION ON EXTENT OF RESPONSIBILITY — For greater certainty, a panel, in making a decision on the extent of responsibility of each respondent party to a specific claim, may determine that any respondent is, or all the respondents together are, not responsible or not wholly responsible for the claim.

56. (1) BASIS AND LIMITATIONS FOR DECISION ON COMPEN-SATION — A panel, in making a decision on an issue of compensation for a specific claim,

(a) shall calculate the pecuniary losses in relation to the claim, to the prescribed maximum, or, if none is prescribed, to a maximum of ten million dollars, based on principles of compensation applied by courts;

---

[477]   Canada, Minister of Indian Affairs and Northern Development, *Outstanding Business: A Native Claims Policy – Specific Claims, Ottawa, 1982.*

Commentary

Paragraph 56(1)(a) makes clear that the Tribunal's jurisdiction to order compensation is limited to "pecuniary losses"; there is no authorization here or elsewhere in the Act for the Tribunal to provide other forms of relief to claimants.[478]

Paragrah 56(1)(a) limits the jurisdiction of the Tribunal, at least with respect to the issues of validity and compensation, to claims for less than $10 million, or any other amount that may be prescribed by the Governor in Council. The original draft of the Act, Bill C-6, contained a claim limit of $7 million that was amended by the Senate. In defending the idea of a claim limit, Senator Jack Austin stated:

> Honourable senators, in the interests of cost-effectiveness, efficiency and fairness to other claimants, the government does not want the Tribunal to get bogged down on one or two extremely large cases and delay access to the Tribunal for others.
>
> The government believes that would defeat one of the purposes for which the Tribunal is being created. Should negotiations on the larger, more complex claims prove unsuccessful, the courts would continue to offer a forum in which the complexities can be carefully examined and where the parties can appeal decisions they feel are incorrect.[479]

Section 24(e) contemplates the parties being able to use binding arbitration – on mutual agreement – to resolve claims of any size.[480]

(b)   may not include any amount for

(i)   punitive or exemplary damages, or

(ii)   any harm or loss that is not pecuniary in nature; and

Commentary

Like s. 56(1)(a), this paragraph makes clear that the Tribunal's jurisdiction in ordering compensation is limited to "pecuniary losses": there is no authorization here or elsewhere in the Act for the Tribunal to provide other forms of relief to claimants.[481]

---

[478]   See also s. 57(2) and the commentary following it.
[479]   Debates of the Senate, Vol. 140, Issue 43 (25 March, 2003) at 1530 (Hon. Jack Austin).
[480]   See also commentary following s. 24(e).
[481]   See also s. 57(2) and the commentary following it.

(c) shall award compensation against each respondent party proportional to the party's responsibility for the losses calculated under paragraph (a).

(2) ONE CLAIM LIMIT FOR RELATED CLAIMS — Two or more specific claims shall, for the purposes of the application of the claim limit under paragraph (1)(a), be treated as one claim if they

(a) are made by the same claimant and are based on the same or substantially the same facts; or

(b) are made by different claimants, are based on the same or substantially the same facts and relate to the same assets.

Commentary

Paragraph (a) is designed to ensure that all of a claimant's interests affected by a set of facts are addressed at once. The section prevents a claimant from submitting separate claims, and thereby avoiding the claim limit, for each potential head of damages arising from any given event or transaction.

Paragraph (b) is designed to ensure that all claims related to any given asset are heard together, provided that the claims are related to the same factual events or transactions. It would have been insufficient to require claims to be heard together based only on the fact that the claims relate to the same asset, as assets can have different owners at different times.

(3) EQUITABLE APPORTIONMENT — If claims are treated as one claim under paragraph (2)(b), the panel shall apportion equitably among the claimants the total amount awarded.

Commentary

While apportionment is possible under this section, it does not allow the Tribunal to make orders that, when added together, exceed the claim limit set under s. 56(1).

57. (1) UNLAWFUL DISPOSITION — If compensation is awarded under this Act for an unlawful disposition of all of the interests or rights of a claimant in or to land and the interests or rights have never been restored to the claimant, then, despite section 39 of the *Indian Act*, all the claimant's interests in, and rights to, the land are extinguished, without prejudice to any right of the claimant to bring any proceeding related to that unlawful disposition against a province that is not a party to the specific claim.

Commentary

Subsection 39(1) of the *Indian Act*[482] states:

> 39. (1) An absolute surrender or a designation is void unless
>
> (a) it is made to Her Majesty;
>
> (b) it is assented to by a majority of the electors of the band
>
> > (i) at a general meeting of the band called by the council of the band,
> >
> > (ii) at a special meeting of the band called by the Minister for the purpose of considering a proposed absolute surrender or designation, or
> >
> > (iii) by a referendum as provided in the regulations; and
>
> (c) it is accepted by the Governor in Council.

By operation of law, the SCRA purports to extinguish a claimant's interests in lands upon the award of compensation for a claimant's losses arising from the unlawful disposition of reserve lands. Specifically, if compensation is awarded under the Act for an unlawful disposition of "all of the interests or rights of a claimant in or to land and the interests or rights have never been restored to the claimant", then, by operation of the statute, all the claimant's interests in, and rights to, the land are extinguished.[483] This extinguishment of rights does not prejudice the claimant's ability pursue a province with respect to the unlawful disposition. The extinguishment of the claimant's rights occurs "despite" s. 39 of the *Indian Act*,[484] which requires, *inter alia,* that a surrender or rights to reserve land be "assented to by a majority of the band" and approved by the Governor in Council. The question that remains is whether extinguishment of First Nation rights to land by operation of statute will be upheld by the courts in the absence of assent by a majority of band members.

(2) UNLAWFUL LEASE — Despite section 39 of the *Indian Act*, if compensation is awarded under this Act in relation to the unexpired period of a lease of land entered into by the Crown in contravention of the rights of the claimant, then, for the duration of that period, the persons who, if the lease had been lawful, would have had any interest in, or right to enjoy, the land are deemed to have that interest or right.

Commentary

Protection of third party rights and interests is at the core of s. 57(2). Subsection 56(1), above, requires that claims heard by the Tribunal be claims for compensation only; however, this subsection demonstrates that in some cases the effect of a Tribunal ruling will be to determine rights in land. It ensures that

---

[482] R.S.C. 1985, c. I-5, s. 39, as amended.

[483] s. 57(1)

[484] R.S.C. 1985, c. I-5.

third parties in possession of lands subject to a leasehold to which a First Nation may have a continuing right or claim will remain in possession of those lands, at least for the term of the lease. At the expiration of the lease, the subsection appears to suggest that the lands could then be restored to the First Nation claimant. Query whether Canada would have further liability to the third party.

58. (1) ACTING AFTER TERMINATION OF APPOINTMENT — A person who has ceased to be an adjudicator of the Tribunal may, with the authorization of the Chief Adjudicator and for the period that the Chief Adjudicator fixes, take part in the disposition of any matter in which the person became engaged while holding office as an adjudicator, and a person so authorized is, for that purpose, deemed to be an adjudicator.

Commentary

The purpose of this section is clear: to prevent the departure of an adjudicator from the Tribunal from having a disruptive impact on any ongoing consideration of a claim in which that adjudicator was taking part.

(2) IF ADJUDICATOR UNABLE TO ACT — If an adjudicator who participates in a panel charged with deciding an issue is, for any reason, unable to take part in the decision, the Chief Adjudicator may, taking into account sections 48 and 52, authorize the remaining adjudicators of the panel to make the decision.

Commentary

The Chief Adjudicator has the authority to authorize a panel that has lost an adjudicator to render a decision, subject only to the rules requiring Tribunal panels to have at least one member qualified to practice law in Canada.

59. (1) NOTICE TO OTHERS — If a panel's decision of an issue in relation to a specific claim might, in the opinion of the panel, significantly affect the interests of a province, first nation or person that has not previously been notified of the claim under subsection 36(1), the Tribunal shall so notify them. The parties may make submissions to the panel as to whose interests might be affected.

Commentary

Subsection 36(1) states:

36. (1) The Commission shall give notice of the filing of a specific claim to each province, first nation or person whose interests a party indicates in writing to the Commission might be significantly affected by the claim.

As any given claim proceeds through preparatory meetings (s. 28), dispute resolution steps (ss. 31 and 33) and interlocutory motions (ss. 47 to 51), the parties' views as to whether third-party interests could be affected may change. Section 59 makes clear that the Tribunal, like the Commission, has the duty to notify third parties accordingly.

(2) EFFECT OF FAILURE TO NOTIFY — Failure to provide notice does not invalidate any decision of the panel.

60. PARTY STATUS — The Tribunal shall grant status as a party in a specific claim to a province that has agreed to submit to the jurisdiction of the Tribunal for that claim.

Commentary

The Tribunal created under this Act is not a court with the jurisdiction to compel or order that a province be joined to the proceedings as a party; this section makes it possible for a province to join itself to the proceeding by consent. Under s. 35 of the *Interpretation Act*,[485] "province" includes the three territories.

61. (1) CONDUCT OF HEARINGS — Subject to this Act, a panel shall conduct its hearings in any manner that it considers fit.

Commentary

While the discretion granted to a panel appears rather broad, presumably it is limited by rules created under s. 45(1).

(2) LIMITATION — In deciding how to conduct a hearing, a panel shall have regard to any submissions that a party has made regarding the manner in which the hearing is to be conducted and to the importance of achieving an expeditious resolution.

Commentary

There is no provision setting out a process for parties to make submissions regarding the manner in which a hearing is to be conducted. Unless and until the Tribunal creates rules under s. 45(1) governing such submissions, parties may be wise to make their submissions at the earliest opportunity and on an ongoing basis.

---

[485]   R.S. C. 1985, c. I-21.

62. (1) PUBLIC HEARINGS — Subject to subsection (2), panel hearings shall be public.

(2) CONFIDENTIAL HEARINGS — A panel may, on application by a party, take any appropriate measures and make any order that the panel considers necessary to ensure the confidentiality of a hearing if the panel is satisfied that the reasons for confidentiality outweigh the societal interest that the hearing be conducted in public.

Commentary

There is no provision setting out a process for making submissions on the need for confidentiality in the conduct of a hearing. Unless and until rules are made by Tribunal under section s. 45(1) governing such submissions, parties may be well advised to make submissions at their earliest opportunity.

Subsection 62(2) is subject to s. 24(1) of the *Access to Information Act*,[486] and is listed in Schedule II of that Act. Subsection 24(1) states:

> 24. (1) The head of a government institution shall refuse to disclose any record requested under this Act that contains information the disclosure of which is restricted by or pursuant to any provision set out in Schedule II.

Therefore it falls within the discretion of the Tribunal to make an order to ensure the confidentiality of a hearing, including the non-disclosure of "records"[487] under the *Access to Information Act*.

63. RIGHT TO CROSS-EXAMINE — A party may cross-examine a witness

    (a) as of right, if the witness is called by a party adverse in interest; and

    (b) with leave of the panel, in any other case.

Commentary

It is the current practice of the Indian Claims Commission to take oral evidence, including oral history evidence, from claimant First Nation communities. Parties to the proceedings are generally prevented from asking direct questions of First Nation witnesses; questions are generally posed by legal counsel to the ICC, and by ICC Commissioners themselves. The rules used by the ICC are generally more flexible when it comes to expert witnesses or witnesses who are not members of the claimant community.

Under the new process, cross-examination of witnesses, especially at the Tribunal stage, will be the norm. The Tribunal will undoubtedly develop rules under s. 45(1)(h) or practices under s. 61(1) to ensure that witnesses, especially

---

[486] R.S. C. 1985, c. A-1.
[487] "Record" is defined in the *Access to Information Act*.

elders from the claimant community, are treated in a respectful and culturally sensitive manner.

64. DEFENCES OF CROWN — Subject to section 54, section 24 of the *Crown Liability and Proceedings Act* applies in respect of a specific claim as if it were a proceeding.

Commentary

This section specifies that Canada is not limited in the range of defences on which it is able to rely in the Specific Claims process, subject to limits established by the SCRA, itself. For example, s. 54 prohibits a panel from taking into account statutory limitation periods and common law doctrines such as laches.

Section 24 of the *Crown Liability and Proceedings Act*[488] states:

> 24. In any proceedings against the Crown, the Crown may raise
>
> > (a) any defence that would be available if the proceedings were a suit or an action between persons in a competent court; and
> >
> > (b) any defence that would be available if the proceedings were by way of statement of claim in the Federal Court.

65. CLAIMS TO BE DECIDED TOGETHER — If a panel determines that specific claims are subject to one claim limit under subsection 56(2) or that they present common issues of law or fact that create a risk that decisions on the claims will be irreconcilable, it shall, unless the parties otherwise agree, decide the claims together.

66. SUSPENSION — If a panel, in considering a specific claim, determines that a first nation has a specific claim or a potential specific claim based on the same or substantially the same facts and relating to the same assets as the specific claim, or that there is any other specific claim or potential specific claim by a first nation that must be before the Tribunal to enable a full resolution of the specific claim, it shall suspend proceedings with respect to the specific claim until, in the case of another specific claim, it is before the Tribunal or, in the case of a potential specific claim, it has been filed under this Act and is before the Tribunal.

---

[488]   R.S.C. 1985, c. C-50.

Commentary

This section ensures that claims, even if related to different claimants or potential claimants, that raise the possibility of inconsistent rulings or outcomes are heard together. Several issues arise in this regard.

This section pertains not only to claims already before the Centre, but also to potential claims. It would appear that should the other First Nation have no intention of pursuing the claim, absent a binding release, the First Nation already before the Tribunal would be frustrated in having its claim heard. It is therefore incumbent on a claimant to ensure to the extent possible that all potential claims and claimants are identified and brought into the process as early as possible.

If another claimant is identified within the operation of this section and that claimant either does not have a claim before the Centre or is in the very early stages of the process set out under this Act, it is conceivable that the claimant already at the Tribunal stage would be made to wait a significant amount of time prior to having its claim heard.

This section does not specify how the claim limit set out in s. 56(2) would apply in the circumstances identified in this section.

67. (1) WITHDRAWAL — A party may withdraw an issue from the Tribunal at any time before the Tribunal gives its decision on it and, in such a case, the panel shall not render a decision on it.

Commentary

"Issue" is not defined in the SCRA. However, the Act makes specific reference to certain "issues" being referred to the Tribunal: "the issues of validity and compensation (s. 23(c)), "interlocutory issues" (ss. 2 and 47) and "any other issue" (s. 51).

(2) COSTS — A panel may award costs on the withdrawal of an issue from the Tribunal.

Commentary

This section is permissive rather than directory, and orders of costs for the withdrawal of an issue will depend on the circumstances of the claim in question.

(3) NOT A BAR — Withdrawal of an issue does not bar any subsequent consideration of the issue by the Tribunal.

Commentary

"Issue" is not defined in the SCRA. However, the Act makes specific reference to certain "issues" being referred to the Tribunal: "the issues of validity and compensation (s. 23(c)), "interlocutory issues" (ss. 2 and 47) and "any other issue" (s. 51).

If any of the foregoing framework forms the foundation for s. 67, no further explanation is required. However, if a different approach is taken to determining the issues that may be withdrawn and later re-submitted, one would do well to be mindful of ss. 65 and 66. These sections are designed to ensure that claims that could result in irreconcilable rulings by the Tribunal are joined and heard at the same time – even at the risk of delay and cost to other parties. It would be surprising, indeed, if issues were allowed to be withdrawn under this section and to be heard subsequently, if the issue would otherwise be caught by s. 65 or s. 66.

68. EVIDENCE NOT ADMISSIBLE IN OTHER PROCEEDINGS — Subject to subsection 71(1), evidence of anything said, any position taken or any admission made by a person in the course of a panel hearing is not admissible in any other proceeding.

Commentary

This section prevents admissions made or positions taken from being used against the party making the admission or taking the position in any subsequent proceeding, such as a lawsuit in a court of law. Such a prohibition prevents claimants from obtaining certain types of information in this forum, which is subject to the claim limit established pursuant to s. 56(2), and then using that information in a different forum to which the claim limit does not apply.

However, pursuant to s. 75(1), documents submitted to the Tribunal are, unless subject to measures taken under s. 75(2), public documents.

69. ADVANCE NOTICE OF DECISION ON COMPENSATION — Not later than 14 days before a panel renders its decision on an issue of compensation, the Tribunal shall give notice to the parties and to the Chief Executive Officer that the decision will be rendered.

70. WRITTEN REASONS AND PUBLICATION — A panel shall give written reasons for its decisions. The Tribunal shall cause the reasons and the decisions to be published in the manner that the Tribunal decides.

71. (1) JUDICIAL REVIEW — A decision of a panel is subject to judicial review under the *Federal Court Act*.

Commentary

Decisions of Tribunal panels are not subject to appeal; however, they are subject to judicial review as authorized by sections 18 and 18.1 of the *Federal*

Courts Act.[489] Judicial review does not allow a judge to substitute his/her own view of the matter for that of the Tribunal's decision. If that decision is found to have been made contrary to well-established principles of administrative law, the remedy, which is discretionary, is usually for the decision to be set aside and the matter returned to the Tribunal for reconsideration.

The pertinent portions of ss. 18 and 18.1 of the *Federal Courts Act* state:

18. (1) Subject to section 28, the Federal Court has exclusive original jurisdiction

(a) to issue an injunction, writ of *certiorari*, writ of prohibition, writ of *mandamus* or writ of *quo warranto*, or grant declaratory relief, against any federal board, commission or other tribunal; and

(b) to hear and determine any application or other proceeding for relief in the nature of relief contemplated by paragraph (a), including any proceeding brought against the Attorney General of Canada, to obtain relief against a federal board, commission or other tribunal.

. . .

(3) The remedies provided for in subsections (1) and (2) may be obtained only on an application for judicial review made under section 18.1.

. . .

18.1 (3) On an application for judicial review, the Federal Court may

(a) order a federal board, commission or other tribunal to do any Act or thing it has unlawfully failed or refused to do or has unreasonably delayed in doing; or

(b) declare invalid or unlawful, or quash, set aside or set aside and refer back for determination in accordance with such directions as it considers to be appropriate, prohibit or restrain, a decision, order, Act or proceeding of a federal board, commission or other tribunal.

(4) The Federal Court may grant relief under subsection (3) if it is satisfied that the federal board, commission or other tribunal

(a) acted without jurisdiction, acted beyond its jurisdiction or refused to exercise its jurisdiction;

(b) failed to observe a principle of natural justice, procedural fairness or other procedure that it was required by law to observe;

---

[489]   R.S.C. 1985, c. F-7.

(c) erred in law in making a decision or an order, whether or not the error appears on the face of the record;

(d) based its decision or order on an erroneous finding of fact that it made in a perverse or capricious manner or without regard for the material before it;

(e) acted, or failed to Act, by reason of fraud or perjured evidence; or

(f) acted in any other way that was contrary to law.

(2) FINAL AND CONCLUSIVE — Subject to subsection (1), a panel's decisions are not subject to appeal or review and, except for decisions with respect to interlocutory issues, are final and conclusive between the parties in all proceedings in any court or tribunal arising out of the same or substantially the same facts.

Commentary

Subject to judicial review under s. 71(1), and with the exception of interlocutory matters heard under s. 47, panel decisions are not subject to appeal and are final and conclusive with respect to any future claims or proceedings based on the same facts. However, subsection 71(3) specifies that a decision that a claim is valid is conclusive only for purposes of the SCRA and it cannot be relied upon in subsequent court proceedings, save for judicial review. This rule prevents a First Nation from obtaining a favourable ruling from the Tribunal and then turning to the courts to have compensation decided.

(3) EXCEPTION RE DECISION OF VALIDITY — Despite subsection (2), a decision of a panel that a specific claim is valid is conclusive only under this Act and, except for the purposes of judicial review under subsection (1), any evidence of the decision is inadmissible before any other court or tribunal.

Commentary

Decisions on validity, made in the context of the claim limit established under s. 56(1)(a), cannot then be used as the basis of a claim for damages in a court of law or other forum.

72. RELEASE AND INDEMNITY — If a panel makes an order that a specific claim is invalid or awards compensation for a specific claim,

(a)   each respondent party is released from any cause of action, claim or liability to the claimant and any of its members of any kind, direct or indirect, arising out of the same or substantially the same facts on which the claim is based; and

(b) **the claimant shall indemnify each respondent party against any amount that the respondent party becomes liable to pay as a result of a claim, action or other proceeding for damages brought by the claimant or any of its members against any other person arising out of the same or substantially the same facts.**

Commentary

A decision by the Tribunal that a claim is "invalid", or a decision on compensation, is intended to be final and conclusive (s. 71(1)) and it settles the claim as between all the parties. By operation of the statute, the respondent parties are released from any further liability to the claimant First Nation or to any of its members as far as any claim based on the same facts as the settled claim is concerned.

Respondent parties are, by definition, the federal and, if added under s. 60, provincial Crown(s).

Further, should a respondent party be found liable as the result of any subsequent proceeding between the claimant First Nation, or any of its members, and a third party that raises the same facts as the claim, and should the respondent party be found liable as a result, the claimant First Nation will be obliged to indemnify the respondent party.

Section 72(2) may have the effect of preventing Canada from having to "pay twice"; it also creates incentive for claimants to ensure that claims are fully developed, all potential respondents identified and the losses properly valued prior to submission to the Tribunal (keeping in mind the required waivers under ss. 32(1)(c) and s. 35(1)(d)).

73. (1) PAYMENT OF AWARD — An award of compensation against the Crown may be paid by instalments, but the award must be fully paid within five years after the date of the Tribunal's decision.

(2) INTEREST — The unpaid balance of the award bears simple interest from the date of the award, at a rate equal to the lowest rate of interest quoted by banks to the most credit-worthy borrowers for prime business loans, as determined and published by the Bank of Canada for the month in which the award was made, which shall be paid together with each instalment.

PART 4

GENERAL

74. ABANDONMENT — A specific claim may not be continued if the claimant

(a) **commences, before another tribunal or a court, a proceeding against the Crown that is based on the same or substantially the same facts as the claim, or that relates to the same assets as the claim and could result in a decision irreconcilable with that of the claim, unless the claimant immediately has the proceeding adjourned; or**

(b) **takes a new step in, or does not continue to adjourn, a proceeding mentioned in paragraph (a) or in subsection 26(3).**

Commentary

The SCRA represents an alternative to litigation and, as such, it is not surprising that the Act does not allow Specific Claims to proceed in the face of active litigation on the same matters.

75. (1) PUBLIC DOCUMENTS — Subject to subsection (2), documents filed with the Commission or with the Tribunal are public documents.

(2) CONFIDENTIAL DOCUMENTS — The Commission, on the request of a party, or a panel of the Tribunal, on the application of a party, may take any measures that it considers necessary to ensure the confidentiality of a document if it is satisfied that the interest of a party or a person that the document not be disclosed outweighs the societal interest that it be public.

Commentary

Subsection 75(2) is subject to s. 24(1) of the *Access to Information Act*, and is listed in Schedule II of that Act. Subsection 24(1) states:

> 24. (1) The head of a government institution shall refuse to disclose any record requested under this Act that contains information the disclosure of which is restricted by or pursuant to any provision set out in Schedule II.

Therefore it falls within the discretion of the Commission or Tribunal, as the case may be, to take measures to ensure the confidentiality of a document, including ensuring that a document is not subject to disclosure pursuant to the *Access to Information Act*.

76. (1) REVIEW — Not earlier than three years and not later than five years after the coming into force of this section, the Minister shall undertake and complete a review of the mandate and structure of the Centre, of its efficiency and effectiveness of operation and of any other matters related to this Act that the Minister considers appropriate. In carrying out the review, the Minister shall give to first nations an opportunity to make representations.

(2) REPORT — On completion of the review, the Minister shall cause to be prepared and sign a report that sets out a statement of any changes to this Act, including any changes to the functions, powers or duties of the Centre or either of its divisions, that the Minister recommends.

(3) TABLING AND REFERRAL OF REPORT — The Minister shall submit to each House of Parliament a copy of the report on any of the first 90 days on which that House is sitting after the Minister signs the report, and each House shall refer the report to the appropriate committee of that House.

76.1 OPPORTUNITY TO MAKE REPRESENTATIONS REGARDING APPOINTMENTS — The Minister shall, before making a recommendation under section 5 or subsection 20(1) or 41(1), notify claimants — which notification may be by ordinary mail sent to their latest known addresses — that they may, during a period that the Minister specifies of not less than 30 days after the date of the notice, make representations in respect of appointments to the office or offices in question.

Commentary

Section 5 deals with the appointment of the Chief Executive Officer of the Centre and subsections 20(1) and 41(1) address the appointment of Commissioners and Tribunal members, respectively. While claimants under the process are permitted to make representations to the Minister, the Minister has no corresponding duty to reply to the representations, or to follow any recommendations he may receive.

The Act does not require broad consultation with all First Nation communities, some of whom may never submit claims to the Centre prior to the making of appointments made under this Act. Nor does it allow for the government to exercise its power of appointment in a completely unilateral fashion there is at least an attempt at striking a balance.

For one year after the coming into force of this Act, "claimant" is defined for the purposes of 76.1 to include claimants under the current Specific Claims Policy, *Outstanding Business* (s. 77.1)

76.2 (1) AVOIDANCE OF CONFLICTING CONDUCT — At no time shall a person who was appointed under section 5 or subsection 20(1) or

41(1) act for any party in connection with any specific claim in relation to which they performed any work or concerning which they obtained significant information during their term in office.

Commentary

The Chief Executive Officer (s. 5), Commissioners (ss. 20(1)) and adjudicators (ss. 41(1)) are prevented from "acting" for any party after having "performed work" or having received "significant information" about the claim during their term of office.

"Significant information" is an imprecise term that, given the intention to limit conflicts of interest, ought to be given a broad definition rather than a narrow or pedantic one.

(2) ONE-YEAR NON-EMPLOYMENT PERIOD — Persons who were appointed under section 5 or subsection 20(1) or 41(1) shall not, within a period of one year after the end of their term in office, accept any employment with or enter into a contract for services with the Department of Indian Affairs and Northern Development or a first nation that had a pending specific claim — before the Commission or the Tribunal, in the case of the Chief Executive Officer, or, in the case of a commissioner or adjudicator, before the Division of the Centre to which the person was appointed — at any time during their term in office.

Commentary

The prohibition on employment and contracts for services applies to the Chief Executive Officer of the Centre (s. 5), Commissioners (s. 20(1)) and adjudicators (s. 41(1)). The prohibition, at first glance, is designed to prevent conflicts of interest between certain employees of the Centre and parties to claims; however, it does not prohibit employment or contracts of service with Provinces that are added as parties under ss. 37 and 60. The prohibition does not treat the Government of Canada as a party to the claim but rather the Department of Indian Affairs and Northern Development.

77. REGULATIONS — The Governor in Council may make regulations

(a) adding to Part 2 of the schedule the name of any agreement related to aboriginal self-government; and

Commentary

Agreements listed in Part 2 of the schedule relate to paragraph (c) of the definition of "first nation" as set out in section 2:

> (c) a group of persons that was a band within the meaning
> of paragraph (a), that is no longer a band by virtue of an

Act or agreement mentioned in the schedule and that has not released its right to bring a specific claim.

(b)   prescribing anything that may, under this Act, be prescribed.

Commentary

For example:

- s. 56(1)(a) authorizes the Governor in Council to prescribe a monetary limit on the jurisdiction of the Tribunal;

- s. 85 permits the Governor in Council to set a day or days for the coming into force of this Act;

The Governor in Council is also authorized to prescribe the form of the waiver a claimant must complete in order to gain access to the Tribunal under ss. 32(1)(c) and 35(1)(d).

PART 5

TRANSITIONAL PROVISION, CONSEQUENTIAL AMENDMENTS, COORDINATING AMENDMENT AND COMING INTO FORCE

Transitional Provision

77.1 MEANING OF "CLAIMANT"— During the period of one year after the coming into force of section 76.1, the reference in that section to "claimants" shall be read as a reference to "claimants under this Act or under the Specific Claims Policy of the Government of Canada".

Commentary

Section 76.1 ensures that claimants are consulted with respect to the appointment of the Chief Executive Officer (s. 5), Commissioners (s. 21) and Tribunal Members (s. 41). Section 77.1 extends the consultation to claimants under the current "Specific Claims Policy of the Government of Canada" (undoubtedly a reference to *"Outstanding Business"*).

The reference to the one-year time frame may be read as a reference to a transition period during which both processes will exist, although it is also possible that the current policy and process thereunder would continue longer than a year.

Consequential Amendments

78. to 83.

Commentary;

Sections 78 to 83 set out amendments to the Access to Information Act,[490] Financial Administration Act,[491] Privacy Act,[492] Public Service Staff Relations Act,[493] and Public Service Superannuation Act [494] occasioned by the enactment of the SCRA.

Coordinating Amendment

84. On the later of the coming into force of section 14 of the *Courts Administration Service Act*, chapter 8 of the Statutes of Canada, 2002, and subsection 71(1) of this Act, subsection 71(1) of this Act is replaced by the following:

71. (1) JUDICIAL REVIEW — A decision of a panel is subject to judicial review under the *Federal Courts Act*.

Commentary

This provision provided for the change in s. 71(1) from the *Federal Court Act* to the *Federal Courts Act,* which was occasioned by the enactment of the *Courts Administration Service Act.*

Coming into Force

85. COMING INTO FORCE — The provisions of this Act come into force on a day or days to be fixed by order of the Governor in Council.

Commentary

At the time of publication, the Governor in Council had not fixed a day or days for the coming into force of this Act.

---

[490]   R.S.C. 1985, c. A-1.
[491]   R.S.C. 1985, c. F-11.
[492]   R.S.C. 1985, c. P-21.
[493]   R.S.C. 1985, c. P-35
[494]   R.S.C. 1985, c. P-36.

SCHEDULE

(Section 2 and paragraphs 26(2)(c) and 77(a))

PART 1

ACTS RELATED TO SELF-GOVERNMENT

Cree-Naskapi (of Quebec) Act
Loi sur les Cris et les Naskapis du Québec
Kanesatake Interim Land Base Governance Act
Loi sur le gouvernement du territoire provisoire de Kanesatake
Mi'kmaq Education Act
Loi sur l'éducation des Mi'kmaq
Nisga'a Final Agreement Act
Loi sur l'Accord définitif nisga'a
Sechelt Indian Band Self-Government Act
Loi sur l'autonomie gouvernementale de la bande indienne sechelte
Yukon First Nations Self-Government Act
Loi sur l'autonomie gouvernementale des premières nations du Yukon

PART 2

AGREEMENTS RELATED TO SELF-GOVERNMENT

Champagne and Aishihik First Nations Self-Government Agreement
Entente sur l'autonomie gouvernementale des Premières Nations de Champagne et de Aishihik

Commentary

Text of the agreement is available at: <http://www.ainc-inac.gc.ca/pr/agr/ykn/casga_e.html>.

Little Salmon/Carmacks Self-Government Agreement
Entente sur l'autonomie gouvernementale de la première nation de Little Salmon/Carmacks

Commentary

Text of the agreement is available at: <http://www.ainc-inac.gc.ca/pr/agr/slmon/lssga_e.html>.

Nacho Nyak Dun First Nation Self-Government Agreement
Entente sur l'autonomie gouvernementale de la première nation des Nacho Nyak Dun

Commentary

Text of the agreement is available at: <http://www.ainc-inac.gc.ca/pr/agr/nacho/ndsga_e.html>.

Selkirk First Nation Self-Government Agreement
Entente sur l'autonomie gouvernementale de la première nation de Selkirk

Commentary

Text of the agreement is available at: <http://www.ainc-inac.gc.ca/pr/agr/selkirk/ssgfa_e.html>.

Ta'an Kwach'an Council Self-Government Agreement
Entente sur l'autonomie gouvernementale du Conseil des Ta'an Kwach'an

Commentary

Text of the agreement is available at: <http://www.ainc-inac.gc.ca/pr/agr/ykn/taansga/index_e.html>.

Teslin Tlingit Council Self-Government Agreement
Entente sur l'autonomie gouvernementale du conseil des Tlingits de Teslin
Tr'ondek Hwech'in Self-Government Agreement
Entente sur l'autonomie gouvernementale des Tr'ondèk Hwëch'in

INDEX

Note: All numerical references are to section and subsection numbers for the Acts and Regulations.

The following abbreviations are used in this Index:

First Nations Fiscal and Statistical Management Act – FSA
Debt Reserve Fund Replenishment Regulations – DRR
First Nations Assessment Appeal Regulations – AAR
First Nations Assessment Inspection Regulations – AIR
First Nations Rates and Expenditure Laws Timing Regulations – RER
First Nations Tax Commission Review Procedures Regulations – TRR
First Nations Taxation Enforcement Regulations – TER
Local Revenue Management Implementation Regulations – LRR
Short-term Pooled Investment Fund Regulations – SPR
First Nations Land Management Act – LMA
Specific Claims Resolution Act – SCA
Framework Agreement – FWA

A

Assessment appeals
- Assessment Review Board
- • attendance at hearing, AAR 13
- • combined hearing, AAR 11
- • constitution, AAR 6
- • decision of, AAR 16(1)
- • deferral of hearing, AAR 10
- • documents, delivery of, AAR 14
- • evidence of value, AAR 15
- • hearing before, AAR 9
- • *in camera* hearing, AAR 12
- • judicial review of decision of, AAR 16(2)
- commencement of appeal, AAR 8
- definitions, AAR 1
- grounds for appeal, AAR 8
- limitation period, AAR 7
- modification of assessment/tax role, AAR 5
- provision for, FSA 5(4)
- regulations, coming into force, AAR 17
- requests for reconsideration, AAR 3
- required procedures, AAR 2
- review by tax assessor, AAR 4

Assessment inspection, *see also* **Local revenue laws**
- access to property, AIR 4
- assessment without inspection, AIR 6
- business hours, AIR 5
- definitions, AIR 1
- notice, AIR 3

- procedures, AIR 2
- regulations, coming into force, AIR 7

Assessment, generally. *See* **Local revenue laws**

C

Canadian Centre for the Independent Resolution of First Nations Specific Claims
- annual report, SCA 18
- appointments to offices
- • non-employment period, SCA 76.2(2)
- • representation opportunities, SCA 76.1
- audits, SCA 17
- Chief Executive Officer
- • absence or incapacity, SCA 8(2)
- • conflicts, SCA 8(6)
- • deemed public service employment, SCA 8(7)
- • full-time appointment, SCA 8(4)
- • functions and powers of, SCA 7
- • part-time appointment, SCA 8(5)
- • rank and status of, SCA 9(1)
- • remuneration of, SCA 8(3)
- • term and tenure of, SCA 8
- claims procedure, *see also* Tribunal Division
- • abandonment, SCA 74
- • admissible claims
- • • grounds, SCA 26(1), (4)-(6)
- • • prohibitions, SCA 26(2), (3)
- • amendments to claim, SCA 29
- • compensation

First Nations Tax Commission
- agent of Crown, as, FSA 18
- local revenue laws, *see also* **Local revenue laws**
- • approval of, FSA 31(3)
- • copy and certificate, FSA 32(2), (4)
- • *First Nations Gazette*, publication in, FSA 34
- • notice of judicial review, FSA 32(3), (4)
- • procedures, establishment of, FSA 35(2)
- • registry, FSA 31(4)
- • restrictions on approval, FSA 32
- • review of, FSA 31(1), (2)
- • review on request, FSA 33
- • standards, establishment of, FSA 35(1)
- chief commissioner/deputy chief
- • appointment of, FSA 19
- • deputy chief functions, FSA 25
- • expenses of, FSA 24(2)
- • full-time status of, FSA 21
- commissioners
- • expenses of, FSA 24(2)
- • part-time status of, FSA 21
- • reappointment of, FSA 22
- • remuneration of, FSA 23
- definitions, FSA 16
- establishment and organization of, FSA 17
- mandate of, FSA 29
- offices of, FSA 26
- powers of, FSA 30
- review procedures
- • affected persons, TRR 15
- • attendance, TRR 21
- • Commission-initiated review
- • • hearing, TRR 42
- • • notice, TRR 38, 40
- • • production, TRR 39
- • • reply by First Nation, TRR 41
- • compliance, TRR 33(4), 34
- • compliance reviews, TRR 4
- • consolidation of hearings, TRR 20
- • costs, TRR 37
- • decision without hearing, TRR 5
- • decisions of Commission, TRR 33
- • definitions, TRR 1
- • document delivery
- • • address for, TRR 7
- • • Commission, by, TRR 8
- • • deemed, TRR 6(2), (3)
- • • deficient documents, TRR 11
- • • late filing, TRR 8(3)
- • • methods, TRR 6(1), 8(4)
- • • signature and authorization requirements, TRR 9

- • • stamped receipt, TRR 8(2)
- • hearings
- • • adjournments, TRR 27(4)
- • • adverse witnesses, TRR 32
- • • attendance, TRR 28
- • • conduct of, TRR 27(1)
- • • directed hearings, TRR 26(1)
- • • evidence and information, TRR 29
- • • examinations, TRR 31
- • • expedited, TRR 27(2)
- • • notice, TRR 26(2)
- • • tele-conferences, TRR 27(3)
- • • witnesses, TRR 32
- • intervenors, TRR 16, 17
- • local revenue laws, review of
- • • non-conforming laws, TRR 3
- • • referral to panel, TRR 2
- • pre-hearing conferences, TRR 30
- • regulations, coming into force, TRR 43
- • reply, TRR 12
- • response to reply, TRR 14
- • review request, filing, TRR 10, 15, 19
- • settlement
- • • consent order, TRR 24
- • • informal resolution, TRR 23
- • • recommencement of review, TRR 25
- • • settlement conferences, TRR 22
- • statutory declarations, requirements, TRR 18
- • time periods, TRR 35
- • variances, TRR 36
- • rules of procedure of, FSA 27
- • staff of, FSA 28

Fiscal and Statistical Management Act
- Aboriginal groups, regulations re non-bands, FSA 141
- Aboriginal rights, non-derogation clause, FSA 3
- coming into force, FSA 155
- compensation, restriction on, FSA 135
- conflicts of interest, FSA 132
- conflicts with other First Nation laws, FSA 138(2)
- conflicts with other laws, FSA 138
- consequential amendments, FSA 147-54
- coordinating amendments, FSA 154
- Crown liability, FSA 133(1)
- definitions, FSA 2, 16, 57, 90, 114
- fiscal powers. *See* financial administration laws; local revenue laws
- financial administration laws
- • additional information on request, FSA 9(5)

**Fiscal and Statistical Management Act
(Cont.)**
- • approval by First Nations Financial
  Management Board, FSA 9(2)
- • coming into force, FSA 9(3)
- • evidence law duly made, FSA 9(4)
- • power to make/delegate power,
  FSA 9(1)
- • requirement to make, FSA 4
- financial management and control
- • audit committee, FSA 128
- • audits, *see also* special examination
- • • annual report, FSA 120
- • • internal, FSA 119(3)
- • annual meeting, FSA 131
- • annual report, FSA 130
- • books and systems, FSA 119
- • corporate plans, FSA 118
- • definitions, FSA 114
- • disclosure of material developments,
  FSA 129
- • financial statements, FSA 119(4)-(6)
- • financial year, FSA 116
- • guarantees by Crown, FSA 115(2)
- • public service, exclusion from,
  FSA 115(1)
- • revenues, expenditure of, FSA 117
- • special examination, FSA 121
- • • auditor as examiner, FSA 123
- • • Auditor General, consultation with,
  FSA 124
- • • information, right to, FSA 125
- • • opinion, restriction on, FSA 126
- • • qualified privilege, FSA 127
- • • report, FSA 122
- First Nations Finance Authority
- • annual budget, FSA 73
- • annual general meeting, FSA 70
- • annual report, FSA 88
- • board of directors
- • • constitution of, FSA 61
- • • duty of care, FSA 68
- • • majority vote, FSA 65
- • • powers of, FSA 75
- • • quorum for meetings, FSA 64
- • • remuneration, FSA 67
- • • terms of, FSA 63
- • borrowing member
- • • application to become, FSA 76
- • • ceasing to be, FSA 77
- • by-laws, FSA 71
- • *Canada Business Corporations Act*,
  application of, FSA 66(2)

- • *Canada Corporations Act*, non-
  application of, FSA 66(1)
- • credit enhancement fund, FSA 85
- • Crown, not agent of, FSA 60
- • debt reserve fund, FSA 84
- • default by First Nation, FSA 86
- • defined terms, FSA 57
- • deputy chairperson, function of, FSA 62
- • establishment of, FSA 58
- • financing, restriction on, FSA 80
- • head office, FSA 72
- • infrastructure loans, limitations, FSA 79
- • mandate of, FSA 74
- • membership of, FSA 59
- • president of, FSA 69
- • priority of, FSA 78
- • regulations, power to make, FSA 89
- • security issuance provisions,
  FSA, 75(1)-(6)
- • short-term loans, limitations, FSA 81
- • short-term pooled investment funds,
  FSA 87, SPR 1-2
- • sinking fund, FSA 82, 83
- • surpluses, declaration of, FSA 83
- First Nations Financial Management
  Board. *See* **First Nations Financial
  Management Board**
- *First Nations Gazette*, publications in,
  FSA 34, 55(4)
- First Nations Statistical Institute
- • board of directors, FSA 94
- • chairperson
- • • appointment of, FSA 95
- • • part-time status of, FSA 98
- • chief statistician, FSA 102
- • Crown corporation, as, FSA 92
- • Crown, not agent of, FSA 93
- • defined terms, FSA 90
- • directors
- • • appointment of, FSA 96
- • • part-time status of, FSA 98
- • • qualifications of, FSA 97(2)
- • • reappointment of, FSA 100
- • • staggered terms of, FSA 97(1)
- • establishment of, FSA 91
- • federal data, disclosure of, FSA 107
- • head office, FSA 101
- • information
- • • disclosure, FSA 108
- • • privileged, FSA 109
- • • protection, FSA 108
- • • sharing, agreement re, FSA 106
- • mandate of, FSA 104
- • oath of office, FSA 103

T

Taxation. *See* **Assessment appeals; Assessment inspection; First Nations Tax Commission; Local revenue laws; Rates and expenditure laws**

Tribunal Division. *See* **Canadian Centre for the Independent Resolution of First Nations Specific Claims**